Game Design Perspectives

Game Design Perspectives

Edited by

François Dominic Laramée

CHARLES RIVER MEDIA, INC.

Hingham, Massachusetts

Publisher: Jenifer Niles
Production: Publishers' Design & Production Services, Inc.
Cover Design: The Printed Image

CHARLES RIVER MEDIA, INC.
20 Downer Avenue, Suite 3
Hingham, Massachusetts 02043
781-740-0400
781-740-8816 (FAX)
info@charlesriver.com
www.charlesriver.com

This book is printed on acid-free paper.

François Dominic Laramée. *Game Design Perspectives.*
ISBN: 1-58450-090-5

All brand names and product names mentioned in this book are trademarks or service marks of their respective companies. Any omission or misuse (of any kind) of service marks or trademarks should not be regarded as intent to infringe on the property of others. The publisher recognizes and respects all marks used by companies, manufacturers, and developers as a means to distinguish their products.

Library of Congress Cataloging-in-Publication Data

Laramee, Francois Dominic.
    Game design perspectives / Francois Dominic Laramee.
        p. cm.
    ISBN 1-58450-090-5
    1. Computer games—Programming.   I. Title.
    QA76.76.C672 L365 2002
    794.8'1526—dc21

                            2002004679

Printed in the United States of America
02 7 6 5 4 3 2 First Edition

CHARLES RIVER MEDIA titles are available for site license or bulk purchase by institutions, user groups, corporations, etc. For additional information, please contact the Special Sales Department at 781-740-0400.

Requests for replacement of a defective CD-ROM must be accompanied by the original disc, your mailing address, telephone number, date of purchase and purchase price. Please state the nature of the problem, and send the information to CHARLES RIVER MEDIA, INC., 20 Downer Avenue, Suite 3, Hingham, Massachusetts 02043. CRM's sole obligation to the purchaser is to replace the disc, based on defective materials or faulty workmanship, but not on the operation or functionality of the product.

To Julie, for putting up with me all these years.

Contents

Preface

François Dominic Laramée

francoislaramee@videotron.ca

Welcome to *Game Design Perspectives*, a compilation of the wisdom of over 25 of the best designers, producers, and business people in the game industry. I hope you will find the ideas discussed in here stimulating, fruitful, and practical.

Game Design Perspectives includes articles on proper design documentation, user interfaces, design theory, characters and storytelling, quality management, platform- and genre-specific issues, relationships between designers and the user community, and game development project management. The articles were selected because they are thought-provoking, practical, and concise. Some of them overlap; occasionally, they even contradict each other. This is as it should be: interactive game design is a new field, and we have not yet begun exploring its boundaries.

Even within the industry, game designers are often treated with a mixture of awe, fear, and distaste, as if what we did for a living was a sort of weird pseudo-magic. And in a sense, it is: design is not as predictable as artwork production, as tangible as programming, or as easy to measure as advertising expense. More, it is sorely lacking in formal, documented methods for predictable and repeatable success. This book and others like it will hopefully begin to do for game design what the patterns movement is doing for programmers. We could do worse than transforming the art of game design into something approaching an engineering discipline.

In the meantime, you may disagree with what the authors have written, sometimes violently. Good. For now, we need debate more than we need certainties. This is how we will develop our art into a craft, and maybe into a science.

A Word about the Authors

Game Design Perspective's authors represent a wide cross-section of the game development community, from the independent designer working on a wildly innovative project to the acclaimed award-winner, and from the self-starter living on promise and dreams to the veteran with almost 100 published credits. They have worked on games for consoles (from the original Atari VCS to the PlayStation 2), handheld devices, personal computers, online networks, interactive television, cell phones, and even stranger platforms. They live in the United States, Canada, Austria, Sweden, Great Britain, Portugal, or the Netherlands, have seen their writing published in countless venues, and perhaps more important, they care about games and the people who make them. I want to thank them profusely for sharing their wealth of knowledge with our community.

Unfortunately, one man will never be able to do so. Damon Zhao, a college student and avid amateur designer who had agreed to write an article on role-playing game design for this book, passed away in a tragic accident before he could complete it. He will be missed.

Who Should Read This Book, and How

Game Design Perspectives is designed to be read in many ways. Some people will want to scan through it in linear fashion; others will concentrate on a single section. Yet more will choose between the offerings according to patterns all their own.

- **Fledgling designers** should begin with Part 1, which covers several models of design documents, and then read the other sections thoroughly, in sequence.
- **Intermediate and expert designers** will sample the contents of Parts 1 through 6, to complement their expertise or compare their ideas with those of the authors.
- **Producers and managers** should begin with Part 6 ("The User Community"), move on to Part 7 ("Managing a Game Development Business"), and look at Part 1 to select a model of documentation for their own teams.
- **Non-designing members of the team** should read the Part 1 articles that are relevant to their own company (i.e., those selected as models by their own designers), and other articles covering topics associated with the game they are working on, so that they can better understand the concepts underlying their design.

Parting Words

I hope that this book will help you design and develop better games more efficiently and in a more pleasant fashion. Game development is a wonderful way to make a living, but there is no reason not to try to make it easier!

Acknowledgments

Many thanks to the many wonderful people who contributed to the creation of this book. Jenifer Niles and the production staff at Charles River Media made my life so easy that I almost feel guilty for not having to work any harder—almost. To the authors who contributed their knowledge and wisdom: you have my undying admiration and gratitude.

Special thanks to the people and companies who have contributed content for the book's CD-ROM, or images to accompany the articles: Winston Tam of Screenplay Systems Inc., Mucky Foot Productions Ltd., André Vieira, and Filipe Dias.

A big tip of the old stovepipe to the editors and friends who published my borderline-literate articles and jokes, and who encouraged me to pursue this project: Beverly Cambron, Mark Shainblum, Dave Astle—I owe you big time.

And of course, thanks to Julie and to my family for the kind words and much-needed kicks in the tailwagon—I would never have done this without you.

About the Authors

Sean Timarco Baggaley

Sean Timarco Baggaley began his career in the games industry as a graphics artist in the 1980s. He designed and programmed published games in the 1990s, ported a popular PC soccer management sim to the Commodore Amiga long after the platform had already been pronounced dead, and was responsible for the naming of the comp.games.* newsgroup hierarchy. He recently wrote the user guide for *RenderWare Graphics*, a popular graphics middleware product, and currently works as a freelance writer and games design consultant. He may be contacted at stimarco@bangbangclick.com.

Adam Baratz

Adam Baratz is a staff writer at Ars Technica (*www.arstechnica.com*), a contract programmer, and a former columnist and software reviewer for the *Boston Globe*. He was also the one of the youngest beta testers for Windows 95 and other software products. He may be contacted at Adam_Baratz@Msn.com.

Brent Boylen

As a Lead Designer at Vicarious Visions, Brent Boylen directed *Spider-Man 2: Enter Electro* (PSX) and *Wolverine's Revenge* for GameBoy Advance. He has worked with several licensed properties in his career; previous projects include design work on *Spongebob Squarepants*, *Fisher-Price Rescue Heroes*, and *Spider-Man*, all for GameBoy Color. He holds a degree in Electronic Media Arts and Communication from Rensselaer Polytechnic Institute.

Chris Campbell

Chris Campbell has worked as Quality Assurance Lead on the *Age of Empires* game series. He has also worked in the quality assurance field in several different sectors, including telecom, supply chain, and finance. For fun, he runs a videogame trivia mailing list, and has been an avid gamer for more than 20 years. He may be contacted at torgo@home.com.

Ben Carter

Ben Carter has been working in the games industry since 1995, initially as a freelance writer, then moving into development. Having completed three titles to date, he is currently working at Lost Toys as a programmer on various console projects. He may be contacted at ben@gunk.demon.co.uk.

Charlie Cleveland

After working for a few Boston area game companies including Papyrus, CogniToy, and Stainless Steel Studios, Charlie Cleveland formed his own team and is innovating in the area of online first-person "social" strategy, with a title tentatively called *Natural Selection*. Information about Charlie and his work can be found on his home page, *http://overmind.org*. He is also an occasional contributer to *Game Developer* magazine and facilitates monthly game developer socials, called the Postmortem, in Boston. He may be contacted at flayra@overmind.org.

John Dennis

John Dennis is currently Lead Designer at Team 17 Software, the developers responsible for the *Worms* games. In his four years since joining the Yorkshire, England-based developer, he has worked as lead designer on five titles and in other respects on another six. His design experience takes in such varied aspects as AI system design, level design, board and card game design, production of concept artwork, all aspects of design documentation, and the running of a seven-strong design department. Before beginning work at Team 17, John was an art teacher. He may be contacted at John.Dennis@team17.com.

D. Sim Dietrich

D. Sim Dietrich Jr. has been creating games as a hobby since 1985, and has been professionally engaged in technology and design capacities since 1995. Sim served as Graphics Display Editor for *Game Programming Gems 2*, and was a contributing author to *Game Programming Gems 1 & 2*. He currently works at NVIDIA Corporation in the 3D Tools & Technology group. He may be contacted at SDietrich@nvidia.com.

Markus Friedl

Markus holds a Master of Media Communications Design degree, for which he has written a thesis on online games, and works as Live Team Designer at Maximum Charisma Studios. He also freelances for several different game projects. He may be contacted at friedl.markus@onebox.com.

Joe Hitchens

Joe Hitchens entered the game development industry in 1986 as an artist; his first project was the sprite animation for a Commodore 64 game entitled *Intergalactic Cage Match*, which was published on cassette tape and for which the animation was created with a joystick. His most recent project was as the sole software engineer for a multiplayer, online blackjack game, complete with game server, support for real-money accounts, etc. He may be contacted at joe@sleepless.com.

Geoff Howland

Geoff Howland is the Lead Programmer and President of Lupine Games, a small independent game development company. He has driven several budget commercial games to completion and written many articles on the trials and tribulations of our evolving craft. He may be contacted at ghowland@lupinegames.com.

Wayne Imlach

Wayne Imlach is currently resident game designer at Muckyfoot Productions in Guildford, Surrey, in England, where he recently completed work on the critically acclaimed *Startopia*. He began his career at Bullfrog, quickly proving his design abilities by contributing to some of the core game elements of *Dungeon Keeper*, before moving on to develop the game mechanics, levels, and interface behind *Theme Hospital*. Later, at Psygnosis, he worked on a number of projects as lead designer, culminating in the release of the BAFTA award-winning *wipEout 3*. He may be contacted at wimlach@hotmail.com.

François Dominic Laramée

A full-time freelancer since 1998, François Dominic Laramée has designed, programmed and produced more than 20 published games for half a dozen platforms over the past 10 years. He has also written more than 40 articles and book chapters for and about game developers for a variety of online and print media, holds graduate degrees in management and computer science, and moonlights as a comedy writer. His Web site can be accessed at *http://pages.infinit.net/idjy*; or he may be contacted at francoislaramee@videotron.ca.

David Michael

David "RM" Michael is co-owner of Samu Games (*http://www.samugames.com*), a game company focused on creating Internet-based multiplayer games. David has been actively involved in designing and running multiplayer online games since 1996. He may be contacted at davidrm@samugames.com.

Ruud van de Moosdjik

Ruud van de Moosdijk is cofounder and vice-president of Engine Software, a small independent developer based in the Netherlands. He has been involved in game development since 1991, beginning on the 8-bit MSX home computer, and has worked on such different aspects of game development as design, graphics, and music and sound effects. Eventually he began producing Engine's latest Handheld games, including *Rescue Heroes: Fire Frenzy*, *Kelly's Clubhouse*, and *Spongebob Squarepants* for Gameboy Color, and *Power Rangers: Timeforce* for the Gameboy Advance. He may be contacted at ruud@engine-software.nl.

Joshua Mosqueira

Joshua Mosqueira spent several years working for the pen-and-paper role-playing game (RPG) industry as a writer and designer. From there he migrated to computer game design, working for a Montreal startup as Creative Director, and later at Vicarious Visions where he worked on *Spider-Man 2: Enter Electro* as Co-Lead Designer. Currently, Joshua lives in Vancouver and works at Relic Entertainment, Inc. He holds degrees in Cinema Studies and English Literature. He may be contacted at jmosqueira@relic.com.

Bruce Onder

Bruce Onder is CEO of Digital Arcana, Inc., a developer and publisher of online entertainment. His award-winning game design work includes *Spycraft: The Great Game* for Activision Studios, Inc. and, more recently, *KISS: Immortals*, a Webisodic rock 'n' roll adventure that plays on such sites as WarnerBros.com. He and cofounder Jeffrey Sullivan are currently developing and publishing *Net League Baseball*, a fantasy sports title that uses e-thletes(tm) instead of MLB statistics to offer a more compelling, immersive, and year-round baseball simulation experience. He can be contacted at bonder@DigitalArcana.com.

Stefan Pettersson

As Director of Development at Picofun, a Swedish-based wireless game developer and distributor, Stefan Pettersson is involved with both development and design. He may be contacted at stefpet@algonet.se.

Jay Powell

In his four years as an agent at Octagon Entertainment, Jay Powell has arranged numerous deals for clients in Europe and North America. Jay regularly puts his 17 years of game industry expertise to the community's service by answering questions and providing advice through GIGnews.com; he presented a lecture on contract negotiations at the 2001 Game Developer Conference. He may be contacted at jay@octagon1.com.

Sheri Graner-Ray

Sheri Graner-Ray began her game industry career as a writer and designer on the *Ultima* series at Origin Systems, where she became known for her mantra, "But what if the player is female?" Sheri has worked in the game industry as everything from writer/designer to producer to head of product development and finally CEO of her own development house. She may be contacted at sheri@silvar.com.

Alexandre Ribeiro

Alexandre Ribeiro is a Senior Programmer at Mind S.A.—Games Division, where he is developing games for such small platforms as Microsoft's Web TV and mobile phones. He is currently developing a next-generation RPG that will be playable from a wide range of devices. He can be contacted at alex@mind.pt.

Jonathon Schilpp

Jonathon Schilpp is a member of Gamedev.net's staff, working on the *Game Dictionary project*, as a game designer and a writer. He can be contacted at Jonathon@gdnmail.net.

Drew Sikora

Drew Sikora, aka Gaiiden, is a member of the Gamedev.net staff, does PR work for the online-learning Game Institute, and runs his own independent developer, Blade Edge Software. He always loves to hear from his readers; he may be contact at gaiiden@hotmail.com.

Tom Sloper

Sloper's game business career began at Western Technologies, where he designed LCD games and the Vectrex games *Spike* and *Bedlam*. There followed stints at Sega Enterprises (game designer), Rudell Design (toy designer), Atari Corporation (director of product development), and Activision (producer, senior producer, executive producer, creative director). In his 12 years at Activision, Sloper produced 36 unique game titles (plus innumerable ports and localizations), and won five awards. He worked for several months in Activision's Japan operation, in Tokyo, and is perhaps best known for designing, managing, and producing Activision's *Shanghai* line. Sloper is currently consulting, writing, speaking, and developing original games. He may be contacted at tomster@sloperama.com.

Marcin Szymanski

Marcin Szymanski is finishing a Computer Science degree at the University of Wisconsin Madison, where he previously obtained a degree in Genetics and created content for a new videogame technology course. He has been critiquing games for over 10 years. He may be contacted at mszyman1@students.wisc.edu.

Daniel Tanguay

Daniel Tanguay works as a game designer at Vicarious Visions, Inc. He began his career as an artist on *Terminus*, an ambitious space simulation, which he completed as Lead Designer three years later. He also led the design effort on *ESPN Winter XGames Snocross*. Daniel holds a degree in Biomedical Engineering from Rensselaer Polytechnic Institute. He may be contacted at dan@vvision.com.

Barbara Walter

Barbara Walter, owner of Walter & Company, based in San Diego, California, is a Certified Personnel Consultant who recruits full-time staff members for game developers throughout the United States. A recruiter since 1988, she is a member and Web site forum moderator for the International Game Developers Association. She also writes a career resource Web page, *CareerLink*, for *San Diego Magazine Online* (*http://www.sandiego-online.com/forums/careers/*). Email Barbara at walterco@ yahoo.com

DESIGN DOCUMENTS

1.0

Introduction

Above all else, game designers are communicators. Not only must they create (and uphold) the grand vision toward which the development effort will inch over many months, but they must also make sure that every member of the team, including the publisher and management, buy into it. Doing so effectively requires exhaustive design documents written with the utmost clarity: when multiple interested parties and large sums of money are involved, any ambiguity of purpose can lead to disaster.

Design Documents As Planning Tools

Developing modern interactive entertainment software is a huge undertaking, which routinely involves 10 or more specialists trained in fields as different as programming, art, marketing, music, and acting over a period of months or years. Unless the designer's ultimate vision is clearly and precisely codified on paper, where every member of the team can refer to it as needed, discrepancies and incompatibilities are bound to slip in, adding unnecessary work to the beta testing phase.

Besides efficiency, clarity of purpose also promotes team motivation. Precise knowledge of the contribution of one's work to the finished product creates a sense of ownership and responsibility; whenever work has to be thrown away because of a shift in focus, this personal relationship between developer and product is weakened.

Risk Reduction

No contractor will ever attempt to build a house without a complete set of plans, and no engineer will ever engage in bridge building without the proper specifications, even if they have built many houses or bridges before. *Especially* if they have built many houses or bridges before. For that matter, few visual artists will ever begin applying paint on canvas without sketching their subject several times in pencil or otherwise studying it thoroughly. These professionals know that a single, seemingly insignificant mistake can lead to catastrophic consequences—and relying on human memory to perform in flawless fashion without any outside assistance is just too risky.

Of course, the consequences of design flaws in computer games are far less dire than those of haphazard public works projects; no lives will be lost if a game's release slips by three months because of playability issues raised in beta testing. However, such a mistake can actually destroy a company. [McConnell98] states that an error inserted into the development process early and fixed at the end of the project can cost 50 to 200 times more than if the error had been corrected soon after it was made. While the game remains on paper, changes are essentially free.

Risk Management

An effective design document will guide the lead programmer in his architecture, the lead artist in planning his team's workload, and the producer in making sure that the project will ship on time and under budget. During preproduction, the lead programmers and artists will also scan the design document for possible sources of project delays and failures. These may include:

* Reliance on features that have not yet been delivered by the research and development team.
* Reliance on expected hardware and software standards (i.e., a new release of OpenGL or a next-generation console) that may or may not achieve sufficient market penetration by the time the game ships.
* A long, critical path of technologies and other components that are prerequisite to each other; any delay in delivering one element of the critical path implies identical delays in the deliveries of all subsequent components.
* A project size that may overflow the available time frame, financial resources, or staff.

The designer may then plan for these contingencies; for example, by adjusting the design so that it can be compatible with existing technology, or by scheduling last the development of features that can be removed without compromising the game's integrity, in case the entire project proves impossible to realize on time.

In theory, a design document should be thorough enough to allow production to go on without any ambiguity even if the designer left the project immediately after delivering it. In practice, this scenario is rarely possible, especially for larger games, which may evolve during development, but the amount of crucial information that remains locked in the designer's head should still be minimized.

Design Documents As Production Control Tools

During development, the design document serves as a benchmark to measure progress—and to ensure that what ends up being delivered actually fulfills the initial requirements. Again, any discrepancies between specifications and implementation must be resolved as quickly as possible, because the interrelations between the various components of the game can magnify an error's impact in unpredictable fashion.

For example, let us assume that an error in scripting the behavior of Proximity Mines causes them to explode when the player character steps within a 5-foot radius instead of the 10-foot radius specified by the document. Level designers who use the mines in their maps will have to use more of them, positioned closer to each other, to provide the player with the expected level of challenge. Later, if someone fixes the original mistake, the mines will regain their long-range sensors—and the levels designed with short-range mines will instantly become unbeatable.

Version Control

Even seemingly benign changes can spawn cascading effects throughout the project. If the player character seems to move too slowly, designers can be tempted to increase its running speed. However, moving obstacles and pursuing enemies will then automatically become weaker, because the player's ability to avoid them has increased. The level designer may then decide to up the number of goblins in a scene from four to six to restore the balance. But now, the six goblins crowd the room, wreaking havoc with each other's path-finding algorithms—they step on each other's toes, so to speak, and effectively provide even less opposition to the player because they cannot move. And what about the graphics engine? If the 3D artists have created magnificent goblin models that push the platform's limits, adding 50 percent more monsters to a scene may destroy the engine's ability to render it at all.

In terms of ability to change, a design document has three stages:

- During the **design phase**, changes cost nothing beyond reflection and typing time; therefore, they can be performed as often as needed.
- During the **prototyping phase**, testing a proposed design change requires a minimal amount of implementation effort. Any modification that adds to the game's quality should be considered.
- During the **development phase**, a design change can break content that has already been developed, or it may have a negative impact on the schedule. The designer should make substantive changes at this stage only if a severe flaw is uncovered or if a publisher absolutely requires the modification before signing a contract.

There are many ways to protect a game development project against late, substantive changes. A solid iterative design and prototyping effort before production begins will ensure a quality product. A modular design, which allows most of the game's behaviors to be controlled by scripts and tables of numbers, will minimize the time and effort required to fine-tune the product during beta testing. However, one of the most important ways to keep a project under control is an ability to let go. If, 12 months into production, the designer comes up with a new feature that would transform a so-so game into a guaranteed best seller, then every effort should be made to realize it. But if the new feature would merely be "cool" (or even "really cool"), then it should be saved for the sequel—when the team will be able to better analyze its impact on the rest of the gameplay, through a new design and prototyping cycle.

Design Documents As Contract Management Tools

Not only can a well-crafted design document facilitate the development process, it can also make a game easier to sell—and help prevent misunderstandings between developer and publisher.

Selling to Publishers

Unless a development house is building a game on assignment from a publisher (usually because the publisher holds a license and already has a good working relationship with the developer), a complete design document will have to be provided and reviewed before a contract can be negotiated. Obviously, the publisher needs to know what they are buying. More important, a detailed specification on paper is a prerequisite to a solid evaluation of the game's budget, timeline, and resource requirements—not to mention of the developer's ability to deliver it within these parameters.

In practice, the relationship between design and budget is often an iterative, circular process. Frequently, business considerations will constrain the creative process from the start: the publisher needs the game at a specific time to fill an empty slot in their release schedule, or they are looking for a product that can be made for a specific amount of money because they want to acquire six more games during the same quarter. A good document will help determine if these constraints can be satisfied by the existing design, and if not, how the project can be altered to do so.

Selling to Consumers

Once the publisher has acquired the rights to a game, they must prepare for its release into the consumer market. The design document will help the publisher's marketing staff identify the game's target audience and key selling points, which will allow them to plan packaging, advertisement, manual text, and press campaigns accordingly. The marketing process provides one more reason why late changes to the design must be avoided: a game that fails to deliver on its promises is a publisher's nightmare, and one that ends up focusing on mature content when its prelaunch hype campaign focused on magazines for 8 to 10 year olds is unlikely to please parents.

Maintaining Harmonious Relationships

Finally, a complete and unambiguous design document submitted during contract negotiations may prevent unnecessary friction between developer and publisher.

Signing a contract based on a vague design can be dangerous, because if there is any discrepancy between what the publisher thinks they are buying and what the developer thinks they are selling, the party with the most to lose (usually the developer) will have to fix the problem—at their own expense. Precision will help prevent these conflicts or, at least, show the publisher that they have approved the features they now want to see changed, which may lead them to give the developers extra money or time to perform the work.

Design Document Taxonomy

Designers have a number of different documents to create as part of the design process. Not every project will require all of them, and some companies organize them differently; however, the following nomenclature applies to most of the game development efforts to which I have contributed over the years.

Design Treatments

The first step in the design process is to produce a *treatment*, usually a short document presenting a very rough outline of the project: which genre the game falls into, what makes it unique, what intellectual property it will be based on, what its target audience will be, how long it will take to develop, etc. The role of the treatment is twofold: ensure that a seminal idea (i.e., "Wouldn't it be cool if . . .") has enough substance to evolve into a game; and serve as a project's calling card with publishers and whoever else is involved in deciding whether to go ahead with a full design.

Article 1.1 in Part 1 of this book presents a template for a design treatment, so we will not go into much more detail here. However, designers should keep in mind that most treatments never lead to full designs, let alone retail products; therefore, spending too much time on a given one is a losing proposition. A five-page treatment written in seven to 10 hours is often enough.

Also, if the treatment is to be distributed to publishers, the development company's marketing department should be consulted before the document is written—some publishers have specific needs and tastes, and submitting a treatment that meets those needs will increase the odds of success. For example, there are publishers who want to see artwork at this stage, while others will prefer to focus on market analysis; yet others will require a walk-through of a gameplay sequence to get a feel for the final product. Marketing specialists will know how to prepare treatments that will attract the attention of the companies they want as partners for the project.

Preliminary Design Documents

Once a project has received the go-ahead for design, a document listing the game's intended feature set must be written first. This document is known as a *preliminary design* (or PDD), usually weighs in at 20 to 50 pages, and can require between 75 and 150 hours of effort over a period of several weeks.

While the designer is ultimately responsible for the PDD, other people should be involved in the process early on:

- **Marketing:** To help focus the design into a sellable product.
- **The lead programmer:** To make sure that the ideas represented in the PDD are technically feasible.
- **The producer:** To make sure that the resources necessary to the project are available or can be acquired.

Of course, the exact content of a PDD varies by genre and scope, but its main purpose is to paint a complete picture of the game the designer wants to build. As an example, the preliminary design of a small 2D arcade shooter I delivered some years ago contained:

- A description of the intellectual property, including characters and storylines.
- Technical specifications: target platform, screen resolution, frame rate, color depth, etc.
- A list of all the weapons, vehicles, ammunition, and power-ups in the game.
- A brief enumeration of the settings, goals, and key features of each level.
- A preliminary bestiary of opponents.
- A list of the actions influencing the score.
- A description of the screen interface and of the user commands.
- A glossary of the terms employed in the document, to ensure clarity of communication.

Preliminary designs tend to be qualitative in nature: they explain *what* the game will do, not *how* it will do it. A feature's internal mechanics should be described in a PDD in only two cases:

- **It is a highly unusual gameplay concept that may either constitute a key selling feature or impact the product's position in the marketplace:** As an example, suppose that the player is controlling a robot whose arms extend proportionally to the amount of pressure applied to a dual-analog joystick: no pressure means "arms to the side;" full pressure equals full extension in the direction pointed to by the joystick, and the hand moves closer or further in real time. Depending on how the controls are implemented, this could make the game very responsive, or very hard to master.
- **It is a risk factor that must be studied thoroughly before the game's budget can be established:** If the game absolutely needs to accept vocal commands as input, a discussion of the types of commands (i.e., single words, complete sentences, size of vocabulary) and context (i.e., very silent environments, in the middle of a navy battle) must be supplied before the lead programmer can know whether the project is feasible within the constraints of available technology.

Revised Design Documents

The preliminary design process yields an ideal list of features; the *revised design document* (RDD) will order them by priority.

Any long-term project must be able to deal with the unpredictable, and games are no exception. Employee turnover, sickness, market conditions, technology changes, and any number of other outside factors can impact a project's schedule. Therefore, designers must be prudent and design in such a way that a sellable product will be shipped on time, even if events beyond their control prevent the game's entire vision from being realized.

In addition to the designers themselves, people involved in design revision should include:

- **The lead programmer and lead artist:** They estimate the amount of work necessary to deliver each feature, identify deliverables that are prerequisite to each other, and evaluate risk of failure.
- **The producer:** The producer knows what additional resources can be acquired, if any.
- **Marketing:** Marketing knows the importance of each feature from a market standpoint.

If all goes well, the process will last a few days and result in a document which tags the features listed in the PDD as "indispensable," "high priority," "low priority/sequel," or "discarded." However, if the revision shows that some critical features might be impossible to deliver within the project's constraints, remedial design work can be required. Extra design work is not to be seen as a setback: better to find out about these issues right away than when the game is in beta testing.

Once the RDD is delivered, the game's core feature set should be cast in stone, and the list of additional materials that will be added if time permits has been sorted by priority. The RDD can thus be used as a solid basis for negotiations with a publisher and for complete game prototyping.

Final Design Documents

The *final design document* (FDD) details the features listed in its predecessors. The FDD is often an organic entity, to which material is added throughout production as the programmers and the artists become available to build new content; as such, it is a prime candidate for implementation as an online document, such as the one described in Article 1.2 of this book, especially because few people outside of the development house will ever need or want to see it.

The only way to characterize the contents of an FDD is: "Whatever is needed." Final designs I have delivered have included combat tables (with weapon ranges and hit resolution systems), a detailed statistical model simulating the behavior of baseball players on and off the field, short stories, a complete specification for a text-to-speech system (including grammar and vocabulary), a summary of the current theories explaining the formation and structure of solar systems, and sample fantasy quests based on Native American mythology. There is really no limit here, and while as much of an FDD's content as possible should be written before production begins, there is no reason why its creation cannot continue for months afterwards.

Level Design Guides

The final task of the game designer (or, in highly specialized studios, of the chief level designer) consists of preparing a guidebook for level design. The guide should include:

- A basic description of each level's goal, environment, structure, and key features.
- A complete description of the moves, power-ups, weapons, and other items at the player's disposal during the game.

- A complete bestiary of monsters, obstacles, traps, and other scriptable objects to be included in the game.
- An introduction chart, listing which of the above will first become available in which levels, which will help ensure that new content will appear at regular intervals.
- A progression chart, listing which of the above should dominate which levels, and when they should fade away. For example, goblins could be common in the first few levels of a fantasy dungeon, with goblin parties increasing in size as the player roams deeper, and become less prevalent later on because they pose little challenge to strong players. Meanwhile, Highly Potent Scimitars of Universal Maiming will only be available in the deepest caverns.

Derivatives

Several other deliverables will be created from the design document, sometimes concurrently, sometimes later. Designers should make sure that their documents contain sufficient information to allow the contributors to do their work, and to provide any required assistance. On any given project, these *derivatives* may include:

- **A visual design guide:** The lead artist will prepare sketches of characters and objects (often complete with color palettes), collect photographs of interesting locales, etc., to create the look and feel of the game.
- **A software architecture:** The lead programmer will prepare a thorough analysis of the software components required by the project.
- **A project schedule:** The producer will identify all tasks that must be performed, calculate their durations with the help of the leads, and schedule them using project management software.
- **An interactive screenplay:** The writer will create the dialogue, and the actors will give their own interpretation of the game's mood.
- **A press guide:** Marketing or the publisher will prepare "sell sheets," mock interviews, and other materials that will be distributed to game magazines and Web sites to create interest in the product.
- **A user manual, and possibly an official strategy guide:** Sometimes, the designer will be directly involved in the production of these end-user documents; in other cases, the design document will be used as a basis for their creation.

Other Perspectives

Design documents are the foundation of the game development process. The articles found in this section contain various document models appropriate at different stages of development, and provide further advice on the writing process:

- My own article, *Writing Effective Design Treatments,* describes the short document that will become a project's calling card when making first contact with publishers and financial backers.

- Drew Sikora's *Online Design Documents* explains how to structure ideas using Web programming techniques, thus facilitating access and updates.
- Bruce Onder's *Writing the Adventure Game* describes, in exhaustive detail, the content of a typical design document in a specific genre, along with the iterative design process that should be implemented by all designers before production even begins.
- John Dennis' *The Designer's Best Friends* explains how to structure a design document (and the creative process itself) for maximum efficiency, while his *When Good Designs Go Bad* discusses ways to prevent development disasters during the design stage.

Beginning designers and producers will want to read through all of Part I and pick a document model suitable to their own teams' needs before they move on to particular topics elsewhere in the book.

Bibliography

[McConnell98] McConnell, S., *Software Project Survival Guide*, Microsoft Press, 1998.

1.1

Writing Effective Design Treatments

François Dominic Laramée

francoislaramee@videotron.ca

Every game design project, whether it is an epic console role-playing game (RPG) or a 30-minute online puzzle, should begin the same way: with a design treatment.

A *treatment* is a document containing the *smallest amount of data that can allow a reader to make a reasoned decision on whether he wants to be involved with a project*. The concept originated in Hollywood and on Broadway, where treatments typically take on the form of one-page (sometimes one-line) summaries of stories. In the game development business, things are rarely as simple because of the number and variety of people expected to make decisions based on the treatment. Still, successful designers know how to pitch concepts in a clear, concise, and powerful manner. You would be surprised how often management and investors make important decisions in less than five minutes.

ON THE CD

This article will outline the content of an effective design treatment; a sample titled Mephistophoria *is included on the companion CD-ROM in the Article 1.1 folder and will be used to illustrate the concepts.*

Why Bother with a Design Treatment?

The design treatment's purpose is manifold, and reflects the complexity of the game industry's decision-making process. A successful treatment will generate enough excitement to secure support for the project from the following groups of people:

- **Yourself:** Not surprisingly, a vast majority of the ideas that, at first glance, seem suitable for development into games, will later turn out to be impractical, insufficient, or otherwise lacking in whatever is needed to make the idea work. If the designer is unable to flesh out a seminal concept into a well-rounded three-page proposal, or if preliminary analysis reveals that the project would require more resources that the team can reasonably expect to obtain, then the idea can immediately be put aside or discarded. No harm done.
- **Your Team:** Whatever the reason, it seems that development teams work together more efficiently when everyone buys into the product's vision, or at least believes

in its potential for success. A near-unanimous disapproval from fellow developers does not necessarily mean that a project is worthless, but it does indicate that the project and the team are not well suited to each other, which can actually be worse. Trying to force a team of diehard shooter fans to develop an edutainment title for preschool children definitely qualifies as a recipe for disaster.

- **Publishers:** The typical publishing house receives hundreds or thousands of unsolicited proposals every year. Obviously, their acquisitions staff do not have the time to review that many 200-page design documents or install and play that many complicated demos. Publishers can only afford to devote significant time and effort to projects they are already interested in. A treatment, on the other hand, can be read in 10 minutes; use it to hook the publisher, and they willl ask for your demo.
- **Financial Backers:** Whether you are seeking venture capital, asking publishers to fund your development, or trying to convince your company's CEO to invest in a full design document and demo for your project, you will need to paint a clear picture of the product you wish to release and of its odds of success in the marketplace.

The best thing about a treatment is that it can be written in a couple of days, sometimes even in a couple of hours. If it fails (and most will, make no mistake about it), you will be able to cut your losses early and move on. But eventually, one idea will succeed, and your project will start on a much firmer footing.

The Introductory Scene

Nine out of 10 creative writing instructors will agree: a hurried reader (such as a magazine editor or an acquisitions specialist at a publishing house) must be hooked quickly or they will toss your submission away and move on. How quickly? Within a single paragraph, preferably in the very first sentence.

One way to do it is to open the treatment with a dramatic scene, as if you were writing a short story. For example, look at *Mephistophoria*'s opening line:

"I assure you," said the Devil with a smile, "there has been no mistake."

Makes you want to read on, doesn't it? If you only retain one idea from this article, let it be this: your odds of success will be far more favorable if you make the reader's job easy and pleasant. Remember, they likely have several other treatments to evaluate today. You cannot afford to give them the slightest motive to toss yours aside.

A dramatic scene also gives you a chance to demonstrate the tone of your game explicitly. In *Mephistophoria*, the Devil shows up in the player's living room, explains that he owns 21 percent of the poor sap's immortal soul thanks to a dubious technicality, and welcomes him to the family. The scene is far more effective at conveying an impression of weirdness, whimsy, and surrealistic insanity (and at showing whether or not the author can deliver it) than a simple assertion such as: "We want to do a weird and funny game."

Game Concept

Now that your reader is hooked, it is time to explain how you will realize the vision hinted at by the opening scene. Begin with a one-paragraph summary of the game's plot and goals:

> Mephistophoria *is an action/adventure game in which the player must accomplish a number of missions under duress from the Devil, in order to reclaim the 21 percent of his immortal soul that the Dark Lord has acquired by nefarious methods.*

Then, spend a page or two explaining your game's unique selling points:

- **Gameplay features:** What does the player get to do in this game that he could not anywhere else? In *Mephistophoria*, a tiny demon is always offering to bail the player out of delicate predicaments. Sometimes, this help is more than welcome; some quests may actually be impossible to solve without cheating. However, it comes at a steep price: the demon claims a fraction of the player's soul. The net result is that, because the player's ultimate goal is to reclaim the part of his soul already in the Devil's possession, he can finish the game and still lose if he accepts too much supernatural assistance. Not only must he perform the job, but he must also do it *well*, in a moral sense. An unusual balancing act to say the least.
- **Rules and mechanics:** Is anything special happening behind the scenes in this game? Does it need special physics? A stochastic simulator? What makes the setting unique?
- **Story, plot, and characters:** One-paragraph biographies of the key characters may help the reader identify with them if the rest of the document is insufficient to convey the information implicitly.
- **Structure:** Will the game be organized in short levels, major missions, or geographic areas? Are they independent, or do they follow an overarching plot line? How will you provide replay value? Is that even a relevant question?

Look and Feel

While the introductory scene demonstrates the tone of the game, additional information may be required to convey the entire experience more effectively. For example, you may wish to include:

- **Sketches of characters and landscapes:** Does your game adopt a North American cartoon look, with round characters and flat colors? European comic-book style? Photo-realism? Manga?
- **An explanation of the camera system:** Do you favor a free camera, one under the control of the player, or fixed camera angles to help nonplayer characters hide behind obstacles?

- **Controls:** How will the player interact with the game? With a small number of easily learned moves, or through long secret combinations unleashing deadly attacks?

Of course, you will want the entire document to support the game's look and feel. If you are pitching a horror game, you may want to print the document on red paper or choose a gothic font. A treatment for a comedy game about insurance adjusters selling protection against abduction by space aliens might include a sample contract, complete with fine print asking the reader why he bothers reading fine print when he is willingly buying insurance against *alien abduction!*

Business Model

Now that you have explained your game to the readers, you must demonstrate its chances of success in the marketplace. Topics you may want to discuss in this section include:

- **Development budget and timeline:** Obviously, decision processes vary with project scope. While no one expects a precise estimate at this point, readers do need to know whether you envision your game as a simple, six person, one-month project or a multimillion dollar AAA behemoth.
- **Platforms:** Is this a console, PC, or online game? Single-player or multiplayer? Do you need to acquire technology (i.e., a 3D engine) or will you develop everything in-house?
- **Followups:** Will this project create assets that can be used in further projects? Is the intellectual property well suited to sequels? How much of the code base (engine, tools, scripting language, etc.) can be applied to other product genres?
- **Target Audience:** Who will buy this product? Can it be sold overseas? If so, will localization be a problem? For example, most Western cartoon characters have three fingers on each hand. However, in Japan, a missing finger is a sign of underworld connections, so a cartoon game for kids may need all new character art to cross the Pacific.
- **Special Assets:** Why is your team uniquely qualified to produce this game? Have you ever done anything like this before? Do you own a valuable license? Do you have access to a unique source of information? *Spycraft's* producers retained former heads of the KGB and the CIA as scenario consultants, thus providing their game with tremendous credibility. Of course, such superstars may be out of your price range, but someone on your stock car racing game development team may have worked on a pit crew at a local track, and that's a start.

Conclusion

A well-written treatment can act as your project's business card, architectural mockup, and Constitution all in one. However, remember that its chief value lies in the fact that it is inexpensive to produce: most treatments will never lead to full designs, let alone retail products.

The wise designer does not get too attached to their ideas. The key to success is to mine enough of the mind's coals to find a diamond once in a while. Then, the real work can begin.

1.2

Online Design Documents

Drew Sikora

gaiiden@hotmail.com

Every game requires a design document.

Today's gaming industry has grown to Hollywood proportions. No longer does a solitary person locked in his garage turn out the latest action adventure. Games produced today are huge, many times larger than those made in the past. Projects of this magnitude must be planned to fine levels of detail, because large undertakings have a tendency to get out of hand without proper guidance. It is the job of the design document (or design specification) to lead the team of programmers, artists, musicians,and so forth, in making a game.

The trouble with design documents lies in their size. Documents can run into hundreds of pages these days, and what developer has time to read through all that? Imagine being a producer, and having a stack of papers a foot high dropped on your desk. *Wham!* You stare in dumbfounded silence as your project manager explains that this is the full design spec, and it must be read completely in order to put together a schedule for development. Twenty hours and twice as many cups of coffee later, your desk is littered with papers. You pick up a handful and sift through them, seeing the page numbers jump from 15 to 105 back to 43. Wait a minute, where is the rest?

Okay, so this scenario is an over-exaggeration (we hope), but given the size of today's design documents, you need a smarter way to make them available to the rest of the team. Online design documents provide the perfect solution, *if implemented correctly*. A designer with no common sense will simply create a Web site and post each page in sequence with links to the next and previous pages. Ta da! Now everyone can go online and spend five hours clicking Next to get to page 351!

ON THE CD

Before you read on, see the companion CD-ROM for the sample online design document provided as a companion to this article.

Open index.htm, located in the Article 1.2 folder on the companion CD-ROM, using your favorite Web browser. Take a few minutes to scan through the document, and keep it open as you read the rest of this article, so that you can reference it whenever you need to. If you are reading away from the computer, do not worry; this chapter contains images for reference as well. Let's begin.

General Design

As you look through the document, you should notice its simplicity, ease of navigation, and finally the presentation of the information. If you were to open Explorer to look at the files, you'd also notice that the document has a set file structure. We'll cover these topics in more depth later, but first you should know exactly what you are trying to accomplish with an online design document (versus a paper version). Your goals should be to:

- **Keep it simple:** Think of your target audience. You aren't trying to sell this document to anyone; therefore, you have no need for snazzy graphics, interactive animation, or page transitions. All your team members want and need is the design document itself.
- **Provide easy access to information:** Ease of access lies solely in your navigation interface. The best part about an online design document is that the user can jump from section to section easily. If you take away this freedom, you miss the point of an online document. In short, the user should *never* have to use the browser's Forward or Back buttons. The links you build into your pages must be self-sufficient.
- **Provide information in various ways:** You must take into account what a team member may need from the design document. Will he need to view an entire chapter? Or does he only have to focus on a subsection? Build the document so that people can easily reach information at various levels of detail.
- **Maintain good file structure:** This is for the sake of the person in charge of maintaining the document, whether it be you or anyone else. If you place pages just anywhere and name them haphazardly, updates will be next to impossible.
- **Avoid mixing media:** If you need to augment your document with multimedia content, such as videos, sound clips, tables, or even pictures, do not embed them directly into the text. Define external links that open new windows for the new content. This lets the viewer focus on one or the other, and minimizes confusion.

In the following sections, we will discuss how the sample design document overcomes these design issues.

Page Layout

If you look at any page in the design document provided, you will notice that it satisfies the first criterion, "Keep it simple." As Figure 1.2.1 shows, the page has a white background, text, links, and horizontal rules. The design of the page itself separates the various sections effectively, keeping everything neat and easy to locate.

The top of the page contains the document header, or the name of the design document. Next, below a horizontal rule, is the title of the current section and its subtopics. After another horizontal rule, we come to the navigation bar, which allows you to browse the document (and will be covered in the next section). Under yet

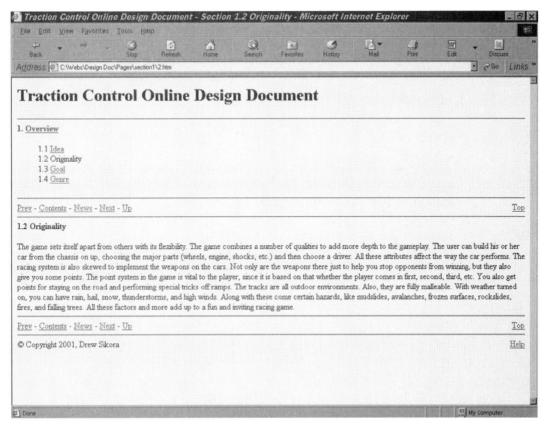

FIGURE 1.2.1   *Online design document cover page.*

another horizontal bar is the main body of the page, which displays the section text. Finally, you have another copy of the navigation bar, followed by a footer, which contains the copyright and other relevant information.

Not only is this page layout simple and effective, it also applies to all sections of the document. In other words, the description above outlines a *template* that can be used and reused to create every page needed to hold the entire design document. Having a template for your online document is the best way to build it quickly and easily, and also ensures that the style of the document will remain uniform, which makes users comfortable. Figure 1.2.2 shows the page displayed in Figure 1.2.1, in template form.

Navigation

Now that you are familiar with the look and style of the page and know where everything is located, look next at the navigation bar in Figure 1.2.3. If you'll recall, criterion number two was to make navigating the document easy, to keep the user from

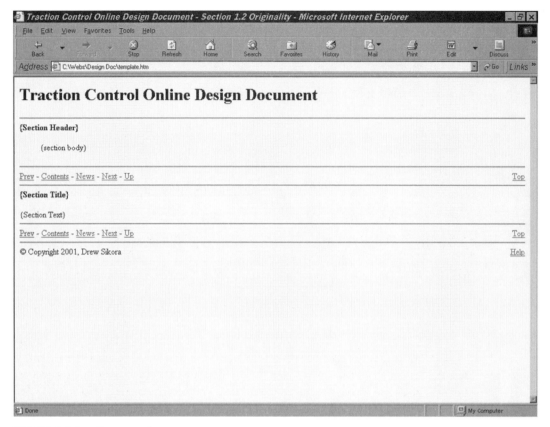

FIGURE 1.2.2   *Page template.*

having to click on the browser's Forward and Back buttons. It sounds like a tall order but, as you will soon discover, all it takes is a little planning and a well-structured document.

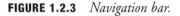

Prev - Contents - News - Next - Up   Top

FIGURE 1.2.3   *Navigation bar.*

First, let's cover the basic navigation scheme developed for this document. In order to satisfy the second constraint outlined above, you need a model that is effective, able to transport the user around the document with ease, and familiar. Thus, you will follow the well-established model of a file tree structure, like the one you deal with in Windows Explorer, as shown in Figure 1.2.4. You can view or open a subfolder, obtain a list of all the subfolders, list the contents of the main folder, and so forth. Fortunately the structure of a standard design document lends itself very well to this model, as it is divided into sections, subsections, sub subsections, etc.

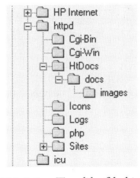

FIGURE 1.2.4 *Tree-like file hierarchy.*

Now that you have the model, look again at the navigation bar. You'll see four links: Prev, Contents, News, and Next. Getting the middle two out of the way first, because they are not really that important to the model: the Contents link, as you may have guessed, takes the user straight back to the table of contents, which is located on the cover page. The News link whisks the user off to a page that lists all of the recent updates that have been made to the document.

The Prev and Next links deserve more attention. These links are the tools that let the user jump from section to section within the document. One important point to clear up first: These links do *not* take the user through the document one section at a time. In other words, if you clicked these links you would not traverse the entire document. Instead, you would traverse the *depth level* you are currently exploring. For example, if you click Next while viewing the contents of Section 1, you will be taken to the page listing the contents of Section 2, not to Section 1.1. Similarly, if you hit Next while perusing the contents of Section 1.1, you will move on to Section 1.2. The Prev link does the same as Next, only in reverse. Before you go any further, spend some time navigating through the document to get the feel of how it works in various situations.

The next navigational feature to cover is the Up link. This link only appears in subsections of the document (such as 1.1 or 2.3.1) and completes the file tree model. If the user is way down in Section 2.8.1.2, then by the navigation rules he can only traverse that section (2.8.1.1, 2.8.1.3, 2.8.1.4, etc.) using the Prev and Next links. However, what if he wants to return to 2.8.1 or 2.8 instead? Enter the Up link, which will bump the user up one level until he reaches the main section (Section 2, for instance). The Up link disappears at the top level, because the next level up would be the table of contents, and you already have a link to that.

The navigation model is almost done, but not quite. Even with this wonderful navigational model there still may be times when the user just doesn't want to have to deal with hitting Prev, Next, or Up to get where he wants. Therefore, each page contains a listing of all the subsections within the section to which it belongs, with all the topics hyperlinked to their respective pages.

Finally, the user may be reading content located towards the end of a long section in the main body of the text, and he may want to return to a previous subsection of the same text to check up on an unclear concept. To save him from having to scroll all the way back up, anchors (the **Top** links) bring him back to the top of the page, where a list of hyperlinks to the page's subsections is located. Figure 1.2.5 has these three navigational elements highlighted.

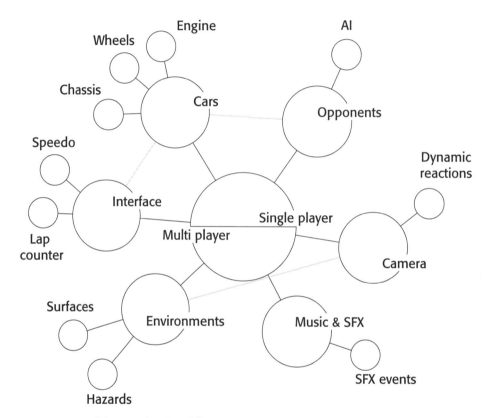

FIGURE 1.2.5   *More navigational features.*

That sums up the navigation used in the sample document. To prove it satisfies the goal, pick a random starting point within the document and then take a minute or two jumping around randomly. Once you are totally lost, get back to where you started using only the links within the document. (Don't cheat!) As you will see, it takes you no time at all to find your way back home, and you do not even need those browser buttons.

Information

The third design point is to present information in various ways. In a well-structured team environment, each person has a unique job that requires them to focus on specific aspects of the document. Artists and musicians will look at sections dedicated to graphics models and sound. Programmers, depending on their task, will focus on various other areas of the document, such as control, graphics, physics, or explanations of certain gameplay features. Whatever the case, it makes sense that a person should not have to wade through information that he can not use.

To this end, the online document should be able to break down information into simpler and simpler forms, until it reaches a point of absolute explicitness. This can be seen in the design document if you drill down to lower and lower sections. For example, in Section 7, the page's body contains a complete listing of the contents of every subsection of Section 7 (see Figure 1.2.6). If you were to select a subsection, say Section 7.3, the body would now list only the contents of Section 7.3. Finally, if you were to go even deeper and select Section 7.3.1, you would see *only* that section in the body (see Figure 1.2.7).

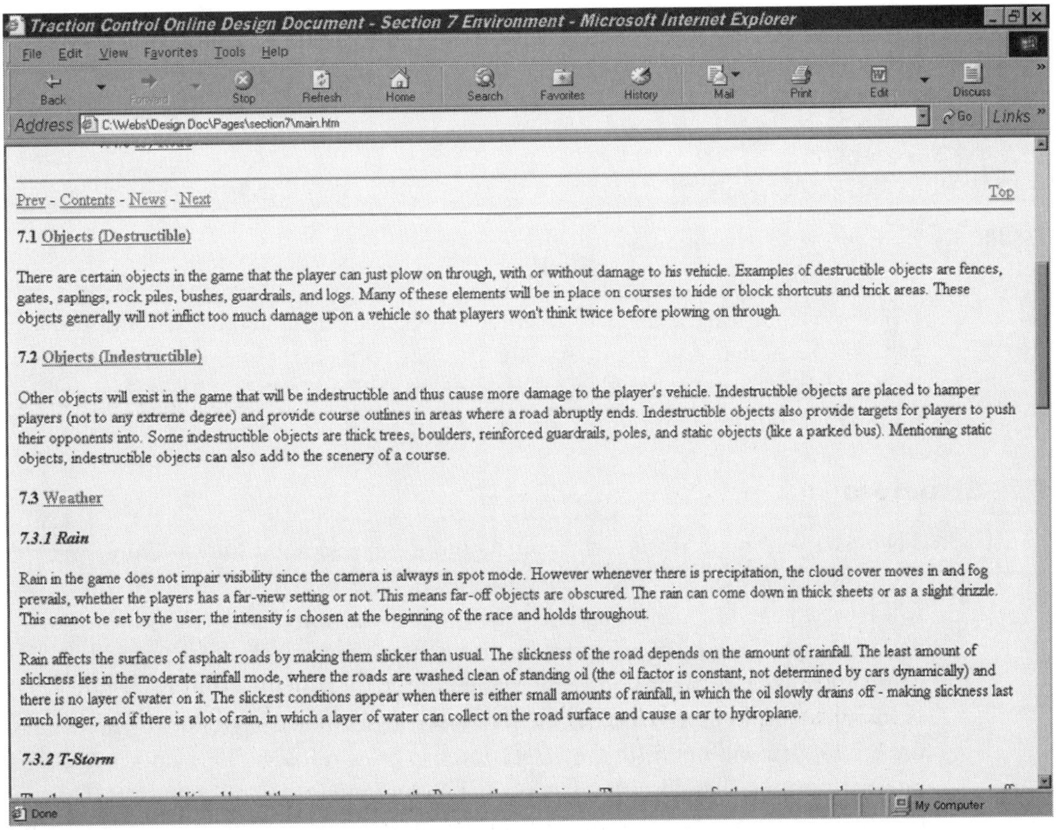

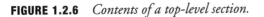

FIGURE 1.2.6 *Contents of a top-level section.*

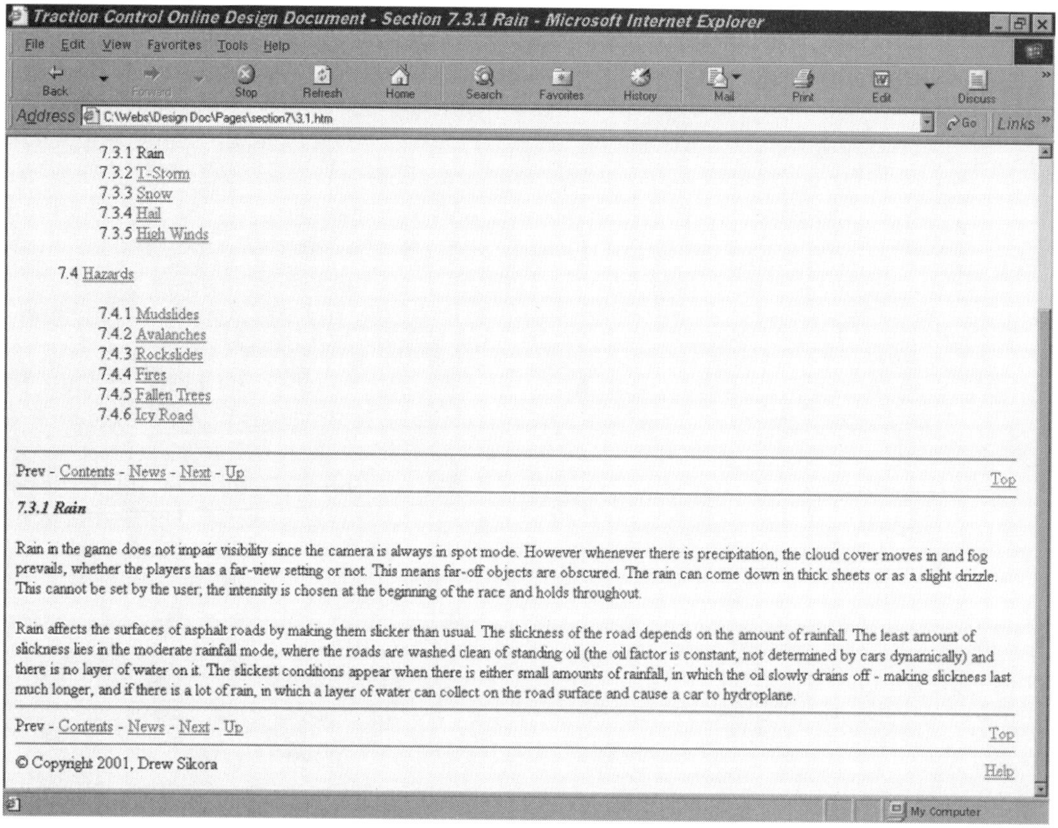

7.3.1 Rain
7.3.2 T-Storm
7.3.3 Snow
7.3.4 Hail
7.3.5 High Winds

7.4 Hazards

7.4.1 Mudslides
7.4.2 Avalanches
7.4.3 Rockslides
7.4.4 Fires
7.4.5 Fallen Trees
7.4.6 Icy Road

Prev - Contents - News - Next - Up Top

7.3.1 Rain

Rain in the game does not impair visibility since the camera is always in spot mode. However whenever there is precipitation, the cloud cover moves in and fog prevails, whether the players has a far-view setting or not. This means far-off objects are obscured. The rain can come down in thick sheets or as a slight drizzle. This cannot be set by the user; the intensity is chosen at the beginning of the race and holds throughout.

Rain affects the surfaces of asphalt roads by making them slicker than usual. The slickness of the road depends on the amount of rainfall. The least amount of slickness lies in the moderate rainfall mode, where the roads are washed clean of standing oil (the oil factor is constant, not determined by cars dynamically) and there is no layer of water on it. The slickest conditions appear when there is either small amounts of rainfall, in which the oil slowly drains off - making slickness last much longer, and if there is a lot of rain, in which a layer of water can collect on the road surface and cause a car to hydroplane.

Prev - Contents - News - Next - Up Top

© Copyright 2001, Drew Sikora Help

FIGURE 1.2.7 *Contents of a subsection.*

Dishing out information in this manner allows users to focus their attention on the parts of the design document that are relevant to them. Thus, the programmer in charge of implementing weather can drill down to Section 7.3 and be presented with nothing but information on weather in the game.

File Structure

There is a very good reason why you should develop a good file structure, and that reason is *maintenance*. Using the level-of-detail access method described above, you will have a page for every single section in your document. As you can imagine, if you just stashed these pages in a folder and named them incoherently, assembling the complete document would be a nightmare.

If you open Explorer and look at the file structure for this design document (see Figure 1.2.8), you will notice that each section has its own folder. This alone helps separate the various files into a well-organized configuration, and provides an added bonus: You can give the same names to files located in different sections. This helps you in two ways:

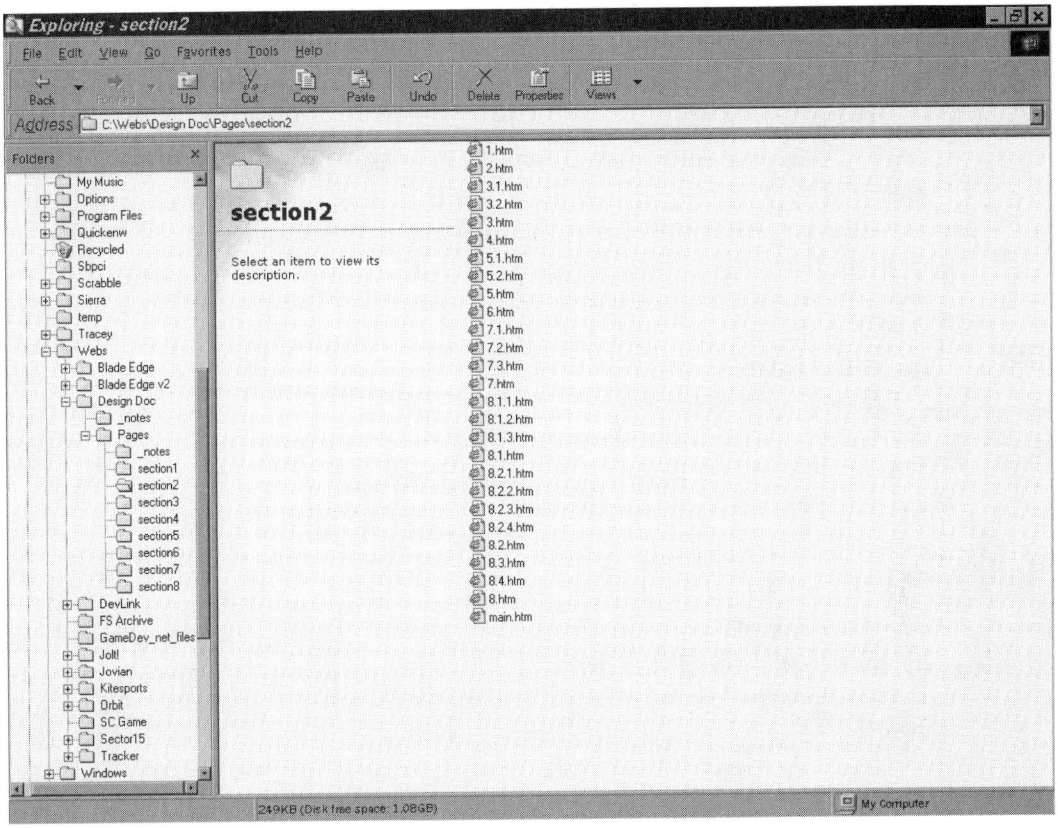

FIGURE 1.2.8   *Online design document file structure.*

- **Uniformity:** There is always one main.htm page in each section, and every file is named by section. Therefore, when linking to pages from within the document itself, you only need to remember the section number to know which file to point to.
- **Error prevention:** Once the files are in the correct folder, it's very hard to mix them up, because if you accidentally drag a file into another folder, chances are that folder will contain a file of the same name. Windows will then prompt you for a replacement, allowing you to cancel the operation. Obviously this is not a foolproof method, but it is a nice caveat, nonetheless.

As you can see, a systematic file structure provides many benefits because it is easy to use and maintain—all wonderful qualities when you need to update the document. As long as things are organized, easy to find, and well named, everybody wins.

Multimedia

When you distribute the design document, you may have to consider other things besides the text. You may have created videos, images, or sound clips that support the explanations you have written into the document itself. Although you can easily embed such content into Web pages, it is best to keep multimedia content as separate, external elements.

The reason for keeping multimedia separate actually goes back to design points two and three: presenting easy access to information and presenting information in various ways. Providing external links that open new windows on demand lets the user focus his attention. Better yet, the user can open several of these support materials at the same time, or keep a multimedia window open while traversing the document, in case the material is referenced somewhere else. This prevents you from having to embed the multimedia element in two or more separate pages, which saves both space and load times.

Although no multimedia elements are included within our sample design document, it should be noted that, in keeping with the orderly file structure we have defined, all multimedia content would be stored in a folder labeled Media, which would contain subfolders for images, sounds, videos, and so on.

Modifications

You may think you can create the perfect document, and you may be right; however, it's unlikely you will create a perfect document on your first try. Sooner or later, you will have to upgrade here, tweak there, overhaul elsewhere, add, remove—all on your own.

Updates

To make sure everyone *else* is on the same page, a very important part of your design document is the *Updates* section. There are three rules to follow when creating this all-important area:

ON THE CD

- **The Updates should be the first thing people see:** Or, at least, there should be a link to the Updates from the main page. If you look at the sample design document's index.htm page on the CD-ROM, you will see that it lists the date of the last update and provides a link to obtain more information.
- **Updates should list every change made, where it was made, and why it was made:** This is common sense—you have to inform people of the where, what, and why so they understand *what* the new feature is or *why* a feature was removed or *where* a section was added.
- **The Updates page should take the user back to where he previously was:** Remember design point number one—we do not want to use the Back button. Add a simple JavaScript link with the statement `history.goto(-1)`, and the user will zip right back to where he came from.

Look at the Updates page in the sample design document to see how these rules were implemented.

Design Notes

As a designer, it is important to note *why* you make gameplay decisions. Explaining yourself can help others understand your thought processes better, not to mention prevent mistakes from cropping up. (The *Traction Control* sample document I provided does not have a section for design notes, mainly because it was never truly meant for production, which is when certain things usually pop up that should be noted.)

As with multimedia content, the Design Notes section should be implemented as a separate page that is linked from the main page as well as from within the document itself. Each individual note should also contain hyperlinks that take the user to the section of the design document relevant to the note.

Feedback

Although you may think your design document has reached the level of perfection, always remember that beauty is in the eye of the beholder. Other members of the team may find an explanation lacking or discover a broken link, and you have to make sure to listen when they tell you.

Constructive criticism is an important part of design and implementation. You should provide a forum or email address that lets team members point out mistakes that need fixing. The goal is to make the design document accepted by everyone, so that everyone likes and uses it. To do this, you will have to take good care of reader feedback, making changes here and there to satisfy the needs of your audience so that in the end, everyone is happy.

Conclusion

You probably never thought so much could go into designing a simple online document. We covered a lot of ground in this article, but fortunately you have a working online document to reference, which should make things muchclearer when designing your own documents. Now that you are done, take some time to peruse the *Traction Control* document and explore it fully. Feel free to use the pages as a template for your own online document, or to develop your own style. Just remember to stick to the goals established at the start, and all of your team's members will be browsing your design documents with ease—and thanking you for it.

1.3

Writing the Adventure Game

Bruce Onder

bonder@digitalarcana.com

There are many ways to write an adventure game, and what follows is an attempt at defining the best practices in this difficult endeavor. Whether you use this particular methodology or not, you should at least use some kind of methodology, or you will be in for some very long nights, indeed.

An Iterative Approach to Game Design

In software development, one of the best and most successful approaches to building applications is called *iterative development*—you build a little, you test a little, you release it to the client.

When working in the financial services industry, my job was to help design and develop new releases for a company's loan processing software. At the beginning of the job, the software was somewhere around release 14, and at the end of the time there, it was around release 25. To keep the revisions working well, the programming team was given a list of the most important features users wanted, and then the team had to determine how many of those features could be developed in a month. The revision was then built, tested, and delivered to users at 600 branch offices around the country. (This financial software is still in production, and continues to process about $15 billion in loans every quarter.)

This article puts forth the proposition that you can—and should—use the same sort of diligence in your own work designing adventure games. Designing adventure games, after all, is not much different than designing any software: you need some sort of assembly line for getting from point A (an idea) to point Z (final polish signed, sealed, and delivered).

Definitions

This article uses a few terms that may require explanation:

- **Story Beat:** A story beat is an abstracted chunk of story that boils down the essential story elements. The classic "Boy meets girl/Boy loses girl/Boy finds girl" describes three story beats. The beats themselves could be fleshed out in any number of ways, but the key concepts of each beat are easily understood—in simple terms.

- **Scene:** A detailed story unit told at a particular location at a particular point in time. For instance, if your hero goes to a seedy bar to find a clue, that is a scene. If he goes back the next night to track down his suspect, that is another scene.

Milestones

Getting from point A to point Z, as mentioned earlier, is another way of saying "hitting your milestones." *Milestones* are nothing more than something tangible (a document, a prototype, or a baseball cap) delivered on or before a specific date. A typical set of design milestones might include the following:

- **Conceptual Design Phase:** Game Overview Document (GOD), GOD Review and Brainstorming Session(s), GOD Revision(s), GOD Sign Off
- **Initial Design Phase:** Initial Design Document (IDD), IDD Review Session(s), IDD Revision(s), IDD Sign Off
- **Expanded Design Phase:** Expanded Design Document (EDD), EDD Review Session(s), EDD Revision(s), EDD Sign-Off
- **Final Design Phase:** Final Design Document (FDD), FDD Review Session(s), FDD Polish(es), FDD Sign Off

We will now describe each phase in detail.

Conceptual Design Phase

This stage of the process is like the first step in organizing a game of touch football—before anything else happens you must find the playing field and make sure all the players are on that field. This requires determining three things:

1. What sort of game you are going to create?
2. What sort of game you are not going to create?
3. What it will look and feel like to play it?

To accomplish these steps, you should gather everyone's thoughts, organize them by topic, synthesize, and publish the summary as a Game Overview Document (GOD). What should be in a GOD? Enough to answer the following questions:

- Executive Summary
  - What kind of game is it?
  - What kind of game is it not?
  - Why will people want to buy it? Why does the publisher want to publish it?
- Game Elements
  - What sort of gameplay will it have?
  - What sorts will it not have?

- Give an example or two of the types of gameplay or puzzles the game will have.
- Story Elements
  - What is the synopsis of the story (in one or two paragraphs)?
  - What is the setting?
  - What is the tone?
  - Provide a few short descriptive scenes with major characters in a major setting.
- Interface
  - What sort of perspective is used (first person, third person)?
  - How will the interface work? (Direct manipulation? Inventory window?)
  - Write a few quick examples of how the interface is used.

The GOD can have a more comprehensive outline than this, but it should remain simple. After all, the GOD is only the first of a series of documents that will spiral outward in terms of complexity and depth.

The Game Overview Document is an alternative to the model presented in Article 1.1.

Reviewing the GOD

When a draft of the GOD is ready, you should submit it to the project's stakeholders (those involved and potentially involved in publishing the game) for review. The process may include, but is not limited to, the producer, the lead developer, the prospective publisher if any, the company's sales staff, and the project's financial backers. Try to contain the review process for the GOD to one day of individual review, and two or three hours of group review and idea capturing. This document should be short so your team members should be able to read and comment on it quickly.

Each section of the document should include all the ideas that everyone on the team can agree upon. You should review, revise, and republish the document as many times as necessary before moving into the initial design phase. Each time you review, you should be striving to revise the concept and add additional ideas about which everyone on the team agrees.

The GOD is a living document until everyone agrees that it accurately describes the game to be designed, and then you will no longer need it. Copy the file, name it "Initial Design Document," (IDD) and begin fleshing out the next level of detail of your game design.

Initial Design Phase

The initial design of your game describes story and interactivity in general, qualitative terms. You are *not* writing full scenes with dialog and detailed scene description and interactivity elements at this stage—you are merely outlining the general flow of events and the types of gameplay the game will offer at any given point.

While no hard and fast rule exists for how long the initial draft of an adventure game design document should be, a safe range would be from 75 to 125 pages. By the time you revise the draft once or twice and get to the final design phase, the document might reach as much as 500 to 1,000 pages.

The major sections of a good IDD are described in the following sections.

Part I: Story

The story section outlines the game's plot line, characters, settings, and structure.

Story Overview

The Story Overview is a short, compelling pitch describing, in the most exciting terms possible, what the rest of the IDD is going to explain. Although the Story Overview is short relative to the rest of the document, you should spend as much time as necessary on it in order to produce the best overview possible. Aim for a single paragraph of three to five sentences that best encapsulates the story. You should commit this part of your document to memory, so that you will always have a quick description of your entire project on hand if necessary.

Story Organization

You should decide how you want your story to be organized and presented to your audience. Possible structure elements include chapters, episodes, acts, and so forth. Alternatively, you might decide that your story should not be delineated in any way, but rather be presented as a continuum along which the player can meander freely. A well-defined structure augmented with the option to save the game at any point within a story unit achieves a good balance between both alternatives. A game built on this structure might have the feel of a novel or television series but at the same time retain the flexibility of software.

Story Outline

The outline tells the story at the level of the *beat* or sequence. The story outline should provide enough detail to allow meaningful comments, but no more: there is a strong possibility that the outline will have to be rewritten several times, so going too deep too soon will waste effort.

Here is an example of a story outline: "You leave the space station aboard the *SS Fistulous* only to be immediately attacked by Antarean space gangsters. You have to *fight the gangsters* in order to survive and continue your quest to find Princess Lulu the Snide."

Your story outline should fit (loosely) within the organizational structure you have decided upon. Over time, story elements will move from one chapter or episode to another as the story and game evolve.

It is useful to underline references to major elements of gameplay. These references will be described in more detail in the Puzzle/Game Descriptions section of the document. Underlining (or actual hyperlinking, if you use a word processor that supports it) is a good way to show a relation between the story and gameplay sections of the document.

Characters

Your job in this section is to capture every detail about each character that might be relevant to the story. Each character is given its own subsection, which contains a paragraph or more covering each of the following topics:

- **Who the character is:** This section will tell anyone reading the document about the character's role in the game. This description becomes useful when revising the document, because any character who does not have a compelling description probably is not doing all they can in the story—at this point, the character can either be enhanced to have a greater role in the story, consolidated with other characters to reduce the number of characters to be produced, or simply cut entirely.

- **What he/she/it looks like:** It is important that the artists know what you have in mind for a character before they start doing sketches. Here's your opportunity to describe exactly what it is you want to see on screen. Keep in mind, though, that the artists bring incredible expertise and creativity of their own to the design process, so be open to their suggestions.

- **Specific design notes:** Sometimes, it is critical that the character have (or not have) specific features for the story to work. For instance, if it is important that a giant multitentacled monster be able to capture all four of your lead characters, the final monster should not emerge from production with only two or three tentacles. Detailing any and all specific design needs in this section can prevent such problems.

- **How he/she/it speaks, and what he/she/it sounds like:** Even if your game will use a text-driven dialog system, it is important to be able to describe the character's speech mannerisms. For instance, if your six-inch tall imp from another dimension speaks with a Bronx accent for some reason, note that here (and provide reasons, so it is clear why this has to be so).

- **When and where he/she/it appears in the story:** This section is not as important as the others, but you can use it to estimate how much screen time the character will have. When you begin scripting the actual scenes, you will be able to go into character appearances in much more detail, but for now, a simple description, such as "Jimbo the Zombie is resurrected by the player in Episode 2 and is with him until the final Episode, when he sacrifices himself out of friendship and boredom with the life of the undead" will suffice.

- **Backstory:** Sometimes it is important to know what happened to the character before your story started. While you should only pepper little bits of backstory here and there to help you write scenes, dialog, or even game or puzzle descriptions, there is never any harm in giving your major characters a deep and detailed backstory.

- **Relationships with other characters:** This section provides probably one of the most important parts of the character description: who likes who, who is falling head over heels for whom, and who is going to knock so-and-so's teeth out if given half a chance. While you w ill not have time to do a Cartesian product on how the characters feel about each other, you can and should note all of the important relationships each character has to the others.

Locations

You should describe the various locations you will be using within your game, as well as any specific sets within those locations. Consider fleshing out the following categories of information for each location:

- **What is the location?** A creepy Scooby-Doo-esque graveyard? Describe it.
- **Special design notes:** As with you did with characters, if there are any special attributes of the location that must be executed a certain way, describe them here. For instance, if the name on the graveyard gates is "Forever Restful" and this fact appears elsewhere in the game, note that here.
- **Which sets are located within this location?** One scene might be the rickety gate at the front entrance; another might be a crypt someone has broken into recently. If your structure permits it, consider listing all of the various times the player will visit these sets, and how these sets need to be dressed or programmed differently. For example, in a space opera game, you might have much of the space ship "locked down" due to a self-destruct virus infecting the ship's computer. Later, the player might have access to the sick bay, and, later still, the escape shuttle. You could list the sick bay and escape pods, noting that the sick bay is only available when the player has deactivated the virus, and the escape shuttles are available only at the end of the game, when the player and the villain are fighting it out.
- **Special dressing or programming for the scenes or location:** For example, the graveyard would look very different at high noon than it would at sunset or midnight. However, you would only describe these variations if you needed the player to be there at those alternate times.

Other Story Notes

This is a catch-all section of the document where you capture miscellaneous bits of information about your story. Some of the subsections under this heading might contain:

- **Tone/Mood of the Story:** A comedic space opera will not be written the same way as a splatterpunk horror game. It will be important for all of the creative members of your team (artists, director, writers, and game designers) to understand the mood in order to produce the game the way you see it.
- **Backstory:** This is the story that happened before the beginning of the game's story. The story notes section is a good place to capture all the backstory that is not specific to a single character in a single place. (Keep backstory for a single

character with that character's description in the Characters section.) For example, in the story notes you would write about the history of the galactic empire, but you would put notes about Fred the Space Cadet's years at Galactic Empire Cadet Academy in his specific description in the Characters section.

Part II: Interactivity

The Interactivity section describes the ways in which information is presented to the players, what the players are expected to do in the game, and the means at their disposal to influence the game world.

Perspective

Unless your game is a pure text adventure, it needs to have perspective; in other words, a way in which the player views the world you have created for him. (Even in pure text adventures, there is a perspective—second person—in which the player is described as "you.")

Traditional perspective options include audience, isometric, bird's-eye, Over the Shoulder (OTS) ,trailing camera, and first person.

- **Audience:** This viewpoint is a flat scene done in a 2D style/technology. This perspective looks to the audience like a television show: the players are the audience, watching the action play out on the stage.
- **Isometric:** In this perspective, you look down on the game world at an angle. Think of the *Diablo* titles and you will have a perfect example (not of an adventure game, but of a perspective).
- **Bird's-Eye:** This perspective looks straight down on the action. You rarely see this style anymore, and with good reason—the perspective is not very effective. If you recall the freeware Jedi Adventures game from LucasArts, it was done in Birds-Eye perspective.
- **Over the Shoulder (OTS):** This perspective gets the player close to the action from the perspective of a character, without giving the player the sense that he actually *is* the character. This perspective is best when the player might be following more than one character through the story.
- **Trailing Camera:** Is similar to OTS, but the view is pulled back even farther, so you can see all of the physical antics of the character. *Tomb Raider* and *Max Payne* provide examples of this perspective.
- **First Person:** In this persepctive, the viewer Looks at the world through the main character's eyes. This perspective provides the most immersive feel for the game player.

Historically, most adventure games have used a first-person perspective. However, you can and should use the best perspective for your game, even if that calls for mixing and matching the different styles to achieve a desired effect.

Interface

In the Interface section, you should describe the look and feel of your game and the ways in which your players will interact with it. For example:

- **Goal**: What is the overall objective you are trying to achieve with your interface? Is it to be as unobtrusive as possible? To be funny? To be as detail-oriented as possible? Capture your goals in the document so that you can refer to them as you progress to see how well you achieve them. Check new interface elements against the goals to decide whether the new elements need to stay, go, or evolve a bit.
- **Character Control:** Does your player control the movements of one or more characters in the game? If so, which one? If not, how does the game impart a sense of action?
- **Basic Movement:** How does the player move around in your game world? With a mouse? Keyboard? Joystick? Game console controller? All of the above?
- **Specific Movement:** Will there be different environments in the game interface, such as underwater exploration? Space walking? Mountain climbing? If so, how does the player move the character(s) through these special environments?
- **Object Manipulation:** How will the player interact with objects in the game? What does clicking on an object do? What does a click-drag action do?
- **Player Help:** How does the player get help if he is stuck? For example, does the player hold down the Control button to see all the interactive spots in the game? Or does help arrive in the form of an on-screen character who points out possible ways to overcome the current problem?
- **Hidden/Visible Interface Elements:** Which elements of the interface can be hidden until requested by the player? Which need to be on screen at all times?
- **Inventory Management:** How will the player get things in and out of his inventory collection? Do you even want an inventory collection?
- **Object Interactions:** How can the player explore the ways in which objects in your world interact? For instance, if the player has a paper clip and nail file (good makings for a lock pick), how can he use these two inventory items in combination to pick the lock on a door?
- **Dialog:** How will the player talk to, or otherwise interact with, the various characters in your game? Will you implement dialog trees? Initiate conversations based on showing inventory objects to characters? Or something entirely different?
- **Other Interfaces:** Your game may have interesting new ways for the player to interact with the world, and the Other Interfaces section is where you need to describe them. For example, if your game has a special in-game rationalization for Save and Restore, you would describe that here.

Story Beat Diagrams

Remember that a *story beat* is a collection of scenes that play out a specific plot point, such as "chase through asteroid field" or "shoot-out with Nazi zombies." A story beat description helps "roll up" the action into chunks that make it easier to discuss the story at a high level.

A *story beat diagram* is a collection of ovals and arrows that help show the flow (or alternate flow) of the story at a high level. Figure 1.3.1 shows a simple story beat diagram.

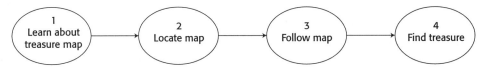

FIGURE 1.3.1   *Story Beat diagram.*

As you can see in the figure, the story at this level looks entirely linear, it lays out very important information. The diagram gives us a 50,000-foot view of the story. We are definitely telling a story about finding a lost treasure, and we see the proper sequencing of story elements: you have to know about the treasure and the map before you can actively find it, you have to locate the map before you can search for the treasure, and you have to search for the treasure before you can locate it.

So far, our sequence diagram does not show any real interactivity. Now look at Figure 1.3.2, which fleshes out the detail of the second story beat.

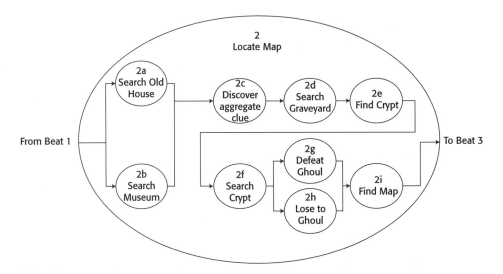

FIGURE 1.3.2   *Detailed story beat diagram.*

In this figure, we describe in more precise detail the ways in which the player can look for the treasure map. We see that the player can search either the old house or the museum, before discovering a new clue aggregated from both of those experiences which will lead the player to search the graveyard. There, the player finds a crypt that contains a ghoul. Whether they beat the ghoul or lose to it, they will find the map (but in different ways, with different scenes playing out).

How far is far enough? If you flesh out each of the major beats to one level below the high-concept description presented in Figure 1.3.1, that is probably good enough for the initial phase. But only you and your client can agree on this.

Puzzle/Game Descriptions

Remember the Story Outline section of the document, where you underlined references to gameplay? In the Puzzle/Game Description, you will now fill in all the details.

What sorts of puzzle and gameplay should be broken out of the storyline and moved here? Anything that would detract from the story being told in the outline section, and anything that involves a multistep process. These elements can be described as follows:

- **Title:** The title should match the title described in the story outline.
- **Goal:** Provide a brief description of the objective the player is trying to reach.
- **Difficulty Rating:** Use Low, Moderate, and High (based on the "average" gamer in your audience).
- **Details:** Provide a detailed description of the tasks and events that need to be completed in order to finish the puzzle or complete the game.

Gameplay Matrix

The *Gameplay Matrix* shows game element distribution within your story. Use it to balance gameplay within your story and to get a sense for the difficulty levels of different parts of your game. The Gameplay Matrix should take the form of a simple table in your document, with the following column headers:

- **Chapter (or Episode, etc.):** Chapter number, episode number, etc., listed in sequential order.
- **Title:** The title of the game or puzzle.
- **Difficulty:** Difficulty level of the game or puzzle.
- **Location(s):** Location(s) used as a backdrop for the game or puzzle.

Once you have created your Gameplay Matrix, you will be able to answer the following questions:

- **How balanced is the gameplay?** Are there periods where the game is too linear?
- **Are some areas of the game too easy, or too difficult?** Or is the variance in difficulty from one part of the game to another designed that way?
- **How diverse are the backdrops of the different games and puzzles?** Will the player get bored by endless repetition? On the other hand, could you move certain scenes to locations visited earlier, in order to benefit from player recognition—and cut development costs in the process?

Object List

As you describe the gameplay and story, the need for certain devices or objects will become obvious. List them in a table, including any special description of the object or state changes the object might experience (before/after being blown up, for example).

Part III: Appendices

The third part of your initial design document includes appendices supporting the concepts described in the previous parts of the document.

Examples of Gameplay

It is usually a good idea to write step-by-step walkthroughs of selected parts of your game. Focus on the two or three sequences that will create the most excitement about the project—especially if you are pitching the project, and not already under contract—or that expose specific design issues that would best be examined within a specific case in point. You can write these examples simply as alternating paragraphs of text: "First you see this," "Then you do this," "Then you see this," and so forth.

World Maps

You may find it helpful to provide maps that show the geographical range of your story. Maps can take many different forms, from the simple "ovals with arrows" diagram to detailed maps and illustrations of your environments.

Inspirational Works

Are there any specific works that you used, or would like people to use, as inspirational "leaping off" points in your story? Some types of inspirational works you could list are:

- **Music Recordings:** What types of music inspired you when creating this game? What music do you think would put other team members in the same "zone?"
- **Posters/Paintings:** Did any wall art strike your fancy while you were creating the game?
- **Novels:** What books might get the your team's right creative juices flowing?
- **Movies:** Did major motion pictures inspire you to write your game? What about independent films?
- **Television:** Would watching *Twin Peaks* put your team members in the right mood? What about *Dexter's Laboratory*?
- **Board Games and Paper Role-Playing Games (RPGs):** What table-top games might help set the appropriate atmosphere for your team?
- **Other Games:** What other games, if any, tweaked your creative urge?

Reviewing the Initial Design Document

At this point, you may want to start pruning the list of team members included in the IDD review meetings. The IDD is probably quite large, and some people might not be able to dedicate the time needed to review it properly. Also, the more people in a review meeting, the more difficult it can be to get things moving, keep everyone on track, and meet goals.

The IDD is likely to require one day for individual review, and a half day (broken into two parts, separated by lunch or dinner) for discussion. Some open issues from the GOD will get resolved, others will be opened up for discussion, and others will remain unresolved.

All of this is okay, as long as you have a plan for moving toward resolution of all open issues by the time you get to the Final Design Document (FDD). If you fail to plan, then you are planning to fail, as many a personal development guru are wont to say.

Expanded Design Phase

When you, your team, and your client are satisfied with the initial design document, it is time to move on to the next stage of detailing, which takes the form of an interactive screenplay in the Expanded Design Document (EDD).

As with the IDD, you still will not be writing full scenes in the EDD. However, you will create placeholders for the scenes you will write in the Final Design Document.

The following elements from the IDD will be expanded into greater detail in the EDD phase. You will likely need to add, modify, and delete items from these lists as you work through the EDD.

- **Cast List:** Reference characters by name and additional modifier (for example, Morty in suit, Morty in pajamas) from this list.
- **Location List:** Every scene you write will be "shot" in a location from this list. Make sure you capture any permutation of the location (night, day, etc.).
- **Object List:** Every object that is used in a scene or by the player should be listed here. Keep track of any changes in the object's state (locked, unlocked, etc.).
- **Story Sections:** The first step is to cut and paste your Story Outline section of the IDD into the EDD document. Each chapter, episode, or part should get its own subsection, with a page break between subsections. Next, create a template for laying out and describing an interactive scene. You will paste this template into the document numerous times, so be certain you are satisfied with it before you use it. Unless you are a programmer, global formatting changes will be too challenging to make once you are under way. The following are some essential items you should include in your interactive scene template:
  - **Scene Reference Number:** An ID number that will uniquely identify every scene in your adventure. The simplest scheme would be to use sequential numbers; however, numbering can become confusing if scenes are added or deleted during the design process. A more robust and usable scheme would be to use the chapter number, the beat number, and the scene number of each scene. This way, if someone references "scene A4C," you will immediately know that they mean "Chapter A, Beat 4, and Scene C."

- **Scene Location:** A reference to the location list in your IDD. If the location has multiple dressings (night/day, before/after specific event, etc.), make sure to specify which one to use.
- **Cast Members:** A list of the characters that appear in this scene. Again, this list will refer to the cast description in your IDD. As with locations, you should specify any particular costume or physical condition needed.
- **Objects:** A list of objects that appear in the scene. These objects are either plot relevant, game relevant, or both.
- **Scene Description:** An outline of the events that occur in the scene.
- **When Available/Played:** A description of the conditions under which the scene is played; for example, "after player has discovered the Pink Armadillo matchbook and visits the Pink Armadillo location." You should also reference any game variables that define this availability.
- **Clip Table:** Interactive scenes can be thought of as a collection of movie clips that play or do not play based on player's actions and the current state of the game. This table lists all of the movie clips that are available in the scene and under what conditions they will play. Playing a movie clip can update the game state, so you should also track that. For example, if a character delivers some clue via dialog, you could track this knowledge using a simple true/false variable.
- **Event Table:** A table of action/result entries that describes what happens in response to each player action inside this scene. For instance, if the player clicks on the "redial" button on the desk phone, a phone number will be dialed and a voice mail machine will answer. Or, if any of the player's potential inventory objects would have interesting interactions with other items in the scene, you would describe those here. *Dependencies* can also be listed among the entries in the event table; for example, "if the player redials the phone and enters the three-digit code, then the message will play."

    Once your template is set, make copies of it for each scene you have identified. Do not be overly concerned if you have to insert, delete, or move scenes once you get started. Just remember that you should never reuse scene numbers. If you delete a scene from your document, change all the text for that scene to strikethrough and add the words "SCENE DELETED" after the scene number. If you need to insert scenes, you can either use the next available scene number, or implement some simple A/B numbering scheme; for example, the scene inserted between B12A and B12B would be B12A1. If you are "moving" a scene, consider deleting the old scene and inserting the content in a new scene in the correct place. You can mark the old scene "SCENE MOVED TO . . ." to be more descriptive, if you like.
- **Puzzle and Gameplay Sections:** This section of the EDD document should contain detailed descriptions of the various puzzles and games you intend to

pepper throughout the story. At this point, you should seek to nail down as many details of the gameplay as possible. Note any game objects needed to complete or advance the puzzles and games. You should also consider refreshing the Gameplay Matrix from the IDD phase and ensure that you still have a good mix of gameplay across your story units. Last, if any of your gameplay elements seem unsatisfactory, now is your last chance to fix them. You can take one of three approaches to fix less than satisfactory elements:

- **Replace them:** There are a few dangers inherent in this solution. First, coming up with new gameplay elements will take time, and possibly the result will be no better than what you had before. Second, you will have to spend additional time "wiring" your new gameplay into the story, making sure that all the conditions and events are right. Adopt this approach only if your project's stakeholders will be satisfied with no other solution.
- **Cut them:** Obviously, cutting elements will only work if your game is already too big. If size is not an issue, cutting content may raise some eyebrows from your clients. If you are lucky and persuasive, you might be able to make cuts, if you can prove that they will increase the product's quality.
- **Improve them:** At this point in the project, fixing whatever problems exist in your already designed content may be the safest and quickest way to success. Sometimes, cosmetic alterations will be enough to make a weak scene acceptable. Other times, a novel spin on a basic premise might eliminate the problem.
- **Variable List:** This new section of your EDD contains a simple four-column table which details, for every variable in the game, the variable name, data type, initial value, and description of purpose. This table describes all of the "state" in your game, such as whether the player has picked up an object, met a character, or asked a specific question.

Reviewing the Expanded Design Document (EDD)

Your first delivery of the EDD should, at a minimum, fully flesh out the basic story and the most important interactive elements and alternate storylines. However, as with the GOD and the IDD, it is perfectly fine to annotate your draft with open-ended comments, questions, "what-if" scenarios, and the like. However, make sure that the comments stand out from the main document in some way—use your word processor's built-in commenting features, or change the font's color, or highlight the comments, for example.

In general, successive drafts of the EDD should focus on resolving these comments in ways that are compatible with the core beliefs captured in the GOD. If the revisions violate those beliefs in any way, make sure that the team accepts the revisions and that the client accepts and signs off on the changes.

The EDD can serve as a readthrough script that your team can examine for continuity, consistency, and internal logic. For instance, one member of the team can read the scene descriptions, characters, and objects out loud, while the other members of the team read out various player actions.

Usually you conduct a readthrough simply to ensure that all your scenes work correctly, but occasionally this sort of play-testing will unearth an interesting bit of gameplay or interactivity that has not previously been thought of. If everyone immediately agrees that the new idea is valuable, then you may justify upsetting the game design schedule to build it into the game.

At the end of the expanded design phase, you will have a fully fleshed-out EDD that will serve as a solid foundation for producing the Final Design Document (FDD).

Final Design Phase

In the final design phase, you will (or at least, should) be concentrating on three things:

- Screenplay writing all scenes you have laid out.
- Refining the gameplay, mostly by fleshing out the details of your puzzles and by fixing faulty game logic.
- Defending the design against major revisions.

Story Sections: Writing Scenes

You can write scenes in any format you, your team, and your client are comfortable with, but the Hollywood screenplay format was developed over many decades to be easily read and easily marked up. See [Nicholl02] for a tutorial on screenplay formatting.

This article will not attempt to teach you how to be a good (or even marginal) screenwriter. Many books are available on that subject. However, remember that most of your final design document (FDD)time and energy will be spent writing the movie clips in your scenes. Therefore, all other design elements (such as the Gameplay Sections, discussed next) should be as complete as possible in the expanded design phase.

Refining the Gameplay

- **Detail Gameplay Elements:** In this section, nail down any outstanding gameplay issues that have been raised, and to make sure that all loose ends have been tied up.
- **Catch and Fix Game Logic:** Once the first draft of your FDD is written, you should set aside time to run through the game to look for mistakes (story continuity, missing props) and faulty game logic (puzzles that cannot be solved, logical dead ends). The following list several ways to play-test your creation:

- **Conduct a script reading:** As in the EDD document review, have your team start reading out loud. Have someone read the stage direction, have others people read various characters, and assign one person to track the state of variables on a pad of paper. Have someone else check off the steps of completing each puzzle or game in the FDD.
- **Wire frame the game:** If you have any skill with HTML, consider developing a set of Web pages with hyperlinks representing various player options from any particular scene in your game. The only thing you will not be able to track with plain HTML is the game's state. If you know how to script dynamic Web pages, you can build a simple "state" machine that can set variables for you when you click certain links. If you do not know how to set up dynamic pages, you can obtain the same basic effect by creating multiple hyperlinks for each possible state combination out of a scene.
- **Develop a prototype:** If your development team can create a prototype, it is a good way to walk through the design as you go, even as far back as the IDD. Prototypes take planning and dedication from developers, though, so if you use this option, try to get the developers to commit the time up front.

Defend Against Major Revisions

One of your chief goals in the final design stage is to keep things under control. The changes you should be making at this point ought to be detail-oriented: correcting faulty logic or detailing scenes. Any change that does not directly address a simple scene note, for example, "I don't think Ace would shoot Jake just because he looked at him funny—have Ace say something funny instead" should be avoided at all costs.

Remember that the bigger the change is at this stage, the more potential impact it can have on the game as a whole. The more work you have to do, the more harm you can do.

If you can get contractual agreement that the final design phase will be dedicated to fleshing out what has already been designed at a higher level and nothing else, do so. You will be glad you did, and so will the fans of your adventure game.

Bibliography

[Laramée02] Laramée, F.D., "Writing Effective Design Treatments," *Game Design Perspectives*, Charles River Media, 2002.
[Nicholl02] Nicholl Fellowships on Screenwriting, "Screenplay Format Sample." Available online: *www.oscars.org/nicholl/format.html.*

1.4

The Designer's Best Friends

John Dennis

John.Dennis@team17.com

Why is it so difficult to both design a game and write a good design document? And why does the final game design document never seem to really capture the excitement of your concept? This article will try to answer just that question and provide you with ideas on how to create the most effective design document you can.

The Trouble with "New"

The concept of a *design* and the problems inherent to it are uniquely modern ones. Here is an example to illustrate: Picture yourself as a Bronze Age man wishing to build a hut for yourself and your family. Your tribe has been building huts in the same way for a hundred generations: first a shallow circular pit is dug in the ground, then reeds and branches are arranged in a circular shape around the pit to create the walls. Last, a roof of reeds, branches, and straw is added, which includes a hole in the top to let out the smoke from the fire. The reeds and straw keep warmth in and the wet out, while the round shape gives you the most room inside the hut for the least amount of building.

You must do the work of collecting the reeds and branches and putting them together, but you do not have to worry about whether the hut will work: it is a tried and tested formula, passed from generation to generation. The problems that face you as a Bronze Age man, problems like keeping warm and dry, have been addressed in an evolutionary design process over a very long period of time. The design of the hut has been refined, each generation adding or removing some aspect, and the unsuccessful changes discontinued, while the effective ones are added to the formula. The process ensures that the house you build is based on tested ideas that you know will work.

Fast forward to the present day. You are a game designer, and your boss wants a game design finished in six months. Not only do you not have the time to evolve your design slowly, but you are also dealing with a design problem that is arguably much more complex than constructing a Bronze Age hut. This is the challenge for the modern designer: a problem that requires a complicated solution and not enough time to implement an evolutionary design process.

But, there is help for the beleaguered designer. Let's look now at our best friends in the battle to get that design to our boss in time.

Your Best Design Friends: Structure and Modularity

A game is a massive construct, with many different parts that fit together in many different ways. Given the level of detail required, even seemingly small games can spawn large design documents. The problem for the designer is to divide the design effectively and make sure that all the parts are kept separate.

What we, the designers, must do at this stage is use a mental knife to cut our designs into neat pieces. The best way to start doing this is to make a *spider diagram* of the idea.

To begin, make a list of all the main elements of your game. For example, in a car racing game the list may include the cars, the environments, the interface, music and sound effects, the opponents, and so forth. Now, draw a circle around each of these elements, as shown in Figure 1.4.1

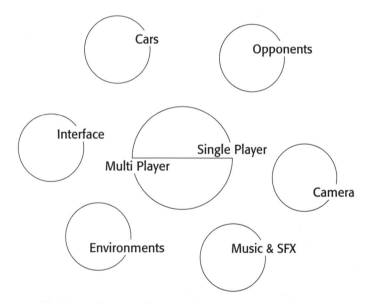

FIGURE 1.4.1   *The basic elements of a game design.*

After you have completed this exercise, think about the components that make up those main elements. For example, for the cars, you might have engines, wheels, chassis, etc. List all of the components, and draw a smaller circle around each, then connect the smaller circles to the car circle. Carry on like this, linking circles that are connected in your game's logical structure. In Figure 1.4.2, the car and interface circles are connected because the interface will be dependent on the classes of vehicles. You should end up with a large spider diagram showing you all the elements you have in your game, and how they are related, as in Figure 1.4.2.

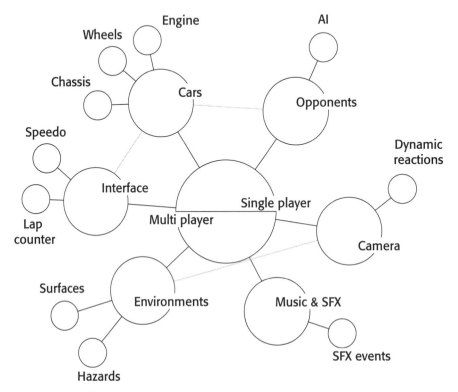

FIGURE 1.4.2   *All elements of a game design and their relationships to one another.*

Of course, there is nothing to stop you from dividing the smaller circles into even smaller circles—divide and subdivide as much as you need to, until there are no aspects of your design that have not been dealt with. The diagram only really represents the first couple of cuts with our mental knife; on a large design you may need to use many more.

What does this exercise teach you to do? Three things:

- **Organize the design document:** If you start with the main modules of your game and then add smaller circles describing their components, then the spider diagram will define the hierarchy of your design's elements. The bigger the circle, the higher the level a component is, and the more smaller elements it will contain. The diagram helps you write your design, starting with the large elements first and dividing these sections to incorporate the smaller elements that compose them.
- **Organize your work:** The spider diagram forces you to divide the game into self-contained logical components and shows you which pieces are in fact parts of

other pieces. The modular design helps you see where aspects of your design might be missing or lacking detail, and aides you making design changes.

- **Identify dependencies:** The spider diagram helps you see the relationship between all the elements in your design. This is invaluable when you revise content—when you make a change to one section, you will have a good idea how this change will affect other sections, which might need changing as well.

Unfortunately, use of our mental knife has its drawbacks as well as benefits. If you used a knife to dissect an animal, you can gain a better understanding of the unfortunate subject, but the animal itself is not only killed but completely cut apart. This analogy can be carried through to a game and its game design document. Show potential customers pictures or animated cars on screen, and they might be convinced that your game is the next big thing. However, show them a 400-page design document, and they stare at you blankly. Dividing a concept into many little pieces can make it much harder for others to see the big picture, and the process can, unfortunately, remove the "wow" factor.

The loss of "wow" factor can be remedied, however. Pictures help retain some of the attractiveness of the game, while clear and concise introductions to each section, coupled with summaries, help paint a more complete picture of what the game is about. While a design document is never going to capture the immediacy of an executable prototype, it is a necessary part of the game-building process. Having a design document that is attractive and captures the "soul" of the game might be a little less daunting for the poor folks on your team who have to read it.

Another Good Chum: Clarity of Language

Always remember that your design document is about communicating your ideas: if people can not read or understand it, you have a problem. Use plain language, written in the present tense, and use plenty of imperatives. It is always better to write, "The car stops when it hits an obstacle" than "The car should stop when it hits an obstacle." If the car only sometimes stops when it hits an obstacle, the conditions for when it does not stop need to be clearly explained, in imperatives. Uncertainty in language often betrays uncertainty in the idea you are describing, so if you find yourself using many "coulds" and "shoulds," think again about your game design and make sure you have certainty in your idea.

In addition, a game design invariably defines its own internal vocabulary. The words and phrases unique to that game design should be standardized and used consistently throughout the document.

The Rest of the Gang: Formatting, Prioritizing, and Managing Document Versions

After you have finished structuring your design and writing it in clear language, you may well find that you have created a 400-page monster. Be aware that if the document is formatted incorrectly, the rest of your team will not be particularly interested in reading it.

Formatting

It might sound obvious, but you must do everything you can to help the reader through your design document. Page numbers, indexes, a glossary, and so forth provide your readers with a document that is easy to navigate and that allows quick access to information. Be sure to cross-reference any part of your document that refers to another section. A design might stretch to several hundred pages and readers will have difficulty picking through a huge document to find an important aspect of the game that is hidden away in a mass of 10-point design gibberish. (If you have followed the rules for making your game design document modular and have written it in clear, concise language, you should not have this problem at all.)

Prioritizing

Make sure that you draw attention to the most important aspects of your design. Here are two reasons why prioritizing the document with key design points is a good idea:

- **Preparing for the worst:** Unfortunately, designs often have features removed at some point through the production process. Flagging parts of the design that are absolutely vital and must not be changed identifies to yourself and the other team members the aspects of the design that are simply not scalable. (Try and be reasonable here, though.)
- **Maintaining focus:** A design document often evolves, and flagging aspects of the game that you defined as key in the early stages makes sure that the design will not wander too far from what you envisioned.

Document Versions

An undertaking as large as writing a game design can take months, depending on game size and designer motivation. Invariably, passages will get written and rewritten and probably rewritten again. Saving different versions of the document and creating a version history helps you and the rest of your team keep track of what has been changed and what is still evolving. This is particularly important if you are keeping the design in electronic form, as described in [Sikora02]: it is vital that the people who are reading your design are actually reading the right version.

Conclusion

The use of analytical thought to break a subject down into understandable chunks was described in [Pirsig74]. In this book, Phaedrus' Knife is viewed as a form of destructive examination, whereby the beauty (or, in the terms of a novel, the quality) of the examined thing is destroyed in the process of the examination.

Dividing an artistic undertaking into smaller understandable pieces is also the subject of [Alexander64], a seminal work by Christopher Alexander, the 1960s architect who invented Patterns—which have since been resurrected by object-oriented designers, making Alexander a bit of a cult hero. Alexander explains how primitive societies had no architects but still created successful designs that lasted centuries. Alexander's ideas can be applied equally effectively to game design as to architecture and programming.

We have arguably come a long way since the time of our friend, the Bronze Age man—dealing with the problem of creating something as complex as a game design is a fine achievement. However, because of the limited time we have in which to produce a game design, we need a few techniques to help us out. Dividing the design into manageable pieces and being able to view those pieces at once both separately and as a whole is crucial. Getting our idea into a readable, attractive, and easy-to-navigate document that facilitates the design's implementation is just as important.

So do yourself, your boss, and your idea a favor, and make use of the game designer's best friends to write a design document that does your idea justice.

Bibliography

[Alexander64] Alexander, C., *Notes on the Synthesis of Form.* Harvard University Press, 1964.

[Pirsig74] Pirsig, R. M., *Zen & The Art of Motorcycle Maintenance.* The Bodley Head, Ltd., 1974.

[Sikora02] Sikora, D., "Online Design Documents," *Game Design Perspectives.* Charles River Media, 2002.

When Good Design Goes Bad

John Dennis

John.Dennis@team17.com

For anyone who has ever feverishly poured their best ideas into a game design document, it is very likely that you will have encountered the bitter moment when your design suddenly goes "bad." You realize that your beloved work will never make it off paper—and if it does, it will be a shadow of the game you thought it would be. The rest of the team are arguing, your boss wants to talk to you, and the deadline becomes a reason for removing large chunks of what you have written. Often these signs indicate the end of a project altogether, and the only things you have to show from your hard work are a badly mauled design document, perhaps a few half-built levels, and the experience of what happens when good design goes bad.

Why is it that so many games do not make it to completion? We would certainly save much wasted time, effort, and heartbreak if we could spot designs that will go bad early.

Of course, there can be many reasons for good designs failing (far too many to list in just one article) and while many problems are inflicted upon the design by management or external sources, many of the more common reasons are rooted in the design document, the design process, or the implementation itself. Spotting the danger early gives you a better chance to catch problems before it is too late. This article will present some of the most common problems that can cause a design to go wrong.

The Initial Concept

The most common error for designers is attempting to include far too much in their initial design document.. For example, some designers simply patch together the best parts of their favourite games: here is a segment where you fly a plane, then you get out and shoot enemies, then move on to a puzzle-solving, role-playing game (RPG) section, while music and 3D effects are played in the background. Although games of this scope are possible (*Shenmue*, for example), it is unlikely that a game this large can be programmed without a team of less than 1,000 people.

It is difficult to understand why some designers want to include so many features at one time. They might know such a game is unrealistic, but a "designer syndrome" drives them to create "the best game ever." This powerful (but misplaced) motivation makes many designers lose sight of the focus of their design and ignore the project's deadlines and available resources. In isolation, each part of the design might be good, but when put together, the result is a monster. Luckily, there are ways to deal with this problem.

The simplest way of taming the "monster" is to ask someone who is not emotionally attached to your design to regularly review what you have written. An ideal reviewer is one of the people who eventually will be implementing your design. It is unlikely that they will be as enthusiastic as you are about having a swarm of a million aliens appear on screen for the finale, because they will know how much work such a scene would entail. Listen to what they say. Make sure that this person has no emotional involvement in the design at all—even programmers or artists who know how much work will be involved can suffer from *designer syndrome*, or the tendency to overlook the practicalities of what we are doing and the demands it will put on manpower.

This review approach is best formalised and incorporated into your design process by allocating a *risk officer* to the project. Ideally, the risk officer is an experienced person with technical know-how who is working on a different project or at least is not closely involved with the game's design. It also helps if the risk officer is pessimistic about what is achievable inside your project deadline. At the beginning of the design process, and every week thereafter, have the risk officer review the content of the design and document the features they see as potential problems.

The risk officer should limit their input to the likelihood of implementation of any given feature; the nature of the content or gameplay are off limits. You and the rest of the team should devise solutions to the problems that the risk officer identifies, and act upon them. This process should result in a game design that, although less ambitious than the one you might have written, will ultimately be more achievable. The earlier you identify problems with your design, the easier they will be to fix, and the less likely you will be to run into terminal design problems further down the line. Remember that the role of the designer is not just to design a good game, but to design a good game that may be developed with the current staff, budget, and available time.

Committing the Design to Paper

Anyone who has ever written a game design document will tell you that what should seem like a dream job is in fact a massive amount of work that details fairly unexciting aspects of the game, from the inner workings of the artificial intelligence to the front-end menu system's functionality. And, unfortunately, such a massive undertaking is also a massive opportunity for mistakes.

A bad design document can create many problems for a team. Make the document hard to read, and nobody on the team will bother, or be able to discern what the design is about. Make the document unattractive enough, and your boss and the marketing people will not be convinced that the proposed game has merit. Structure the document poorly enough, and as soon as one feature has to be removed, other aspects of the design fall apart. If you do not include relevant details, the rest of the team will make them up as they go along. In other words, no matter how good the concept for your game is, the key to success lies in the details. A bad game design document can not only betray the weaknesses in your thinking, but it can lead the project into crisis.

Writing a good game design document is a skill that can be learned. The following sections list some simple rules that may help you avoid problems later.

Design Modularly

Obviously, something as complex as a game design must be divided into component parts so that you, the designer, can think in sufficient detail about each of them. But it is also important that you consider each aspect of the game in relation to the whole design along with all the other elements that make it up . See [Dennis02] in Part 1 of this book for details.

Prioritize

Consider each of the modules in your design in terms of importance. Label the key parts as vital, and the less important ones as expendable. A game design is rather like a building: a skeleton is needed to hold it up, while other materials can be removed with relatively little impact.

Identifying the important parts will not only help point the other members of the team in the direction of the "must-know" parts of your design, but also help ensure that vital parts of your design are protected, preventing them from being removed later if the project has to be slimmed to fit a deadline.

Pay Attention to Detail

Your design document should also include enough detail in order to enable the artists, sound technicians, and programmers to extract the requirements needed to build your game. Of course, not all detail is good: it is very interesting knowing that "Thraaag the Mighty" was born on the planet Zorn, but this detail will not help your team make the design a reality. The detail you need to include in the design document is about the functionality of your game: if you have context-sensitive music, for example, what are the events that change the state of the music? If your game includes alien enemies, how do they attack, what is the range of their attack, and how much damage do they do?

The right kind of detail helps flesh out your design; the wrong kind does not move your concept forward, but simply buries the vital information in the design.

Show, Don't Tell

Remember that you are writing your design for people who are not as familiar with your ideas as you are. Consequently, some of the more complex features of the design may need demonstrating. A hard-to-explain aspect of your design may benefit from a drawing, a cartoon strip, or even better, an animation. It may be useful to animate a 10 or 20 second period of typical play: such a demonstration can express your idea better than writing ever could, and it helps communicate the play experience as you visualise it to the members of the team who actually have to create the game.

The Audience

Last, think about the team members who have to read your design. Make the document attractive, communicate your ideas through pictures where you can, and make sure the document is easy to read and contains the information that the rest of the team needs to create the game. If you are not sure what information they are going to need, then ask them, and make sure you write this information in a form that they are prepared to digest. Creating a relevant and readable design document is a big step towards preventing your design from going bad.

Implementing Your Design

By now you have made sure that your design is not completely unrealistic and you have committed it to paper in a way that contains all the relevant detail in an easy-to-understand format. Surely you have done everything you can, and the game is heading for the best-seller's list, right? Unfortunately not. Despite the design document being pretty much finished, you still have plenty to do—thus we find ourselves at the last stage of the design process: implementation.

Many things can go wrong in this stage of development, but for the designer, one landmark looms large on the horizon: *level design*.

Many people consider the skills for designing levels in some way inferior to those required to write a game design document. This is simply not the case. The levels designed for a game are at the sharp end of the design process, and are the embodiment of the game design that the player actually experiences. For this reason, it is imperative that level design work be done well, because no matter how good the design document is, bad level design equals a bad game.

As before, while designing levels for your game is a complex art, there are some guidelines that will help you avoid serious problems.

Identify Your Aims

The first thing to remember is that each level has a goal: that goal might be to further the story in a particular way, to introduce a new play style, or to introduce a new enemy to the player. Identify what you want the player to obtain from each level and how that fits in with the game as a whole. Once established, do not deviate from this plan: if you change the goal, it may well impact the success of another level you have designed. Therefore, the first rule is to identify what you want from each of your levels and how that fits into the whole game experience. And, once you have done this, do not change your mind.

Set Up the Conflict

When you have decided what you want a level to achieve in the game, think of each of your missions as a little story that your player lives through. The initial setup presents the player with a situation and some sort of conflict or puzzle to solve. For example, your character might find an ogre that can not be tackled head on; however, a mighty sword rests on a balcony and if the player can climb up there without the ogre seeing her, the battle would be won.

Basically, you set the scene for the player's escapades during each level by laying out its various elements, such as enemies and their behaviour, rewards, and architecture. Once you have set the scene, the story itself unfolds through the player's actions. By creating problems with one optimal solution and several possible solutions, you will cater to players of all styles and abilities. The best players will find the optimal solution; less able players may still succeed but perhaps sustain more damage or not gain all the rewards that the best player does.

Resolve the Situation

When the player is finished with the level, it is up to you to make sure that they believe they either won a great victory or failed miserably, depending on how well they played. If they succeeded, give them satisfaction. Did they beat the ogre? Then let them see his castle crumble to dust and the dark shadows that blighted the land lift. If they lost, then make it clear why they lost and how they might have won. If you do not provide a resolution, the player might not be motivated to try your level again. Resolve your levels satisfactorily and the player will feel a sense of achievement, or at least believe they can succeed the next time they play..

Consider Pacing

If you make your game too difficult right from the beginning, less talented players will quickly put it down. Make it too tense early on, and the big ending that you had planned will seem so dramatic. Even worse, if you fail to make the last few levels tense enough (or the conclusion satisfactory), all the players will feel that they wasted their time on your game.

Generally speaking, each level should reach a climax somewhere near the end of it at a moment that the player will remember and tell their friends about. Build the excitement to that point, and when the resolution comes, it will be all the more satisfactory for the player.

High points of the game should get higher as the game goes on. Your first few levels may ease the player into the game, teaching them the key skills they need in order to play, while the last few levels will be tense and difficult, taking the player to the final conclusion of the game and challenging them to the extent of their ability.

Conclusion

So, what do you do if you have done everything right, and your design still goes bad? Unfortunately, circumstances may conspire against you, and even knowing the reasons why designs go bad may not help. You may find yourself trying to retro-fit a design to a project already in development, fighting with a shifting deadline, saddled with poor level design tools, limited to a team too small to develop the game, or even stuck with a group of people who do not like you. The market you planned to release the game into may have died during the development of your game, or insurmountable technical problems may prevent getting the game past the prototype stage.

The first thing you need to know is that it is very common for games to never be completed. Second, even if you do your absolute best, you may not be able to prevent the project from hitting the rocks. And third, if the design does go bad, it is not usually one person's fault.

Ours is a relatively young industry, in which developers often have little discipline, rely on outmoded development strategies, or worse, no strategy at all. But if you are aware of the potential problems described in this article, you will make it much less likely that your team will fail in designing your dream game.

Bibliography

[Dennis02] Dennis, J., "The Designer's Best Friends," *Game Design Perspectives*, Charles River Media, 2002.

GAME DESIGN THEORY

2.0

Introduction

Where does the fun in a game come from? What must we put into a game to make it worthwhile, and what do we need to keep out of it? How do we generate ideas, sift the golden nuggets from the unworkable clichés, and refine the best of everything into commercially viable products?

Designers must answer these difficult questions every day. This section of the book focuses on several aspects of design theory, from the seminal idea to the refinements of playtesting.

Knowing The Audience

Before you can begin design work proper, you must ask yourself: who will play this game, when, where, and how? Each aspect of your design will have to be tailored accordingly. For example:

- **Pacing:** Whereas hardcore gamers are notoriously fond of adrenaline-rush products, most adults get more than enough stress and pressure at work or from the vagaries of daily life; thus, games for the mass market tend to be more relaxed, to feature less overt conflict, and to let the players dictate the rhythm of the action at their leisure.
- **Structure:** Games for handheld mobile devices, such as the GameBoy Advance and cell phones, tend to be played in short bursts, for example between classes and meetings or while riding the bus. Therefore, they require short levels that can be walked through in minutes.
- **Complexity:** Many types of games require simple rules that can be learned instantly; for example, those for young children, those for casual gamers with limited free time, and Web "gamelets" intended to keep visitors on a site for a few extra minutes. Similarly, these products must provide quick, easy, and frequent gratification in the form of small successes and new discoveries.
- **Technological Thresholds:** Mass-market PC game players tend to own older machines equipped with entry-level video cards and limited memory. Games targeted to them must install easily, work on low-end hardware, and require little or no configuration.

Generating Ideas

Truly original ideas are few and far between; after all, human beings have been looking for ways to entertain each other for tens of thousands of years. For game designers, the key to design success lies in finding the optimal balance between novelty, which is required to make a product stand out, and familiarity, without which we run the risk of alienating the audience.

Ideas that could potentially find their way into a game are everywhere, from the funny stories told by friends at parties to the short newspaper filler paragraphs describing the weird events and people in the world to the off-beat low-circulation magazines found in public libraries. Designers, like anyone involved in creative endeavors, must be curious about everything: spend an afternoon at your local bookstore, roaming the aisles at random; listen to people on the subway; attend community outreach lectures on a nearby college campus—and, of course, play as many games as possible, especially the paper kind, because their rules and internal workings must be printed for all to see.

Then, to insert originality into your designs, combine a number of ideas in unusual ways. If you like car racing, mazes, and microbiology, design a game about microbes swimming in the bloodstream and evading antibiotics—or one in which white blood cells must assemble the right antibody ammunition from *Tetris*-like components before attacking the invading disease with big bio-guns. If you prefer real-time strategy and teen movies, how about a high school cafeteria food fighting game?

Let the creative energy flow, but be ruthless with your ideas: if one is not quite perfect for your project, discard it and look for another. Devising new concepts is hard work, but in today's market, even small flaws can doom a project to failure. Besides, coming up with seminal ideas is the best part of our jobs.

Playtesting

Design ideas rarely spring from the mind in finished form. This is why designers spend a great deal of time proofing their concepts, using prototyping in the early stages of the design process, and playtesting later on.

Prototypes

Before production begins, prototypes help the design team test the basic premises of the game. The questions that will be answered at this point include:

- Is this feature necessary? Why?
- How can we give the player easy access to this feature?
- Is this rule ambiguous? How do we refine it?
- Is there enough for the player to do at every point of the game?

Although the term *prototype* is usually assumed to refer to a technical proof of concept, game prototypes do not always require high-tech implementations. If your product's mechanics are similar to those of a board game, or can be made so for testing purposes, a tabletop prototype may be all that you need. In extreme cases, a "thought experiment" imaginary walkthrough process may even be called for.

Remember that the goal of a game design prototype is to allow for quick and inexpensive changes to even the most fundamental gameplay concepts, because at this point, you do not really know what is going to work. Sitting around a tabletop board and making rule changes as you go along costs very little and eases fast turn-around. If you can avoid implementing your design too early, you may save a great deal of time.

Playtesting

Once development is underway, playtesting takes over. This process looks at the actual game build and verifies that the features that could not be validated during the prototyping phase (for example, because they were too difficult to model) work as effectively as intended.

Playtesting involves far more than bug hunting. In addition to quality assurance and the designers, playtesting should include potential players—for example through a focus group—especially when the intended audience is demographically different from the development team.

Immersion

All forms of entertainment strive to create *suspension of disbelief,* a state in which the player's mind forgets that it is being subjected to entertainment and instead accepts what it perceives as reality. Suspension of disbelief does not always require much in terms of sensory stimulation: people have been "getting lost" in good books and campfire stories since the invention of language.

Interactive entertainment can create immersion in a variety of ways. Games focusing on action, hand-eye coordination, and personal identification between the player and the hero will strive to create immersion through sensory input: realistic visuals, positional audio, force-feedback, dramatic acting, and so forth. Games of strategy will prefer intellectual immersion: information is presented as a whole, often viewed from above, and players are fed a constant stream of abstract decisions to make. In both cases, the designer's job is to create a *closed environment,* a set of perceptions that are sufficient to represent an experience and to absorb the conscious mind. Include too little depth in the closed environment, and the players will start noticing the holes, as they would if they were watching a bad movie. Include too much, and they will be overwhelmed and give up.

Causality

Causality is the relationship between action and consequence. In a gaming context, causality must be obvious at all times: the players must know that what happens is a result of their decisions, and why one entails the other, whether immediately (in action games) or at a predictable point in the future. They must be able to identify causes for all in-game effects; otherwise, they will feel like stringed puppets.

Implementing clear causal relationships into a game requires consideration of several factors:

- **Concision:** Possible player actions at any given time must be kept to a manageable number. Otherwise, no analysis of likely outcomes is possible, and the player is forced to act in an effectively random fashion.
- **Emergence:** The interaction of simple rules may lead to surprisingly complex outcomes. While this is a good thing because it adds depth to the experience, emergence is a key concept of chaos theory —and where there is chaos, there is no possibility of understanding causality.
- **Recuperation:** The more crucial an action's consequences, the more important it is to allow the player an "escape clause" to rectify mistakes, especially if these consequences are not obvious beforehand. Players who jump out of a starship's airlock without a space suit should know better, and having their characters die immediate and painful deaths is not unwarranted; however, if there is an angry dragon behind the door on the left and a treasure behind the otherwise identical door on the right, the player had better be able to close doors *fast* after opening them.

Just as players need to identify the consequences of their actions, they must also feel that these consequences *matter*. In early days, games presented players with seemingly crucial choices that all led to the same outcome; for example, being asked to decide between sides in a conflict, and ending up being betrayed or attacked by everyone immediately after. Cheating like this breaks causality from the other end of the equation, because there is no real cause when there is no variation in effect.

Reinforcement

In psychology, reinforcement describes the phenomenon by which acceptable behaviors are encouraged through rewards (*positive reinforcement*) while bad behaviors are eradicated through punishment (*negative reinforcement*). Player learning constitutes an obvious and direct application: when the score goes up or the enemy falls to the ground, the player's most recent decisions and moves are positively reinforced, and vice versa.

However, reinforcement can become problematic if it leads to runaway *positive feedback* loops. The greenhouse effect is one well-known real-life example: high concentrations of carbon dioxide in the atmosphere prevent heat from being radiated into outer space, which causes the Earth's average temperature to rise, which causes the oceans to liberate some of the carbon dioxide dissolved in their water back into the atmosphere, and so on.

In a game, positive feedback occurs when an existing advantage on one side tends to, *by itself*, become greater and greater. In chess, for example, grandmasters will often resign after losing a single pawn, because the subsequent exchange of pieces of equal values widens the gap between the two sides' powers. The same phenomenon may occur in a fantasy role-playing game: a 10th level barbarian is more than a match for

10 beginning characters, and the added experience and inventory items acquired by defeating them in combat will make the mighty warrior even more invincible.

Several techniques can be employed to mitigate the effects of runaway reinforcement:

- **Diminishing returns:** In the game *Diablo*, not only do the experience gaps between consecutive levels grow exponentially, but killing an opponent of much lower stature earns no experience at all.
- **Negative feedback:** In empire-building games, the player who is in the lead tends to become the target of alliances between the others, until the gap has been narrowed. The structure of the game itself makes it harder to maintain the lead, unless a player has achieved overwhelming superiority.
- **Machine learning:** Artificial intelligence techniques can teach the computer how to counteract a player's favorite strategies, thus mitigating any advantage acquired through repetitive use of the same trick.
- **The nemesis:** When all else fails, introducing a unit, monster, or mission that is invulnerable to popular solutions will force the player to give up reliance on acquired knowledge and to learn new ways to make progress.

Thus, effective use of reinforcement is the key not only to player learning, but also to game balance.

Non-Linearity

Unlike passive forms of entertainment such as movies and books, which establish boundaries between the audience and the characters and take the audience along for the ride, games cast players in the starring roles. Therefore, while the players will inevitably experience the game in linear fashion (the human brain being what it is), they must not feel *linearly constrained*: games require valid choices, with valid outcomes.

Multiple Solutions

The ultimate form of non-linearity occurs when players can choose the game's victory conditions, and thus effectively take control of the evaluation of their own performance.

The tabletop game *Illuminati*, by Steve Jackson Games, implements this feature in a most unusual way: in addition to the standard take-over-the-world criterion, each player can also win the game by fulfilling a unique objective, which is selected at the beginning of the game *and kept secret from everyone else*. Not knowing what your opponents are trying to achieve creates very strange gameplay dynamics indeed: players never really know if an adversary's move indicates a secret plan, or if it is a red herring intended to draw their attention away from the real machinations.

Multiple Means

Even if the victory conditions are fixed, non-linearity can be built into a game by allowing players to earn success in many different ways. The puzzle game *The Incred-*

ible Machine, in which players solve simple problems by assembling any number of bizarre contraptions into Rube Goldberg devices, is the ultimate non-linear experience: no two people will ever come up with the exact same Machine for the same task, except in trivial cases.

Temporal Relationships

Nothing breaks down the illusion of non-linearity faster than forcing an arbitrary order on game events. In some early adventure games, for example, Character X was programmed with the assumption that players had engaged in prior discussions with Character Y; if they had not, their conversations with X (which were driven by a list of questions no one could have imagined without Y's help) made absolutely no sense.

If a temporal relationship between two events is crucial to the game's plot, it must be physically impossible to violate: lock the second event behind an impenetrable barrier, and give the players the key only after they have confronted the first. Otherwise, preserve non-linearity by giving context information to game entities; sometimes, a single line ("I don't know, why don't you ask Y?") will be sufficient.

False Non-Linearity

In the early days of gaming, non-linearity was often faked by using tricks that did little but annoy the players:

- **The choice of doom:** Go to the left, and win. Go to the right, and die automatically without any hope of salvation. Save, move, die, and reload.
- **The false choice:** Think long and hard, make a move, and end up in the exact same situation no matter what you did.
- **The run-around:** This happens when the designer imposes a rigid order on player actions, and then locates consecutive events at opposite corners of the game world to mask the linear structure.

These techniques should be avoided—unless you wish to use player frustration as an actual gameplay device. I once used variations of the run-around technique in an insurance claims game, to give players first-hand knowledge of the fact that the inhabitants of the (thankfully fictitious) town of Broken Carriage, Arkansas, were dimwits who had little love for strangers. The result was satisfactory.

Learning Curves

Unless you are designing an add-on pack for hardcore fans of a specific title, one of your most delicate tasks will be the handling of new players.

Experimental psychology tells us that the human mind can hold but a handful of concepts (approximately 7) in short-term memory at the same time. Fortunately, the brain is an associative device: once a set of related concepts have been thoroughly mastered, they can merge into a "gestalt" and thus take up fewer memory slots. For a novice first-person shooter player, moving around, switching weapons, strafing enemies, and assessing the length of a jump all constitute difficult tasks, so there is little room in the conscious mind for added complexity. Meanwhile, the expert player has assimilated the entire shooter interface as a whole, leaving him with plenty of time to deal with strategic considerations.

Designers must balance the need to introduce new game elements on a regular basis (to maintain interest) with the requirements of the human mind (i.e., enough time to understand and assimilate). Too little novelty, and the players get bored; too much, and they are overwhelmed.

Replay Value

Everything else being equal, players will consider the game that provides more hours of enjoyment to be a better investment. However, creating added value by making a bigger game is rarely cost-effective, except in some genres (like role-playing) where doing so has become a de facto standard. Therefore, most designers must rely on replayability to increase the perceived value of their games.

There are many ways to make the same scenario interesting to play several times:

- **Alternate victory conditions:** In *Master of Orion 2,* players can win by military domination (i.e., exterminating the opposition), by diplomacy (i.e., being elected supreme leader by the galactic council), or by scientific dominion (i.e., defeating the omnipotent forces of Antares).
- **Repeated visits to a familiar setting:** Colorful 3D environments cost a lot to create, but it is often possible to reuse them for several missions at little cost, simply by moving and replacing entities.
- **Alternate tools:** Role-playing games can provide tremendous replay value through character classes: playing as a barbarian and playing as a necromancer can feel like two entirely different games. Other genres can exploit the same phenomenon by changing vehicles, weapons, power-ups, etc.
- **Randomized content:** Of course, if new puzzles are generated at game time, the novelty factor is protected.
- **Differentiating between victory and perfection:** By letting players complete a level without solving every puzzle and finding every gold coin, an incentive to return once the game has been won is created.
- **Multiplayer:** Unlike artificial intelligences, which can become predictable after a while, different human opponents always provide new challenges.

Other Perspectives

Game design is an eclectic field, with many open questions, and so it is hardly surprising to see the Game Design Theory section of the book include articles on such a diverse set of topics. But in a sense, they are not so disparate, for whether we discuss rules, worlds, balance, or pace, we are simply asking ourselves: "Where does the fun come from? How can we make the games better?"

The articles found in this section discuss topics that apply to a wide variety of genres, styles, platforms, and audiences. They should therefore be of interest to most designers. Read them at leisure, one at a sitting, and let them stimulate your thoughts.

- Joshua Mosqueira opens the section with his article on *world building*, in which he describes the holistic design techniques used in the pen-and-paper game industry to create entertainment experiences where rules, characters, and settings integrate seamlessly into a harmonious whole.
- Geoff Howland and Charlie Cleveland examine the interactions between high-level game mechanical concepts, respectively from the perspectives of design equilibrium and of the causal relationship between player actions and game-world consequences.
- Sim Dietrich then examines the concept of the *meta-game*, which emerges when the players willingly "break character" to find ways to work around the game's rules and restrictions.
- Jonathon Schilpp then looks at the importance of the numerical models that we have inherited from paper gaming, specifically hit points, and alternative methods of representing combat injuries.
- One of my own articles discusses several qualitative schemes that reward players and support strategic decision-making more intuitively than experience points and numerical ratings.
- Marcin Szymanski looks at the delicate balance between challenge, boredom, and player frustration.
- I return to discuss sources of *designer* frustration, specifically nine sets of desirable but mutually incompatible design features and goals.
- Joe Hitchens looks at ways to structure an action game, its content, and its difficulty level in ways that maximize player involvement without overwhelming them.
- Dan Tanguay and Brent Boylen draw upon their experiences designing *ESPN Winter X-Games Snocross* and *Spider-Man 2: Enter Electro* to discuss the benefits and drawbacks of using licensed intellectual property as the raw material for a game.
- Sim Dietrich looks at ways to identify a faulty game design early in the development process, and at ways to correct the problems before they snowball to disaster.
- And finally, I survey the basic concepts of level design, and what the lead designer can do to make that job easier.

World Building: From Paper to Polygons

Joshua Mosqueira

jmosqueira@relic.com

Origin Systems, the now defunct developer of some the most original, captivating, and successful games in history (such as the *Ultima* and *Wing Commander* series), had a simple motto: "We create worlds."

These three simple words, filled with infinite possibilities and enshrined on every Origin game box, poster, and splash screen represent the goal to which all game designers should aspire—to build worlds and not just games. Not a simple task, but far from impossible. A game with a properly developed "world," one that provides the player with rich characters, contextual gameplay, and a motivating story, is a game that continues to exist long after the player stops playing. - This is the magic that world building offers to designers.

Overview

As game technology and content grows more complex, games become more than a simple pastime: they become entertainment experiences. However, as games evolve into the realm of mass media, publishers require game developers to design and produce games that are not only accessible and entertaining, but that do not require obtuse game mechanics or gameplay. The market's focus has shifted from arcade-style games to more sophisticated entertainment experiences. Yet, too often games exist within "the box" (its platform) with little or no attention paid to developing a contextualized world to support the game as a holistic entity. While game graphics and stories have evolved, gameplay at times feels tacked on or out of place in relation to the rest of the game and its setting. This distancing may lead to games that are nothing more than a series of haphazard encounters and events existing solely within the game's levels, lessening the player's immersion and serving only to remind them they are playing a game and not taking part in an unfolding adventure.

This article looks into world building as a design tool, introducing a holistic approach to game design. It adopts some of the techniques pen-and-paper roleplaying game (RPG) writers have been using for years and illustrates how these same methods can be applied to video and computer game design.

While just about any style and genre of game can benefit from world building, the focus of this article lies with story-driven games; e.g., shooters, survival horror, real-time strategy (RTS), etc.

Rooted in Paper

The correlation between pen-and-paper (P&P) RPGs and video games is stronger than it appears—many of today's leading game designers and producers (such as Warren Spector) started their careers in the P&P industry. Similarly, top franchises like *Baldur's Gate* (*Advanced Dungeons and Dragons*) and *Mechwarrior* (*Battletech*) first emerged as tabletop games. Although "kissing cousins" to video games, P&P RPGs have evolved into highly sophisticated storytelling experiences, and while the medium and technology differ, the end result does not—the creation of games that combine mechanics, story, and setting into immersive and entertaining experiences. For this reason, it is worthwhile to see how P&P RPG writers approach world building, the bread and butter of their craft.

Pen-and-paper RPGs are the sum of their parts. While the notion of *cabal design* is relatively new among video game development, P&P RPG designers have been employing a similar process since their inception. Cabal design is collaborative in nature. Instead of hermetically sealed teams working in isolation, cabal design encourages all members of a team to work together and share ideas. Cabal design usually takes the form of focused round-table discussions, where key members of the team meet to discuss a particular topic—art, or story, or other related topics. Not only does this collaborative brainstorming allow for a fertile exchange of ideas, it also ensures everyone is equally invested in the game. Cabal design is used heavily in P&P games, as this is the only means through which the usually diverse teams involved in the development can jointly contribute, share, and expand a single vision and evolve it into a playable world. A successful P&P RPG is one that combines design, writing, art, and game mechanics into a seamless experience.

Brave New Worlds—Genres

When discussing world building, a good place to start is *genre*. Genres are prevalent in video game design, but only when it comes to gameplay styles and conventions. Some designers use gameplay genres as a starting point, but more often, genre becomes a barrier. Once a game has been defined as a shooter, a RTS, or RPG, it inherits, whether consciously or unconsciously, all the baggage associated with that genre. Describing a game as a "shooter" evokes, for seasoned gamers, images of endless corridors and rooms, but it means nothing to the casual gamer (who is the ideal target audience of today's games).

Designers should focus on thematic and narrative genres rather than gameplay conventions, because genres like fantasy, sci-fi, cyber-punk, even the Wild West are more evocative and offer a better starting point for both story *and* gameplay. Why should designers look to genres to start world building? For one simple reason: genres sell.

In the past 10 years many successful P&P RPG franchises have been built on thematic genres and not gameplay ones. P&P RPGs like *Vampire: The Masquerade* and *Deadlands: The Weird West* have heralded this shift, either by tapping into existing genres (vampires in the vein of Ann Rice's novels) or mixing two genres to create a new one (the wild west and horror). Any potential player looking at either game on a store shelf has an idea of what the game is about even before reading it. This immediate identification makes the game much more accessible: there is no need for players to translate or decipher what the game will be about.

Thematic and narrative genres also give the designer and player a shared vocabulary. The player already has certain thematic expectations for a genre that the game designer can evolve into setting, story, and game mechanics. There is no better hook with which to draw the player into the game than genre. Genre helps bind a game's elements into a cohesive whole, while at the same time it provides a basic underlying structure and even suggests gameplay mechanics.

Playing God

There are certain benefits that arise from holistic design. World building allows a designer to grasp the bigger picture, to see the game—and its story, events, AI—as part of a collective whole and not isolated sections in a design document. This overview helps the designer identify the three core principles of effective design: context, consistency, and story.

Context

World building is not literally about creating a world, complete with topography, weather, and ecosystems. Granted, it *could* lead there, but few games require that level of detail (thankfully). Instead, the focus of world building is context—to create a supporting framework upon which every other element of the game hinges, from art, to mechanics, to story.

Context, in many ways, kick-starts a game. It answers the most important questions:

- **Who is the player?** A lone marine, a commander, a father looking for his daughter?
- **What is she trying to do?** Escape? Command armies? Survive?
- **How does she win or lose?** Who is her nemesis? How can the player stop him?
- **Where is the action happening?** A small mid-western town? Tau Ceti?
- **And, most important, why?** Why is the player crawling through corridors? Why is she gathering resources to build armies? To win, yes, but for the game to be an experience, the *why* needs to be less about game mechanics and more about interaction and, yes, story. Context serves as the starting point for this.

Finally, context serves another critical role, one that helps mesh the game into a self-contained experience. Context helps sustain and reinforce the player's suspension of disbelief, a key factor if the player is going to buy into and immerse himself in the game. The moment the game forces the player to perform some arbitrary action for the sake of "gameplay," the game's context is broken and all suspension of disbelief is lost.

Consistency

As games become more sophisticated, the player's expectations increase with regard to consistency. If the game allows the player to break a window, he then expects to be able to break every window he comes across. The player demands a certain level of consistency, and every time the game fails to deliver this consistency, he is further reminded he is just playing a game.

Consistency is at the root of immersion. Allowing a player to break certain windows and turn some faucets off and on does not make a game immersive. What makes a game immersive is having the environment react to the player's actions in ways the player *expects* them to react. This is what consistency achieves and what world building helps create. Consistency is not to be confused or replaced with predictability. A consistent game world is not devoid of surprises; however, it implies that a game's internal logic governs and underpins those surprises.

In the end, consistency creates an illusion of a real world for the player. Granted, he may not be able to open every door or break every window, but once the illusion is achieved, the player believes in the world enough that he either overlooks these shortcomings or ignores them all together. This is root of immersion.

Story

Story actualizes context and consistency—it is the "big bang" that serves as the game's genesis. Stripped to its bare minimum, story, through context and consistency, helps motivate the player and provides the impetus for playing the game to its conclusion. Today, story (and its cut-scenes and animatics) has replaced points and high scores as the player's motivating reward. This makes story a key part of the experience and one that benefits from world building. Stories that are two-dimensional and cliché usually fail to maintain the player's interest. World building helps a designer craft a story that, if nothing else, helps underpin the game's mechanics and maintain interest. Story helps a designer fill in the blanks and lead the player from one mission, level, or encounter to the next.

Story, and its characters, is also what players remember and identify with. Craft a well-detailed story with memorable characters, and you will have created a game that lives beyond the monitor.

Gameplay

What about gameplay? Context, consistency, and story on their own do not constitute a game; perhaps they could constitute a novel or script treatment, but little else. However, together, the three will suggest appropriate gameplay styles and mechanics through the process of world building.

Gameplay, while seldom thought of in this manner, is the delivery medium for the game and its world—it is the link between the player and the game (and its story).

Without gameplay, there is no interaction and hence no access to the unfolding story. Too often "game" and "story" are thought of as distinct and sometimes mutually exclusive entities. However, to create a satisfying experience that evolves beyond a game, gameplay and story need to be symbiotic. Both need to reflect and support each other, which results in convergence. Together, context, consistency, and story create a diagetic environment, from which emergent gameplay evolves—gameplay that is contextualized, consistent, and mutually supportive with the story.

In this case, context answers the question: why is the player doing this? Consistency ensures that the consequences of the player's actions are reasonable and understandable. Finally, the story motivates the player into performing the action, and then into continuing through the game.

Holistic Design

Creating a game environment with built-in player motivation, context, and supporting gameplay creates an overall experience that lives and breathes beyond the monitor or television screen. Think of games as sandboxes, defined spaces where anything and everything is possible. World building helps define this sandbox—is it a strange far-off world where creatures of pure energy stalk a crew on a crippled spaceship, or a desert dotted with ruins and tombs filled with treasures to be discovered, or a wasteland where desperate armies clash, with the fate of a whole planet in the balance? This is the potential of world building.

The Toolbox—World Building in Action

We have established that consistency, context, emergent gameplay and story are goals of world building, but how does the process actually work? The answer varies from designer to designer, and is dictated not only by personal preferences, but also by outside limitations (such as technology and money). Fortunately, there are no hard and fast rules, no secret set of commandments. World building requires only that a designer think beyond the game in an organized fashion, and begin building from the ground up.

There is a reason why world building is not called "world design" or "world creation." The process of world building is more akin to building a house and, as such, it requires blueprints, a solid foundation, and tools. There is a definite methodology at work, but just like every house is a unique entity, so is each game world. The following guidelines are just that—suggestions and recommendations, not a recipe to be followed to the letter. There is no right or wrong way to approach world building, but it never hurts to start with the basics.

Foundation

No matter how complex a game becomes, it always begins with a single core concept, the foundation that ties everything together—*the essence statement*. The designer needs to start with this foundation and build from that. While world building emphasizes a holistic approach to game design, going from the general to the specific, in truth it starts with a single premise and snowballs from there. Without this initial premise, there is no catalyst for world building. The key is not to get lost in the details—what is needed is a brief description (no more than a few sentences) that captures the essence of the game and defines as well as refines the vision behind the project without shackling it.

This description should work as a springboard; if it limits or constrains the project, it is an indication that the game's foundation is not solid.

Vision over Details

World building does not concern itself with details. The whole process serves as a framework for game design and not as the final product. World building is about vision. Furthermore, world building is an iterative process; each revision will naturally add more detail. It is best to think of world building as peeling the layers of an onion. One starts with the skin and pulls back each successive layer until the core is exposed.

If detail is the focus early on, the danger is that world building will lose its focus (literally drowned by too many details) or balloon in scope—the bane of any project. Keep it simple, keep it focused and the details will emerge on their own.

A Question of Origins

One of the aims of world building is to create a fictional space where the game exists in a believable manner. This "space" can be defined by asking a simple question: *In what setting would the game's premise naturally evolve and emerge?*

This is a classic chicken-and-egg argument, but it is crucial to think about world building in this manner. It is a question of diagetics: the game's premise should emerge from the world and its supporting foundation, not the other way around. Sometime is it difficult to divorce the two, but a designer should always strive to find a happy medium.

Crafting the Illusion

World building is about crafting an illusion for the player, who must have the sense that the game exists within a larger context when in truth it does not. This illusion is fundamental, not only to world building and games, but to movies and books as well. Four elements are crucial to the game illusion: genre, style, setting, and mechanics.

Genre

Genre, already discussed above, is crucial to world building because of its underlying structure and the point of reference it provides. Moreover, genre brings thematic unity and atmosphere.

Theme (setting aside 8th grade English nightmares) is especially important in world building. This does not mean a designer needs a Shakespearian grasp of symbolism and complex themes. Theme provides cohesion—it becomes a measuring stick with which to judge and evaluate other elements of the game's world. Theme does not have to be complex either, often just a simple word will do; for example, *revenge, hope, love*. As always, keep it simple.

Style

Even at this early stage it is important for the designer to already have a visual grasp of the world. A game style is often just as important as theme and genre, because games are largely a visual medium. Visual reference is key; use design sketches or images from movies, comics, or anything else that conveys the intended meaning. The goal is to begin to develop the game's visual language, which the team's artists will craft into the final project.

Game Mechanics

Game mechanics are crucial to developing a proper game world and maintaining its illusion. Designers need to be aware of how gameplay relates to the world if they want to craft a diagetic environment, because game mechanics and interface are the media through which the player interacts with the system. Without gameplay, there is no interaction. A player's immersion rests solely upon the seamless integration of the game's mechanics into the world. World building often suggests appropriate mechanics, the result of having a fleshed-out vision of the game's environment and setting.

Game mechanics do not need to be invisible; on the contrary, the player can be keenly aware of them as long as the mechanics do not add more layers the player must decipher. In a perfect game, game mechanics should seem, even though they are artificial constructs, as a natural extension of the game world and, in turn, of the playing experience.

The Player

Even while we are thinking at a high concept level, we must not forget the one critical ingredient without which there is no game—the player. Whoever they may be (hardcore, casual, male, female, under 12, over 25, etc.), they are active participants in game development and should never be very far from the designer's mind.

A designer is engaging in world building for the benefit and entertainment of the players. A game will not grab and absorb players simply because they are playing it. On the contrary, the designer needs to entice them, to lure them into the game. Above all, the player needs to be the focus of the game, and a designer needs to be conscious of this. Reduced to its essence, world building is all about creating a motivating context and immersive environment for the player.

Character

A game's main character (the player's alter ego) is crucial in creating player attachment. A well-designed and developed character completely immerses the players in the game and creates real emotional attachment.

The main character needs to be, on some level, heroic, no matter how dark and gritty a game is. Of course, this does not mean they have to be squeaky clean, cardboard heroes. Quite the contrary, they can be complex and tragic figures, but they must possess enough redeeming qualities to make them appealing and identifiable. A cold-blooded killer, no matter how "cool" he is, is still a cold-blooded killer.

Avoid stereotypes. Not every main character needs to be an ex-marine betrayed by the government. In fact, the more vulnerable the character is, the more believable he becomes for the player. *Half-Life*'s Gordon Freeman, though devoid of characterization in the game, is still a strong character because he is simply a scientist caught in the wrong place at the wrong time.

Archetypes make excellent starting points for main characters. If you do notunderstand what archetypes are, look at the original *Star Wars* movie to see them in action: Luke is the reluctant hero, Obi Wan the mentor, Darth Vader the dark villain, etc. Another excellent character springboard is the "Hero's Journey" archetype found throughout mythology; it provides an excellent starting point for creating character arcs and gameplay situations.

Rewards

Rewards motivate. A designer should be aware of how he plans to reward the players—what they will get out of the game by playing it—is the game's intention to make the player laugh, feel smart, cooperate with others, or cry?

The Game

World building attempts to create a rich and vibrant setting. However, at the end of the day, designers should never forget that they are designing a game. Genre, setting, mechanics, and so forth are worthless unless the player is having *fun*. A detailed and dynamic backdrop for a game adds untold levels of immersion and player attachment, but if it is not entertaining to play, then there is no point in world building.

Blueprints

World building is all for naught if the designer cannot communicate his vision to the rest of the team. This point highlights the need for thorough documentation—the blueprints of the world and game. The level of detail in documentation can vary from project to project—in some cases, a simple overview is enough; other times a designer needs a weighty design bible to communicate all the essential information. A *primer* is often all that is needed for world building.

A primer is a designer's mission statement. It outlines the game's essence and touches upon elements which, while crucial to world building, are not critical to game development. Theme, mood, style, character bios, and locations are the subject matter of a primer; no need to get into level schematics or damage matrices. Often times, the primer's only audience is the designer himself.

The primer should help answer all the high-level conceptual questions and guide the development of the design document. The primer eventually gets incorporated, in whole or in part, into other design documents, but initially it should serve to communicate vision and design intent.

Tricks of the Trade

Like any craftsman, a designer should have a toolbox by his side. Everyone has different preferences, which means no two designers will have the same tools. Of course, we are not talking about physical tools like hammers and chisels, nor dictionaries or Strunk and White's *Elements of Style*. A designer's toolbox for the task of world building should contain a vocabulary, a language, to help him refine his vision and communicate it. Game design and world building are nine-tenths communication. A designer who can articulate game context in a straightforward manner, no matter how complex, stands a better chance at seeing those elements implemented. The following "tools" allow a designer to find ways to articulate the previously discussed guidelines into a working design.

Brainstorming

It is rare that only the designer has a say when it comes to game development. In reality, game design is a collaborative effort, and while the designer is the torchbearer, he needs to work closely with artists and programmers in order to execute his vision. The most common medium for the collaborative work is brainstorming sessions.

Games, and their worlds, are not designed in isolation. Getting the input of other team members is not only beneficial, but critical in sharing vision on a project. The most obvious advantage of brainstorming is the rapid exchange of ideas in an open environment. Even though a designer can have a vivid vision for the game, during a brainstorming session someone can make a suggestion, or offer a critique, that strengthens the overall concept of the game. This results in the *ping-pong* or snowball effect.

The ping-pong effect occurs when ideas bounce from participant to participant, each adding his or her own twist, allowing the concepts to germinate and evolve in a collaborative way. While someone, normally the designer, sets the ball in play, the ownership of the idea or concept becomes shared in the end, thanks to the back-and-forth process.

Of course, brainstorming has its drawbacks. First, it requires a high level of maturity and respect between the participants. Participants need to understand that the designer will have the final word. By the same token, the designer needs to know when to design with the door closed and when to design with the door open.

While the door is closed, the designer retreats to the comfort of his office and hammers out the basics without outside interference—design by committee rarely works. This closed-door approach is required at the beginning of any project, and world building is no exception. Other team members need to respect the designer when the "door is closed." However, the designer cannot keep the door closed indefinitely—this breeds resentment and leads to a lack of communication (remember, communication is the core of game design). Once ready, the designer needs to open the door and allow the team to provide feedback, usually though brainstorming sessions. While the door is open, it is the turn of the designer to respect his teammates and take all their critiques, suggestions, and ideas seriously and with due diligence.

Context Tree

The context tree (or plot tree) is a writing trick used to outline ideas and concepts and find underlying connections before starting to write. The simplicity of the context tree belies its benefit as a design tool, especially when it comes to world building: once complete, it allows the designer a bird's-eye view of the key concepts he is working with.

To build a context tree, start by writing down the principal idea in the center of the page. This can be a single word (*gothic*) or a sentence (*a tale of revenge set in Paris during WWI*). This written idea will form the center of the web. From there, jot down ideas around the core concept, like the branches of a tree. Ideas that are strongly related to the hub are written near the center. All other ideas are placed toward the edge, and links are drawn between related or codependent concepts to show how they interact.

Depending on the level of detail required, the same process can be applied to individual ideas, each spawning their own tree. Once all the ideas, (and subideas) are on paper, lines are drawn linking the various concepts and the key concepts that emerged are circled. See Figure 2.1.1 for an example.

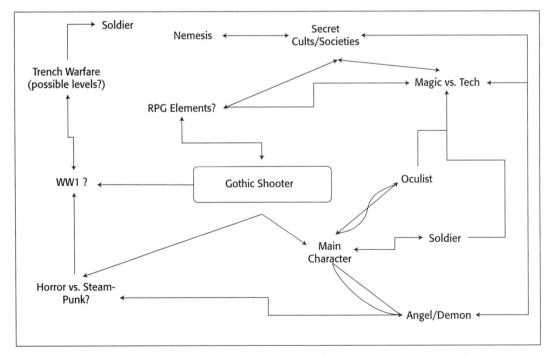

FIGURE 2.1.1 *Context Tree for Trench, a fictitious WWI shooter. Copyright 2002 Joshua Mosqueira.*

Example of Play

Given world building's emphasis on abstract concepts such as theme, style, and genre, it is always good practice, at the final design stage, to outline a small example of what a typical playing experience would be. There is no need for actual mechanics; the example is a narrative, told from the point of view of the main character as he "plays" the game. Player input can be included, but usually as boxed text or footnotes.

The example does not need to be long, but it should cover the core game elements. If the game focuses on character interaction, exploration, and combat, the example of play should highlight each of these.

The key, however, is not to replicate the game through text, but to give a sense of its setting, style, and atmosphere and how these will impact and affect gameplay.

Conclusion

World building is full of potential for game designers. Today's games are reaching new heights of sophistication, both in terms of technology and content. For this reason, as game designers, it is crucial that the games we produce exist beyond our (and the player's) monitors and television screens. If games are truly going to become a viable form of mass-market entertainment—along the lines of novels, television programs, and motion pictures—they need to move away from clichés and stereotypes, and aim at crafting experiences that are unique to the medium. This requires designers to think beyond gameplay genres and create living and breathing worlds with characters and situations that exist within a consistent context.

World building by itself cannot accomplish this, but it is a good start. The more sophisticated games become, the greater the player's expectation becomes for consistency and context with regard to both gameplay and story. Many gamers are not interested in wandering endless hallways shooting things, collecting mana crystals to power spells, or jumping from one crate to the next. They want games that will transport them into a mythical make-believe place where they are heroes, not cardboard cut-outs fighting the same faceless thug again and again.

In the end, one cannot forget that, world building or not, games must be entertaining. After all, what we do as designers, is create sandboxes—worlds that other people play in.

Bibliography

[Hale99] Hale, C., *Syn and Syntax*, Broadway Books, 1999. *Excellent companion to the eternal* Elements of Style.

[King00] King, S., *On Writing*, Scribner, 2000. *Stephen King's thoughts on the process of writing.*

[Mosqueira97] Boulle, P., Brochu, S., and Mosqueira, J., "Tribe 8," *Dream Pod* 9, 1997. *The "Hero's Journey" in action.*

[Rollings00] Rollings, A., and Morris, D., *Game Architecture and Design*, The Coriolis Group, 2000.

Balancing Gameplay Hooks

Geoff Howland

ghowland@lupinegames.com

After you remove the graphics, any license brands, the theme, and the characters from any game, what is left? What holds the player's attention and creates the possibility for them to be entertained? What goals do the players perceive or try to create for themselves?

What is left as the basis of all games is *gameplay*, and gameplay is centered on the *hooks* that focus the player's attention on the game.

What Is a Gameplay Hook?

A *gameplay hook* is anything that requires the player to make a decision that relates to the game, and thus keeps them playing. Any activity that the player performs for the purpose of furthering their playing can be a hook. Likewise, activities that distract or deter the player from playing are not hooks but barricades—essentially, anti-hooks.

A gameplay hook is different from a marketing hook, which is designed to attract the player to buy the game, or from the style or gimmick hooks that may entice initial play. Gameplay hooks are distinctly about interactivity within the game. They are the focuses of the player's attention and the keys to holding it. Gameplay hooks do not literally need to be interactive—it is completely valid to present the player with information in such a way that they believe they have to plan things when it really will not matter one way or another, as long as they never find out their decision did not have an impact on the results.

Gameplay hooks can take on several different forms:

- **Action Hooks:** Action hooks require the player to move their controls, characters, or pieces around, or to interact with the game explicitly. Talking to a non-playing character about a quest is an action hook, as is avoiding being shot with missiles from a helicopter.
- **Resource Hooks:** Resource hooks are elements that the player does not directly control in terms of actions, but that affect how actions work or affect the game state. Decisions regarding ammunition or health are basic examples of resource hooks. Ammunition (or lack of it) can limit the player's ability to interact with the environment by requiring a decision on whether to use a weapon. Similarly,

the player's health conditions will determine how he approaches certain tasks; he may have to abandon his current goal in favor of finding ways to cure injuries.

- **Tactical and Strategic Hooks:** Tactical and strategic hooks are subtler than other kinds of hooks and may not be present in every game. Far more than mere gameplay decisions, tactical hooks actually change the way the game works. For example, in a car racing game, getting behind another car and using their draft can allow you to accelerate faster and pass them. This is not a separate activity from normal acceleration, because you are still using the same controls in the same way, yet it provides a tactical decision the player can use to be interactive with the game and affect the outcome. Further examples of tactical hooks include deciding when to perform a move, and allocating resources to a task. A truly effective tactical hook would allow players to accomplish goals, through use of tactics, that could not be achieved otherwise—at least, not through the same basic commands and controls.

- **Time Hooks:** Time hooks include anything that has to do with making the player deal with future events. A player waiting on a weapon to be spawned must keep that process in mind and check on it from time to time to see when it can be used. The most basic forms of time hooks include counters that mark the end of the game and timers that determine how quickly the player completed his tasks. Never underestimate the power of giving the player a clock to watch. The simple fact that time spent is increasing (or a counter is decreasing) puts the player under pressure to complete their actions faster, and gives them a clear watermark for improving their actions in the future. If the last lap or level took them 1:32 last time, they can shoot for 1:15 next time.

A Look at Hooks in Game Genres

Table 2.2.1 shows the types of hooks commonly found in popular genres.

Table 2.2.1 Gameplay Hooks by Genre and Category

Genre	Action Hook	Resource Hook	Tactics Hook	Time Hook
Any	Exploration, Communication with other players	Points or Score		Timer or Countdown
Action	Navigate, Avoid/Follow, Combat	Ammo, Health	Weapon Choice, Map Memorization	
Real Time Strategy	Asset Layout/Map Painting, Unit Selection and Orders, Combat Assessment and Unit Targeting	Resource and Money, Accounting,	Repairing and Upgrading Units, Grouping and Positioning	Waiting for Builds

(continues)

Table 2.2.1 Gameplay Hooks by Genre and Category (*Continued*)

Genre	Action Hook	Resource Hook	Tactics Hook	Time Hook
Driving	Navigation, Avoid/ Chase, Stunts	Damage Control, Fuel, Upgrades	Drafting	Speed and Other Time Records, Incremental Time Extensions on Checkpoints
Jumpers	Navigation, Skilled Jump Control	Item Collection		Incremental Time Boosts on Counter with Item Collection
Puzzle	Unique Puzzle Element	Special Limited Actions (Super Bombs)		Timer or Speed Increase
Role Playing Game	Heavy Exploration, Quests and Missions, Conversation and Story	Stats, Skills, Spells and Item Collection, Health, Ammo, Quest Management	Character Type Selection, Useful Skill Upgrades	

Creating Your Hooks

You can begin your game design in one of two ways. You can base your design on similar games, and then add unique elements; alternatively, you can start from scratch, determine what hooks you want to use as the main focuses, and begin to design the game from there. Each of these strategies has its advantages.

Building upon a well-established base helps target your audience from the beginning. You can attract players by identifying the key hooks of their favorite current games, and then tailoring those hooks, or adding new ones, to obtain the desired effect.

Building your hooks from the ground up can be compared to discarding the current genre expectations and starting from scratch. You might end up making many of the same decisions that other designers have made—because they are the best solutions to the problems at hand—but along the way you will learn a lot about how your games' mechanics work.

Hit Points As Hooks

An interesting example of a hook is the use of hit points in role-playing games (RPGs). If you were to remove hit points, which are the basis for determining the overall strength of a player-character and the damage he has sustained, from your game, what would you replace them with to create a minimally working health and damage system?

I recently tried, with the goal of developing a more realistic human response to combat, including the ability for one-strike kills and the lingering effects of damage, to develop a game without using hit points. The best solution I could come up with was a 5-point system, consisting of injuries, mobility, will power, stamina, and stun:

- **Injuries:** Bodily damage.
- **Mobility:** The ability to move appendages and location.
- **Will power:** The likelihood of staying conscious and refraining from running away under the influence of intense pain.
- **Stamina:** The amount of energy a character had left, and the speed and power that could still be given to actions.
- Being temporarily at a loss for reactions.

This system became much more complicated than a hit points system, but removing any component seemed to reduce its effectiveness. However, after examining this system under play conditions, and seeing what the player would have to keep in mind, it became obvious that my design had two major flaws.

First, this system is significantly more complex than a hit points system. Its metrics change rapidly in the middle of a fight, and dealing with the changes effectively would require the player to divert his attention from the action, right when he can least afford to do so. .

The second flaw was in the premise of my goal itself. A system where any hit can mean death removes an entire field of resource management that has been a backbone of computer RPGs. Calculating how much deeper a character can go into a dungeon based on current hit points, number of spell points one can use to heal with, and number of items left that have healing power is a large part of the RPG player's strategy. Taking it away would dramatically change how people play the game. In one sense, players would not bother to go deep into the game levels because they would always be one potential hit away from death. In another more realistic sense, it would radically decrease the player's range of actually play and increase the number of saves or other non-playing activities to protect their characters against death. Having a simple accounting formula for hit points allows players to see the buffer between when the character is still relatively safe from death and when they must start playing very carefully.

I ended up scrapping the goal and sticking with hit points. However, the exercise was very informative as to how RPGs function, and was a valuable lesson on what major hooks I was looking for in my game.

Key Hooks

In every game, players spend the majority of their time on a small set of actions. These *key hooks* are the meat and potatoes of every game and often define its genre. In a first-person shooter game, for example, the hooks typically include navigation, avoid/chase, combat targeting, and dodging, health, and ammo.

Supporting Hooks

While the key hooks often define the genre and basic activities in a game, the *supporting hooks* usually differentiate a game from others in its genre. Almost all car driving games deal with primary hooks of navigation, steering control, and time limits, but the supporting hooks, like those in *Midnight Club*, in which the players race for pink slips to increase their car resources, make it stand out from other racing games. Likewise, *Need for Speed: Hot Pursuit* differentiates itself from other racing games by including evading the police as a major supporting hook of the game. The player's key hooks are to race their cars faster than others, but through the addition of police that more actively try to detain the player, the gameplay in *Need for Speed* is differentiated and new strategies emerge.

"Old Reliable" Hooks

When all else fails, there is a plethora of *old reliable* gameplay hooks available to a designer. While these hooks might appear cliché and trite when they become the main focus of the player's attention, they can be used as filler to keep the player busy between more interesting activities.

Old reliable gameplay techniques are reliable because they appeal to people at a basic level. One reliable gameplay hook is to require the player to have more money or higher skill points for any given level or activity. This kind of hook provides a reason for the player to continue the game between more significant story points or conflicts. Many players will spend hours doing tedious things for the brief moment of joy when they reach their goal. For example, the game *Gran Turismo* requires that the player earn money through racing to buy better cars. Much of the lure of playing *Gran Turismo* is to attain new and better cars, and you have to race many times to earn the money to buy a car that is a significant step forward from your current vehicle.

The trick to using old reliable hooks is to minimize tedium by keeping the player's attention on the key hooks they will face in the future, and not the supporting tasks they must settle for in the meantime.

Balancing Your Hooks

The most important aspects of hook balancing lie in understanding who your audience is, what their goals are, and the pace at which you want your game to move. Adding more action hooks can means making the game more complicated. Adding resource hooks can speed up the feel of the game, because the player must keep vigilant and make sure their characters have enough of the correct supplies. More tactical hooks can add layers of complexity to action or resource management. Time hooks can keep the player focused on making precise movements, and can force him to concentrate on a single end goal.

Too Much

"Kitchen sink" design is a problem most designers face. Too much of a good thing not only causes development problems but can also dilute the purpose of the game.. What is the point of a game where you can do anything? Where is the drive to continue once the novelty that the world is 100 percent interactive has worn off? Games are about their limitations, not their freedoms.

For example, take the physical game of American football. Football is a game because of its rules and structure. If you were to design football from scratch, but decided that you also wanted the players to be able to fly, dig through the ground, and not have side lines or scheduled handovers, then the game is no longer football. It has now devolved to a game of tag with points. Because of the varieties of movement between running on the ground, tunneling, or flying, a coach can no longer design detailed plays, as there are simply too many possibilities to take into account. How can you do a right sweep if the opponent could be coming from underneath you or from above, and without handovers, when would you have time to initiate plays anyway?

Placing too many hooks of any type actively or inactively on the player can overload their ability to manage them all, and may lead to them ignoring all but a few basic ones. Thus, they will not be able to enjoy your game to its full potential. Games with too many hooks may also be harder for players to learn, which can dissuade them from playing in the first place.

Too Little

The downside of having too few gameplay hooks is that the game's novelty will quickly wear off as the player gets used to the limited hooks. Once the learning curve is complete, the game falls flat.

Some hooks are strong enough to bypass this issue, especially in games targeted toward players looking for simple fun. *Tetris* is a good example of this; it features only a handful of hooks for manipulating the pieces, increasing speed, and scoring more points. This simple combination works, and the game can entertain for long periods of time. However, usually this limited type of game will not satisfy all audiences.

Hidden Hooks

One way you can continue to challenge players in a game is to hide some hooks so that they are not immediately obvious. These *hidden hooks* can either be exposed to the player later in the game, or built into it from the beginning but never described as one of its functions.

Hiding hooks is not the same as having hidden Easter eggs or hidden rooms in a game (though those cases could be considered an extension of the exploration hook). Hiding a hook is more akin to not telling players in a driving game that they can draft behind other cars to gain speed. Then, as the players see that they drive faster than normally possible in certain conditions, they eventually figure out the hook on their own.

The hidden hook has the double benefit of giving the player something new to focus on while playing, as well as rewarding them with the thrill of discovery.

Conclusion

Will there ever be a "just right" game? Finding the perfect balance of hooks for your game is more likely to be done on the joypad, keyboard, and mouse rather than in a notebook. Games that endure are modified hundreds or thousands of times to become balanced, so never expect your game to roll off your pen perfectly balanced. Plan for experimentation, and leave room for adjustment.

2.3

Meaningful Game Mechanics

Charlie Cleveland

flayra@overmind.org

There are few practical tools available to game designers. Game design is hard to quantify, and remains largely based on trial and error and designer intuition. This article explains two specific design criteria—intent and consequence—which together make up the concept of *meaningful game mechanics*. The tradeoffs of using meaningful game mechanics are discussed, and examples from well-known games are given.

The techniques described in this article are applicable to most types of games, but less so in "instantiated" games, such as most adventures and linear story-based games, which are built to be played once through, in a certain way.

Definitions

For the purpose of this discussion, meaningful game mechanics are rules, player choices, and other designs that have been created with *intent* and *consequence* in mind.

Intent

For a game mechanic to have intent, it needs to make obvious to the player that a decision can be made, and that the player's choices will have direct influence on the outcome of events.

When there is clear intent, the player knows he is making a meaningful choice, and has a reasonable chance of predicting the general outcome of that choice. A real-time strategy (RTS) technology tree, where each branch is labeled with technology descriptions and costs, shows intent. The same technology tree without this information shows no intent, because the player can not reasonably predict the results of his choices. Similarly, in a shooter game, the choice between a path that ascends a mountain toward a dark castle and a path that descends to a misty lake, also shows intent. Choosing between two identical doors in a game does not show intent, because while the player knows he is making a choice, he has no idea what differentiates the two doors, or what could be behind either of them.

Consequence

To have consequence, a game choice must not be able to be trivially reversed. Advancing a pawn in chess has consequence, for it can never be moved back. Toggling a standard light switch does not: if the player switches the light off and then realizes that it must be on to complete the level, it is easily switched back on. However, if that same light switch is located at the top of a pedestal surrounded by lava, activating it has greater consequence, because of the time and risk involved.

Together, intent and consequence allow the player to commit himself and the game state to a path, action, or future that he has a reasonable chance of forecasting, and one that is not trivially reversed. Game mechanics that are designed with these factors in mind, are what we define as *meaningful*.

Advantages of Meaningful Mechanics

When choices are explicit, failure is more easily accepted, because the player clearly understands what he did wrong and what he could do to prevent the same outcome in the future. This facilitates growth of player skill, and the game is perceived as being fair.

Player comments like "If only I hadn't chosen to reload without taking cover first," or "if only I had something that could attack airplanes," show a clear understanding of explicit choices. However, it is more difficult to understand the effect of more abstract decisions, such as researching +3 range instead of +2. A game will remain interesting longer if the player knows how to improve.

Meaningful mechanics also lead to memorable games. When player actions really matter, individual play sessions are easier to remember, and players tell better stories of their exploits. Such memorable games will affect a person more deeply and for longer. Conversely, as choices decrease in meaning, eventually there is no reason for the player to be there at all.

Meaningful choices also promote interesting multiplayer interaction. For players to interact with each other in a multiplayer environment (whether cooperatively or competitively), they must be able to detect and recognize each other's influence over the game world. With vague or overly subtle game mechanics, the outcome of other player's choices are less noticeable. This is especially important for multiplayer strategy games, where a skilled player will make choices directly from an opponent's actions.

Examples

In the science-fiction, real-time strategy game *Starcraft*, some units can operate in different modes. For example, siege tanks can either choose normal movement and attack or to deploy their turrets in "siege mode," which allows them to inflict more damage and reach more distant targets. However, tanks in siege mode are stationary and cannot hit close targets. Other units have the ability to burrow, making them mostly hidden and invulnerable, but unable to attack. The fact that it takes time and player attention to switch a unit between modes and the fact that choosing the wrong mode can mean great loss adds strategy to the game. Making the modes more similar (e.g., reducing intent) or cutting the time it takes to change between them (e.g., reducing consequence) would make the feature dull and pointless.

In the shooting game *Counter-Strike*, if a player dies, he is out of the game for the entire round. This sometimes means players have to wait for several minutes, watching the others from the grave and chatting with their fellow deceased. It is not an uncomfortable existence, but it is not as fun as playing. The fact that the game adds this meaningful consequence to player death increases enjoyment of actively playing the game.

These principles of meaningful mechanics work in traditional non-electronic games as well. In modern backgammon, the doubling cube is a great example of a meaningful device. Players can sometimes force an ultimatum: double the stakes or immediately forfeit. This is quite powerful, because the doubling is cumulative and the stakes are valuable. Personal risk is the foundation that gambling is built on, and perhaps the most meaningful game mechanic of them all, because a player's performance in the game can directly affect his happiness and welfare outside the game.

Games that involve pain or physical consequence also rely on the principle of meaningful mechanics. Examples are numerous: playground games like dodgeball, tug of war, being subjected to the "paddling machine" after failing to capture the flag, and children's card games where the winner gets to rap the loser's knuckles with the deck, all colorfully illustrate this concept. Then, there is the probably fictional grim game of chance, Russian Roulette. What could be more memorable than this? (Except for the loser, of course. . . .)

Disadvantages of Meaningful Mechanics

If meaningful game mechanics are so great, why not use them everywhere?

First, game choices with too much intent can become simplistic and boring. A game with perfect intent would have to give the player complete information about the outcomes of every choice so he could make the decision that fit his intent exactly. In a computerized chess game, for example, the game would have to tell the player exactly how the computer would respond as the player mulls over each potential move, or maybe even show the player's precisely calculated odds of victory for each choice. An element of uncertainty (often related to opponent responses) must remain, or the game devolves into an endless repetition of the same optimal strategy.

In the two-door choice example mentioned above, the game design with perfect intent would show the player a map of the area beyond each door, including all threats and treasures. The player would certainly be well informed, but the choices are no longer interesting and the game ceases to be entertaining.

It is also possible to over-use consequence. Consider a one-minute delay while switching weapons in a first-person shooter. In this case, not only is this heavy consequence extremely frustrating, it works against the primary goal of the game, which is to promote an action experience in which reflexes are important. Having consequences that are too stiff can also stress players and discourage newcomers. Game consequences that cause severe player anxiety (like gambling games for instance) move the focus of the game away from entertainment and toward competition and outcome. *Starcraft* is sometimes criticized for its harsh consequences for even the tiniest of mistakes.

High consequences may be great for tournament or rated play, but often are not fun for games that are more social or casual in nature. Games for children and other non-hardcore markets, like many console games, are probably better served with fewer consequential mechanics.

Conclusion

There is a balance worth looking for, where game choices have just the right equilibrium of intent and consequence. This balance varies accordingly with the game genre and target audience. By understanding how intent and consequence in game mechanics affect the game and its players, this middle ground can be more easily attained.

For further reading on similar topics, see [Church99].

Bibliography

[Church99] Church, D., "Formal Abstract Design Tools." Available online: *www.gamasutra.com/features/19990716/design_tools_07.htm, 1999*. Members only.

Special thanks to Brian Sharp for his many insightful comments during the preparation of this article.

2.4

Know Your Meta-Game

Sim Dietrich

SDietrich@nvidia.com

Meta-gaming occurs when players "play the rules" instead of playing their roles. Meta-gaming involves aspects of the game-playing experience that usually are not designed as part of the main gameplay session, but that heavily influence the actual gameplay nonetheless.

This article will attempt to help game designers identify the meta-game aspects of their own creations, avoid the sometimes negative feedback that meta-gaming can create, and rid their games of these unfortunate side effects whenever possible.

Pac-Man's Meta-Game

Let's start with a very simple videogame and explain how even it has a meta-game, and how the meta-game affects the overall gameplay experience.

A Pac-Man Primer

Pac-Man, by Namco, was a huge arcade hit during the videogame craze of the early 1980s. Players moved Pac-Man around a simple maze, in which Pac-Man had to eat dots and avoid four ghosts that could kill him on contact. There were four special dots, known as "Power Pills," near the corners of the maze; when eaten by Pac-Man, a Power Pill caused the ghosts to temporarily become edible and run away. When Pac-Man ate all the dots in the maze, the level was over, and a new level would begin. Each successive level had a bonus item, typically a piece of fruit or candy, that would appear at the ghost-spawning area and then wander around the maze. Last, players started with three lives for their Pac-Man, but could gain more upon reaching certain scores.

Learning the Game

Pac-Man has two meta-game aspects. One is the simple process of learning the game. The controls are easy enough, involving nothing more than a four-way digital joystick, but there are still techniques that players can learn over time to improve their score. For example, players benefit from learning how long the Power Pills last, how to use the wraparound tunnel, and the pattern of the ghosts' movement:

- Ghosts typically only change direction at intersections, so players can exploit this by waiting at a wall juncture until they see which way a threatening ghost is headed.
- Most of the time, Pac-Man is moving forward, but it is possible to pause in a corner, or to quickly move Pac-Man back and forth with the joystick so that he effectively stalls in place. This way, the player can wait for a bonus item or ghost to change directions, and then decide his next move.
- Expert players like to attract ghosts and get them to follow Pac-Man, so that when they eat a Power Pill, more edible ghosts are within range. This way, they can score more points.

The meta-game aspect of learning is common to all games, and is almost completely positive. Where a game cannot be learned, and tactics cannot be developed, it can be argued that there is not much of a game to begin with. Tactics add subtlety, allow players to make progress even after the basics are mastered, and provides a mechanism for players to develop their own unique playing style.

Patterns

The second meta-game aspect of Pac-Man is that of the *pattern*. The best Pac-Man players learned that they could achieve higher scores by moving Pac-Man around the maze in a set pattern that allowed Pac-Man to avoid the ghosts and eat all of the dots, thus completing the level without losing a life. This way, they achieved astronomical scores not through superior skill, but through knowledge of a breakdown in the game's rules. This strict adherence to the pattern allowed them to conquer level after level; some were able to go for so long that they would voluntarily quit with Pac-Man lives remaining.

The pattern meta-game aspect is worrisome, because it changes the fundamental structure of the game. Pac-Man, ostensibly a game of avoiding ghosts while clearing a maze of dots, becomes an exercise in repetitive pattern-matching. Clearly, pattern players are not really playing Pac-Man as designed. The question remains, is that good, bad or something in between?

In the case of a game designed for video arcades, a pattern player is mostly a bad thing. First of all, a pattern player can tie up a machine for hours on a single quarter. That revenue loss can at times be mitigated by the fact that a high-scoring player can attract a crowd and raise other players' interest levels in the game, but it is not especially exciting to watch someone perform the same maneuvers over and over, as there are no tactics or tricks besides the pattern itself for spectators to learn.

So, now that the pattern is identified as a negative meta-game aspect, what should a conscientious game designer do to avoid the problem in the first place?

The pattern tactic works in Pac-Man because the ghost movement is deterministic, and because the level layout is fixed. If the maze and/or ghosts were more random, the pattern approach would be impossible. If the maze were random, the players would have to rely on tactics alone, so beginning players would likely be totally lost unless they could practice on the same level for a while. Perhaps the first five levels should be fixed, and then later levels would be more and more randomized to challenge better players.

However, if the ghosts' movements were truly randomized, the game would become much more difficult. Even if players do not know a pattern for a certain level, they quickly develop a feel for where ghosts are likely to turn that aids them in their play. Thus, in order to keep the game at roughly the same difficulty level, some other aspects of the gameplay would need to be tweaked. One possibility would be to tie the ghosts' strategy to the immediate area of the maze they occupy. If the levels were randomized, ghost movement would be predictable within a certain level (or at least within a well-known component of that level), but moving on to the next level would require the player to study ghost behavior all over again.

So, we have analyzed a seemingly simple game, and extracted both positive meta-game aspects (like learning tactics) and negative game-breaking tactics (like the pattern), and proposed a solution to mitigate or eliminate the negative meta-game.

The Meta-Game of *Counter-Strike*

One example of a meta-game in *Counter-Strike* is the process of buying weapons from round to round. Players can purposely choose a weak weapon in the first round to save up cash for the next round. This way, even if the player's avatar dies during the round, he still retains the cash and can buy a superior weapon in a subsequent round.

For a terrorist or counter-terrorist, this is an unnatural way of thinking. The very knowledge of the fact that there will be a "next round" whether your character lives or dies, and that you can maintain a bank account after death for your next life, is unusual indeed.

Designers should be very careful with the type of game they are creating, and especially careful with the player's actual role in it. If the game is designed to be an immersive experience, then the meta-game aspects should be carefully controlled, and possibly eliminated. On the other hand, if the game is designed to work on multiple levels (like *Counter-Strike*, which functions as a resource management and virtual terrorist/anti-terrorist training simulation), the meta-game aspects should be used to balance gameplay and foster strategic thinking.

Going back to the example of an avatar in *Counter-Strike* leaving money to his reincarnated self—this may not have been the intent of the designers. However, they seem to have made several design choices that justify this odd tactic. For example, the same level repeats several times in order to amortize long load times. This allows players to learn the levels, and lets the gameplay develop enough stability for players to produce meaningful tactics. Also, the ability to save up money from round to round was likely added as a way to reward better players and teams with better weapon choices over time.

Of course, a savvy player can take advantage of these perfectly valid design choices to somewhat subvert what, at first glance, seems to be the fundamental idea of the game—"You are a Terrorist bent on destruction!" or "You are a SWAT team member seeking to prevent chaos!" Instead it becomes "You are an abstract manager of resources, including weapons, ammo, and money, and you must control a series of avatars through several rounds of play, trying to make your team win the most rounds."

Designing the Meta-Game

Counter-Strike and its clones are clearly going for a strategy/tactics/action mix, so the meta-game aspects are part of what works in the game. However, let's assume that the designer's intent was instead to create an immersive, realistic simulation of terrorist or anti-terrorist actions. What parts of the game and meta-game would change?

First, the game levels would have to be randomized, because terrorists rarely attack in the same place twice in the real world. This would introduce a significant gameplay adjustment: not knowing a map from previous games would radically change the way in which players would plan their missions. Players would have to either rely on maps or blueprints before the game round started (as in the game *Rainbow Six*), or go blindly into the area and creep along in search of the enemy. This design change appears to make each encounter more unique, and potentially more exciting, so we will retain it for now.

Next, the level would only be played once—the encounter is won or lost in a single round. A potential downside to this would be that if a player's avatar got shot right away in the beginning, it would be a long wait before the player could play again in the next level. Here, the designer may choose to introduce a meta-game aspect in order to improve gameplay. Perhaps a certain number of the terrorists and/or SWAT team members are "hidden" in the level, and can come out of hiding to be used by players killed early in the contest. Such a feature could introduce other negative meta-game aspects, however, such as a player purposely committing a suicide run with her avatar in anticipation of coming right back as one of the "hidden" avatars. So, we will discard this design choice: getting shot is bad in the game, just like in the real world, so we want to penalize kamikaze tactics and encourage players to work together to keep from getting killed.

Because there would only be a single round of play, the weapon load-out system would have to change as well. Rather than starting with a fixed amount of money before the level, which adds a resource-management meta-game aspect, perhaps the designer would choose a limited set of weapons and equipment for each team during scenario design. For instance, when designing an encounter in a mountainous setting, the designer would allow a certain number of SWAT players to use rappelling equipment; an underwater setting might have scuba gear and harpoon guns. Players could use an in-game chat system to negotiate which players get which weapons and equipment.

Given a single round of play per level and the designer's control of weapon and equipment choices, it seems prudent to eliminate the monetary aspect of the game, including the pause before rounds that allows players to perform weapon and equipment purchases. Instead, these items should be placed in the level's starting area for each team. This way any unused weapons, ammo, or equipment becomes a strategic asset that the other side could potentially claim or sabotage.

This new game design more faithfully represents our hypothetical designer's goal, that of creating an immersive, realistic simulation of terrorist or anti-terrorist operations.

The Game As a Training Ground

The new game resulting from our changes to *Counter-Strike* may be more realistic, but, on the other hand, it may also be too difficult. Meta-game aspects such as level replay and load/saving present the advantage that the entire game plays out like a training exercise for the player. Let's look at this metaphor briefly, and then see how reducing the meta-gaming can make learning a game too hard.

In a police firearms training course, a policeman walks through a simulated urban environment, where wooden people-shaped cut-outs pop up at various intervals. Some cut-outs represent "bad guys" who should be shot, while others are innocent bystanders. The policeman in training has a short, fixed time interval in which to react before getting "shot" himself. This exercise is designed to teach policemen how to quickly recognize the difference between friend and foe, and provides more realistic training than a traditional firing range.

If a policeman goes through the training course again and again, his reaction time and shooting skills may improve, but what is he really learning? Because the course's layout is relatively fixed and there are only so many cut-outs to work with, he would learn, over time, the places and times where the "bad guys" tend to pop up. The cues that assist him in are artificial, in that they are part of the training course, and are also counter to the purpose of the training—being able to react properly and quickly in a realistic, dangerous situation. Of course, putting policemen in jeopardy for simple training exercises is impossible, so such exercises as the "friend or foe" course are a reasonable approximation.

In a virtual game environment, however, the training can be an almost exact replica of the "real thing," except that the player does not face negative consequences when he fails. The role-playing game *Deus Ex*, from Ion Storm Austin, features an extensive training section at the beginning of the game to help teach its mechanics to the players.

Meta-Game Aspects of Game Saves

In order to make each level or mission more interesting to play, a game designer may choose to nullify as many meta-game elements as possible, by randomizing levels, ending the mission (at least for that player) when the player's avatar dies, and by taking away information that the player's avatar would not have. Another technique employed by some games is to allow only one save per level, in case a player needed to turn off the game system for a while and come back to it later. Having only one save per level, and ensuring that a player must reload from that save point, prevents certain types of "cheating," such as running around the level on a suicide run, not fighting but looking around for clues, knowing that they can just reload the game later.

However, restricting the load/save system may make the game too difficult to learn and play. One of the key techniques of gameplay training is to keep most of the scenario constant and vary just a few factors at a time, so that it is easier to discern which elements are dynamically affecting the situation. However, a real game environment may be too difficult as a training ground, unless players can access it in a special training mode, wherein loading, saving, and restarting are unlimited.

It is also beneficial to make the training system available throughout the game, and not just before level 1. Having the training system always available compensates for the fact that the player is no longer using the game itself and the load/save system as a training tool.

The net result is a model whereby a game contains two modes:

- A **training mode**, which is set up for players to learn how to succeed in the game.
- A **gameplay mode**, in which a player attempts a level or mission only once, relying on his or her wits, skill, and training to succeed.

Hopefully, this will provide a richer overall game experience.

Complex Games Lead to Meta-Gaming

Another example of meta-gaming occurs when a player gets stuck in a difficult action game. The player may save the game before a difficult battle and replay the fight over and over in order to complete the battle with the maximum amount of ammo or the minimum health loss before continuing the game. In this case, the player is using knowledge (the characteristics and timing of upcoming battles) and abilities (load/save game) that are not available to the player's in-game avatar.

Clearly, many difficult action games (such as *Quake 3: Arena* and *Max Payne*) encourage this pattern of behavior. The trends toward better enemy artificial intelligence (AI), longer levels, and complex level design actually work in symbiosis with frequent game saves: because a reload minimizes the cost of failure, it makes very difficult challenges (and the search for multiple possible solutions to a problem) safe to experience.

The more difficult the environment and behavior patterns are to master, the more important this type of meta-game activity will be for the majority of players.

Adding a Meta-Game to Your Game

It is sometimes advantageous to remove gameplay concepts from the actual game and move them into the meta-game instead. For example, in multiplayer, online role-playing games (RPGs), powerful magic items and equipment are highly sought after, because they contribute to character success as well as to a player's sense of uniqueness and power. However, if a player obtains such coveted items from another player through thievery or murder, huge animosity and frustration is created; if the situation happens often enough, the entire game world may devolve into chaos.

Let us assume that a designer wishes to focus her game on questing with other players, rather than on squabbling over treasure or inventory. One approach would be to make it impossible to take items from players or their corpses, but to provide an in-game market or an out-of-game user interface where they could be traded freely. Another idea would be to emphasize the roles of spells and skills, which cannot be stolen, to reduce the reliance on in-game items to differentiate avatars.

Conclusion

Gameplayers are resourceful. They will use any technique available to succeed. If there are meta-game "cheats" in a game, players will find and use them. Designers should understand the effect the meta-game has on the core gameplay experience, and ensure that that the meta-game works in the game's favor.

2.5

Pros and Cons of Hit Point Systems

Jonathon Schilpp

Jonathon@gdnmail.net

Hit point systems have been a common feature of computer games for a very long time, and for good reason. But there are a number of disadvantages of using hit points, and every game designer should be aware of them.

While the topics discussed in this article may be applied to any game that uses hit points, we will focus here on how hit point systems are used in role-playing games (RPGs).

A Typical Hit Point System

Death is an important concept in computer game design. The threat of character death can be very useful in making the player's progress in the game depend on the quality of the decisions he makes. Whether it is the death of a beloved character, or the destruction of a player-controlled spaceship, death provides a useful feedback mechanism. Consequences, such as restarting a game level, that result from poor decisions help the player learn how to more effectively play the game. And the possibility of such setbacks helps to challenge the player, while increasing his desire to play well.

But what should cause death? If a player's character is attacked by a wounded bear, it is reasonable to expect that he might die. But what if a character is hit in the face with a pie? It hardly makes sense for the hapless character to die as a result of that!

Objects in the game world may be treated in a similar fashion. For instance, an army attacking a castle may try to force its way in by using a battering ram. The gates will most likely not break open at the first attempt. Yet every attack on the gates should weaken them to some degree.

If you have purchased this book, you are probably already familiar with the basic concepts of hit point systems. But each game has its own system, and each may be very different from the others. So, let's quickly review the most basic features common to most hit point systems:

- Each character is assigned a certain number of hit points.
- When something occurs that "harms" the character, some of these points are lost.

- The more harmful the source of injury, the more points are lost.
- If the number of hit points reaches zero, the character dies.
- It is usually possible for the character to be healed through various means, in which case the number of hit points for the character increases.
- There is a ceiling to the number of hit points which may be gained through healing, which is usually equal to the character's original assigned number of hit points.
- To simulate character growth, the character's maximum number of hit points is periodically increased. This increase makes the character less vulnerable and rewards the player as well.

Advantages of Hit Point Systems

Hit point systems can have a number of advantages, including ease of use, versatility, and player familiarity

Ease of Use

One advantage of using a hit point system is that the system is easy to implement. The math involved is simple, and the mechanics of these systems makes them easy to understand. A hit point system does not place a great burden on the computer's hardware resources, and it can be implemented with trivial algorithms. The system's inherent simplicity saves time and makes the games less expensive to create.

Versatility

Second, a game usually features many diverse creatures or objects. Anticipating every possible combination of interactions is a daunting task. What happens if an elephant crashes headfirst into a tree? What if the tree falls on a grass hut? What if an elephant crashes headfirst into a grass hut? Could a tree possibly fall on an elephant? There are only three objects in this example, and already the situation is getting out of hand.

Using a hit point system, it is possible for the designer to assign a value to something such as the elephant's behavior. He might decide that "elephant crashes headfirst into something" should result in 120 hit points' worth of damage to whatever the elephant crashes into. When the elephant crashes into a tree, 120 hit points are subtracted from the tree's total. If this reduces the tree's total to zero, the tree will fall. (But if it is a sturdy old tree, and has more than 120 hit points to begin with, the elephant will have quite a headache!)

Player Familiarity

Because hit point systems are so common, most players are familiar with them. The typical player does not have to spend much time figuring out how his character gains hit points, or how to tell whether his character is in danger of death. The player can jump right into the game, enjoying it without reading the manual, which makes the game more user friendly. Intuitive understanding can also make the difference between a game demo that is easy and fun to play and one that is frustrating and confusing. Ease of play can directly translate into better sales.

Disadvantages of Hit Point Systems

However, hit point systems also do have a number of disadvantages. They can distract the player from the game's objectives, eliminate the thrill associated with risk, create absurd situations in the gameplay, and even alter the game's balance.

Player Distraction

Because there is usually a cost associated with character death, the player must remain constantly aware of his current hit point total. Using the hit point system may distract the player from more important aspects of the game, which can have a negative impact on the overall game experience.

All forms of entertainment share one goal: suspension of disbelief. In our field, this concept means that, in order to create the most memorable, effective game experience, the designer must be able to make the player forget that it is "only a game." What is a computer game, anyway? Really, it is simply a person sitting in front of an appliance, pressing its buttons and waiting to see what happens. Hardly exciting, is it? The more the player thinks about the game in this way, the less he will enjoy it. The designer's job is to make the player forget how bored he should be.

In order to help the player forget that he is just tinkering with a machine, the designer should limit any unnecessary details that remind the player that the experience is not real. Such details include requiring the player to navigate game menus or change CDs in the middle of the game. Unfortunately, having the player keep track of his character's current hit point total can be just as distracting.

No Fear

Another problem with the typical hit point system is that it can limit the player's experience of certain emotions, notably fear.

Players feel a natural attachment to their characters, because through these characters the player experiences the game. It is sometimes useful for the designer to make use of this emotional attachment for dramatic purposes.

Suppose the designer intends to have the player visit a particularly frightening environment. He goes to great lengths to create a mood of mystery and danger. From the beginning of the game, the player hears tales of horror about the unholy happenings at a dark temple in the mountains.

Having both dreaded and anticipated this moment for hours, the player is finally about to explore the fearsome temple. He knows that it is dangerous, and that his character is bound to meet with some formidable obstacles. The game's music, background sound effects, and weird lighting combine with the stories he has heard to put him ill at ease. The player is enjoying the same sort of experience one gets from watching a good horror movie.

Everything is going well, from the designer's point of view. The player does not really fear death, of course. The game is not so convincing that the player believes that whatever happens to his character will also happen to him. But he is very attached to his character, and is reluctant to allow him to venture into the temple unprepared. He identifies with his character to the point where he fears for his character's life, which is precisely the experience the designer hoped to convey.

Then the player checks his character's hit points and realizes that his character is in excellent health. Because the character has a high number of hit points, it is in no immediate danger of death. "Even if I am hurt," the player says, "I can just come right back outside and heal myself." And so the player ventures into the temple, no longer fearful. The entire mood is lost, and the work the game's designer spent so many hours agonizing over has been wasted. Much effort has been dedicated to creating a powerful experience, but because the player knows that his character is in no immediate danger, the quality of that experience is greatly weakened.

Absurd Situations

The use of hit point systems can also lead to bizarre, nonsensical situations. As an example, let's meet Thog the Invincible. Thog is a warrior who has 50 hit points. He is currently sitting in a tavern, where he has spent much of the day drinking great quantities of ale to celebrate his theft of a small treasure from a local adventurer.

Having imbibed more ale than is good for him (or for anyone else), Thog stumbles out the back door into an alley. He believes he is headed home. He is, in fact, headed in the opposite direction. As he stumps along, his finely tuned senses tell him he is being followed. Perhaps this awareness is the result of years of training. More likely it is the arrow that whistles past his ear. To his dismay, he discovers that he has left his sword at the tavern. Just as startling, he realizes that he is not wearing his lucky armor, either.

But Thog is a crafty warrior. With a hearty shout for the guard, he follows his dependable instincts and soon finds himself trapped in a blind alley. He turns around and comes face to face with the adventurer from whom he has stolen. Thog is weaponless, unarmored, and the cramped alley and his intoxicated condition are not conducive to escape. Realizing he is hopelessly trapped, Thog decides to accept his fate, and face death calmly. He stands tall, and lets the arrows hit him as they may. This looks like the end for Thog. But is it?

Of course not. This is one of those quirks of a hit point system. Before the local guardsmen arrive, Thog's assassin has just enough time to shoot eight arrows into him. Each arrow cause a maximum of six hit points' worth of damage. Even if the adventurer hits Thog with each arrow, and even if every arrow causes the maximum possible damage, it is impossible for Thog to die. Eight arrows times six hit points equals 48 hit points. But Thog has 50. (This is why he is called Thog the Invincible.)

Thus, the hit point system has created an unbelievable situation in the game.

Game Balance

In a typical hit point system the player's character grows more powerful by gaining hit points, which makes the character progressively less vulnerable to once-lethal dangers. The Slimy Slitherers, which once caused the player such alarm, become nothing but a nuisance once the player's character has enough hit points. In order to maintain the player's interest in the game, the designer must create new, more dangerous challenges.

Of course, this involves a lot of work. The designer must wrack his brain to come up with further exotic creatures and characters, and he must somehow make them fit together to create a cohesive, consistent game world. And each entity, from subversive pirates to icky Squeechums, must be individually developed. Finally, the game must be tested to ensure that the creatures and characters are well balanced.

If the game is too easy, the player becomes bored and loses interest in playing. If the game is too difficult, the player becomes frustrated and likewise loses interest. And if the game is inconsistent, with some pieces too easy and others too difficult, the player is bound to be disappointed.

Here is an example of the type of problem an unbalanced game can cause. Suppose the game's designer wants the player to discover a subterranean civilization. The designer decides that in order for the player to reach this mysterious land, he must venture through a vast network of caves. Of course, the player cannot simply stroll to the underground city. His journey must be exciting and adventurous. So, he will be attacked by cave-dwelling goblins. The goblins are relatively weak, but in great number, they pose a serious threat to the character's safety. After a long struggle, the player defeats the goblins and makes first contact with the underground culture.

So far, there does not seem to be a problem. But what happens when the player is ready to return to the surface? If he takes the most logical route and returns through the caves from which he came, he will have to fight more goblins. But he has already met these critters earlier, so the return trip does not instill the same feeling of exploration the player experienced the first time. He has also spent some time in the subterranean city, and his character has gained experience. This means that he has more hit points than before, and that the goblins are no longer a challenge. Instead of being nervous or excited when his character faces a goblin, the player is bored and frustrated. Each battle with the goblins is a tedious affair which the player is impatient to finish. The caverns, which were once exciting and intimidating, are now boring and stale. The player is eager to progress from the underground city, which is interesting, to the next interesting part of the game. Unfortunately, the caves stand in the way.

There are a number of ways in which the game's designer could overcome this problem. He could make the goblins stronger on the player's return trip. But this does not make much sense, and seems unfair. He could populate the caves with a more formidable creature, but this also seems strange. Where have all the goblins gone? Could the entire goblin civilization vanish overnight? The designer might make the player's progress to the next interesting area of the game world quicker by allowing him to travel there directly. Perhaps the player's character is teleported? But is teleportation consistent with the game's mood and setting? Perhaps the best solution is to have another exit from the underground city. While the player enters through one system of caverns, he might leave through another.

So there are certainly ways to work around this problem. But if the player's character did not gain any extra hit points in the first place, there would be no problem to work around at all, because the goblins would remain as challenging as ever.

Some Alternatives

Although a reliance on traditional hit point systems is often justified, it is possible to build different mechanics into a game. A few examples of alternative solutions follow.

No Hit Points

Although hit point systems are very common, not every game uses them. Many games of a nonviolent nature do not use hit points at all. Simulation, sports and racing games usually do not use hit point systems, even when opponents can be eliminated by nefarious methods.

It is also possible to make violent games that do not use hit points, for example, fighting games in which characters engage in duels with swords. Because it is reasonable to assume that a successful attack will lead to the other character's death, hit point systems are unnecessary, even in a game that could hardly be more violent.

Hidden Hit Points

It is also possible to create a game with a hit point system without allowing the player to know how many hit points his character has at any given time. This method helps to create uncertainty in the player with regard to his character's vulnerability: because the next blow always has a chance to kill the character, the player will have to be more careful than he would be otherwise.

For example, consider a game in which the player must judge his character's health by observation. A character who wears a painful facial expression, speaks in a weary voice, and staggers is obviously in trouble. Just *how much* trouble, however, is unclear, and that is exactly what we want.

In an earlier section, I mentioned that when the player is constantly assessing how many hit points his character has, he may become distracted from other, more important aspects of the game. When using hidden hit points, this is not such a concern, because the player is not focusing on abstract hit points, but on his character's very concrete health. This strengthens suspension of disbelief, tightens the emotional bond between the player and his character, and helps to draw the player deeper into the game world.

Fixed Hit Points

If a player character's hit point total does not increase during the game, the unbalancing effects of typical hit point systems are eliminated, because an adversary that was formidable in the beginning of the game will still provide a challenge later in the game.

Remember the example in which the player's character had to pass through caverns on his way to and from a subterranean city? We established that the return trip was bound to be boring, because the goblins would no longer pose a serious threat. But without the increase in hit points, the return trip is still somewhat of an adventure.

When using a fixed hit point system, it is important to allow the player's character to improve in some other way. Players appreciate watching their characters grow, becoming more competent and better able to influence the game world. Most players are used to the power and gradual invulnerability that comes from increased hit points. Eliminating this common source of character growth without providing something in return is bound to disappoint the player.

As an alternative, consider allowing player characters to learn useful skills. This takes a little more work on the designer's part, but it results in a more interesting game. While increasing a character's hit points will be appreciated to some small degree by the player, it is not exactly thrilling, and does not open any new avenues of gameplay. On the other hand, allowing the character to learn how to swim creates many more opportunities. Now, the player can reach the island he can just barely see from the shore, or he can explore the flooded ruins of an ancient fortress. For the player, this newly discovered freedom is much more enjoyable than a 5 percent hit point increase.

Other avenues of character growth include learning to cast magic spells, gaining possession of powerful items, upgrading wealth and social standing, making powerful friends, or learning the secrets of the game world. These skills and many more are good substitutes for increased hit points. Is a player more likely to be thrilled by an extra five hit points, or by the ability to cast a fireball spell?

A Combination Approach

Of course, some of these alternative approaches may be combined to enhance one another. It is certainly possible to create a game in which the player's character has a fixed number of hidden hit points, and where character growth may consist entirely of learning new skills and making friends. Such a system avoids most of the major disadvantages of the typical hit point system.

Even using this system, absurd situations may arise. And a character in good health may still make the player a little overconfident. But as long as the game designer takes these issues into account, he can minimize the problem of unlikely situations.

Conclusion

Hit point systems would not be used in so many games if they did not bring some important assets to the table. They are easy for designers to use, easy for programmers to implement, and easy for players to understand.

But in order to make the best game possible, designers must be aware of hit points' potential drawbacks. Careful examination of the character health system will not only avoid problems, but also encourage entirely different styles of gameplay.

Alternatives to Numbers in Game Design Models

François Dominic Laramée

francoislaramee@videotron.ca

Numbers are everywhere. From the 6th-level fighter in the fantasy role-playing game, to the 2,500 experience points earned at the end of a battle, to the 65 percent health score in a first-person shooter. No matter where you look, numbers pervade the game playing landscape.

In the old days of board games and paper role-playing games (RPGs), there was no alternative to numbers. Continuity and suspension of disbelief had to yield to the need for human players to throw dice and look at cross-referenced tables. How else could gameplay mechanics be resolved? But in the age of the computer, the nitty-gritty details of the game's rules can be hidden deep inside the machine. Players can and should be isolated from implementation details. Thus, there is no reason to confuse your player with such concepts as "level 5 turning ratios" and "92% pass rush ratings" that they have difficulty comprehending and that destroy the immediacy of the game.

In this article, we will look at a handful of ways in which we can masquerade the numerical models used by game software to turn them into symbolic, qualitative, or fuzzy representations that make more intuitive sense to the player. As we will see, some of these representations can even have a dramatic effect on emergent styles of gameplay.

The Case for Numbers

Of course, there are many situations in which showing numbers to players is perfectly legitimate. For example:

- **When the game concept is represented by numbers in real life:** Baseball is notorious for compiling statistics on everything. On-base percentages and earned run averages are an integral part of the sport, and should be treated as such.
- **When the need for precision outweighs the need for realism:** If the player must collect all four-leaf clovers scattered across a level in order to open a portal, she should know exactly how many there are.

- **When victory conditions depend on it:** An arcade game in which players are trying to beat a high score must clearly label the point value of every action.
- **When everything else fails:** Numbers are familiar, and they come with a built-in ordinal relationship. A 75% rating is obviously better than one of 48%; one glance, case closed. The relationship between "ion drive" and "meta-flywheel engine" is not so obvious. If there is no other obvious way to convey meaning, numbers provide a safe fallback mechanism.

There are also situations in which a mixed model works best. Ammunition is an interesting case: while a soldier usually will not know (or care) whether there are 356 or 357 rounds in the clip currently attached to his machine gun, the difference between 1 and 2 is a lot more significant. Thus, the ideal representation for ammo may include precise figures for numbers up to and including, say, 12 bullets, and fuzzy evaluations like "running out" and "plenty" when the quantities are higher.

Qualitative Achievement Schemes

Most role-playing games, from *Dungeons and Dragons* to *Diablo*, allow characters to grow in power by acquiring experience points and levels. Defeat enough goblins, pilfer enough gold, run enough errands for the rich and powerful, and you will become virtually indestructible. A perfectly valid solution, as long as it fits the type of gameplay that you want to encourage.

But is it always what you want in, say, a massively multiplayer online world? What about the player who prefers diplomacy to violence and crime? His character will never amount to anything in the game world's grand scheme of things. And what about the cheater who hacks into the system and turns his mild-mannered elf into a 100th-level assassin with 17 million hit points? By the time you find out about him and banish him from the game world, he may have driven dozens of paying customers away for good.

Let us look at alternative rewards for player achievement (in online worlds and elsewhere) that may sidestep some of the problems associated with the standard numerical way of "keeping score."

The "Boy Scout" System

Using this method, you would, instead of awarding experience points, award badges of achievement for specific quests or tasks. For example, a character who brings the scalps of 20 bugbears back to the captain of the guards will receive the title of "Bane of the Bugbears" and the right to wear a medal, badge, or ribbon on his character's uniform and profile sheet.

The badges do not grant the character any specific privileges in terms of hit points or fighting ability. Their impact is purely psychological: the player is proud of his work, other players who see his badge collection are impressed by his prowess, and nonplayer character (NPC) townsfolk may hail him by his new title from time to time.

You may even want to consider taking the idea one step further: instead of rewarding the character, give the badges to the *players* themselves. For an action-oriented game, this would be a little extreme. However, a historical game based on role-playing (in the theatrical sense) and on a quasi-educational experience of life in the past may benefit from a close adequation between the player and his character.

For example, consider an online world re-creating the realities of 17th century North America, where players are expected to sample a variety of experiences (including the myths and legends of the First Nations, exploration and hunting, crucial historical events, and daily life) instead of building up specialist characters. By giving them the chance to earn a great number of badges relatively easily, you could build strong incentives for this type of behavior into the core of the game's reward system.

The Guild System

This system organizes each area of activity into a guild, and rewards players for achievement in that field by giving them titles and access to guild resources.

This method is somewhat akin to the medieval "trade guild" system, where a craftsman would join a single guild and toil away for years before achieving the rank of master. However, we cannot force players to specialize to this level, or we would drive away all but the most single-minded in short order. Our players must be allowed to join as many guilds as they want. However, a guild-oriented reward scheme lets dedicated players benefit from sustained efforts: while anyone can become an apprentice and participate in the guild's activities, it takes more effort to become a companion, partner, or guild master.

The guild system has many interesting effects on an online world's dynamics:

- **Self-organization:** The exact type and level of achievement required to attain higher ranks may be determined by guild members themselves. The Guild of Thieves may decide to test candidates with specific quests. The Guild of Elder Statesmen may elect new partners through a voting process similar to the one used by the Baseball Hall of Fame.
- **Privileges:** High-ranking members of the Guild of Hunters receive higher prices for their pelts at the town market. Anyone who reaches companion status in the Guild of Healers is immune from attack, unless they attack first.
- **Meta-game support:** You can easily imagine a Guild of Architects whose members are real-life 3D artists; periodically, the Guild will hold contests (say, to design the town's new cathedral), and the player who wins the contest receives the rank of Senior Master in addition to seeing his creation added to the game world. The Guild of Bards may hold weekly "open stage" meetings, during which players are encouraged to post their own poetry on a chat line.
- **Player-supplied content:** High-ranking guild members may be allowed to design quests related to their area of expertise.

The Martial Arts System

While badges and guild ranks reward an ongoing process of achievement, a system inspired by martial arts will award belts and degrees (possibly many for each area of expertise) based on formal examinations.

If you decide to use this method, make sure that the nature, timing, and content of the examinations is well known, and advertise that players are expected to devote significant effort to practice and preparation. After all, once a player has earned a belt, it is his for life.

The main difference between a system like this and traditional experience point gathering is that the player will need to achieve a definite level of prowess before passing an examination. With experience points, a patient player could theoretically reach level 10 by killing a great many lowly kobolds, and thus attain power and high status without ever doing anything significant. Not so when the Black Belt exam consists of slaying a red dragon single-handedly.

Characters obtaining prestigious belts do not necessarily receive special powers along with them. In a traditional experience point system, character improvement is the reward for obtaining experience; in a martial-arts system, *the marker of experience is the reward for character improvement*. In a sense, the relationship between achievement and capability is reversed—which portrays reality far more accurately.

The Proficiency System

This method is a variant of the martial arts system in which the player must periodically requalify to keep his high rankings. This system is similar to common military and police procedures, where marksmen, for example, must pass weapons-proficiency tests every few years to maintain their rights to the title.

In a proficiency system, the titles held by the player accurately reflect his current prowess instead of past achievements. This added accuracy, however, comes at the cost of requiring the player to keep practicing his skills, lest they erode, which may be seen as an annoyance, and so should be approached with caution.

Fuzzy Evaluation Schemes

In strategy games, gameplay is based on decision-making. The information supplied to the player and which he uses to justify his decisions may be complete (as in chess) or incomplete (as in poker). The way this kind of data is modeled and presented determines how accurately the game simulates a real-life experience.

Scouting Reports

In professional sports, assessment of a player's talent is an art. Most of the relevant factors (such as passing ability, awareness, leadership, or ego) are unsuited to quantitative evaluation. Trying to force numerical representations on these features is not only awkward, but also voids several interesting gameplay opportunities.

Consider the following example, taken from a professional American football simulation. The gameplayer, as general manager of his team, must determine whether to invest his first-round draft pick in a promising defensive tackle or a cornerback. In real life, a scout would be likely to provide a report containing comments such as: "This kid has an instinct for the game, and he's always chasing the ball." Or: "He may be a great tackler, but he's a headcase who will disrupt the team."

The scout would also probably evaluate each player's resistance to injury in qualitative terms, like "below average" or "exceptional," rather than with precise numbers: there is no such thing as 34 percent endurance. Unfortunately, most computer games ignore this fact, and merely show the numbers they use in their simulation engine to the users. This makes little intuitive sense, and implies a level of precision that human scouts can never achieve in reality. Thus, a game that maps the internal numerical representation to words before presenting the data to the user (for example, transforming anything more than one standard deviation above average into "very good") clearly provides a more immersive experience.

Better yet, not only is the fuzzy, qualitative evaluation more intuitive than the numbers, but it also provides *more* information. If you do not know the average skill of the football-playing population, a rating of 76 tells you little about the relative value of one prospect versus another, while "clearly above average" certainly does.

One possible drawback of the scouting report approach is that improvement is not always immediately obvious. Minute changes, like an increase from 200 to 201 hit points, are easy to communicate with numbers. However, in a scouting system, 200 and 201 may both map to "very strong," which hides the improvement. On the other hand, if 200 maps to "strong" and 201 to "very strong," the scouting report will overstate the relative importance of the change. One way to alleviate this problem is to use fuzzier and overlapping evaluations (such as strong, strong to very strong, and very strong) instead of clear-cut categories.

Fame and Fortune

A fuzzy alternative to character levels can be implemented using a *fame database*. Here is how it works: instead of making characters inherently more powerful when they solve quests, improve their reputation among the NPC population. Thus, friendly NPCs will be more likely to collaborate with a hero, while enemies will be afraid of him and will fare poorly when meeting him on the battlefield. On the other hand, dastardly players will attract attention from high-ranking city guards and bounty hunters, while honest shopkeepers will deny them service.

Advantages of the fame system include:

- **Foiling hackers:** Information travels slowly in large worlds, so fame should be implemented as a time- and space-sensitive distributed database. Only kings and legendary heroes should be famous everywhere; most people only manage to acquire a small measure of local notoriety, and remain unknown outside of their home areas. Thus, the database can detect a hack by looking for unwarranted discrepancies in a player's reputation over geographic areas, or for a very quick rise in his local fame over a short period of time.

- **Reinforcing appropriate behavior:** So-called "player killers" prey on the less powerful (often new players) and wreck the game for everyone. Obviously, this is easier to do when their own characters are much stronger than those of their victims. However, in a fame-based system, characters do not gain actual power, but instead rely on their reputations to make their jobs easier—and fame has no effect on other human players.
- **Maintaining challenge:** For a 12th-level wizard, dispatching a dozen trolls is boring. In a fame-based system, anyone who wanders outside of his "sphere of influence" is going to have to work harder to achieve the same thing.

Conclusion

Of course, in many cases, choosing the middle ground between traditional experience points versus more symbolic representations of character advancement will be the most effective solution. For example, consider a role-playing game in which characters acquire a small amount of power as they gain experience, and also enjoy the fruits of fame and guild associations. Such a game would let players build characters with significant clout, without making them so powerful that all of the game world's quests and other content becomes boring.

All games need numbers. Computers, after all, are digital devices. However, human beings are not, and in many cases, transforming digital representations into analog values before presenting them to the user can result in a more intuitive and immersive experience.

2.7

Increasing Challenge without Frustrating Players

Marcin Szymanski

mszyman1@students.wisc.edu

The warrior steps around the remains of the enemies he has just defeated, happy with his victory. He notices the treasure on the altar just ahead. Knowing that traps may abound, he pauses, and his eyes begin to scan the floor, the walls, and the pillars. Something simply does not feel right. Without warning, a huge demon teleports into the chamber. The monstrosity informs the warrior that he took too long before grabbing the treasure, and proceeds to annihilate him with powerful energy spells—game over.

Does this make for a good challenge? Certainly, the player has been beaten, and must change his tactics in order to survive and obtain the treasure. By learning more about the game environment, the player will be able to make better decisions and take more appropriate actions next time. However, this scenario shows a misinterpretation of challenge. The scene might have been fun for the game designer, but such a misrepresentation can quite easily turn the player away from the game for good.

If misunderstood, challenge can lead not to a feeling of satisfaction, but to frustration. This article describes a variety of potential sources of player frustration, explains why they are introduced into a game in the first place, and proposes solutions that remove the frustration while maintaining or increasing challenge. By making the appropriate modifications, which can be as simple as adjusting a single number in the game code, the designer can fundamentally transform the dynamics of the player experience.

Total Control

One of the most fundamental elements of gameplay is the controls. A game's control scheme shoulders a tremendous burden: it must provide the player with complete power while also remaining practically invisible. For these reasons, it is important to ensure that a game's controls (keystrokes, mouse-clicks, joystick maneuvers) do not frustrate players. Having to wrestle with controls can destroy suspension of disbelief and, even worse, lead to a frustrating experience [Saltzman00].

Controls can be frustrating to players for a variety of reasons. Maybe they were intentionally made difficult in an attempt to add to the game's challenge. Another possibility for frustration is when controls are designed to be drastically different in each game area instead of being consistent. Also, controls can become frustrating when too many different actions are mapped to the keyboard or controller. Players should not be forced to scan a reference card every time they want to perform a game action.

A useful solution to this problem is to use context-sensitive controls—for example, button presses that are automatically translated into different moves by the game according to the state of the player character. Context-sensitive controls require the game to be smart enough to understand what players are likely to want to do in any particular situation, which is a difficult problem to solve, but the smaller command set associated with context sensitivity allows for a much smoother play experience.

It is also a good idea to provide video and audio feedback when commands are executed. If context-sensitive controls are implemented, a player will become comfortable with the controls more quickly if she knows that her choices are being understood properly by the game. For example, if clicking the right mouse button on a building's icon will start construction, the game should react with text or speech to that effect.

Finally, if possible, design controls that are similar to and/or compatible with the schemes used by other games in the same genre.

An interface that follows these guidelines allows the player to communicate efficiently with the game. This efficiency eventually leads to a mastery of the controls, and the designer can increase the challenge of the game as a whole.

Sudden Death

Many games threaten the player's character or vehicle with damage and/or death. Some game do so without warning, which may be seen as increasing the game's challenge. However, it ceases to be a challenge when a player has no way of predicting, evading, or surviving a dangerous game situation, such as the warrior's dilemma presented above [Saltzman00].

The "unavoidable risk" category includes a variety of game mechanics that cause frustration. An action game may have an area where the ceiling is so low that the player cannot jump over enemy bullets. An adventure game may have a switch that, if activated at the wrong time, instantly disintegrates your character, forcing the player to reload the game.

A player should not have to figure things out by constantly dying and retrying the level [Rollings00]. One solution is to have visual or audio cues that an attack is coming or an enemy is near. Alternatively, if the game must feature instant deaths to provide an accurate simulation, it should also allow for an instant restart at the same puzzle or in the same area. Or, the game may provide infinite lives, which is a great way to encourage exploration and creativity, and allows for more challenging gameplay because players are more willing to experiment with new tactics or items when the consequences of failure are limited.

Basic Training

A game may periodically reward the player's character with new items or abilities. However, it is frustrating to have to learn a new ability in a high-pressure situation, such as a fight with a level boss. Now the player is suddenly faced with two problems at the same time: she has to fight a new enemy, and she has to learn how to use a new ability or item. The player will not have the confidence that she is using the new game mechanic correctly and will begin to lose trust in the game's fairness.

A good way to avoid the problem of the player having to learn new abilities or to use new items too quickly is to include specific training areas—easy tasks or safe zones—where the player can learn how the new skills or items work under low-pressure conditions. Providing such training areas can allow for more challenging scenarios later, because the designer can be fairly sure that the player understands his game mechanics and is using them correctly.

Advance Notice

As a player advances through a game, he becomes aware of hints the designer has pro-grammed into the game's environment. For example, noise and lighting levels may help the player learn how powerful the nearby enemies are. However, it is very impor-tant for the designer to communicate such information to the player effectively, just as it is critical to ensure that players cannot enter areas that will be impossible to solve at given stages of the game.

It is also important to foreshadow enemy abilities and to build a consistent (although not necessarily smooth) difficulty curve [Hallford01]. This way, the designer can introduce very challenging situations into the game and be sure that the player will know what to expect—and be well prepared to confront the challenge.

For example, assume that the player faces an extremely devious opponent in bat-tle and barely manages to finish it off with his last bullet. Later, while crawling in the shadows, the player sees the enemy's four bigger brothers patrolling an area, unaware of his presence. His experience will tell him to avoid them. Allowing the player to anticipate his later challenges increases his trust of the game, which lets him enjoy himself and, when the time comes, overcome challenging situations. If the four broth-ers had instead materialized in front of the player immediately after the first battle, the challenge would have turned to a hopeless and losing situation, and the player might have responded with disgust.

Saving Grace

Allowing a player to save his game lets him return to the game after a pause, or allows him to create a "backup" in case the foray into a new situation ends in death. How-ever, be aware of two major issues associated with the typical game save. First, when saving becomes an in-game mechanic, such as when the game requires the player to collect potions or other items in order to save, suspension of disbelief is destroyed.

Second, when "save spots" are extremely far apart, such as in one recent game where the player can only save once after every three missions, player death leads to unnecessary (and frustrating) repetition.

Placing save spots far apart is a bad idea, and it is even worse to make game saves an in-game mechanic. First, a player may need to leave the game for several days. What if she has no more Save Potions? What if she is too far away from a save spot? Saving the game should be used for its intended purpose: to allow the player to return to the "real world" when they need to. Letting a player save only every three levels is also bad design, because the first two levels may be relatively easy, while the third may be very difficult. In this case, a player may become frustrated and bored when forced to redo the first two missions a dozen times only to die in the third. Or, a player may have time to complete the first mission or two, but may need to stop playing before beginning the third. Requiring her to replay the first two missions punishes the player for not having unlimited playing time.

Instincts of Self-Preservation

Many games provide players with the opportunity to protect a vulnerable target or sidekick. This can be an interesting game design element, as players must balance their own survival with the mission's objectives. However, if the player is expected to protect or save artificial intelligence (AI) characters, the AI itself must be up to the task. Nothing is more frustrating than watching a sidekick jumping from the side of a building, or supposedly automated gun turrets stay silent as they are shredded by enemy fire. If there is no way to make the AI do its part, do not require the player to pick up the slack.

If the game is designed to include such AI elements, you can prevent AI deficiency problems in several ways. Sidekicks can be teleported to safety if they fall off a cliff. If they get lost in a maze, they can be teleported to the player's general area. AI agents that are designed to fight should have reasonable combat capabilities. For example, the AI characters should fire their guns and move around well enough to defend themselves if under direct assault. In general, anything that is not under direct player control should be efficient enough not to cause the players additional problems. [Saltzman00].

Try It Again, I Dare You

Part of some games' challenges is the threat of death. Even if the game is well balanced and avoids frustrating design elements, it is always possible that a player's character will die. That said, when a player's character dies, the player should be allowed to try the game again as soon as possible. With video game consoles especially, load times can be frustrating if the player has to go through several menus and loading screens to return to where they were when they lost the game. It is not difficult to add a "Try Again?" screen, which can make a tremendous difference to alleviate player frustration.

Naturally, this advice applies more for some genres (action games) than for others (strategy games). Nevertheless, where a player might expect to be able to try again immediately, he should have a chance to do so. Having to wade through an entire level or game only to die for the twentieth time dissipates any real sense of challenge.

Careful with Those Numbers!

Some of the most frustrating gameplay elements arise from simple mistuning of numerical parameters in the game code. For example, if an RPG's enemy encounter rate is so high that the player gets attacked every 5 seconds, he will spend less time exploring. Or, if a robot player character's turning rate is so low that it takes too long to reverse direction, it becomes impossible for the player to pursue a fleeing enemy.

A more subtle problem occurs when the main character runs too slowly. Few players will complain that they get to their destinations too fast, but they will quickly get frustrated if it takes an unjustifiably long time to traverse a room.

The best way to fix parameter issues is to watch people play the game during development. If they attempt to do things in novel ways but are slowed down by the game's mechanics or assumptions, then the rules are too restrictive and should be changed. If players cannot move because they are always surrounded by swarms of easily defeated monsters, decrease the enemy encounter rate while increasing the strength or intelligence of the enemies in each encounter. If players in an action game simply back their characters against a wall to fight in each encounter, their character's turning speed might be too low.

The entire dynamics of the game can depend on the seemingly innocent numbers in your parameters. If you have an early prototype of your game tested, and listen to your testers, you can find and correct many problems associated with numerical parameters.

Avoid the Inevitable

The current state of the art in AI still cannot compete against the reasoning of a human brain. Therefore, tricks are often used to allow in-game enemies to pose a challenge to the player. Some of these tricks, such as giving enemies perfect aim or a head-start on building defenses, are better left out, because players quickly recognize that their computer opponents are "cheating."

Always let the player hope that they might be able to dodge the next shot. If the player knows that the next time they run into a certain enemy they are guaranteed to be hit five times for major damage, they will simply avoid that enemy (which means the enemy may as well not have been put there in the first place), and if that is impossible, they will get frustrated.

The easiest solution to this problem is to make enemy units fallible. The game can introduce a random factor that makes it possible for enemies to miss a shot, or to build the wrong unit, or to go the wrong way when chasing a player. Players themselves are fallible, and if they see the computer making some of the same mistakes that they are, they will feel more fulfilled when a challenging opponent is vanquished.

Nobody's Perfect

Many games require the player to play with perfect technique to win through a certain level or area. For example, a designer may place several ledges in a row above a fiery pit. If the player misses a jump and falls, the character dies and the player must start over. However, it is a bad idea to require that each jump be perfect. Simply put, players are not perfect, and they might not press the button at exactly the right time. What makes this scenario worse is that every additional action that must be done perfectly in a sequence makes it more unlikely that a player will accomplish the entire task.

There are two main solutions to this problem. The designer could redesign the environment; e.g., place the ledges a bit closer together, so that the player can make the jumps despite slight timing miscues. The designer could also build a more gradual challenge: if a player misses a jump, she falls to a floor a few meters below instead of plunging to her death, and only needs to climb a ladder (not necessarily from the very bottom step) to try again.

In general, requiring perfection may discourage all but the most hardcore players, because requiring perfection makes the game inaccessible to the casual gamer [Hallford01]. It is useful to watch players with a mix of skill levels test your game—it will become clear where average players are having trouble. In addition, having players test a prototype will reveal areas where every player is able to perform a task with equal ease, which will uncover spots where the game's challenge should increase.

Conclusion

Of course, rules are made to be broken, which includes the guidelines specified above. However, these guidelines should be broken with care, and only if doing so makes a specific scene or game concept memorable.

When the sources of frustration illustrated in this article are combined, the effect can overwhelm the player. The fewer frustrations encountered, the less likely the player is to give up the game, and the better the odds of a challenging and fulfilling gameplay experience.

Bibliography

[Hallford01] Hallford, N., *Swords & Circuitry: A Designer's Guide to Computer Role-Playing Games*, Prima Publishing, 2001.
[Rollings00] Rollings, A., and Morris, D., *Game Architecture and Design*, The Coriolis Group, 2000.
[Saltzman00] Saltzman, M., *Game Design: Secrets of the Sages*, 2nd Ed., Macmillan Publishing, 2000.

2.8

Nine Trade-Offs of
Game Design

François Dominic Laramée

francoislaramee@videotron.ca

Deciding what to leave out may be the most difficult part of the game designer's job. (It certainly is the most heart-wrenching.) Each of us, deep inside, harbors a personal conception of the "Ultimate Game," a perfect product capable of satisfying the needs of every player until the end of time. Unfortunately, deadlines and budgets impose limits on our creations, and perfectly good ideas must be pruned from our designs before they have a chance to blossom.

Cutting features from a game design because of external constraints is difficult, but it is nothing compared to having to do it because of internal incompatibilities. Sometimes, worthwhile and desirable design goals simply cannot coexist, at least not entirely, and the designer must sacrifice one or the other—or perhaps both.

This article describes nine such sets of conflicting goals.

Balance versus Enjoyment

Developers expend considerable effort tweaking their games until they reach the perfect level of challenge, adding a monster here, increasing hit points there, speeding up a timer elsewhere. Unfortunately, there are as many definitions of "perfect level of challenge" as there are players.

What seems like perfect balance to you will be far too easy for those who like to set the difficulty level of every game to "impossible" before they even begin. At the other end of the spectrum is the novice player buying his first game and completely unaware of the basic conventions of the genre. And of course, we cannot forget about the players who demand +15 Diamond Blades of Universal Slaughter midway through level 1, because they have more fun when the game is safe and easy and they possess clear advantages over their enemies. Satisfying all three types of players at the same time can be impossible.

Study your target audience, not only for skill, but also for preferences. Then design your game's standard difficulty level to provide them with a suitable amount of challenge. Do not spend too much time tweaking "easy" and "hard" settings; changing monster speeds, adjusting the rates at which computer opponents in strategy games acquire new technology, and the like, are more than enough. After all, you are much better off making 30 good levels for your core audience than to redesign 10 levels three times each to try to please everyone.

Realism versus Understandability

Some inherently complicated phenomena must be simulated accurately for a game to be interesting. For example, an economic simulation must rely on highly sophisticated algorithms to encode the behavior of the stock market, supply and demand, and so forth. Most of its gameplay is, in fact, based on discovering the hidden relationships between player actions and their consequences in the game world.

On the other hand, equally complex phenomena cannot be represented accurately in an entertaining manner. For example, an arcade game of science-fiction dogfights must provide immediate satisfaction. Therefore, it cannot afford the intricacies of an accurate physical simulation, and must simplify reality to hook the player instantly.

Finding the perfect balance between accuracy and abstraction is difficult. A racing game in which the car never skids when turning at high speeds breaks player expectations; while technically "simpler" than one with more realistic physics, it will leave the player far more confused.

Structure versus Freedom

This is the eternal quandary: should the player be free to do anything, at the risk of getting hopelessly lost, or should he be taken by the hand and led through a mostly linear story that may make him feel stifled?

Games can aim for any point on the structure/freedom continuum. For example:

- **Persistent online worlds** are as close to ultimate freedom as possible. While they invariably contain a number of structured quests and a social hierarchy, players can choose whether to pay attention to them or not. In fact, many game worlds implicitly encourage players to spend hours in unstructured conversation.
- **World-building strategy games** allow the player to perform a large number of different tasks, within the constraints of the rules.
- **Adventures and role-playing games** typically feature a well-defined final objective. Players may be allowed to divert their attention to side issues for a while, but they are ultimately expected to make progress toward the goal.

While many designers would like to do away with linearity, it must be stressed that stories have entertained human beings for millennia . Unless you are designing a truly open-ended multiplayer environment, you should err on the side of structure.

Mood versus Playability

Some experiences cannot be represented accurately in a computer game without compromising the player's ability to enjoy them. For example, dark, foreboding caves filled with monsters and eerie sounds are a staple of fantasy role-playing games. In the pen-and-paper game *Dungeons and Dragons*, player characters must either carry their own sources of light, acquire infrared vision, or work in the dark. This is acceptable because *Dungeons and Dragons* is a conceptual game that takes place in the players' minds. On a computer, however, excessive darkness makes a game unplayable. In fact, if the lighting in a given scene is too low, the player can and will adjust the monitor's settings to make the room look brighter.

The bottom line is that some situations are not pleasant in real life, and would be no more interesting on screen. Fighting unseen opponents is one of them. Even worse: in reality, sounds, winds, shifting shadows, and temperature gradients could help locate enemies, but most of these clues are unavailable on the computer.

On the other hand, fear is a very useful tool in the designer's repertoire. Turning the lights off is a far better way to convey urgency than merely reducing the character's fighting efficiency, and a detective game totally devoid of graphics because the main character is blind would be a most unusual experience. But always make sure to avoid causing intractable problems to the player merely for the sake of ambiance.

Completeness versus Manageability

Completeness is related to realism: where *realism* describes the way in which the game handles non-obvious causal relationships between player actions and game events, *completeness* denotes how closely the *process* of communicating player decisions to the game mimics its real-life counterpart.

Flight simulators are notorious for trying to re-create the experience of piloting an aircraft in minute detail. As a result, they provide the player with a highly realistic impression, but at the cost of a steep learning curve: learning to fly an airplane requires significant amounts of training and practice. The above-mentioned arcade dogfighting game, on the other hand, will likely abstract ship launch sequences to a single button press, even though an actual starfighter pilot would probably have to go through a 30-minute checklist before he could leave on a mission.

Real life is filled with boredom; include too much completeness in your game, and some of the boredom is bound to sneak in along with it. On the other hand, dilute the real experience too much, and you may lose cognitive resonance with the phenomenon you are representing.

Innovation versus Familiarity

In recent years, standard interfaces have emerged in several genres, notably in first-person shooters and real-time strategy games. Thanks to these genres, players of a new game can quickly get started, because its basic control scheme is familiar. However, the presence of such conventions effectively restricts the designer's freedom of innovation: if players expect a certain set of common functionality to be present in every game of the same genre, it is impossible to design one that departs so radically from the norm that some of this functionality becomes inoperable or obsolete.

The same phenomenon manifests itself in many other areas of game design. A wildly innovative game is hard to explain to players, hard to sell to retailers, and even harder to playtest. Licensed intellectual property is well known to players, but their expectations (not to mention those of the licensor) restrict what the designer can do with the property.

Familiarity makes the designer's work easier—until he needs to break out of the mold. Make sure that your game upholds player expectations, or at least provide plenty of justification when it does not.

Scope versus Concision

The more elaborate, detailed, or varied the gameplay, the longer the game will take to complete. In some genres, this is hardly a problem; online role-playing worlds, for example, are built on the premise that they should last forever. Designers of multi-player games with clear winning conditions, on the other hand, must consider the scope of their game very seriously.

During an online gaming session, participants can leave at any time because of technical problems, boredom, fatigue, or real-life interruptions. On the Internet, time zone considerations are also a factor: if it is three hours later where your opponent lives, she is far more likely to drop out of the game and go to bed than you are. The probability that all of the players who start a game will still be there at the end is inversely proportional to the length of the game and to the number of players itself. So is the probability that you will be able to get everyone back to finish a saved game another day. Thus, short games involving few people (i.e., a 10-minute death match) stand a much better chance of being played through than 10-hour strategy epics.

If multiplayer functionality is crucial to your game, make sure that a self-sufficient and consistent gameplay session can be completed in the shortest possible amount of time—at most, two hours. Sometimes, as in a death match, this chunk of gameplay will consist of a full game. In other cases, a single level, quest, or scenario is the best you can hope to achieve in one sitting. If you are designing a strategy game whose grand campaign game normally takes 10 to 12 hours in single-player mode, consider including a simpler, faster version of the game for Internet play—or leave the multiplayer functionality out altogether.

Violence versus Isolation

What kinds of meaningful interaction can a human player and a computer-operated NPC have? Not many. Artificial intelligence (AI) in the broad sense is still in its infancy, and it is very difficult for end users to teach anything to the machine, to conduct a free-form conversation with it, or to rely on its assistance for help, because the algorithms driving the machine's behavior are just not advanced enough for these purposes.

Game AI technology is very mature, however, in the area of combat. Collision detection, pathfinding, formation-based motion, and the like have been refined to a high degree of efficiency. Therefore, the one type of meaningful interaction that is easiest to provide is violence.

As a result, nonviolent games tend to feature highly abstracted experiences, where the player is alone in a world of rules and inanimate objects. *The Incredible Machine, Tetris,* and most classic games fall within this category. Meanwhile, the majority of games featuring interesting nonplayer characters pit them against the user in mortal combat. As a side effect of this phenomenon, most multiplayer games are also based on violence, because there is no easy way to build a single-player training mode for a nonviolent multiplayer game.

Thus, designers are faced with the dilemma of making games based on conflict and combat, or making games where a single player is stuck in a solipsistic world. This seems like a wasted opportunity; games like the *Creatures* series have begun to bridge the chasm, but there is still a lot of work to be done.

Breadth versus Depth versus Pace

The three desirable qualities of breadth, depth, and pace are mutually conflicting; at most, you can hope to maximize two of them at the same time.

- **Breadth** describes the variety of actions that the player can undertake. *Civilization,* for example, is a very broad game: the player conducts diplomacy, manages an economy, commands armed forces in combat, directs scientific research and urban planning, and more. Typically, a broad game will require the player to perform many different tasks in parallel.
- **Depth** describes the level of detail with which an activity is portrayed in the game. Flight simulators and shooters are depth-oriented games. Usually, different tasks in a deep game are performed at different times; for example, the character in a shooter will fight, then clean his gun, then look at a map, instead of mixing all three activities.
- **Pace** defines the rhythm of the game, specifically the amount of time required to perform a complete set of actions compared to the work load that must be handled in that time period. A turn-based game with no turn duration limits has slow pace, while a shooter in which the player can fire a round every 0.2 seconds has fast pace, and a real-time strategy game where the player must control 250 units on the battlefield may have very fast pace.

A deep and broad game, for example an empire-building simulation with lots of micro-management, would require a slow pace to let the player perform his job without undue pressure. It would also be targeted towards a very patient audience. A deep and fast-paced game, like a first-person shooter, cannot afford to distract the player with side issues: the fight is the game, period. Keep it short and to the point. Most real-time strategy games are broad and fast-paced, so they must restrict the strategy element to management of a handful of resources and buildings—nowhere near the complexity of a turn-based product like *Civilization*—and reduce actions to very high-level abstractions.

A broad, deep, and fast-paced game would overwhelm any player; there is only so much that the human brain can handle at one time.

Conclusion

Game design can be a frustrating job, because many good ideas are incompatible with each other or financially impractical. Knowing when and where to leave concepts out is a difficult but crucial skill. For some genres, player expectations make the decision process easier: shooters, for example, usually require a fast pace, while world-building strategy games can sacrifice speed for breadth of experience. But remember: sometimes, breaking player expectations may be the key to success!

Pacing in Action Games

Joe Hitchens
joe@sleepless.com

Agood action game will be much like a roller-coaster ride. It will begin with gentle action, slowly build up tension, reach a point where a combination of excitement and fear intermingle, then build to a fevered pitch, and end with a powerful and fulfilling climax. This article describes methods for building such a pace that will captivate players and hold their interest until the end of the game.

Pacing

When we discuss "pacing" in an action game, we are usually talking about how the various game elements are presented to the player over the course of the game. These elements include the rate at which new enemies and characters first appear or how common certain objects or power-ups are, and determines how quickly the game's difficulty level rises.

If pacing were simply a matter of increasing the excitement and action at a steady rate, the designer's job would be easy. You could simply take all of your game elements, determine their values or powers relative to one another, and spread them evenly across the entire game. This method works, up to a point, but it is not the best approach, because it does not take into account the human psyche and the differences in skill and ability among players. One person's slow, steady build-up is another's frantic, out of control, mad rush. Go too fast, and you might frustrate or overwhelm some players. Go too slowly, and they may get bored and lose interest.

So how do you please everyone? You cannot. It will be virtually impossible to design a game that satisfies all audiences. Some people will always enjoy solitaire; others enjoy the danger of hand-to-hand combat.

However, you *can* make your game appeal to a larger audience by providing the player with some control over the difficulty level and by distributing the game elements carefully to provide the most interesting, engaging, and satisfying experience possible.

Player Skill Level

Let's look at the tried-and-true method of "skill" levels. A simple menu with "novice," "regular," and "expert" settings will help players find their skill levels, and in most cases such settings are not difficult to set up. For example, if your game stars a horde of slobbering, saber-toothed roto-vipers, ask your software engineer to provide some with lower skill level to the monsters, so that they think more slowly, occasionally forget what they were doing, or sometimes aim their radioactive spitballs erratically.

When a player tries your game for the first time, it should rapidly become apparent to them whether they need to choose another difficulty level. Allow them to do so quickly and easily so that they will be able to get right back into the game.

Providing three levels of difficulty should be sufficient for most games. More than three probably will not be helpful. Remember that the skill levels exist onlt to adjust the game to within the broad range of a player's skill, so that the game can appeal to a broader audience with minimal effort.

Self-Adaptation

Another way to address the comfort level of your players is to design the game to adapt to their ability dynamically. This solution is currently more theoretical than practical and it is very hard to implement satisfactorily.

For example, suppose, in your game, the player shoots at a swarming horde of 8-foot tall, greenish-blue, Ganymedian cyber-ants. The player controls a master with a 100 round-per-second, high-caliber mini-gun that he took from the wreckage of their drop ship, and the game decides that the player's skill level is very high. Therefore the game boosts the skill level of the ants in direct, real-time proportion to your player's "skill." Thus, the challenge is effectively eliminated and the entertainment level drops. A challenge will not be perceived as a challenge if the game magically inflates to meet your player's ability. Challenges are only valuable to the extent that they can be overcome and the player can get some feeling of accomplishment from overcoming it.

Self-adaptation techniques have occasionally been used in games in the past. But even so, I am still a strong proponent of the simple, coarsely divided skill menu. People are stubborn, creative, and flexible. As long as you can give your players a challenge somewhere in the general area of their ability, they will be satisfied. Do not go any further, because your players *will* find a way to solve the challenge. They will think it through or find an alternate route, and when they do, they will find the a satisfying feeling of accomplishment.

Distribution of Game Elements

The game designer can truly be creative when it comes to distribution of game elements. There is a definite art to balancing the elements in your game and introducing them in the most interesting and exciting ways.

It is always best to lay out the elements across the landscape of your game during the initial design phase and not after development has begun. Once development begins, the game develops an inertia of its own, and it will be much more difficult and costly to make changes. Begin by building a stable of characters and objects for your make-believe world, but write only a superficial description of how they interact, or how they fit into the story (if there is one).After all the landscapes, buildings, weapons, objects, and treasures are ready, you can weave everything together into a game.

A true work of art in pacing will *not* be a simple linear progression. A straight line from 0 to 100 percent across a chart is not entertaining, because it's too predictable. What want is something that is, in an abstract sense, akin to a tree, to the human voice, or to the path that a river takes across the land—in other words, something that varies in detail, but has similar overall, emergent qualities. Think of a game, especially one built on a strong integral story, as following a path or thread from beginning to end. Take that thread, twist and turn to it, overlap it here and there, maybe make it backtrack upon itself from time to time, but always move it in the general direction of the goal.

Think of the straight line on a chart as the raw material for your thread. Bend it by introducing surprising and unexpected elements that appear out of nowhere and become crucial to the completion of the game. For example, a troll leader that you defeated earlier, but to whom you showed mercy, may later rush to your side to help you overcome an otherwise invincible foe. Or a weapon that was found in a previous level and that was only minimally useful at the time will suddenly become the perfect way to penetrate a barrier.

Turn the thread back on itself by requiring the player to return to a previously vis-ited (but subtly changed) place to get an object or a piece of information. Perhaps you reach a reactor core only to find that you cannot get in without a retina scan from your commander, who is lying dead back in the drop ship.

Backtracking can be cost-effective because you get more mileage out of existing maps, monsters, and objects. Use it sparingly, however, because backtracking can become obvious to the player if you abuse the trick. Backtracking can also be useful for giving the player a sense of progression: they may find that enemies that were pre-viously difficult to overcome are now much easier to fight, which can be both satisfy-ing and provide a respite between challenges. But, no matter how you vary your thread, make sure to always move it toward the goal.

Many older games were structured as a series of levels and level bosses. The level bosses were subbosses, more challenging than the smaller enemies experienced during the level, but nothing like the ultimate enemy that was the climax to the game. This method provides a good rough sketch to follow, but it is a little too predictable; stir it up using methods described above without destroying the overall pattern.

Do not forget to reward your player. Once the player has killed a boss, solved a major quest, or gained a new weapon, give him a short, easy area in which to rest, enjoy the victory, and release the adrenaline of the hard-fought victory.

Conclusion

For the best pacing, look for the perfect balance between order and chaos in the dis-tribution of your game elements. Prepare your pacing in the design phase, before development begins, and provide a simple three-level difficulty adjustment system. Build up the players' expectations, make them shiver with anticipation, and then completely surprise them. Do these things and your game will be better than a roller-coaster.

2.10

Adapting Licensed Properties

Daniel Tanguay and Brent Boylen

> *They're making a game out of that?*
> *Just what we need—another [insert popular genre] game.*

Almost every day another press release heralds that the latest film, comic, or television show will soon be released as a game. The industry reaction often mimics the exchange above. After all, many games based on intellectual properties from other media fail either critically or commercially.

Yet these licensed properties continue to be developed, and with good reason: as expenditures rise, publishers must find a way to guarantee the success of their product. They negotiate for licenses to mitigate risk; licensed property carries with it a receptive audience, which translates to higher sales. Furthermore, a licensed property can create increased market awareness, which is especially important for products competing in an already crowded marketplace.

Licensed properties attract developers as well. A licensed property can provide an immediate universe of references to help the team focus on gameplay instead of ancillary content. Knowing their licensed product could sell well also can boost team spirit. And for some, licensing provides a chance to work with a property they have tremendous respect for.

However, developing a game based on licensed property comes with a price: a designer will encounter more limitations when creating the game's feature set. The goal of this article is to make designers aware of these limitations and introduce possible methods of successfully developing within them.

Key Issues

A number of key issues with regard to licensed property need to be addressed as discussed in the following sections.

Target Audience

The publisher must know the game's target demographic to estimate development and marketing costs. However, the designer must further define this *target audience* into the three following subsets in order to craft the game experience:

- The **general audience** represents the mainstream market. Its size and age vary with the platform, and with the current stage in the platform's hardware lifecycle.
- The **genre audience** comprises fans of the genre(s) that define the game in development. Sales data help describe this audience.
- The **core audience** describes fans of the licensed property itself.

Identify the intersection between these three audiences, and then balance the game experience for each, using the techniques described in this article.

External Limitations

The publisher and licensor will define limitations for adapting their property, in order to protect the brand as much as possible. The parameters of this control should be specified in the contract.

The reasons for these limitations include maintaining consistency while developing the property itself alongside the game, and the creator's desire to maintain artistic control. A licensor's reaction to new content varies based on these two points. Some licensors will insist that the designer add no new content to the property's universe, while others only bar irreversible changes, such as killing a major character, and others will merely rubber-stamp any changes to ensure consistency. How does the designer work within these limitations without severely compromising the game's vision?

Staying True

The designer can still have a great degree of freedom within any external limitations; however, this freedom can prove problematic. A licensed game that does not adhere closely enough to its source may infuriate a licensor, while one that adheres too closely may alienate gamers. Where should the designer take liberties in the adaptation to ensure the best player experience?

The Tools

A designer has the following tools at his disposal to deal with these key issues (this is by no means a comprehensive list, merely a foundation for an individual tool set):

- Immersion
- Layering
- Discretion

Each of these tools will be discussed below. Also, recent Vicarious Visions projects, including *Spider-Man 2: Enter Electro* and *ESPN Winter XGames Snocross*, will help illustrate these tools.

Immersion

When setting about to create the feature set for any game, the designer traditionally immerses himself in the target genres to understand the competition. He plays as many games in those genres as possible and reads the reviews of any competing products.

However, when adapting a licensed property, the designer should also become an expert on that property. Whether film, print media, or sport, he should examine the property in excruciating detail. He should also research the history of the licensed property and any media that surrounds it, ultimately generating a comprehensive library of references. Effectively, the designer should attempt to become the property's biggest fan.

Spirit

During this research onslaught, the designer must isolate the *spirit* of the licensed property. He must understand why people like it, even though he might not. Reviews often help in this regard, as do other core audience opinions. He should take both positive and negative criticism into account, as well as any suggestions for improvement, and communicate both this spirit and possible improvement to his team.

Documentation alone cannot convey the spirit of the property to others. During research for *Spider-Man 2: Enter Electro*, it was necessary not only to buy issues of the various *Spider-Man* series, but other series too. Much of the team had little or no experience with comics and needed to understand the "feel" of comic books. These references communicated to the team the spirit of Spider-Man and the comic book medium. Without them, the spirit would never have shone through to the player, and the game would have seemed inconsistent with the property.

Innovation

While digging for references, the designer should isolate the licensed property's unique features. Using his genre expertise, the designer can then create hooks that catch a potential player's eye, making his game stand out from the competition. In *ESPN Winter XGames Snocross*, for example, interviews with actual Snocross athletes revealed that maintaining stamina during competition is vital to winning. The designer used this idea to create several game features centered on the concept of stamina; the most prominent feature was the stamina bar. Racing games usually track vehicular damage, sometimes in a complicated overlay. However, in the Snocross game, the bar easily communicated the abstract concept of stamina while retaining the familiar gameplay of managing "damage" and emphasizing the athlete's risk in racing a snowmobile. Furthermore, the designer tied trick performance to the stamina bar and devoted several snowmobile upgrades to boosting a racer's stamina.

Troubleshooting

Immersion aids the designer when problem arise while they are adapting the property to a feature set. And problems *will* crop up, because the game and the property are different media—one cannot entirely translate to the other. The more the designer knows about the licensed property, the more likely he will find a seamless solution to most problems.

This in-depth knowledge of the property also becomes invaluable when dealing with technical limitations. In *Spider-Man 2: Enter Electro*, several boss characters proved difficult to implement, especially Sandman. Finding references for Sandman attacks in the comics reduced the guesswork and tension involved in designing a state machine for a boss that can morph his body into almost anything.

Immersion may seem like an obvious step to take, but the designer often uses this tool less than he could. Command of the game's genre(s) and the licensed property gives his footing when dealing with the publisher, the licensor, and his own team. Furthermore, immersion creates the foundation for the other design tools in this article.

Layering

The overall target audience of a game can grow to monstrous proportions. After all, a product targeted to a larger audience can result in better sales. Ideally, the general, genre, and core audiences will have significant crossover, permitting the designer to easily tailor the game experience to suit the needs and expectations of a significant part of the playing population.

In practice, however, the age and interest range of the target audience is most likely too wide for a focused design. To avoid creating the game for the audience's lowest common denominator, the designer can instead *layer* the game experience. Basic layers offer gameplay to every audience type while advanced layers target specific members.

All games feature layers to some extent; layers allow the player to discover new gameplay as he becomes more adept at the game. These layers give the game *depth* because the player now has several means to overcome the game's challenges, which encourage him to replay the game. The designer can integrate the licensed property in a similar fashion: in *Spider-Man 2: Enter Electro*, the general audience knows Spider-Man spins webs, swings from them, and thwarts evildoers. This knowledge is all they need in order to enjoy the game at its most basic level. However, the game slowly introduces other details of the *Spider-Man* universe as the player progresses, allowing them to assimilate new layers to appreciate the property as a core Spider-Man fan would.

License-specific layering can assist the designer in many prominent areas, including gameplay, game modes, characters, and story.

Gameplay

License-specific gameplay can draw from the more obscure aspects of the licensed property, the history of the property, or the fandom surrounding it. This gameplay should not be essential to win the game: its purpose is to entertain the core audience and educate the non-core audiences. For example, collecting the Spider-Man comics in

Spider-Man 2: Enter Electro is not required to complete the game, but it gives the player more to do if they have mastered the rest of the game and adds to the replay value. The designer chose the issue for each collectible comic to appeal to Spider-Man fans.

Game Modes

License-specific layering is not limited to in-game elements: game modes themselves can benefit from it. In *ESPN Winter XGames Snocross*, the player can choose between XGames Mode and an assortment of arcade-style modes. All modes use the same tracks, yet the game experience for each varies. XGames Mode features tournament-style play founded on real-life Snocross events, as well as an upgrade system based on the sizable demand for aftermarket sled parts. This mode appeals more to the core and genre audiences. The arcade modes, on the other hand, feature more colorful elements, such as floating hoops for the racer to jump through. These modes appeal more to the general audience. The player can choose how he wants to play the game based on his understanding of the sport of Snocross.

Characters

Many licensed properties, such as Spider-Man, have distinctive characters that embody their uniqueness. Using these characters creates an obvious connection to the property that satisfies both the general and the core audiences. The designer then can layer situations that take advantage of the lesser-known attributes of these characters, or can use secondary characters familiar to fans of the licensed property without alienating the general audience. The villains featured in *Spider-Man 2: Enter Electro* included a mix of both the popular and not so popular: Sandman, for instance, is well known and was strongly desired by the core audience, while the Beetle is virtually unknown by younger Spider-Man fans.

Story

For years, Hollywood writers have used story layering when adapting a licensed property to a film. A story with a traditional progression, such as the hero's journey, creates a familiar framework with an accessible end result. If the story is self-contained, someone without a working knowledge of the licensed property can understand it immediately. The designer can then work in details the core audience will appreciate.

Staying true to the property's timeline and locations, and showing evidence of knowledge of past events outside of the game universe, will keep the true fans happy while presenting a fleshed-out world to immerse the uninitiated. In *Spider-Man 2: Enter Electro*, the story is episodic to instill a sense of reading individual Spider-Man issues. Also, the team referred to real-life photos of Spider-Man's hometown of New York City when constructing levels to make the player feel as if he is actually swinging through the skyscrapers of Manhattan.

Layering can be a powerful tool, but the designer must use it wisely. If layering gets out of control, the team may very well end up creating two different games for the price of one. The team can minimize the amount of additional content created for layering by reusing as many assets as possible. After completing a game in *Spider-Man 2: Enter Electro*, for example, the player unlocks new suits for Spider-Man to wear. Each suit modifies Spider-Man's attributes in some way, creating a new experience for future play. The decision to unlock suits, which is implemented in the game as simple texture swapping, eliminated the need to create secret characters, models, and animations.

Discretion

Quite simply, the designer must make responsible decisions. He must use *discretion* when deciding where to adapt the licensed property, and again when scoping the game's feature set so that the team can complete the game on time. He must also employ it when resolving any conflict with a publisher or licensor.

License Consistency

A designer adapting a licensed property is in an awkward position. He has a responsibility to both the player and the licensor when adding, removing, or refining features in his design.

In the beginning, the publisher and the designer should decide how closely to translate the licensed property into the game. The key to this decision lies in the size of the core audience. If fans of the licensed property can make the game a commercial success, the designer can tailor features more closely to the property. If the core audience cannot financially support the game, the designer should take more liberties with the adaptation and target the general audience to ensure sales.

A football license game is an example of a property with a core audience that could support a comprehensive, license-oriented simulation. On the other hand, the snowmobile-racing audience might not create this support, which is why the snowmobiles in *ESPN Winter XGames Snocross* behave with "heightened realism." They catch rise higher in the game than in real life, to exaggerate a sense of height and danger, and to give the player more time to perform tricks.

Internal consistency is ultimately more important than external consistency for a simple reason: a game is a different medium than the licensed property. As such, it is an interpretation of that property that exploits the interactive medium's strengths. An internally consistent vision will generate suspension of disbelief in a player, regardless of external consistency. Therefore, the designer should not shy away from adding gameplay that is not quite true to the license, but adds more fun or keeps the game competitive.

To continue the Snocross example, the team faced a dilemma with the trick system in *ESPN Winter XGames Snocross*. In real life, no one performs tricks at Winter XGames Snocross except across the finish line—it is too risky during the race. On the other hand, snowmobilers do perform tricks outside of competition, the most successful extreme sports games feature elegant trick systems, and, of course, the opportunity to perform tricks is just too much fun to pass up. The pro-trick argument proved stronger; thus, the player can perform tricks in any *ESPN Winter XGames Snocross* race. The team also implemented a system to justify trick use during a race: a driver's popularity points increase as he performs tricks, pleasing his sponsor who later converts those points to cash. This points system introduced internal consistency for a feature that is externally inconsistent.

Conflict Resolution

The designer must always keep in mind that his publisher (directly) and the licensor (indirectly) are paying his company to deliver a product to them. He should handle any design disagreements with the publisher or the licensor with the utmost professionalism. Maintaining this respect and consideration is essential to successful project completion.

Many times, a licensor requires certain features in their contract with the publisher. The designer should avoid fighting over these requirements, because changing the contract during development is not practical. His efforts should focus instead on adapting his vision to those requirements. In the case of *ESPN Winter XGames Snocross*, Konami's contract with ESPN required that any ESPN game feature licensed athletes. However, the design team felt strongly that fictional characters enhanced the appeal to the general audience by providing them archetypes to relate to. The team professionally conveyed their objection, and then adapted the game design to include the aforementioned XGames Mode like that seen in *ESPN XGames Skateboarding*. XGames Mode would feature the requested athletes, thus meeting the licensor requirements. The other game modes took more freedom with the property and included playable fictional characters.

When the designer disagrees with the licensor or the publisher on a possibly controversial feature, he must have evidence, such as a referenced precedent, to support his argument. Without precedent, the feature will seem incongruous with the license, and will cause friction in those relationships where the licensor thoroughly scrutinizes any content. As previously mentioned, the development team for *Spider-Man 2: Enter Electro* researched the comics for past examples of Sandman's abilities on which to base the character's attack moves. Some moves in his design did not exist in the comics, while others did. Marvel cut those moves without precedent in the comics for consistency with the property. The others that had precedent survived into the final product.

Disagreements with the publisher or licensor can be difficult, but do not need to be. A flexible designer will understand the spirit of the publisher or licensor request, all the while selling his point of view. Frequently, the publisher and licensor will accept an alternate solution that fulfills the spirit if not the letter of the request.

Exercising discretion over which battles to fight with licensors and how to fight them has far-reaching effects on the entire project. Not only can disagreements impact the success of the game and the developer's relationship with the publisher and licensor, but it also influences team morale and the overall office atmosphere. Ultimately, discretion can win or lose the battle of making a and enjoyable and well-selling game.

Conclusion

The truth is unfortunate—many games based on licensed properties do not live up to their potential. Sometimes, circumstances outside of the developer's control result in the demise of a promising design. At other times, however, the developer is at fault.

Many developers are concerned exclusively with satisfying the publisher and licensor. The developer, especially the designer, must keep the best interests of the player in mind when making decisions. If the designer does not champion the player and their experience, no one else will. By keeping this in mind while behaving professionally, a developer can craft an enjoyable, innovative game based on a licensed property.

2.11

Warning Signs of Faulty Game Design

Sim Dietrich

SDietrich@nvidia.com

Creating and producing games is a long process. Without proper design review, it is easy to let unplanned interactions slip into the final product. In addition, some aspects of a paper game design may not translate well to the actual game. This article describes several warning signs that indicate that a game design may need tweaking, and includes potential solutions for each of them.

Warning Sign #1: New Players Can't Play the Game without Assistance

When demonstrating a game to an outside party, the development team is constantly called upon to explain the controls, the user interface choices, or the roles of in-game objects.

Potential Solution

Having to convey a certain amount of information is natural, because the demo may be insufficiently documented and/or the game may feature novel or complex gameplay. However, excessive player difficulty may be caused by a clunky user interface whose problems have become unnoticeable to the development team after long months of use.

If you find that a specific part of the game requires frequent guidance, you should consider ways to eliminate that feature, or make it easier to understand, or defer its introduction until later in the game.

For example, in *Star Wars: Rebellion*, the tactical game design originally called for six combat formations for capital ships and star fighters. However, new players had trouble figuring out which formations were supposed to be used in which situations, and some of the alternatives did not seem to make a difference in battle.

Over time it became clear that, due to the lack of terrain or effective defense in empty space, only two of the originally planned formations were any more effective than a random swarm. One was a spherical formation around a ship. Around a friendly ship, it was guaranteed to provide the best offensive screen in any direction.

Around an enemy, it allowed the maximum number of ships to attack the enemy at once. The other useful formation was linear, and played on various ship types' firing ranges: the line of ships positioned themselves to be able to fire while staying out of range of their opponents' weapons.

Eliminating the other formations caused some wasted code and artwork, but it simplified the game and its interface. The reduction in confusing options greatly increased new players' ability to pick up the tactical game.

Warning Sign #2: New Players Don't *Enjoy* the Game without Assistance

When demonstrating a game to an outside party, the development team often looks over their shoulder and guides them to the "fun" areas, or instructs them as to the best way to get started, in an effort to prevent frustration.

Potential Solution

If the "non-fun" scene is a weapon load-out screen or a map of potential areas to explore, it can add to the depth of a game considerably, but it can also confuse new players. If you must guide players to the fun areas, it is probably because they are overwhelmed with the game's complexity and do not know what they are supposed to do. Help them by getting rid of the non-fun areas completely, or at least by changing the starting position to a simpler, more interesting locale.

Consider restricting the choices available at the beginning of the game. Players likely cannot make meaningful choices early in the learning process anyway, because they do not yet understand how the game elements interact. Give players more freedom and more choices over time: the new player needs simplicity during the first few hours of gameplay, while the advanced player needs variety in order to maintain his interest. These restrictions not only simplify the learning curve, but additional complexity can be presented as an additional reward for competent play.

The designer should orchestrate the fun in the first few areas or levels, then step back and get out of the way of the advanced player, who likely has developed her own "fun" playing style.

Warning Sign #3: Load/Save Syndrome

Excessive loading and saving during certain sections of a game typically indicates the game is too difficult.

Potential Solution

Sometimes, the excessive load/save problem originates from the player and not the game itself. A number of shooter enthusiasts routinely save their games after killing each enemy, and reload them whenever their avatars sustain damage. One way some games inadvertently skirt the issue is to limit the number or alter the timing of save games. Many console games, for example, can only be saved in a few select locations, or after successful completion of well-defined tasks. Such a game-saving scheme also allows the designer to tune the gameplay around the save points: to make a level harder, making its save points sparser, and vice versa.

But while limiting the player's ability to save may teach him to play carefully instead of relying on the load/save cycle as a crutch, it does nothing to fix the problem of a game that is really too hard.

Players will often revert to constant saving and reloading to relieve frustration with the core gameplay. Discover the source of the frustration, and find ways for the player to anticipate danger through their in-game avatar, or through the user interface. Make it your goal to ensure that it is theoretically possible for a player to survive any situation the first time through.

Real-time games strive to create drama and suspense. Neither of these are achieved when a player is too surprised to react meaningfully, or when the need to repeat the same impossible sequence over and over again bores him. Instead of forcing the player to learn by trial and error, have the avatar visibly react near danger. Consider giving the avatar a "sixth sense" to let the player know that a tricky situation is coming.

For example, consider the interface in Konami's *Metal Gear Solid*. *MGS* featured a far-away third-person perspective camera—one so far away that the art could not be detailed enough to show enemies' facial emotions or body language. So, the interface was graphically enhanced with an overlay that showed the player which guards were alerted, and with an overhead radar screen that showed the positions and fields of view of the enemies. Although not "realistic" in the sense that a real spy would not be privy to a guard's field of view, this interface provided key information the player needed in order to succeed.

Warning Sign #4 : Unpopular Characters

If playtesters choose the same characters and/or strategies again and again, it may indicate an imbalanced design in which one character or strategy trumps all others. In the extreme case, this imbalance can render all other characters or strategies worthless. If a certain character in a fighting game always dominates, then players will learn to choose it all the time, making all the time and energy put into creating the other characters wasted.

Potential Solution

Create a tracking system on your network that uploads the game stats of each session, what characters or sides were chosen, who won, etc., and compile statistics. If specific choices prove to be very popular (or very unpopular), ask the players why they make their decisions. Be careful not to overreact early on, though: players learn from each other, and some characters or strategies are only good when used in certain ways, so there will always be some flux in the decision patterns as the gameplay is explored.

Alternatively, you could study the most popular characters and tactics and design enemies specifically to beat them—while making them vulnerable to other, under-used choices. An example of a "nemesis character" is Dhalsim, in Capcom's *Street Fighter 2*. Dhalsim excels at long-distance attacks and can slide under projectiles, which allows him to counter the common tactics employed by the Ken and Ryu player characters. Because Dhalsim is so unique, he takes time to master, but is considered by many to be one of the most powerful characters in the game, and serves as a nice balance to the more popular characters. Try to design a strategy, opponent, or item that nicely counterbalances every popular gameplay choice.

A good treatment of counterbalancing gameplay choices through a "rock, paper, scissors" approach is explored in [Rollings00].

Warning Sign #5: The All-Offense Syndrome

One way to make an action game level easier for players is to add more health packs. But if the player needs so many healing devices, we should ask ourselves whether he has enough ability to avoid damage altogether. Is there ample warning of an impending attack? Can the player find out what type of attack is coming and from what direction? If so, is there enough time to react? As we have seen while discussing Warning Sign #3, being constantly surprised is frustrating. Worse, there have been numerous fighting games in which blocking or defensive moves took too long to initiate to be effective.

Potential Solution

Instead of helping the player heal after he has been hit, provide effective defensive moves (such as dives, blocks, or rolls) and shielding. For example, in first person shooters, the "strafe" command acts primarily as a dodging mechanism: with strafing, good players can get through the entire first episode of *Doom* virtually unharmed, while otherwise copious amounts of armor and health packs are required to survive.

Tune a level assuming that the defensive moves are obvious and available, or tune it assuming no defensive moves at all. Use these hypotheses about defenses as a learning curve option, as explained in Warning #2. Perhaps the first levels of the game contain numerous health packs, and later levels not only contain few health packs, but feature sections that encourage players to learn dodging and defensive maneuvers.

Warning Sign #7: Players Frequently Reconfigure Controls

Many games now offer the ability to reconfigure controls, in order to accommodate a plethora of joysticks, mice, keyboards, and other input devices. If the majority of players reconfigure the default controls, it may be a sign that the default controls are inadequate. Remember that beginning players may not understand that the controls can be reconfigured, or may be unwilling to do so.

Potential Solution

Rather than forcing the player to compensate for a poorly designed control scheme, or one that does not scale well with player ability, try to find a default configuration that will require as little tweaking as possible. PC game designers should also look at localizing default keyboard controls for various markets, because international keyboards vary considerably in layout.

Console designers have less of a problem with this due to rather strict guidelines set by console manufacturers on which buttons should perform which actions, but the PC game space has no real standard. However, many PC action games now support "Quake WASD" controls as an option, while real-time strategy games offer a "Warcraft-like" interface. These quasi-standards have the advantage of being easy to learn for players familiar with the original games—but if you have no need at all for new controls beyond those employed in a previous game, it may be a sign that your game is not bringing any new gameplay to the genre.

For more thoughts on control design, see [Dietrich02].

Warning Sign #8 : Winning or Losing

Some games feature a gameplay cycle where players start off weak, get a few power-ups and become invincible, then become weak again when the power-ups wear off or the player characters die. Taken to the extreme, this routine leaves players either completely helpless, or totally invincible.

The vulnerability-invincibility cycle can work for some games; for example, *Pac-Man*, in which the gameplay is based on alternating between long periods of perilous normalcy and short bursts of supercharged lethality. However, the cycle can also make games uneven and hard to tune.

Potential Solution

It can be argued that the most interesting gameplay occurs when a player teeters on the brink of victory and destruction. The ability to anticipate danger, have time to appreciate it, and then circumvent it is paramount.

Seek ways to balance the player's abilities and challenges, through clever level and item design, as well as programmatically. Try keeping track of a player's rate of progress through the game, and throw challenges at her that match her skill level.

One approach, first suggested to the author by Hugh Sider of Coolhand Interactive, is to have the computer identify a nemesis character that could appear repeatedly to challenge the player. This nemesis could be chosen specifically to exploit certain aspects of the player's gameplay style. The nemesis does not have to be a specific character, but could be a unit type, or simply a challenge or situation that arises on occasion to balance a player's overconfidence. Alternatively, periodically presenting a character with a simple challenge can help her regain confidence.

The principle at work here is one of balance. The computer has the ability to actively improve the gameplay experience for the player. Instead of spending time developing invincible AI routines, invest it in making the game itself act as a responsive playmate whose goal is to provide a fun experience by keeping the game in balance.

Conclusion

It is almost impossible for designers to predict all of the consequences of their choices for game design. The best way to ensure that your game design is free of major flaws is to observe players testing it during development, and noting any unintended patterns in their behavior.

Bibliography

[Dietrich02] Dietrich, S., "Six Principles of User Interaction," *Game Design Perspectives*, Charles River Media, 2002.

[Rollings00] Rollings, A., and Morris, D., *Game Architecture and Design,* The Coriolis Group, 2000.

2.12

Elements of Level Design

François Dominic Laramée

francoislaramee@videotron.ca

In recent years, *level design* has increasingly come to be considered synonymous with 3D art. Level editors have been merged into general-purpose 3D modeling tools, and most writers who have discussed level design have done so in terms of visual arts and architecture.

This article will focus on the nonvisual aspects of level design: how to structure a game into effective subdivisions, organize progression between levels, and build the gameplay of the levels themselves. For the purposes of this discussion, the term *level* will include:

- Maps in shooters
- Scenarios in strategy games
- Quests in RPGs and adventures
- Levels in arcade games
- Any other self-contained units of gameplay of comparable scope

Level Duration

While there are many valid ways to split a game into levels, one quasi-universal rule is that the average player should be able to complete at least one level of any game in a single sitting (or gameplay session). The exact definition of a sitting, however, is enormously variable:

- **For young children**, who like to frequently move from one activity to another, a game session may often last no more than 15 minutes.
- **For casual gamers**, who divide their few hours of free time between interactive entertainment and a variety of other pastimes, the duration of a television show (i.e., 30 to 60 minutes) is a good benchmark.
- **For hardcore gamers**, daily sessions of two hours or more are not unusual, but levels that require more than two hours of continuous concentration should be avoided unless the game's scenario absolutely demands them.

Whatever the game's audience, a single gameplay session should be enough to obtain closure on a level—or, at the very least, some satisfaction. Exploring a large, open-ended environment or completing a very long mission (for example, a full *Civilization III* game) requires a significant commitment of time and effort on the part of the player; if your game requires such a structure, make sure that:

- **You provide milestones of achievement on a regular basis:** *Civilization III* allows the player to build "wonders" of the world, advance between epochs, etc.
- **You allow the player to save the game as needed:** When levels are short, lack of ability to save the game midway through is often not much of a hindrance, because the end of a level is a natural milestone; in an open-ended environment, the absence of such intuitive boundaries makes it more important for the player to be able to end and resume play at will.
- **You make it easy for the player to resume a saved game after a pause of several days:** *Civilization III* is a turn-based game, so the players can spend as much time as needed reacquainting themselves with the state of the world before making any difficult decisions. In an action game, resuming play is not as obvious; this lack of reacquainting time is one more reason to make resuming games easy.

Concurrency

Concurrency refers to the number of levels that are "open" or available at any given point in the game. This issue arises most obviously in role-playing games (RPGs), in which several characters may bestow quests upon the player at the same time, but it can also occur in implicit form in other genres. Possible solutions to this issue include: allowing only one open level at a time, allowing a handful of these levels, or allowing an arbitrary number of open levels.

Only One Level at a Time

This linear structure is most appropriate in games that require unwavering focus, such as those plunging the player into first-person immersion, and those that do not attempt to create a sense of non-linear progress through a storyline, such as puzzle games (e.g.., *The Incredible Machine*) and abstract/arcade titles (e.g., *Pac-Man*).

A Handful of Levels at a Time

Role-playing games create an illusion of vastness and freedom of choice by providing players several quests to fulfill, some of which may be mutually exclusive, in an order of their choosing. This approach lets players shift their focus from a difficult problem and concentrate on an easier (or merely different) task; this focus shift alleviates frustration, especially because the subconscious mind will keep looking for solutions to the original problem while the player's attention is elsewhere.

Make sure not to open too many complicated quests at once, though; *Diablo II* strikes a great balance between freedom and ability to handle multiple tasks by offering one to two major quests and a handful of random wilderness environments at any one time.

Many Levels at a Time

Allowing many open levels can be dangerous because of the confusion it can cause in players. However, if we choose to define a *level* as a task to accomplish, allowing players to juggle many of them can be a powerful gameplay attractor: real-time strategy games such as *Starcraft* and world-building games like *SimCity* are based on selecting which potentially profitable activities to perform and which to ignore because of a lack of resources, and the best players are those who manage to accomplish the most with the same toolkit.

Relationships between Levels

Genre and audience may also influence the ways in which the connections between levels are structured. Possible models include: unrelated levels, a loose global structure based on an overarching storyline, and campaigns.

Unrelated Levels

This model is the classic puzzle game structure, in which consecutive levels are completely independent and have no obvious interconnection, save perhaps a vague increase in difficulty as time goes by.

In addition to puzzles, many action and arcade games can also benefit from this model: each environment can be developed independently, thus cutting down on schedules, and the list of levels sorted by difficulty during beta testing.

However, such a lack of designed structure may lead to confusion and loss of interest; make sure that it is appropriate in your case.

Overarching Storylines

This is the classic television model: each episode is self-contained, with its own internal plot line and conclusion, but some or all of the episodes also relate to a long-term story arc.

This model is perfect for casual gamers: it is familiar because of its television origin, the global storyline helps sustain interest, and the self-contained levels are well suited to occasional playing sessions. For the same reasons, it is also ideal for episodic Internet games.

Campaigns

The basic campaign structure, inherited from board games and implemented in such successful titles as *Age of Empires*, consists of a series of scenarios connected to each other in strict linear fashion: completing mission A grants access to mission B, and so on. It is also the implicit structure in most modern action games.

The *Wing Commander* series implemented a variation on this method: a linear subset of missions was played in the same solar system, and the next subset was selected (usually from two alternatives) depending on the player's success.

Campaigns provide tremendous immersion:

- They support detailed, high-stakes backgrounds.
- In a campaign, the player is under constant pressure to perform.
- Finally, because the order in which the player will experience the campaign's content is highly predictable, it is easy to augment its dramatic appeal with screenwriting techniques such as the ones described by [Timarco02].

However, a campaign's cast-iron structure can be its undoing, because the player may feel trapped in it. A shrewd selection of background can alleviate this problem: in *Wing Commander,* for example, the players are starfighter pilots attached to a carrier group, and it is natural for them to follow the mother ship wherever it goes. A game based on free traders or lone-wolf gunslingers will usually demand a more open-ended structure, because these types of characters should not be subjected to outside control.

Reusing Environments

Developing interactive 3D environments is a costly enterprise; therefore, many studios have chosen to multiply the number of levels and missions that take place within the same virtual world. *Mario 64* was the quintessential example: each of the worlds contained in the game could be visited several times as players received new missions—and better still, the worlds themselves changed in subtle ways between visits, giving the player the illusion of an organic, evolving universe.

In addition to the obvious cost reductions, reusing environments presents several interesting gameplay-related advantages. The familiar settings create *cognitive resonance* during return visits: the players know what to expect, can put experience to good use, and will be pleasantly surprised by the small changes that have happened since their last visits. They also stimulate *associative memory*: clever players may remember that the large crates that they used to climb to the police station's roof last time can now be combined with the new trampolines to reach the bonus life floating on top of a flagpole.

However, beware of staleness: too much cognitive resonance is equivalent to repetition.

Organizing Progression

One of the trickiest aspects of level design is deciding how to pace the introduction and phasing out of content over the course of the game, and how this impacts the player's learning curve. We will examine the two aspects of this issue separately.

Difficulty Curve

Providing players with the ideal level of challenge at various stages of the game requires a substantial amount of playtesting. However, some general models can guide the effort:

- **Flat curve:** In this model, the game's difficulty does not change from one level to another. Many edutainment titles of exploration, in which "levels" are replaced by different activities such as a coloring book and a sing-along, are targeted to a very narrow age group with specific knowledge and ability expectations. Collections of puzzles and card games also fall into this category; as such, *flat* often means "flat and low." It may also be possible to design games that are uniformly difficult, somewhat like the books of chess problems used by masters in their training, but they would likely have a limited audience and require a few learning levels as well.

- **Linear progression:** In this model, the challenge increases steadily from the game's beginning to its conclusion. While easy to implement, the linear model is risky, because it leaves the player with little time to master the game early on and may lead to an unreachable conclusion: if the game's difficulty reaches a player's talent limit in the penultimate level, the climax will forever remain out of reach.

- **S-curve:** This model begins with a relatively flat section, during which the player learns the game. This may consist of a few training levels, a tutorial campaign, etc. Then, the difficulty curve's slope grows steeper throughout the core of the game, before flattening again two to five hours of gameplay before the conclusion is reached. This provides players with sustained challenge, while allowing those who "survive" through the first 80 percent of the game to finish it eventually.

Content Life Cycle

The first time a player sets foot in a *Diablo* dungeon, a skeleton is a powerful foe. However, it does not remain so for very long; if the player had to keep hacking away at basic skeletons throughout the game, boredom would soon set in.

All types of content are subject to the same life cycle, from novelty to boredom to resurgence. Once a monster's power has been selected or a helpful device's capabilities have been scripted, deciding which levels to populate with it becomes the next crucial step. The steps in a game entity's life cycle include:

Stage 1: Introduction

At this stage, the player has never seen the entity; he may not know how it works, how much damage it can sustain, what its offensive capabilities are, and so forth.

Stage 1 entities should be introduced sparingly, often in isolation, to give players the opportunity to study their behavior—especially when it is not obvious. (It is pretty easy to guess how a skeleton will act; not so for a self-aware alien computer.)

For example, the Butcher in the original *Diablo* game was a powerful opponent of a previously unseen type who was the key to a low-level quest. New players did not know his strengths and weaknesses; it took significant trial and error to find the best way to defeat him, especially with one of the lightly armed character classes. Therefore, the designers gave him no minions and no special powers beyond its cleaver, so that the players would be able to study his behavior and learn how to beat him. When players later met similar creatures in groups deeper in the dungeon, they knew what to expect.

Stage 2: Familiarity

Once an entity's basic traits have become familiar to the player, it is time to make it common and let it adopt standard behavior: wolves hunt in packs, monsters use their favorite attacks, several trampolines can be assembled into a makeshift ladder, and so forth. At this stage, the player is expected to learn and apply the entity's typical uses and behavior, thus painting the picture sketched during Stage 1.

Stage 3: Prevalence

At this stage, the entity is well known to the player and presents no new challenge. Thus, it fades into the background and/or becomes "cannon fodder": the player deals with it matter-of-factly, without too much attention.

Step 4: Variations

Now that the entity is so well known that the player hardly notices it any more, it is time to introduce variants: the lowly kobolds are now led by a spell-casting shaman, the lightning bolt spell can now turn corners, an incompetent but gentle vampire emerges from the ranks of the evil dead, etc.

The key here is to break the assumptions that you have so carefully crafted in the players' minds in the earlier stages. Surprise the players by violating stereotypes, and your world will seem more complete, complex, and realistic.

Step 5: Fading Away

Once you have presented several variations, the entity should be allowed to disappear because it holds no more secrets for the player—and, in the case of monsters, no more challenge.

Step 6: Resonance

Finally, after the player has forgotten about an entity, you might want to bring it back in a different context to create resonance, thus tying the elements of the game world together in the player's mind. For example, the kobolds and their shamans who appeared in Stage 4 may have been enslaved by a demon and forced to fight the player under its orders; destroying the demon will free the kobolds, who will ally themselves with the player and protect him from the next menace.

Designing Effective Levels

The lead designer is responsible for creating the framework within which the level designers are expected to work. The previous sections describe his part of the work; now, let us delve into the realm of the level designers themselves.

Optimal Use of the Game's Features

Levels should be designed around the game's core features. This statement is less obvious than it seems. In a game of ancient warfare, rivers and mountains are key strategic elements, because foot soldiers will be unable to cross the first without bridges, and catapults cannot be pulled over the second. However, the same landscape features become minor hindrances to modern vehicles, and completely irrelevant to aircraft (unless we are talking about the Himalayas). Similarly, in a war game where troops must be supplied from their home countries, seaports and mountain passes must be secured before any large-scale assault can take place, whereas games that ignore supply lines leave armies free to roam the countryside at will.

Examine the player character's moves and the palette of entities available in a given level, and design tasks that reward original thought. Suppose that your player character is a futuristic soldier equipped with a body suit that can absorb the concussive force of most explosions and collisions—maybe not entirely, but enough to let the hero survive with minor injuries instead of being shredded into tiny pieces. In this case, explosives can become a locomotive device: the player can set a charge on one side of a cliff, jump on it to set off the explosion, fly across the cliff (riding the explosive wave front) and land relatively unscathed on the other side. The shrewd level designer will take advantage of this by giving players the choice of going the long way and finding a bridge (probably under heavy enemy surveillance), or thinking of the original solution and saving both time and ammunition.

Finally, give monsters knowledge of the world in which they live. The classic example of an inane enemy is the ghoul that fights with its bare hands when it has the Ultimate Sword of Death in its stash—the player should earn critical resources, safe hiding places, and similarly useful knowledge by having to defeat enemies who take advantage of them.

Balancing Gameplay Styles

Players like to imprint their own styles on a game. Some like to use their dexterity to avoid problems, while others like to think things through, and still others prefer to lower their heads and bash everything in sight. All of these gameplay styles are valid, and they should be encouraged at various points in the game—especially if you are designing an RPG with multiple character classes.

For example, consider the case of a powerful vampire bat. This monster strikes for heavy damage and flies at high speed, but it can only sustain a few hits before it dies. At first glance, this looks like a well-balanced opponent. Now, consider how that monster will interact with two different character classes: a sturdy barbarian and a necromancer. Against the barbarian, the bat's speed is wasted: the barbarian will be running *toward* it, not away from it. And in any exchange of blows, the barbarian's superior endurance and power will lead to a quick victory. On the other hand, the necromancer relies on summoned undead creatures to fight for him; but these minions are slow and cannot reach the bat. The necromancer cannot flee either, because the bat is just as fast as he is. By the time his feeble blows have dispatched the enemy, he will have sustained critical wounds.

The solution to a problem like this one is to balance the level with another opponent whose characteristics give the necromancer a chance to defeat it: for example, a giant poisonous slug that can be surrounded by his undead minions and slowly pounded into oblivion while the wizard himself rests in a corner. (For the barbarian, a high-endurance poisonous opponent is far more dangerous than any vampire bat.)

Balancing Resources

Any critical resource should be expensive to acquire and difficult to keep. This rule applies to safe positions in shooters, mines in real-time strategy games, powerful weapons and spells in RPGs, and so forth.

For example, if there is a single gold mine on the map in a multiplayer strategy game of ancient warfare, it should be:

- Located on an island equidistant from all players' starting positions;
- Defended by NPC towers and wild animals, so that the first player to conquer it will sustain massive casualties;
- And the island itself should be almost indefensible, so that gaining control of the mine does not ensure victory—the player will have to spend time and effort to maintain his dominion over the critical resource.

Be especially wary of resource imbalance if your game supports random levels. A warrior who has fought tooth and nail through 10 perilous levels and earned a constant stream of fire-resistant magical items will not enjoy coming face to face with a horde of acid-spewing demons on Level 11.

Balancing Victory Conditions

Contemporary games sometimes push the support for various gameplay styles one step further by allowing players to select their own ultimate objectives: *Black and White* allows the player to be either a benevolent god or evil demon, *Civilization 3* can be won by conquest, cultural domination, political rule, or scientific advancement, and so forth.

Within levels, allowing players to select objectives has rarely been done: whatever the players do in the first 90 percent of the level, success is measured by whether or not they manage to overcome the "boss" sitting in the last room. This time-honored tradition still has its place, but it has been overused. Even in quest-driven RPGs, there must be room for alternate solutions: a thief should be able to retrieve the object of the quest by sneaking behind a sleeping dragon, a wizard by telekinesis, and a trickster by showering the dragon's face with red pepper and inducing a sneezing fit. Really, how likely is it that the dragon will be holding the Gem of Ten Thousand Faces in its tiny paws all the time?

Conclusion

If general design is a game's backbone, level design is its flesh and blood. Level design has become a specialty in itself, and rightly so, but effective level design requires a commitment on the part of the lead designer to create gameplay devices, entities, and opponents that can take on a multiplicity of roles.

Bibliography

[Timarco02] Timarco Baggaley, S., "Show and Tell: Applying Screenwriting Techniques to Video Games," *Game Design Perspectives*, Charles River Media, 2002.

USER INTERFACES

3.0

Introduction

No matter how strong our desire to make our work as vivid as possible, a wide chasm remains between the real world and the alternate realities we create for our games. The computer is one side of the chasm, with the user stuck on the opposite side, and only the flimsiest of bridges connects the two. This bridge, built from flat screens, keyboards, mice, and joysticks, is the user interface.

It is impossible to overstate the importance of good interface design to entertainment software. Without a fluid and effective control scheme, the most captivating game concept is reduced to an unplayable source of frustration. Without a proper display of information, the player becomes a helpless victim of circumstance. In a very real sense, the interface defines the game, because it is the designer's sole means of communicating with the player.

The Many Faces of The Game Interface

Development companies have been known, on occasion, to hire one person to design a game and a second to design its interface. This is extremely dangerous practice, for several reasons:

- **In some genres, the interface is the game:** In a fighting game, mastering the keystroke combinations that lead to special moves is the heart and soul of the gameplay, and making sure that the players receive appropriate sensory feedback to assess their performances is crucial.
- **An ineffective interface can ruin a good game:** For example, consider the delays imposed by navigation between game screens. As a rule, if reaching a state in which gameplay can occur takes up a measurable share of the total game session, the interface is flawed.
- **A game is a holistic experience:** If the interface somehow clashes with the rest of the game, whether in terms of visual style, rhythm, or competition for the player's attention, the experience will be diminished.
- **The interface requires significant resources:** Any CPU time, memory, or screen space devoted to the interface is unavailable for anything else. In flight simulators, buttons and controls can occupy half the display's real estate. And in the future, spoken interfaces may demand their own dedicated hardware.

Also, the interface includes far more than a few counters and sliding gauges. The load/save cycle, the input controls, the screen layout, even the rendering engine can be considered parts of the interface, because they contribute to the interchange of information between software and player.

Human Visual Perception

[Monk84] describes the human visual system (i.e., the eyes and the parts of the brain that control sight) as an active low-pass spatio-temporal filter, which means that there is much that the eye does not see, and much that it constructs on its own from imperfect information. This is extremely fortunate for us game developers: in a very real sense, the eye helps us deceive it.

The Retina

Sight depends on two types of light-sensitive cells:

- **Rods,** which are very sensitive to light but saturate at low intensity levels, are mostly located in the peripheral regions of the retina.
- **Cones,** which work best under high luminance, are concentrated at the fovea, an area of the retina less than half a millimeter in diameter. The human eye actually contains three varieties of cones, each of which is optimally designed to detect a unique wavelength; this is why we perceive color.

When we focus our attention on an image, the eye's lens concentrates light on the fovea, where a large number of cone cells analyze the image at high resolution. Anything outside the center of attention is perceived at much lower resolution—to illustrate this principle, keep your eyes on one word of this sentence, and see how far to the right or left you call still read.

Conversely, because there are few rod cells at the fovea, many people find it easier to "see out of the corners of their eyes" rather than to focus on particular objects in dark environments. This is because the rods, which handle peripheral vision, are more easily stimulated than cones. The same phenomenon explains why we tend to see in shades of gray instead of in color when there is insufficient lighting: rods are color-blind.

Visual Sensitivity

Evolution has given the eye characteristic abilities that served to protect our distant ancestors from the perils of the prehistoric world. These special talents and quirks have made their way to us. For example:

- Sensitivity to rapid movement (including flicker) is highest in the areas of peripheral vision. This allowed for quick detection of incoming predators.
- Depth perception is mostly limited to a small area centered on the eyes' point of interest.
- Visual acuity decreases with distance from the center of attention, but more so vertically than horizontally, because most attacks on proto-humans came from

ground animals. This is the reason why computer monitors and movie screens are wider than they are high.

Screen Luminance

When we look at a brightly lit screen, the eye's pupil is constricted. This reduces distortion, increases visual acuity, and reduces the discomfort associated with reflected glare. Unfortunately, it also increases sensitivity to flicker. Thus, whether by design or by chance, many early 3D game developers (who did not benefit from special-purpose hardware to ensure high frame rates) mitigated the flicker problem by setting their games in dark, foreboding environments with low light levels.

Of course, when the frame rate is high enough (i.e., over 50 Hz for most people), this is no longer an issue, and game settings become a matter of taste.

Visual Display Rules

The eye's characteristics influence the effectiveness of our interface schemes. Here are a few rules that will help you maximize yours:

- **Stimuli away from the center of focus should be based on variations of luminance instead of color, and vice versa:** Consider the problem of informing the player that his health is dangerously low in a fighting game. Usually, the "health bars" are located at the top of the screen, away from the center of attention. Thus, the message will be more effective if the bar blinks, or if its length is reduced (with the lost health being represented by black space), than if it simply faded from green to yellow to red.

- **The larger the display, the higher the frame rate that must be achieved:** Remember that flicker sensitivity is highest in peripheral vision. This is rarely an issue in computer games, because the monitor occupies only a few degrees of the visual range, but the designer of arcade games with extra-wide displays may have to contend with it.

- **Avoid overfilling the screen:** [Monk84] suggests that only 25 percent of the display area should be devoted to significant information (i.e., anything except backgrounds, which are easily dismissed by the brain) or else the information will overflow the mind's ability to process it.

- **Put alarm signals in the upper-right quadrant of the screen:** The eye is most sensitive to changes there. Similarly, information that should be ignored unless the player wants to focus on it explicitly should be located in the bottom-right quadrant, where the eye is least sensitive.

- **On PC games driven by keyboard commands, you may want different visual interfaces for newbies and experienced players:** Moving your head up and down is tiring, so new players who keep looking at the keyboard will prefer to receive feedback at the bottom of the screen, while veterans who know the commands by heart will prefer to get important information at the top of the screen and secondary material (i.e., status reports) at the bottom, where it is least obtrusive.

- **Avoid excessive granularity in visual indicators:** A color-based gauge conveys information effectively, especially when the code is well known, like the red-yellow-green progression of traffic signals. However, five different colors represent an upper limit on what the eye can process quickly and effectively. For indicators based on size or length, like bar charts, four or five levels is optimal. For indicators based on angles, like a clock or a compass, players may be able to discern up to 24 different orientations easily.

Interfaces And Children

A few simple rules govern the design of interfaces for younger players:

- If the target audience includes children under 8, use no written text unless it is accompanied by voiceovers.
- The younger the player, the larger the active areas of the screen (buttons, etc.) should be, because young children's motor skills are not fully developed.
- Be wary of depth layers and 3D when designing for the preschool crowd. At this age, mastery of the third dimension is imperfect (which partly explains why young kids fall down so often). The same rule applies to subtle shifts in color: kids like saturated, uniform color blocks because this is what they perceive most easily.

Interfaces And Platforms

Input Sequences

A computer keyboard has over 100 keys, while console controllers usually have about 10, including the Start and Select buttons but excluding the directional pads. (The Game Boy Advance only has six.) The consequences of this fact are twofold:

- PC games can support a large number of different commands with single keystrokes, but doing so requires a lot of hand movement on the part of the player.
- Console games that need many commands will require multiple-key command sequences, or context-sensitive commands, or both.

As a result, if a game features a large command set, *initiating* a command entry will take a little longer on a PC game (because the player needs to position his hands on the appropriate keys, which may force him to look down), but *completing* the entry will be faster.

Precision

A mouse is a high-precision input device, because it is designed to support negative feedback from the human body's error-control systems. Put simply: if you move the cursor too far, you can bring it back with a simple flexion of the wrist. There is no need to move the fingers, and no measurable delay between wrist movement and cursor movement: the hand's position maps directly to what you see on screen.

Console game controllers provide less precision. If you miss your target with a digital game pad, you will need to move your finger to press another button. You will also be forced to initiate the button's release a fraction of a second before you reach your destination, because of the button's activation threshold. And while analog controllers mitigate these issues, they can do nothing about the low resolution of the television screen or the size of the Game Boy Advance display, which can severely limit the number of game objects that can be shown at the same time.

As a result, titles that require very precise input, like real-time strategy games where the player must give individual orders to several small units, do not work well on consoles. Similarly, because of interface limitations, most console titles adopt fairly lenient rules of activation: enemy bounding boxes (which determine whether an attack hits or not) will tend to be large, while player characters are given acrobatic abilities that allow them to grab the edge of a cliff and pull themselves up when the player times a jump imprecisely.

The Future

In recent years, we have seen the emergence of force feedback technology and analog console controllers. Special-purpose interface devices have also grown in popularity; whereas they used to be limited to steering wheels and flight sticks, we now see dancing pads, fake snowboards, and a host of other gadgets in consumers' homes. In the future, aural interfaces and emoting game characters may narrow the gap between game and player even further.

Aural Interfaces

Whereas today's games accept hand-triggered input and provide visual feedback, those of the near future will augment their capabilities by accepting spoken commands and returning information encoded in sound.

Positional 3D audio and interactive music have already begun the process. Advanced speech recognition and synthesis will complete it, provided scientists can refine the technology:

- Speech recognition will become suitable for mainstream action games only when it is able to support very noisy environments. Today's technology barely works with hands-free cellular phones; it would have no chance in the typical PC shooter war zone.

- On the output side, speech synthesis will need to incorporate changes in tone, rhythm, prosody, and other forms of modulation, which often carry as much information as the words themselves.

For a longer discussion of spoken game interfaces, see [Laramée00].

Other Forms of Communication

Humans communicate through far more than discrete commands and formal speech. [Picard97] discusses how to make computers fake emotion—and ultimately feel it as well.

In the near future, providing game characters with nonverbal communication skills will be as much a matter of art as one of design. Ways to enhance their expressive power include facial movement, gestures, posture, pupil dilation, sweat, respiration rates, and muscle twitches. For example, behavioral psychology tells us that people who lie have trouble making eye contact, and that the added flow of blood to the head that accompanies a lie makes the nose itchy; if the players see an on-screen character scratch the sides of his nose repeatedly, their subconscious minds will recognize the signal and raise suspicion. Books on nonverbal communication contain many examples of such cues.

Other Perspectives

The other articles in this section cover a variety of topics related to game user interfaces:

- Sim Dietrich discusses general user interface principles, including input and output concepts.
- Special issues related to the design of interfaces for 3D games is discussed by Sean Timarco Baggaley.
- Wayne Imlach presents an innovative camera control scheme.
- Adam Baratz discusses using artistic expression techniques in game mechanics.
- Finally, the ins and outs of the load/save cycle and its influence on gameplay is presented by Wayne Imlach.

Bibliography

[Laramée00] Laramée, F.D., "Speech Interfaces for Games," Parts I through III. Available online: *www.gignews.com/fdlspeech3.htm, Gignews.com, 2000.*
[Monk84] Monk, A. ed., *Fundamentals of Human-Computer Interaction*, Academic Press, 1984.
[Picard97] Picard, R., *Affective Computing*, MIT Press, 1997.

3.1

Six Principles of User Interaction

Sim Dietrich

SDietrich@nvidia.com

The user interface is one of the most overlooked areas of game design, but one that truly feeds into every other aspect of the design. Developers and testers become so used to the controls, sounds, and display of a game that deficiencies in these areas are often hard to detect. This article presents a series of principles regarding display, sounds, and controls that will help illuminate problems and opportunities to improve your game's user experience.

1. Consistency

Designers must always strive for consistency. One example of consistency in a game is a steady frame rate—the rate at which the video display is refreshed—especially important in action games. It is much less distracting to players when a game runs consistently at 30 Hz compared to frame rates that vary wildly from 60 to 20 Hz.

That said, some game engines strive for consistency in one area to such a degree that they lose consistency in others. For instance, some level-of-detail polygon reduction schemes will actively change the number of triangles displayed on a frame-to-frame basis, in order to achieve consistency in frame rate or perhaps polygon count. Unfortunately, these schemes tend to disrupt object silhouettes and vertex lighting intensity to such a degree that they compound the distraction during rapid frame rate shifts. This is a major problem, since the human eye is very sensitive to silhouette changes. In general, the best approach is to use a static level-of-detail system in which the transition points are all but undetectable. This solution wastes some graphics power but more than makes up for the slight frame rate loss by promoting visual consistency.

Consistency should be high in areas such as frame rate, art style, sound style, model and texture quality, object silhouettes, and lighting/shadows. Having a single object in the scene with a gorgeous shadow, for instance, begs the question of why the others do not—and the result will be worse than if the scene included no shadows at all. It is important to strive for a consistent level of detail in every aspect of the game's interface in order to keep players immersed.

2. Rhythm

Rhythmic patterns often emerge during gameplay. Some games, such as *Parappa the Rappa* or *Dance Dance Revolution*, exploit them directly. Most other real-time games, however, feature implicit rhythm, often enhanced through the timing of sound effects or music. For example, Mario jumping over barrels in *Donkey Kong* follows a rhythmic pattern, reinforced by the accompanying musical trill that follows with the points display. Players also pick up on the rhythms of enemy movement and attack patterns in games such as *Doom*, in order to avoid incoming fireballs while shooting the enemy demons at will.

Let us explore how a control scheme can help a player develop a rhythmic feel for a game such as a dragon flight simulator. In such a game, the player controls a winged dragon that can perform such actions as flying, diving, and breathing fire.

One obvious control scheme for such a game would have the player press buttons to speed up or slow down the flying, use the joystick or mouse to control flying direction, and press the fire button to use the dragon's fiery breath. A dragon is not an airplane, however, and controls like those described above would fail to capture the unique character of a dragon's flight.

A better scheme emerges from considering the fact that a dragon flaps its wings in order to stay aloft. In this new paradigm, the player would press a button to extend the wings from the dragon's sides. Letting go of this button would cause the wings to flap once. By timing the flapping of the wings, the player can control the speed and height of the dragon. Holding the flap button causes the wings to remain extended, and the dragon, to glide. Letting go of the flap button completely makes the dragon fold its wings, begin to lose altitude and dive. By tying the control to the natural rhythms of the dragon, the control becomes more immersive.

A similar idea can be used to add rhythm to the dragon's breath weapon. When the breath weapon button is pressed, the dragon begins to inhale. The longer the breath button is held, the more oxygen catches fire, thus increasing the breath's power. When the breath button is released, the weapon is fired.

Better yet: if the button is held too long, the dragon will black out due to a lack of oxygen! Finally, the dragon's breathing should be audible, and a tired dragon should breath heavier, thus making its breath weapon less effective. This would encourage the player to tie her use of the breath weapon to the dragon's breath cycle.

By designing the control timing to match visual and audible cues in the game, such as the dragon's wings flapping or breathing, players can more easily time their actions.

3. Expressiveness

The human need for self-expression often finds release in many games, especially multiplayer contests. Players will use whatever forms of communication and expression are available to them, however limited. Examples of expression methods in a multiplayer action game like *Quake Capture-the-Flag* include custom player names (including clan affiliations with text-animated logos), preset phrases bound to a key, player colors, player model type, built-in taunts and salutes, weapon choice, primitive dancing, play style, and finally, chat.

The more methods available through which players can express their uniqueness, the more invested they can become in the game. *Ultima Online* takes this to an extreme: players can even build and decorate their own virtual homes in the game world, as well as control every aspect of their avatar's appearance.

4. Orthogonality

Cluttered controls can be an indicator of a confused game design. Good designers try to minimize the control set as much as possible. One key to usable controls is *orthogonality*, which means that distinct actions should be separately controllable without interfering with each other. One example of an orthogonal control device would be the A-Z keys on a keyboard. Pressing one of the A-Z keys does not have any effect on any of the other keys.

A four-way digital joypad is partially orthogonal. Pressing Up is orthogonal to pressing Left or Right. Pressing Down, on the other hand, is not orthogonal with respect to pressing Up: the two commands are mutually exclusive. This inherent non-orthogonality in the control device itself can be exploited in the control scheme of the game. For instance, it would not do to have the Up and Down buttons correspond to two unrelated commands that might be issued together, such as "fire" and "dodge." If the player wished to fire while dodging, she would be unable to make that maneuver, due to the control scheme itself. However, mapping Up to something like "jump" and mapping Down to something like "crawl," is fine, as it does not make sense to jump and crawl simultaneously. The trick is to map non-orthogonal commands to non-orthogonal control states, so players can never even issue a nonsensical command.

The desire for fully orthogonal controls must be weighed against the need to keep the number of buttons in use to a minimum. Clearly *Ultima II* took orthogonality to an extreme, where every key on the keyboard mapped to a unique command. Although this allowed savvy players to quickly choose from many options, it required a much steeper learning curve than an equivalent hierarchical menu system.

5. Context

In order to reduce control complexity, contextual control schemes attempt to infer what the player wishes to do based on the context of her environment or nearby objects, thereby reducing the number of different controls and helping players remember what they are.

Contextual control was deployed in *Hubie*, a real-time action puzzle game by Serendipity Software. One of its design goals was to fit the entire interface on a digital game controller with only two buttons and a directional pad. Since there were three movement modes and three action modes, they overloaded the Up-Left and Up-Right controls to mean "Helicopter Jump" when there was nothing in front of Hubie and "Climb Up" when there was something in front of Hubie (see Figure 3.1.1 for an example). This method worked because it matched what a player most likely wanted to do. There would be no point in jumping if a wall were in front of you, andno point climbing if there were nothing to climb.

FIGURE 3.1.1 *Hubie is next to and facing a boulder, so pressing Up-Left will cause him to climb. If nothing were in front of Hubie, then he would perform a "Helicopter Jump" instead.*

A similar approach was used to distinguish between "Blow Left" and "Push Left"—the command was also contextual, based on the object (if any) that was closest to Hubie. These contextual controls especially worked well because of the tiled nature of the boards—it was very easy to tell what action Hubie would take because the context was clear and orthogonal.

Designing effective contextual controls is much more difficult in a more freeform 3D environment, because the player's avatar may be within range of several objects simultaneously. This issue comes up in 3D action games with a contextual "Use" key. For example, in *Max Payne*, having a sniper rifle enables the player to use the Sniper Scope to zoom in on enemies in order to aim better. When Max, the avatar, wields the sniper rifle, the "Use" key is overloaded to mean "Zoom." However, the same key is also required to open doors and manipulate switches, so confusion can occur in situations in which more than one possible interpretation is valid.

6. Fluidity

As gamers demand more role-playing and strategy elements in their games, including the ability to select from an inventory or give out commands, it becomes even more challenging for the designer to keep the interface fluid and natural. This is especially important on a console, where the control options are limited and textual menus require large portions of the screen in order to be legible.

For example, here is a way to implement a "list item selection" control with a single button press followed by a move with the directional pad, instead of having to move a cursor through traditional menu options. Consider a scheme whereby pressing a button on a controller brings up a semi-transparent menu similar to a flower, as in Figure 3.1.2. The Cancel option is in the flower's center, and each petal of the flower contains an option. The player can push the directional controller in one of up to eight directions and then release the button to confirm his choice. Releasing the button before moving the directional pad cancels the action. This way, not only can many options be displayed in a small area of screen real-estate, but choosing an option takes almost no time at all.

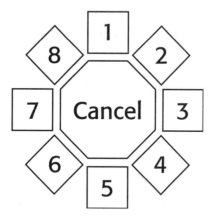

FIGURE 3.1.2   *Flower Gesture Control.*

Alternatively, if the game does not exploit either the digital or analog controller, the menu button can be eliminated completely, and a choice made simply by moving the directional controller.

Conclusion

The preceding principles all encourage developing and maintaining player interest. By providing consistency, a player is less distracted by clashing game elements or varying frame rate. Rhythmic interaction helps players learn the controls and, if the rhythm is tied to visual and audible cues, it adds to game world immersion. Expressiveness enhances the players' ability to emotionally invest in their avatars, and the game playing experience as a whole. Orthogonal controls are simpler to combine, thus allowing gameplay to be more complex and expressive. Designing controls with context allows a large number of options in a simple format, thus making games easier to learn and enjoy. Last, fluid controls are simple to manipulate, allowing the player to dwell on the task at hand or ahead, rather than on the user interface.

3.2

Breaking the Looking Glass: Designing User Interfaces for 3D Computer Games

Sean Timarco Baggaley

stimarco@bangbangclick.com

Designing effective user interfaces for games is a difficult task. Designing user interfaces for 3D games is more difficult still. Even something as fundamental as the choice of, say, a first-person or third-person viewpoint can make or break a game, yet there has been little explanation as to why this is the case.

The most difficult user interface design issue for all games is balancing the information flow between the game and the player. 3D user interfaces may provide a more realistic viewpoint, but the information they transmit to the player is dramatically different from that of a 2D interface. This article discusses the relative merits of 2D and 3D interfaces.

Entering the Twenty-First Century

The problem with 3D games is that, even though videogame technology has improved dramatically in the last 30 years, game displays themselves have failed to keep pace. The humble television set has remained essentially the same since the mid-1920s, with only the advent of color and cosmetic improvements appearing in the last 80 years.

We currently have no holographic projectors—no science-fictional holodecks or holocubes. Computers are now quite capable of manipulating fully 3D environment databases in real time, but these environments are still usually projected onto a 2D screen.

The result is that a 3D game displays a world on a 2D surface, but unlike Alice, players cannot break through the looking glass and immerse themselves fully within our three-dimensional wonderland.

The popularity of 3D graphics in games today means videogame designers face an important dilemma: how to design user interfaces for games set in 3D environments, when those environments can only be rendered onto a 2D display. The art of the game designer is therefore to create a user interface so intuitive that the player forgets that that glass barrier exists—in effect, letting the player take that metaphorical step through that looking glass and into our world.

All this begs the question: given that all consumer games use 2D displays, how do we define a video game?

Videogames: A Definition

A videogame is a simulation designed with the aim of providing the end user with interactive entertainment. Like all simulations, a videogame includes a database, a logic module, and a user interface. This basic architecture is shown in Figure 3.2.1. This article's primary focus is on the user interface component of the simulation. Because the user interface is the part of the game the player will be concentrating on the most, it is therefore the most important part to get right. A bad user interface will *always* result in a bad game.

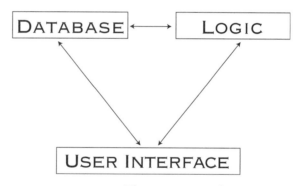

FIGURE 3.2.1 *The components of a game.*

Computer games are nothing special from a purely architectural perspective: any experienced programmer will tell you that the diagram in Figure 3.2.1 could be applied to all but the most trivial of computer programs.

The User Interface

The user interface, however, does not begin and end with the 2D elements such as side-panels, dials, and heads-up displays, because—and this is the most important sentence in this article—*the graphics engine itself is an integral part of the user interface.*

The reason for this statement is evident if we examine what user interfaces are all about: communication.

The Art of Communication

The need for a user interface in a game is twofold:

- To communicate the game's database and logic to the player.
- To feed the player's actions back to the logic and database.

In theory, the best user interface is one that conveys the most information to and from the user as transparently as possible. However, many games rely on limitations in the real-world interface itself to provide part of the gameplay. The racing game genre reveals a typical example of this.

A standard racing game contains a car that the player drives and a virtual environment within which the player drives the car. The environment is stored as a database, as is the description of the car. How the car moves within the virtual world is defined by the logic, which interacts with the database.

The user interface connects these elements to the player by presenting the information—usually by rendering the environment in and around the car in some way—to the player in a form that is easily assimilated.

Ideally, the user interface will help immerse the player in the game, so at first glance, creating a 3D racing game makes sense. And it does, up to a point. After all, we do not drive a car from a helicopter's-eye view as in Atari's *Super Sprint*. Instead, we sit inside the car and look out of the window at the road and the traffic around us.

The problem is that the player often starts asking awkward questions like: "What's coming up behind me?" and "Who's driving the car that's trying to overtake me on my right?" These are questions the player needs to have answered. In real life, the player turns his head and looks out of a window or in one of three mirrors. (Expensive arcade games have attempted to simulate this with techniques such as multiple displays that provide a wrap-around environment.)

Atari's *Super Sprint* displays the entire track to the player at all times, which neatly resolves the problems stated above. The player can see his position on that track and see exactly where all his opponents are. This information is difficult to communicate to a player through a 3D interface without the use of tricks such as overlaying the track layout and superimposing a mirror or two.

The video game designer must determine how all the needed information is to be communicated to the player. The player cannot rely on all the wing- or rear-view mirrors that a real car would have. Without the freedom of designing a dedicated cabinet or a full-blown installation for the game, we are stuck with the humble television or monitor. (While virtual reality goggles do exist, they are not currently in widespread use.)

Some racing games involve weapons and even flying in a full 3D environment, rather than merely along a surface, in which case the player also needs access to the information required to establish spatial awareness.

Anyone driving a car in the real world knows that the constant monitoring of the car's surroundings is one of the main reasons why you take lessons and pass a test before you can obtain a driver's license. However, in most cases, a game's logic and database is often adapted to reduce the impact of these limitations—if reality is too difficult to play in, change the reality!

The different ways to perceive reality are illustrated in Figures 3.2.2 and 3.2.3. Figure 3.2.2 shows the information a player would get from a top-down view. Figure 3.2.3 shows the view a player gets from inside a car.

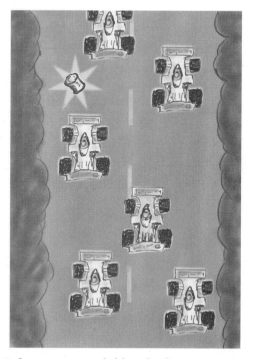

FIGURE 3.2.2 *Information provided by a bird's-eye view of a road with a car.*

The 2D view is clearly limited solely to the information shown in the illustration—the player does not know what lies further down the road. This is obviously going to provide less information than a 3D view, which would be limited only by the horizon of the 3D graphic engine. However, the designer in this case would scale the speed of the player's car to allow for this limitation. (And probably specify smaller cars!)

Figure 3.2.3 omits the information given by mirrors, because it is impossible to stare at all the mirrors and look ahead at the same time. The common racing game compromise of superimposing a mirror onto the main screen is far from perfect and requires obscuring a portion of the forward view, thus keeping the overall information bandwidth about the same.

The fact remains that humans only have two eyes in the front of their heads, so when a driver is watching the road ahead, any information his memory recalls from glances in the mirrors is outdated. In fact, the *only* way for a driver inside a car to obtain all the information in Figure 3.2.2 is to stop time, look out of his windows and

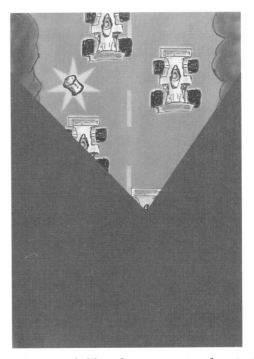

FIGURE 3.2.3 *Information provided by a first-person view from inside the same car, facing ahead.*

check his mirrors, then restart time again, move forward a little and repeat the process again.

This time lag and the resulting requirement for extrapolation is an important feature of many real-world interfaces and is also the reason why road users need to be trained and licensed.

This exposes a key limitation in the real-life user interface of cars and other road vehicles. We do not have eyes in the backs of our heads, so we have to physically rotate our heads to obtain the information required, but the driver is constantly trying to maintain a picture in his head similar to that shown in Figure 3.2.2, and ideally needs to keep all that information as up to date as possible. Driving a car solely from Figure 3.2.2's top-down view is actually easier because all the information is instantly available.

This illustration shows that 3D user interfaces are not always the best interfaces. This conclusion may seem obvious, yet many published games appear to have ignored it. In many cases, a design more suited to a 2D display will be twisted by arguments from technology evangelists who declare that all-singing, all-dancing 3D interfaces are the ideal.

We do not mean that 3D user interfaces should not be used at all. Because most racing games sell themselves—at least in part—on their ability to simulate the experience of "being there," the limitations of a real car's user interface must also be simulated to make the experience accurate.

Talking Back

So far, we have looked at only visual communication from the computer to the player. Audio reproduction technology has advanced a little more than has video and can be used to provide additional information to the user, but a complete discussion of this topic is beyond the scope of this article. Instead, we will look at another aspect of the user interface that is imposed upon us by the display devices of today: communicating the intent of the player to the computer.

Our players cannot enter our world and experience it directly. Every visual experience our games provide is forcibly filtered through a fixed, impassable, impenetrable wall of glass. Even reaching through the glass to manipulate the controls we see before us directly is impossible.

Instead, we are forced to *abstract* this important communication stream, forcing the player to use levers, wheels, switches, and buttons in combination to communicate his every intent to our game.

This explains why most of the best-selling 3D games invariably simulate an experience in which such an abstract user interface is normal. Racing games are particularly suited to this medium precisely because automobiles use such levers, wheels, switches, and buttons in real life. To the racing game player, such controls are intuitive because they approximate the controls used to control an actual car.

Abstracted controls can cause major problems in games that require the player to move a virtual character (e.g., id Software's *Quake*). Although plenty of players are willing to buy these games, much of the potential audience admits to being put off by the unintuitive nature of the controls. In real life, you can quickly glance over your shoulder while running forward and shoot at enemies to your right all at the same time. This is impossible in a consumer video game, so *Quake* and its imitators effectively weld the weapon to the character's head so that turning the head also turns the weapon.

The third-person viewpoint, such as used in the *Tomb Raider* series created by Core Design, is a more intuitive attempt at solving this problem. *Tomb Raider* succeeds only partly because most players are already used to the convention of controlling a visible character with joysticks and the like. The main reason for its success is that the game implements a much simpler control mechanism. Lara Croft aims her weapons automatically, so the player *can* run and jump in one direction while shooting in another.

Reaching through the Looking Glass

Most early 2D games designers realized—whether consciously or not—that the display device's limitations were something to work with, rather than against. The result was games that are clearly tailored to running on a television screen.

Williams' *Defender*, Namco's *Space Invaders,* and Atari's *Asteroids* were all created with the screen's dimensions in mind. The wraparound movement of the asteroids in *Asteroids* simply is not feasible within a first-person viewpoint. *Defender,* and the other scrolling shooters of the time, locates the player in a fixed, two-dimensional plane. *Space Invaders* likewise locks both player and enemies into a rectangular section of space. In real life, spaceships and airplanes are not limited in this way, but without the limitation, the game's mechanics fall apart: the moment you give people the illusion of realism, they start expecting *complete* realism.

The Glass Wall

When a 3D interface renders a scene from the lead character or a camera's point of view, that view provides a window into an environment. Just like Alice and her looking glass, the implication is that there is more of that environment surrounding the player, but the player cannot see it.

Recall the player's view in Figure 3.2.3. When playing a 3D game on a typical home system, the player's view is restricted to that conical volume. The biggest problem is that, unlike Alice, the player is permanently stuck on one side of his looking glass—the television is in a fixed position, so the player cannot turn his head or glance upward or sideways to view more of the scene. Instead, he has to consciously trap such unconscious desires and relay this need to the computer, so that it can turn the view for him and show him new wonders through that magic mirror.

This obstacle is by far the biggest when designing 3D games. At all times, the player's view of your virtual world is limited to what they can see through the small window of the television.

For this reason, designers must think long and hard before deciding to go for a 3D user interface for a game. Some game designs work well within the constraints of such interfaces—others less so. It is the designer's job to ensure that the user interface they choose for a specific game gets out of the way of the player so he can get on with playing the game.

Conclusion

Perhaps the most important thing to realize is that a 3D database does not automatically require a modern, polygon-based 3D user interface to render it. This fact is illustrated by two very similar games. One is *Theme Park World* by Electronic Arts (EA), which used a fully 3D user interface with special effects, full rotation, etc. The second game, released at about the same time, was Hasbro Interactive's *Rollercoaster Tycoon*, which had similar game logic, but relied on a more traditional, isometric perspective engine which did not allow full rotation or other similar user interface features.

Surprisingly, it was Hasbro's game, produced by Chris Sawyer and his small team, which dramatically outsold EA's product, even though *Theme Park World* was developed by EA's Bullfrog label. Even the critics agreed: EA's game may have been technically more advanced, but the 3D user interface just got in the way. Chris Sawyer's game was simply more fun to play.

3.3

Camera Control Systems for 3D Games

Wayne Imlach

wimlach@hotmail.com

This article proposes an alternative camera system for use with the first- or third-person, character- or vehicle-based genre of computer games, and discusses some of the limitations of current camera systems.

Current Camera Systems

The majority of contemporary 3D games use a few well-known camera systems:

- First-person perspective
- Over the shoulder (OTS) third person
- Fixed camera

Let us examine the weaknesses of each of these systems.

First-Person Perspective

In first-person point of view, the game is seen through the eyes of the player character; as a result, hands and feet are the only parts of the character that are ever seen, except when the character steps in front of a mirror or similar device. First-person cameras distance the player from his character—he is, in a sense, playing his own role rather than that of the character in the game. In addition, a player's interaction with objects in the game world has little or confusing spatial feedback. This is particularly stifling in games that use close-quarters combat, adventure-style games in which the player avatar must carefully manipulate objects and scenery (for example, the platforms he must jump on and the levers he must pull) to make progress, and vehicle games where the player must maneuver a vessel in confined or restricted areas.

Over the Shoulder (OTS) Third-Person Perspective

Third person views do help the player associate with her avatar, but at the cost of accurately gauging the avatar's focus of interest. Focus point is particularly important in games that involve accurate projectile placement: the player needs to know exactly where she is aiming, and be able to finely adjust that aim. Third person does not lend itself well to this.

The avatar itself can also become something of a hindrance when it obscures the player's view, particularly in flying vehicle-based games; also the back of any character's head can eventually become a boring vista.

Fixed-Camera Perspective

Fixed cameras offer the most cinematic and varied viewpoints of the three systems discussed so far, but they suffer heavily in the architectural design of the environment. For a fixed camera system to work, areas must either be free of clutter to offer an unimpeded view of the character, or several cameras need to be set up to avoid the player avatar moving out of view behind the scenery.

Where multiple cameras are used, there is also a risk that the player will be disoriented by sudden changes of viewpoint, especially when the controls' reference scheme is tied to the viewpoint.

Combined Systems

Some modern games have overcome the drawbacks of each system described above by using one or more perspectives at different points during the game; for example, using OTS for exploration and interaction and switching to first person when projectile accuracy is required. Others allow the player to manually choose which views they prefer.

However, it should be possible to design a hybrid camera system with all the strengths and few of the weakness of the ones described above, and to take the burden of view selection away from designers and players alike. We will now describe such a system in detail, first dealing with character-based games, then adapting it to vehicle-based games.

Character-Based Hybrid Camera System

Our goal for the new camera system is to combine the best qualities of first- and third-person action games, thus allowing the player to always view her character and its interaction with the environment, while permitting accurate focus of interest for activities such as targeting opponents. Most of the concepts described here have been used in games on the market, but as far as I know, no game has yet combined them in the following manner.

The Camera Halo

The *camera halo* moves a camera along the x-axis within a "halo" that orbits the player avatar as seen in Figure 3.3.1. The halo is flexible and possesses the following properties:

FIGURE 3.3.1 *The camera halo. The top-left panel indicates the camera's positions and orientations in the other images.*

- It can **increase and decrease in diameter** in response to the environment (open areas allowing a larger circle), the camera pitch, or manual adjustment.
- It can **change height** in response to the environment, and adjusts automatically in response to the camera's pitch or manual adjustment.
- Its **center-point can move relative to the avatar's** in response to the environment (for example, where it would intersect scenery), or via manual adjustment. However, the avatar should never be outside the halo itself.
- The camera **always points toward the player avatar** in the horizontal plane.
- **The player moves the camera left and right along the halo,** and changes its pitch or vertical angle with normal up/down controls.

A simple sphere (see Figure 3.3.2) can be used in place of a halo with variable height and a camera that pitches. However, this presents problems when the camera buries itself below ground level, and keeping the character in view when looking skyward is not easy.

FIGURE 3.3.2   *The camera sphere. The top-left panel indicates the camera's positions and orientations in the other images. Note the loss of visual information compared to Figure 3.3.1*

The Avatar

In our system, the player's avatar responds to the position of the camera. The exact response is determined by the avatar's mode–*normal* or *projectile*.

In normal circumstances (assuming a humanoid avatar), the avatar will rotate its head, torso, and waist to look at the camera's focal point. This rotation should be realistic–initially only the head should move, then the torso takes over as the head nears the limit of its rotation. As the torso reaches its own limit of motion, the waist begins to turn. Assuming the normal eye field of view is at least 90 degrees, this scheme should allow the avatar to view all 360 degrees of the scene without moving its feet. Of course, if the new focal point is maintained, the avatar will eventually turn its entire body to face it.

When the avatar holds a projectile device (such as a gun), the weapon will move to follow the player's focus of interest, and the avatar will turn its entire body as soon as the weapon reaches its maximum angle of rotation. Thus, the delay between the player's decision to point toward a target and issue an attack command and the avatar's actual gun fire will be minimized. Figure 3.3.3 summarizes avatar response to the player's manipulation of the camera.

FIGURE 3.3.3 *An example of the player's view and of the avatar's stance. The avatar's orientation follows the player's point of view.*

The Controls

Although visually it appears as though the player is controlling the movement of the avatar, *the player in fact controls the camera* that accompanies the avatar. The player moves the camera, and the avatar responds in a suitable manner to follow this movement. However, the camera is attached to the avatar, and is forbidden from moving too far from it. This actual control scheme can be similar to the standard first-person shooter interface.

Requirements

The flexibility that the hybrid character-based system provides needs to be matched with a more complex yet visually rewarding animation system. Because the player can now view the character from any angle, the designer can not overlook flaws in the avatar's mesh or in its animation.

In order to decrease design effort, animations will probably need to be modular–that is, cutting the player model into head, upper body, and lower body sections, animating each separately, and combining the resulting sequences to produce a wide range of animations. Animation blending between the modular sequences, so that the actions of the legs impact the animation of the torso and arms, can smooth things and improve the "natural" movement of the character.

Additional animation sequences will also be required due to the extended view angle. Where a normal third-person game would only need to detail combat moves to the front and perhaps both sides of the character, this 360-degree view now allows impressive maneuvers to be undertaken to the rear of the avatar, watched in full detail by the player who still has direct control.

Ideally, the avatar will have realistic animation sequences for any shift in position, rather than the simplistic "rotate on the spot" or "snap to this stance" conventions. Realistic animation reinforces the cinematic quality of the experience and maintains the player's suspension of disbelief.

Advantages of the Hybrid System

Our system combines the advantages of the three traditional camera systems:

- **Avatar empathy:** The player can see his character and watch its movement at all times, which reinforces the idea that players are taking on a role, rather than simply playing the game.
- **Projectile Accuracy:** The player retains the accuracy of first-person shooters, because the camera's and the avatar's focal points are co-located.
- **Cinematic Action:** The player can experience avatar animation and interaction from almost any angle, much as a free-floating camera might in a cut-scene, while still retaining direct control.

Vehicle-Based Hybrid Camera System

The rules for a character-based hybrid system can be applied to vehicle-based games, though less will be gained because most vehicle games are simulations that do not benefit from highly abstracted controls. An example of an abstract control would be a simple keystroke encoding a complex move such as jumping or moving forward, activities that in real life require complex thought and timing. On the other hand, the controls in a driving game directly map to the controls a player might use in a car, and these are simple enough to require little or no abstraction.

However, it is still possible to use abstracted controls to drive vehicles. It may be advantageous to do so in games in which the player alternates between controlling a character and controlling a vehicle driven or piloted by the character. And when simulating a vehicle whose actual controls are complicated enough to warrant abstraction, such as a fighter jet, space shooter, or submarine that can move freely in three dimensions, the hybrid camera system is just as useful as it is in character-based games.

The Controls

The controls for vehicle-based games can be similar to those used in the character-based system; the player does not directly control the orientation of her craft. Instead, she moves a camera around the craft, and it only reorients itself on manual command, if the player decides to move to a new location, or if it fires fixed weaponry at a target.

Spot the Difference

While the differences between this scheme and current third-person vehicle games might seem insignificant, the subtle change of control from direct to completely abstract presents the possibility of allowing the player to control very complex vehicles without requiring a deep understanding of physics, because the game takes care of acceleration and attitude automatically. The hybrid camera can be seen as an "always-on" context-sensitive autopilot function, a feature that is increasingly being implemented in contemporary real-life vehicles. Of course, simulation purists will be distressed by the additional layers of abstraction, but unless the purpose of the game is to simulate the control systems of a vehicle, rather than the vehicle's interaction with the game world, simplifying manipulation will appear beneficial to the majority of players.

Additional Tips

Regardless of the intelligence of the camera system, there will be times when the focal point will become obscured, either by the avatar itself, another game object, or an element of scenery. While the camera halo will adjust its diameter to take into account the features of the environment, it would be disorienting to the player to change the diameter (the distance from camera to avatar) too quickly or too often. Thanks to the capabilities of modern graphics hardware, a compromise can be reached.

When a game object obscures view, it should first become transparent so that the player can still see the avatar through the object. The camera should then slowly begin to draw closer to the avatar, eventually clearing the obstruction if the player does not manually move the camera to a better location.

If this method proves too demanding on the hardware, or produces messy results (such as in rendering complex nonconvex objects), an outline of the player avatar can be rendered showing the player its location behind the obscuring object. This method has been commonly used in isometric viewpoint games (such as *Baldur's Gate* or *Age of Empires*) when the characters or units move behind large buildings. Note that this technique will need to be applied to obscured opponents in addition to the player's avatar.

Alternatively, we could deform the halo in response to the environment. An oblong or egg-shaped camera path (as shown in Figure 3.3.4) would, in some situations, allow smoother camera panning for the player. Note this is not the same as having the camera "hug" a wall or object, which can be particularly disturbing as the camera will normally have to change its position very quickly. However, effective use of this technique will require clever and continuous monitoring of the environment.

FIGURE 3.3.4   *Environment-driven halo deformation.*

Conclusion

Although the first- and third-person character-based genres of computer games are well established, there is still room for innovation and improvement in the visual representation and control of the on-screen character and environment, making greater use of 3D technology and bringing the experience of the player closer to a cinematic quality in both look and feel. The hybrid camera system described in this article brings us a step closer to this goal.

3.4

Learning Artistic Articulation without Reinventing the Wheel

Adam Baratz

Adam_Baratz@msn.com

We are on the verge of a very important point in gaming history. Soon, we will witness an amazing transformation: this medium, once solely a hobby for computer science students, is getting ready to emerge as the new century's dominant means of artistic expression.

The twentieth century gave birth to the mass media of cinema and television. While these also began as hobbies for scientists and tinkerers, their ease of distribution (film being relatively easy to duplicate, and TV being ubiquitous) catapulted them to their current positions in our culture.

Throughout the history of Western culture, ease of distribution has played the largest role in forming viable commercial media. The oft-cited milestone of the invention of Gutenberg's printing press quickly democratized the written word. The intellectual monopoly once held by the Catholic Church was broken, and the ability to distribute written works moved to the common people. While it cannot be said that everyone was suddenly penning diatribes and memoirs for global distribution, it became possible for men of reasonable means to afford and to produce literature. Nothing *inherent* to the medium had changed, only the fact that a work could suddenly be duplicated and distributed *en masse*.

Compare the history of printing to that of visual art. Paintings are each unique. Although it is possible to create duplicates of paintings like the *Mona Lisa*, you will only see the original *Mona Lisa* if you visit the Louvre. With photography, however, you can easily make unlimited perfect reprints of a negative; this ease gives photography its mass popularity.

Despite the position photography holds in our culture, it does not touch the cultural dominance held by cinema and television. Cinema and television are narrative forms, and people usually enjoy narrative art much more than static forms such as paintings, photographs, and sculptures. The primary reason for entertainment is to provide an escape from real life, and narrative art provides an easier escape than does staticart. For most people, it is far easier to watch a movie for a couple of hours than to stare at a painting for as long.

However, both -narrative and static art rely on an analog medium. Digital content can be easily duplicated which gives it an advantage over traditional cinema and television. It is true that digital video discs (DVDs) are currently on the market , and HDTV is on the horizon, but every creative asset in a computer game is digital throughout a game's production. Filmmakers and television producers must take time-consuming intermediary steps to convert analog content to digital content. This, in the end, is the triumph of computer games: a narrative digital medium with an unlimited opportunity for distribution.

What We Should Listen To

While gaming has much in its favor from the start (nothing can take away the perfect copying of bits), it will have to fight to conquer the most precious asset of the masters of analog media: *articulation*.

Anyone who has watched a political debate will acknowledge that there is something to be said for a fine orator. When a speaker has a magical way with words, he can captivate the viewer and run circles around his opponents, regardless of ideology. This is especially apparent in a debate between candidates of severely unmatched ability.

The key advantage of analog media is that it translates directly into common, almost instinctive, ways for people to express themselves. Not everyone is a Rembrandt, but most people can draw basic forms with a pen. People see, so people paint pictures of what they see. They can paint a realistic representation, a romantic visage, an impressionistic interpretation, or an abstract expressionistic attack of color and form. As a painter, you can wield a paint brush and hopefully translate your vision into a painting. It is difficult to make a recorded vision worth people's time, but it is definitely easier than accomplishing the same thing on a computer. Should you decide to create a visual image completely from scratch on a computer, you would spend the bulk of the time constructing the means of representing the image in ones and zeros.

When creating a computer game, the majority of the development time is spent not on the final *content* that the user cares about, but on the *means* for delivering that content.

The Power of Licensing

To some extent, developers know that content delivery mechanisms are crucial. A number of companies exist that license third-party engines for their first-person shooter games. While there is little *artistic* worth in these games, you can easily see an increase in content quality in games that use licensed technology. When a mature solution already exists, companies are spending resources and talent on content rather than on creating their own 3D engines..

Likewise, consider the decision to hire a professional (and often external) writer to create a game's content. Designers are beginning to admit that, while they have mastered interactivity, they might not necessarily be good at writing narrative and at meeting the audience's expectations in that area. *Deus Ex,* which garnered critical and commercial acclaim, advertised its reliance on an outside writer, to great success.

Gaming versus Writing

Writing for games brings new challenges to traditional writers. A linear story allows writers to finesse their words to yield subtle qualities, but games do not. Around 10,000 lines of dialog were written for *Deus Ex,* yet a gamer who played the game only once would encounter only a fraction of them. Writers must understand this peculiarity of the game medium and adapt to it Only when writers have adapted to the differences between writing for games and linear writing will they be able to work successfully on a game project. By then, they may have become as skilled at game design as the designers themselves.

Currently, writing and game design are typically handled as separate entities. In the future, the two should probably be handled as one. This fact leads to the next main problem with outsourced writing: *integration.*

Designers often create the game's story by separating writing from gameplay during design. The game design and the writing are often created to exist in their separate spheres, but the result of such a practice is disjointed game design. Playing such a split-designed game will reveal that the design was clearly broken into two separate segments, one for each sphere. Most of the player's time in these games is spent on traditional genre-related gameplay activities. Then, when the player reaches certain plot points, the game switches into the writing sphere. The interface changes and the player engages in dialog whose primary goal is to direct the flow of the branches in the plot. Then, when a new direction has been decided, the player returns to the main sphere of the game. This process is repeated until the plot has ended and a conclusion is met.

This type of game design creates dissonance in the way the player treats the resulting experience. The player's goal is no longer to live through an instance of the story, but to maximize the possibilities the plot branches provide. Near the end of *Deus Ex,* there is a blatant junction where the plot splits into three possible branches for the player to follow. Reading between the lines, one finds the game saying: "At this point, there are three possible endings for you to try. The point now, is not to choose one, but to try to find all three of them."

Other games even make a point of advertising their number of endings, as if this were just another feature to go with photorealistic texture maps and a solid AI. At this point, the story becomes inconsequential. Trying to experience all the different game endings usually devolves into a game in itself.

Current games are too much like theme park rides: the player is given the illusion of existing in a pristine world, yet he is moved along like a cart on rails toward the goals. Sometimes, he has some say in where the rails lead, but he will get to the end of the ride sooner or later, whether he likes it or not. For computer games to be respected as not only a commercial form, but also as a full-fledged art form with the prestige of galleries and exhibitions, and respect from other artists, they must move into the real world, where these rails do not exist. Hopefully, we will all enjoy the highs and lows of this rail-free world, rich and replete with dynamic emotion and change.

The Power of Maneuverability

Game developers are ready to face this world explained above. Their most difficult problem, as mentioned before, is *articulation*. The bulk of game development time is *not* spent on content, as it should be; far too much time is spent on creating the means to *show* this content. But game developers are not the first to have trouble articulating their emotions. As pointed out in the epigraph, the means to show content are often the most hindering factor in a work's creation. Thus, game developers need to restructure their current managerial methods for developing games.

Current game development is structured linearly; the process moves from point A to point B. Because of the heavy financial involvement in developing games, it is unthinkable for the game plan to change completely at any point. Management has come to expect some delays at various points, but they do not expect and will reject any attempts at a complete change in direction.

Another prime benefit of the analog arts is ease in direction change. You are reading an example of this right now. Before this article was even submitted to the editor, it was rewritten several times to try new angles and new ways to articulate ideas and emotions. I had no attachment to the pieces of paper, the same 26 letters are always going to be there, so why not try something new? The work will always be better for it.

Having a change in plan like this in a computer game, on the other hand, would be unthinkable for two reasons. The first and less consequential is the structure of the process: the process of making a game is structured for making a product, one heavily documented in its engineering, and subject to little change. Second, and perhaps foremost, the point of a product is to make money. Even if the end result is terrible, less money would be lost by not restructuring the manufacturing than by improving the game, because the software company cannot predict how positively those changes would affect sales.

The solution to the problem of locked-in development is to build the desired flexibility into the design from the start, rather than force a complete restructuring along the way. In the analog arts, artists have standard tools: brushes, cameras, chisels, etc. The advantage to having a standardized set of tools is that the artist can focus completely on the content; they do not have to worry about building their tools from scratch because the standard set has evolved to the best it can be.

Programmers engineer a new set of tools every time they make a game. As stated earlier, those who license the technology have a huge advantage over those who do not. They get to work with a standard set of tools that have matured significantly.

This enables them to spend most of the development time working on the content, which is what their audience cares about. Even if a designer's goals for a project are not artistic, he can benefit from licensing tools by gaining time to fine-tune gameplay.

What We Must Learn Ourselves

Narrative media, such as film, literature, and theater, have many important lessons to teach game designers.

Computer games have been in existence only for a few decades, and not much effort has yet been spent on artistic development. Game designers' predecessors have been working in their own media for much longer, establishing conventions to facilitate the process of creation. Because there is no point in reinventing the wheel, artists working within these media share many techniques and tools. For example, film, theater, and television (for the most part) use scripts. The format of these scripts is essentially the same across the three media, though there are subtle differences in each, because each media must describe actions that will be recorded using different means. Film scripts often describe camera movement and blocking. In theater, blocking is usually left to the discretion of the director, with the script only indicating important directions. Each piece of documentation evolved to meet the needs of the medium.

Design documents are the scripts for computer games. They borrow from other media: cut-scene scripts are often modeled after film scripts, character bibles are often structured like collections of biographies and short stories, - and so on. All the different parts of a design document have evolved to meet the production goals of games.

Knowing When to Draw the Line

Sometimes the lines between games and other media become too blurred. For computer games to advance to a level of higher cultural distinction, they must become significantly different from other types of narrative.

The history of photography provides an example of differentiating media. When photography began to be recognized as an art form, pictorialism was the predominant photographic school; the goal of the pictorialists was to make photographs look like paintings. Hazy pictures were taken with human subjects often placed in classical poses. These early photographs were an effort not to create an original style, but to emulate one that already existed.

A significant change occurred when photographers realized that photography could be easily used as a documentary tool. Early war photographs were taken during the Crimean War; however, the technology was so crude that the pictures could only be taken of scenes of previous battles. These photographs show pock-marked fields strewn with cannon balls. By the time of the American Civil War, when photographic technology improved, photographer were able to take photos - during battle.

As photography became more realistic, though, it infringed more and more on the artistic niche that painting had held in monopoly on for past centuries. Since photography was cheaper, faster, and more accurate than painting for documenting events, photography quickly replaced paint and canvas as the popular means of recording political and social history. As a result, painting branched out into forms of expression that photography could not duplicate: cubism, surrealism, and abstract expressionism. All these different artistic schools used their medium in a unique way. Yes, there were abstract expressionist photographers, but there certainly no photographer was quite like Jackson Pollock.

Adaptable, and Thus Surviving, Media

Because painting was able to adapt to a new niche, it was able to survive as a notable form of artistic expression. At the same time, photography was able to further develop into an even more unique medium. Both sides won, and the art world in general was able to advance because of it.

A similar battle is beginning now. This time, film and computer games are fighting to determine which will become the better narrative medium. Film currently is one of the most popular forms of narrative. Computer games are trying to achieve a similar distinction. Just as in the case of painting and photography, only one will dominate. However, in this case, the challenger is not better than the current champion.

On the visual end, many of the features that cost film nothing cost gaming dearly. If a designer wants shadows, reflections, environmental mapping, bump mapping, high-resolution textures, and other special effects, he must write intricate code for his engine. Meanwhile, the filmmaker will take out her camera, snap a shot, and have a lab process the film for her. Does the designer want an accurate physics model? More difficult programming. Mother Nature is doing a rather adequate job for filmmakers as it is. Does he want realistic character models? The list goes on and on.

For computer games to survive and prosper, they should take advantage of things their medium can do that cannot be accomplished elsewhere. If a game designer wants to create a "cinematic gaming experience," he should quit his job immediately and learn how to work a motion picture camera. Other media cannot put the audience in the first person, as gaming can, nor can they change as the experience moves along. Game designers need to learn to use the unique aspects of computers to their advantage, rather than trying to force computer games to emulate other media.

Conclusion

The key point to recognize is that for gaming to succeed as a notable form of artistic expression, it must prove itself to be dynamic and adaptable. It must take advantage of the groundwork that other artists have already laid with their combined work, but it also must step beyond that. If games stagnate and become repetitive in style and content, no progress will be made. Designers must realize what strengths games have, and what other media are better at.

The process of artistic creation is an illuminating one, for audience and artist alike. Taking risks to test one's expectations and perceptions is key. Computer games can become more than they are today, but only if designers are willing to try. The designer must become as flexible as the medium itself can be, testing the limits of both himself and the tools he works with.

3.5

The Game Save

Wayne Imlach

wimlach@hotmail.com

This article discusses the impact of the game save method on game design and balance, and offers solutions to overcome the limitations inherent in common game save techniques. In addition, several designs and implementations of the save interface are discussed.

Let us begin by exploring the generic save systems in use in contemporary games, along with a discussion of their respective pros and cons.

Save Triggers

In a trigger-based system, the player must reach specific locations or complete certain tasks in order to save the game. Usually, triggers are located at the end of a level, after a boss encounter, or at the end of a tricky section of gameplay. Saving at a trigger may be carried out automatically or at the discretion of the player.

Advantages of Save Triggers

Using save triggers, the difficulty level of a section of the game can be balanced more accurately, because the designer can assume that the player will have to complete an entire section without using saves to speed up their progress. The player feels increased pressure, as a mistake will send him back to the beginning of the section or to his last save location. Consequently, player satisfaction and sense of achievement at the completion of a section will be enhanced.

Disadvantages of Save Triggers

Because each section must be played in its entirety before the player is allowed to save the game, the length of time between save triggers must be carefully selected so as to avoid frustration and excessive repetition. Save triggers can have a critical impact on game and level design. Remember that players may save because they are unavoidably interrupted which means they will have to repeat the interrupted section from the beginning.

If player stats are carried from one section to the next with little or no modification, ensuring that sections are self-contained or can be replayed is a must. Otherwise, players completing a section may find themselves in such a poor state that the subsequent sections become impossible. Ideally, the location of a save trigger should be surrounded by rewards and/or double as a refresh or recovery point.

Usage

Save triggers are often used in console games. Memory card space is often at a premium, and recording the state of the game only at one of, say, 250 important junctures allows player location to be encoded with a single byte.

Saving time is also a consideration. The smaller the save file, the shorter the "down time" for the player while he waits for data to be written to the memory card. Because saving to a memory card is often a slow process with multiple user prompts, any speed gain is important.

Save Anywhere

In a "save anywhere" system, the player instantly saves her current status, regardless of location or activity.

Advantages of Save Anywhere

Using save anywhere, the player can leave and resume the game at any time. Players can easily choose to replay specific sections of the game at will.

Disadvantages of Save Anywhere

Cunning players can maximize their progress through the game, replaying each encounter until they succeed with minimal loss or maximal gain. Designers tend to respond with levels designed with this strategy in mind, ramping up the difficulty level accordingly and making the save game a vital part of completing a level rather than a convenience.

Further, players can sometimes save the game before running into an untenable situation. Tension and suspense from encounters is often lost, as players will wander into new areas specifically to scout enemies, then reload the game and play the scene again with unfair prior knowledge of what to expect.

Usage

The ability to save anywhere is common in personal computer games. The save process is often (though not always) quick, and the large storage capacity of modern hard drives allows most players to retain an extended number of past saves.

Coded Text Saves

In a coded text save system, the state of the game is recorded in a cryptic text string and shown to the player so that he can note it manually and enter it on a special interface screen at a later time.

Advantages of Coded Text Saves

With a coded text save, no storage medium other than player memory or pen and paper is required to save the player's progress. Short codes also allow for easy transfer of game progress from one machine or player to another.

Disadvantages of Coded Text Saves

Only a limited amount of information can be stored in a string of manageable length. Therefore, the save can often only be made at definitive transition points in the game, such as the completion of a level.

Usage

Coded text saves were most commonly used on older game consoles, where storage devices were unavailable or unreliable. On modern consoles and handheld systems, they can provide an alternative to memory card storage for simple games.

Restrictive Solutions

A number of restrictions can be imposed upon save systems to avoid the negative impact they might have on game pacing and difficulty.

Where

The player can be restricted to saving only in selected areas, such as safety zones or save points. Safety zones would normally be used if the player has free reign to explore an extended environment in nonlinear fashion, while save points or triggers are normally placed after the completion of a difficult area or task in linear, enclosed scenarios.

When

Another option is to limit the number of saves a player can make during any one level. Make sure, however, to allow enough to cover both the need to save game progress and potential interruptions. Possible schemes include:

- **A fixed number of saves,** so the player knows they have only *n* number of saves per level.
- **A variable number of saves,** where the player earns the right to save by completing a task or collecting a token.
- **Time-stamp saves,** where the game allows a save only if a certain amount of time has passed since the last one.

What

Saves can also be restricted to situations where certain game conditions are met. A common condition is that no enemies can be in the vicinity or be aware of the player's presence.

Game Mechanic Solutions

So, how do we give players the convenience of save anywhere without compromising game difficulty or pace?

Randomization

When the player initiates a save, any level elements that have yet to be encountered by the player are randomized. Opponents yet to be encountered are randomly selected from a list of possible types. The guardian behind a door might be one of three types–set only once that door is opened. The troops that guard the gold mine in a strategy game can be selected randomly when first spotted by the player.

Opponent start locations can also be randomized within unexplored areas. In a strategy game, perhaps the units within an area are placed only when the player comes close to the area–and if a save or load is made, the positions of as-yet-unseen units is shifted again.

It is also possible to randomize architecture in uncharted territories. Any area that a player has yet to explore has a number of possible designs, one of which is chosen upon entry. The changes do not need to be dramatic–relocation of furniture, pillars, trees and rocks, and other objects can be made without compromising the overall design of the area or requiring extensive remodelling.

In addition to reducing the negative aspects of any-time saves, the above systems also add to a game's general replay value because each time it is played elements are slightly different.

Forewarning

Use *forewarning* to allow the AI opponents the same luxury the player has when a past save is loaded. If you are not using a randomizing system, the player who has saved, explored, and reloaded now has foreknowledge of his opponents' positions and general tactics. To balance this unfair advantage, allow the AI to know as much as was revealed to the character up to the point the game was reloaded. The AI may then change its tactics or objectives, rendering the player's foreknowledge less of an advantage.

While forewarning has obvious applications in strategy titles, it can also apply to the opponents in a first- or third-person style game–adjusting behavior based on the weapons or tactics the opponent employed just before the most recent game reload.

A Note on Game Balance

It might be prudent to count the number of times a player has had to reload and retry a section of the game. If this count goes beyond a set limit, then the player may genuinely be having problems with the current difficulty setting. In this case, the difficulty of the section should be slowly ramped down (while still retaining any randomization and foreknowledge rules) to avoid excessive frustration from the player–after all, the game is there to not only challenge the player, but to entertain him as well.

The Autosave

Consideration must be made as to the effect the autosave process has on the game. Does the save require extensive processing power? How long does the save process take? Does the game pause while saving occurs?

Unless the save is very quick, intrusive autosaves should be avoided during the normal course of a game. Ideally, the save should take place while some other transitional process is in progress, such as loading data for a new level, or during a noninteractive cut-scene.

If the autosave is transparent to the player, it can be as frequent as desired. Possible rules determining when to save may include the following:

- **Time Based:** Saving every few minutes ensures that the player will not lose much gameplay time if something goes wrong. Time-based saves are also useful for debugging purposes during game development.
- **Location Based:** The game is automatically saved each time the player moves from one room to the next.
- **Task Based:** The game is saved after a major task or story/game element has been completed.

The number of autosaves recorded should also be considered. If possible, a history should be kept of recent autosaves (the exact number depends on storage space and save frequency), thus allowing the player to choose which save to restore. Players may discover they have made a poor game choice, and the most recent autosave may not be far enough in the past to rectify the mistake.

Multiplayer Saves

Two distinct types of multiplayer save exist:

- **Centralized Save:** A single save held on one machine that holds the data for all players, and is broadcast on load.
- **Distributed Save:** Individual saves on each participating machine that must be synchronously loaded to restart a game.

The choice of which type of save to use will be determined by bandwidth limitations and the size of individual saves. A centralized save is for high bandwidth or small file size, while a distributed save requires less bandwidth and can accommodate a larger save game file size.

The centralized save has an additional advantage in that the players restarting the multiplayer game do not necessarily need to be the original players–anyone can take the place of a player because the save information is stored by the host and transmitted to the clients.

Another issue, common to both systems, is that of *interface*. Ensure that the player is made aware which saves are multiplayer, and of the identities of the players who were involved in the game at the time. In today's global online community, it is possible to play a number of multiplayer games with a variety of opponents, and it can be very easy to forget who participated in which game. Manual allocation of nonoriginal players must also be considered if supported.

Save Interface

There is nothing more frustrating than being faced with a number of possible saves to restore and insufficient information on which to base a choice. Make sure that your game save interface contains functions that:

- Allow the player to input a reasonably lengthy title for the save.
- Allow the player to input a separate text description of the save.
- Include a time stamp with the save.
- Include a screenshot with the save.
- Sort the saves chronologically.
- Include game status/info with the save.

In addition, a few common sense conventions are often overlooked. If quicksave and quickload options are available, *do not* place the default keys for these actions adjacent to one another–ensure they are on opposite ends of the controller or keyboard, especially if no confirmation prompt is displayed when the command is triggered. The player should also be allowed to delete redundant saves from within the interface, while they are either loading or saving. Save game management is important particularly with an extended storage medium where many saves can be recorded.

Additional Save Considerations

Minimizing Saves

To cut down on the amount of data to save, consider rounding values that are not visible to the player–health scores of enemies are a good example.

Using just three bits, we can record a health score to the nearest 1/27th of its original value. Thus, an enemy with 3,476 of its original 10,000 health points remaining is stored as 9/27th; therefore, after reloading it will have 3,333 health points, which is a close enough approximation to go unnoticed by the player and have no discernable impact on game balance. This method is particularly useful in games where large numbers of units, each with a variety of numerical characteristics, need to be stored.

Note that keeping game saves as small as possible has other benefits, including time taken to write or read the data from the storage device. This is most noticeable with consoles that may use slow-access memory cards.

Portability

Ensure that saves are stored in a clearly labelled folder, and tagged by player profile. With today's burgeoning number of possible PC configurations, the frequent need to upgrade, and ever-present threats of virus infection, players may have to reinstall their game a number of times during its lifespan. Keeping the saves in an easily accessed form ensures they can make backup copies and continue playing their game with no loss of progress after a fresh install.

Multiple Saves

Given enough storage space, the player should always be allowed to store multiple saves. Multiple saves provide a useful history of the game, and allow players to return to earlier game sections and replay them with alternate strategies, replay sections they particularly enjoyed, or see how making alternate choices would have changed the flow of the game.

Cross-Platform Saves

Another aspect to consider when developing a save system is that of cross-platform compatibility. If the game structure is maintained and duplicated across different platforms, then it can be advantageous to retain a common file format. With many of today's new systems really differing only in graphic power, and the wider availability of online access, a cross-platform multiplayer game is becoming an increasingly realistic model. If you wish to allow players with different machines to compete against one another, it is a simple step to allow exchange of save information across those platforms.

Consumer Expectations

You should consider the expectations of the consumer when deciding what type of save system to develop for your game. Players of personal computer titles have come to expect the ability to save at any point with a simple keystroke, regardless of the effect such a save will have on game balance. If you do not provide such a system, or at least offer a compromise solution, this will be reflected in negative reviews and customer comments.

Games that have been developed on a console platform and then ported to the PC often suffer, in the eyes of players and reviewers, from the lack of this free save feature, which illustrates the importance of the save mechanism in the overall design of the game.

Saving Time

The length of time that a game uses to perform a save will be a determining factor in the frequency of game saves, which in turn may influence perceived game difficulty.

Keep this in mind when balancing your game. Sudden death scenarios where saving takes more than a few seconds should be avoided–if a player finds that frequent saves are necessary to complete the game and they spend half their playing time watching a save/load progress bar, they will soon give up and go play elsewhere.

Player Profiles

Players should be allowed to create or load a profile at the beginning of each game session. The profile is then used to distinguish different players using the same machine. As well as normal game save data being stored separately for each player, other settings can be stored in the profile–for example, common audio and video settings, control configurations, and player game progress.

Ensure the player can return to the profile selection screen mid-game to avoid unnecessarily quitting or resetting of the game whenever a new person wishes to play.

Finally, if possible, this profile data should be made portable in the fashion discussed earlier for game saves themselves.

Spectator and Record Saves

Another type of game save that you may want to consider is a *record function* that stores the last *n* seconds of gameplay. This technique is commonly seen in racing titles as an instant replay facility.

Ironically, the record feature is often missing from the very games that would benefit the most from its implementation. Strategy games are a prime example: allowing a player to watch a recorded battle and review each side's actions is a valuable learning tool in mastering the game. This is true even for something as direct as a first-person shooter: watching individual players to understand their tactics and playing style can often be very educational, particularly to new players lacking experience.

Conclusion

The method and interface for saving games should not be left to the later stages of a project since, as we have shown, they can have a profound effect on the overall design and balance of the game. Ensure that method and interface for game saves is considered early in development, and that the design works around its limitations while taking advantage of its strengths, even if the save system itself is not to be implemented until much later. A little thought early can save a lot of trouble later.

GENRES AND PLATFORMS

4.0

Introduction

The variety of the games released in the past 20 or so years is nothing short of staggering. From the arcade shooters of yesteryear to the world-building strategy games of today, and from the dating and dancing simulations that sweep the Japanese market to the epic massively multiplayer role-playing games being hailed as the future of the gaming industry, we have achieved a great deal in a short time. And now that it is (or is becoming) economically viable to develop games not only on consoles and personal computers, but also on personal digital assistants, cell phones, interactive television set-top boxes, private networks hosted on airplanes, and soon on even more alien platforms, the possibilities will only increase.

Established Game Genres: Pros and Cons

In a growing market, the existence of well-established genres, such as real-time strategy games and first-person shooters, can be seen as both a blessing and a curse by developers, because they carry with them a number of content- and business-related expectations that must be tackled by designers and producers alike.

The advantages of working within the boundaries of a specific genre include:

- **Faster, easier, more robust design:** The creators of games in a given genre have likely already encountered and defeated many of the difficult design challenges involved; studying their work will guide the development process away from potentially costly errors.
- **Conventions:** Real-time strategy (RTS) games and first-person shooters (FPS) have evolved standardized interface schemes. For the designer of a new FPS or RTS, this means that a significant share of the game's feature set is predetermined; for players, it means a shorter learning curve.
- **Ready-made audience:** We know who the players of fighting games are, what they like, and how to present the game to them. For publishers, genre games are easier to advertise and to sell to retailers, who see the established target demographics as a risk-lessening factor.

However, working with common genres also has its drawbacks:

- **Restrictions on creativity:** Once a large "standard feature set" has come to be expected by players and reviewers, departing radically from it can be seen as dangerous from a marketing standpoint.

- **Increased competition:** Sequels, clones, and rip-offs are a fact of life in the inter-active entertainment industry, but successful genres tend to beget extremely crowded marketplaces.
- **Budget bloating:** High levels of competition and standardized gameplay make it difficult to differentiate a game and to increase its odds of commercial success. Historically, the most common solutions to this problem were to make a bigger and fancier game, and to spend more on marketing. Too often, the results of this "financial arms race" have been disastrous for all involved.

Taxonomy of Game Genres

That said, let us look at the common game genres, their audiences, and key design challenges.

Any taxonomy of games is bound to be incomplete, controversial, and at least partially ambiguous, because many games will straddle the fence between two (or more) categories while others will fit within none. The scheme described in this arti-cle may surprise the reader on occasion, because it departs slightly from the norm and regroups apparently disparate games into the same categories. This is done because, from a design perspective, these games present similar challenges despite their evident differences in subject matter.

Within the limited space of this article, we will attempt to paint as complete a picture of the current state of the industry as possible, while taking a quick look at the emerging categories that are expected to achieve prominence in the next few years.

Action Games

By far the largest category, both in terms of product variety and market share, *action games* include such industry staples as:

- Most of the arcade classics (*Space Invaders, Pac-Man*)
- Fighting games (e.g., the *Tekken* series)
- Arcade-style vehicle racing games (e.g., the original *Pole Position*)
- First-person shooters (e.g., *Quake III: Arena*)
- All sports games except those focusing on team management.

All of the members of this hodge-podge category share a handful of defining characteristics: immediate responsiveness, sensory immersion, fast pacing, and a reliance on hand-eye coordination.

Responsiveness

In any action game, all player actions have immediate and obvious consequences. If the player opens fire on an enemy in a shooter, or performs a trick in a snowboarding title, the game must accept the commands, act on them without delay, and present the player with results: a wounded opponent, a high score, a monetary prize, etc. In contrast, decisions made in strategy games often yield no visible results until a substantial amount of time has passed.

Players of action games receive their rewards through the immediate feedback provided by the game. Learning that a certain enemy is particularly vulnerable to spinning heel kicks gives the player an advantage that can be applied right away. Furthermore, since the game usually proceeds at high speed, the player has no time to analyze the results of his actions in abstract fashion: the results must be so obvious that learning does not detract from the need to continue performing. Thus, feedback should be presented audio-visually and in such a way that it is unmistakable; examples include the infamous (but highly effective from a gameplay standpoint) enemy explosions in shooters, and the flashing health bars appearing at the top of the fighting game's screen.

Pacing

Action titles attempt to fool the player's brain into believing that the hockey game, race, or space dogfight in the computer game is actually occurring. One of the tools employed in creating this suspension of disbelief is speed: quite simply, a good action game leaves the player with no time to rationalize the fact that he is only playing a game. The player has just too much to contend at such rapid speeds to have time to worry about metaphysics!

However, while "just enough" action suspends disbelief, "too much" action overwhelms the player. Finding the appropriate balance is one of the action game designer's most difficult tasks; see [Hitchens02] for ways to deal with this issue.

Sensory Immersion

The other half of the action game equation for suspension of disbelief consists of creating an environment that the brain will readily accept as "real" through proper sensory stimulation. Therefore, action games tend to be at the forefront of innovation in graphics, positional audio, and tactile (force-feedback) technology. An action game is first and foremost a sensory experience, and anything that enhances that experience constitutes a powerful competitive advantage.

This does not mean that it is impossible to develop a good action game without advanced technology; indeed, *Space Invaders* was one of the biggest hits of all time, and it originally came out with blocky, 2D monochrome characters flying in a vacuum. However, advanced technology usually enhances the player's experience in action games more than it does in other genres.

Hand-Eye Coordination

Finally, just as the action game must provide visual feedback to let players evaluate the consequences of their actions, it must also create visual stimuli to trigger them. Action games rely on instantaneous reactions on the part of the users; help your players by designing visual cues that correspond to the human eye's behavior. For example, high-resolution sight is limited to a very small area centered on the eyes' focus, while peripheral vision is more effective at noticing movement than color or detail.

Management Games

At the other end of the spectrum from action games are the *management games* that rely on planning and strategy and remove hand-eye coordination from the equation altogether. They include:

- Turn-based strategy games, such as the *Civilization* and *Master of Orion* series
- So-called "god games" such as *Populous* and *SimCity*
- Virtual lab experiments, such as *SimEarth*, Maxis' evolution simulator based on Lovelock's Gaia hypothesis
- Sports franchise management games, such as the ubiquitous European soccer sims, in which the players focus on building championship dynasties instead of hitting home runs or scoring goals

Important design issues in management games include controlling scope, dealing with time constraints, and modeling complexity in software.

Scope

Management games tend to cover a broad variety of topics at the same time: for example, *Master of Orion* requires players to deal with scientific research, diplomacy, population pressures, military campaigns, economies, and planetary ecosystems, among other things.

To keep from overwhelming players and slowing the game to a crawl, implement high-level views of each necessary task: there is no need to choose the menu for the army's lunch (or even to decide whether or not to feed the troops), and hiring each member of the nuclear reactor's maintenance crew individually will be a waste of the players' time in all but the most extreme of circumstances. Also implement the decision-making process in the simplest possible way, ideally with a single click: there are many decisions to be made repetitively, so any time saved will accumulate surprisingly quickly.

Time Constraints

In a management game, *speed* is usually not an issue: players can take as long as they need to examine the state of the game, elaborate plans, give orders, and study the results of their decisions. However, *time management* can still become a significant problem, especially in multiplayer mode, because turn-based games tend to take a very long time to play.

Thus, most management games are single-player by nature. If multiplayer functionality is required, the game should include self-contained scenarios that can be played in two hours or less, while the grand campaigns are left to the solitary players.

Players and Complexity

A game like *SimEarth* requires incredibly complex simulation software "under the hood" to implement the underlying phenomena accurately. However, *being* accurate is not enough: the process must also *appear* accurate to the players, both in terms of correction and of responsiveness to their actions. Therefore, designers must ensure that players have sufficient information at their disposal to learn the consequences of their decisions; otherwise, from the players' perspective, the game might as well be acting randomly.

Fast Strategy Games

Games of "fast strategy" occupy the middle of the road between the action and management genres: they require planning on the part of the players, but usually on a fairly narrow set of decisions, and time constraints force players to choose between goals not only because of a lack of resources and units, but because of their finite ability to supervise execution of many orders in parallel. Real-time strategy games, such as *Age of Empires*, fall within this category; so do time-oriented coarse simulations of real-life experiences, such as *Airport Tycoon*, and many contemporary wargames.

For the designer, a fast strategy game presents the danger of information overload and exacerbates the risk associated with delayed responses.

Information Overload

For the player, the key to a fast strategy game is to be able to juggle many objectives: securing precious resources, raiding enemy camps, protecting weak units, upgrading industrial infrastructure, researching new technologies, etc. Time being of the essence, the game must be designed with two key objectives in mind:

- **A simplified world:** In real-life, there is much more to building a nation than collecting food, stone, gold, and wood. However, in *Age of Empires*, these four resources suffice to build every unit and contraption imaginable, because having to secure sources of even more types of materials at the same time would detract from the rest of the gameplay and frustrate users.
- **Coarse-grained management:** Players cannot afford to micromanage every unit all the time; armies must be able to take initiative, woodcutters need to look for new trees to fell once they have finished turning one into lumber, factories must be able to continue production orders instead of asking for new instructions each time they complete one assignment, etc.

The player has enough to do handling critical strategy decisions; game entities need enough autonomy to handle mundane tasks.

Delayed Responses

In a fast strategy game, it is easy for a player to lose track of what a given unit may be doing. A woodcutter who starts looking for trees to the north when the forest is located to the south may wander to the edges of the map and never do anything useful, effectively depriving the player of two types of resources—wood and woodcutters.

Similarly, in any real-time game, coordinating the actions of several units can be difficult. While *Civilization 3* tells players the number of turns required for a unit to reach a destination, which allows them to plan for the concurrent arrival of infantry, cavalry, and artillery at the point of attack, an RTS army may be delayed by narrow mountain passes, wandering animals, etc. If the result is that the catapults coming in from the east arrive 20 seconds before the southern archers expected to protect them, the well-crafted mission can turn into a disaster. As a designer, make sure to give players the tools to plan effectively—and to quickly alter a plan if outside interference makes it obsolete.

Story-Driven Games

When a game is centered on a character or on a strong plot, instead of abstract tactical decisions or hand-eye coordination, it can be considered to be *story driven*. Examples of story-driven games include:

- Adventures and interactive fiction (the classic *King's Quest* series)
- Role-playing games (the *Diablo* and *Final Fantasy* series)
- Online serials (*Kiss: Immortals* and *Steppenwolf: The X-Creatures Project*, the latter of which I have made a modest contribution to)

For the purposes of this discussion, the essential difference between an adventure game and an RPG is that the former focuses on solving the quest/mission/mystery, while the latter is centered on the process of transforming a normal person, the main character, into an invincible hero. Thus, the distinction is blurry at best.

Much more will be said about story-driven games in Part 5 of this book; for now, let us state the two most challenging design issues involved in creating them: the linearity/nonlinearity conundrum and the character, which is ultimately out of the designer's control.

Linearity

Human perception is linear in nature. No matter how much freedom of action is built into a game, the player will experience it one scene at a time, just like a movie. However, if the game *feels* linear and constrained, the player will become frustrated—but if it seems too loose and unstructured, confusion may set in. Reaching the optimal balance requires concentrated effort.

Characters

As Henry James said, every story is fundamentally about character. However, while classic storytellers enjoy unlimited freedom when it comes to deciding how their characters think, evolve, and reveal themselves, game designers have to live with the fact that their main characters are entirely within the players' control. A game's hero can-not have a sudden change of heart and decide to join the forces of evil against the wishes of the player—conversely, the ideal game would let the players decide which side they want to cast their lots with instead of forcing them along a chosen path.

Simulators

Whereas most games strive to extract the essence of an experience and discard the rest, *simulators* mimic the entire experience in exacting detail. Typical examples include:

- Microsoft's *Flight Simulator*
- Physically correct car racing games
- Military vehicle games, some of which are so accurate that the armed forces use them to train their personnel

Designing simulators presents unique challenges with regard to control schemes and excessive specialization.

Controls

As a designer, it is reasonable to assume that flight simulator enthusiasts will want to play with a flight stick resembling the instruments in real planes, or that car racing buffs will acquire steering wheels and pedals to immerse themselves in the experience.

But what if the game you are designing simulates heavy industrial equipment, like forklifts or forest harvesters? Or robotic remote presence machinery, which may be controlled by dual joysticks (one for each arm)? In such cases, expecting the player to own a facsimile of the actual controls is unreasonable. Thus, the designer must find a way to map the real-life interface to keyboard, mouse, or joypad commands—but because the game is a simulator, any discrepancy between the real machine and the game risks ruining the experience.

Overspecialization

Most real-life activities consist of short bursts of excitement sprinkled into long peri-ods of boredom. For most people, piloting the Space Shuttle would be an enormous thrill—but the hours-long prelaunch checklist, days of nauseating weightlessness, and sleep deprivation are just as much a part of the actual experience as the high-speed landing. In a true simulator, the boring parts likely have to stay in; while this may appeal to the true hardcore fans, it will drive away most of the potential audience.

Therefore, the simulator's designer must find the proper balance between emula-tion of reality (to make the simulation accurate) and usability (i.e., the entertainment factor). Solving this problem is quite difficult; indeed, it can be argued that most experiences are not suited to accurate simulation at all, at least not as commercially viable entertainment.

Abstract Games

When players manipulate symbols, or when a game represents a real-life situation in minimalist fashion, without concern for the realism of the simulation, we have an *abstract game*. This type of entertainment has been around for centuries: most table-top board games, for example, fall within this category. Interactive abstract games include:

*   Adaptations of classic games such as chess and checkers
*   Puzzle games, such as *Tetris* or *Minesweeper*
*   Social games; e.g., multiplayer online versions of *Monopoly* and Bridge
*   Interactive gambling
*   Solitaire
*   The slower-paced arcade classics

Abstract game design challenges are related to their atypical audiences, because they are often targeted to so-called "casual gamers" instead of the industry's core market of male teenagers and young adults. These challenges include a requirement for simplicity and a relative lack of technological innovation.

Simplicity

To attract casual players, a game must be easy to learn (ideally in 10 minutes or less), easy to play in short sessions, and not too hectic in rhythm. This is especially true for Web-based games that cost nothing to play: users who have spent money on a boxed game will invest the time necessary to learn how to enjoy it, but on the Web, leaving the Web page has no consequences.

Technological Neutrality

Abstract games typically cannot be sold at premium prices in retail outlets. The only way to earn a profit on them is through volume: selling many copies, logging large numbers of ad-fueled online connection time, etc. Thus, abstract games must run on the largest possible number of devices—and that means foregoing all of the latest technology, or even any requirement for the user to set up anything by hand. And because "the largest possible number of devices" means, among other things, computers and PDAs equipped with low-bandwidth modems, abstract online game designers must become masters of content reuse: any texture that can be used in two levels, or any game entity that can take on two roles, reduces the game's download signature by an appreciable amount.

Platform Games

Run-and-jump platformers could be considered a subcategory of action games, but their specificities (and their enduring popularity) justify keeping them separate. They include:

- Classic side-scrollers, such as the original *Donkey Kong* and *Super Mario Bros.* titles, which account for a significant share of the games available on Game Boy Advance.
- 3D exploration games, such as the *Crash Bandicoot* and *Spyro* series.

All platform games consist of making a star character perform tricks and find prizes that are hidden within levels. Conceptually, this is trivial: often, the "prize" is simply the other end of the track.

Platformers distinguish themselves from other action titles by their reliance on strong characters, environment exploration, and dexterity puzzles.

Characters

Officially or unofficially, platform game characters have become the mascots of several publishers and consoles: Mario for Nintendo, Sonic for Sega, Crash Bandicoot for the PlayStation, Rayman for UbiSoft, etc. To succeed in the well-established platformer market, a game needs a strong character with an interesting set of basic athletic moves and special powers.

However, unlike role-playing games, which often bestow new abilities on characters on a permanent basis, platformers usually implement special moves and talents as short-term power-ups lasting between 5 and 60 seconds. Thus, it is much easier to predict which moves the player will be likely to perform in a given setting, because he will have to find the necessary power-ups on site. This is also true for players: if they see a "flight" power-up, they will immediately start looking for nearby puzzles that require its use. To keep challenging players, designers must look for ways to make flight difficult (i.e., place many airborne obstacles in the level) or create puzzles that require combining flight with another talent in unusual ways: for example, flight and speed power-ups used at the same time in an enclosed environment can create a wind tunnel, which sucks in the poisonous butterflies barring the player's way to the treasure room.

Exploration

Platformers tap into natural human curiosity: find a way to reach Room X because a prize waits there for you. This curiosity should be fostered by a number of gameplay devices:

- Lure players to out-of-the-way areas (i.e., a high ledge) by displaying the rewards (i.e., a bonus life) openly, so that they can be seen from the heart of the level.
- Clearly indicate the areas that have already been explored and those that remain unseen, for example with a small on-screen map, to make sure that the player will not miss any of the content (except maybe a handful of secret rooms).
- Give the players exact goals to reach within the level (i.e., grab 400 of a specific kind of token) and display progress openly.

Puzzles

Finally, many contemporary platformers have adopted the "game within a game" concept: earn an orb by beating a monster at a simplified game of one-on-one hockey, fly a World War I fighter plane, ride a jet ski across a level, etc. Providing a variety of (easy-to-learn) tasks for the players to perform, each of which comes with its own set of controls and power-ups, keeps the game fresh for a long time—but at a significant cost in development effort.

Edutainment

Edutainment is a generic term for all forms of children's interactive software that combine playful activities with learning, whether the content is related to school curricula or not. Edutainment titles can teach motor skills or elementary art, reading, arithmetic, and language, and many other things—sometimes all within the same product.

Designing edutainment is tricky because it is very hard for adults to guess what children will like. Play testing and focus groups are particularly important in this category. Other challenges include setting an appropriate difficulty level and filtering the content appropriately.

Difficulty

Children's skills evolve very rapidly. The same game will appear incomprehensible to a 3-year-old, challenging to a 5-year-old and boring to a first-grader. Inviting children of different ages to participate in focus groups can help designers identify activities that stray from the level of complexity appropriate for their target demographics; this is especially important in titles made up of a number of different activities, each of which must be balanced.

Content

Because edutainment is targeted at children 10 years old and younger, great care must be taken to ensure that all content is age appropriate. The trouble is, not everyone has the same concept of what constitutes appropriate content: while violence and sex are obviously out, some clients will insist on a certain depiction of gender roles, characters of various ethnic backgrounds, etc.

Of course, despite the designer's best efforts, people who want to be offended by children's entertainment or educational content can always find a reason to be: as was the case in the movement to ban the "devil-worshipping" Harry Potter, the "gay Teletubby" issue, and the battle against the teaching of evolution in some American states. However, this unfortunate reality does not free developers from their obligations to provide age-appropriate material.

Persistent Game Worlds

Persistent game worlds are multiplayer experiences that continue to exist and evolve over a period of years, whether or not a specific player is logged on at any given time. These include:

- Massively multiplayer role-playing worlds, such as *Everquest* and *Star Wars Galaxies*
- Special-purpose communities that emerge around a multiplayer game, such as *Air Warrior* or *Paintball.NET*

Much is written elsewhere in this book about multiplayer games; however, two specific design challenges deserve to be mentioned here: the social dynamics of online worlds, and the persistence of mistakes.

Social Dynamics

Persistent games are social by nature: the denizens of role-playing worlds form clans, get married, start wars, and even evolve their own subcultures. This fascinating phenomenon requires free and easy access to communication with others—which can also be abused by bullies or criminal predators.

The rules of the game also influence its social dynamics, and vice-versa. Games that reward player-on-player violence will beget cruel dystopian worlds where players constantly attack each other, sometimes at the expense of the intended game functionality.

Mistakes and Cheaters

In persistent worlds, characters are expected to last a long time. Thus, a player who obtains an advantage will insist on keeping it, even if the source of the advantage was a bug in the game's programming.

Suppose that a game allows players to set their characters on "auto-pilot" before logging out. Further suppose that an infinite supply of widgets can be purchased in a village at the eastern edge of the game world for one gold piece each and sold at a small profit at the other end of the continent. If the prices are hardwired instead of being submitted to the laws of supply and demand, a player could very well program his character to shuttle back and forth between the two villages, log off for a month, and return to an incredible amount of undeserved wealth.

Some players will even go as far as to hack the game software to obtain unfair advantages. The designer must think of ways to counter this activity (for example, by keeping game logic and databases on servers) lest it ruin the game for everyone but the cheaters.

The Future

So far in this article, we have discussed the types of games that have achieved significant success up to now. Predicting which kinds will emerge in the future, thanks to evolving technologies and audiences, is obviously fraught with peril; however, a handful of emerging genres seem poised to break into the mainstream before 2010.

Invasive Games

Current interactive entertainment is a passive art, in the sense that games wait for players to initiate gameplay sessions. This does not have to remain true.

One of the Japanese crazes of 2000–2001 was a fishing game played on cell phones. Players would log in early in the morning, go about their businesses, and receive phone calls from the system when fish took the bait; they would then have to interrupt their activities and try to reel in the fish—or go on with their lives and lose the catch. In the Europe and America, *Majestic* was an early attempt at such invasive gaming; characters sent players messages via fax, telephone, or email.

In the future, an invasive "secret identity" game that would call upon players to solve missions at inopportune times (i.e., via a sort of "Bat Signal") might become very popular—especially if it were tied to local events, as discussed in the next section.

Event-Driven Games

In other fields, entertainment is all about creating big events: the Super Bowl, the Academy Awards, May sweeps, etc. Games that tie into this phenomenon may be the future of interactive television.

Imagine that the secret identity game mentioned above were operated in partnership with a major television network. The player's "contact" would call him at 6:00 pm informing the player that he has left a clue on the Web site associated with the magazine that will sit on Mr. X's coffee table during tonight's episode of a popular sitcom. Regional operators could also plant clues in city landmarks, at sporting events, and so forth.

Other Perspectives

The rest of Part 4 contains articles focusing on a specific game genre or non-standard platform:

- In two articles, Bruce Onder discusses the design of turn-based strategy games and of interactive television content.
- Stefan Pettersson examines the advantages and limitations of wireless devices such as cell phones as gaming platforms.
- Alexandre Ribeiro explains memory-saving techniques from which artists and designers can benefit when creating content for limited platforms, such as interactive television and handheld devices.
- Markus Friedl studies the patterns of interaction between users and game content (in all possible combinations) in multiplayer game worlds.
- Joe Hitchens looks at the ins and outs of designing effective online games, including how to deal with cheaters, censorship, and game lobbies.

- Finally, Drew Sikora discusses the persistence of online game worlds that exist independent of the players, and how to turn this problematic feature to our advantage.

Bibliography

[Hitchens02] Hitchens, J., "Pacing in Action Games," *Game Design Perspectives*, Charles River Media, 2002.

4.1

Turn-Based Game Design

Bruce Onder

bonder@digitalarcana.com

In today's world of 3D real-time games, is there still a role for the oft-maligned turn-based strategy game? This article will discuss this question and present the design issues, problems, and advantages of turn-based game design.

Description

First, what are turn-based games? Simply put, *turn-based* games are games that have a clearly delineated sequence of events, including order specification (what you want to have happen turn) and resolution (what actually happened during the run).

How are turn-based different from "real-time" games? Real-time games strive to conceal their order specification and resolution behind the scenes as much as possible, in order to give the illusion that things are happening in "real time." One way real-time games achieve this is to have a constant turn-resolution loop that looks for any pending orders and executes them. In a turn-based game with several "units" that need orders for the current turn, the player would take as much time as necessary to enter orders for each unit, and then send a signal that he is ready to continue. In a real-time game, part of the fun of playing lies in deciding which unit should receive the player's precious attention, leaving the other units to fend for themselves.

Why should we care about turn-based games? Turn-based games may soon enter a renaissance in which some very intriguing and entertaining games will be provided on the various platforms that support turn-based games well–Web browsers, the mobile phone, i-mode, and similar devices.

Advantages of Turn-Based Games

Because of their relaxed pacing, turn-based games allow players to communicate among themselves at will, to enter multiplayer games without being forced into continuous presence, and to devote as much or as little time as they wish to preparing their next moves. For developers, the advantages related to turn-based games' technical simplicity include easier and cheaper programming, increased multiplayer scalability, and additional viable business models.

Increased Diplomacy

When games do not need to be played in real time, players have much more opportunity to discuss the state of their positions with other players–in short, they get to conduct *diplomacy*. In fact, one of the longest-running email turn-based games in existence is *Diplomacy Adjudicator*, where you can join many other *Diplomacy* players in many variants of the original game. (See *http://devel.diplom.org/DipPouch/Email/newbie.html* for an overview of the game, and for links to many more in-depth Web pages about it.)

Increased Strategy

The more time a player has between turns, the more time they have to consider their options. Many players enjoy repeatedly reviewing their positions , looking for the best possible future moves.

Increased Flexibility

One of the biggest advantages of turn-based games is that as long as the player finishes his turn by the game's deadline, they can play when it is most convenient or desirable for them, rather than at the convenience of the game or other players. The flexibility of turn-based games also enables players to easily arrange play against opponents who live on other continents .

Reduced Development Costs

In many cases, turn-based games are cheaper to produce than their more complicated and graphically intensive real-time counterparts. In a well-designed turn-based game, in fact, most of the content is created by the players themselves as their turns are resolved and game history is created.

Ease of Building Massively Multiplayer Games

It is far easier (not to mention cheaper) to build a turn-based game that can handle a million simultaneous players than it is to build one game that plays in real-time. When a player's orders need to be processed only once every 30 minutes, his consumption of server resources is negligible.

Business Model Opportunities

Turn-based games are excellent candidates for subscription-based business models. Many existing titles use a pay-per-turn model, in which some amount of money is debited from the player's account balance for each turn processed. Mobile phone operators, who sell access by the minute or by the packet transfer, constitute a natural market for turn-based games.

Examples of Good Turn-Based Games

The following are examples of some popular turn-based games currently in existence:

- *Olympia (http://www.pbm.com/):* This play-by-email game of fantasy empire-building allows players to form alliances, make enemies, create services for other players to use in the game world, spread propaganda, and much more.
- *Sissyfight 2000 (http:www.SissyFight.com/):* A fun, light game in which the player takes on the role of a schoolgirl and tries to claw, tease, and tattle her way to victory. It uses a leader-board metaphor to keep players returning for more schoolyard scrapes.
- *Kung Fu Boy (http://www.KungFuBoy.com/):* Similar to the virtual pets that you downloaded and then fed, watered, and constantly played with to keep them healthy and happy, *Kung Fu Boy* provides players with a little boy to train in the martial arts. The player then sends him out to fight with other boys—players can buy him gear to take into fights with him.
- *Net League Baseball (NLB) (http://www.NetLeagueBaseball.com/):* NLB is a fantasy baseball game in which, instead of tracking real-world statistics and trading those numbers with other players, participants must put together a world-class baseball team made up of simulated ball players with their own skills, personality quirks, and egos.

Design Issues

Designing a turn-based game requires careful examination of the relationship between game time and real time. Designers must ensure that the game can be completed in a reasonable amount of time, and that players will not be unduly penalized if they must leave the game for a time.

Pace of Play: Real World

One of the first design issues to consider in turn-based game design is: how quickly do you want your turns to be resolved? In other words, how often will your games have deadlines?

One option is to place no deadlines at all in your game. For example, in chess–unless you are playing competitive chess—there is no time limit on planning and making your next move. Some -publishers of computer implementations of traditional table-top games offer email-enabled versions of their games without deadlines, so that players can take turns in the same amount of time via email as they would playing the game on the table top.

Unlimited deadlines work fine for certain games or for two very patient people. However, if you wish to create a game in which any number of people can play on a predictable basis, you will definitely need to consider establishing turn deadlines.

Depending on the game, any level of turn *granularity* (the amount of time between turn deadlines) may be suitable. However, as the granularity is reduced, many of the advantages of turn-based design attenuate proportionally. For example: if you are designing a space-based empire-building game and you set your turn deadlines to every five minutes, you will have reduced flexibility, diplomacy, and strategy. On the other hand, if you set your granularity too large, you can easily lose players because of lack of excitement.

Good turn-based game designs typically choose a level of granularity of one day to one week. A day will still provide players flexibility and plenty of time to email allies to coordinate orders. A week is enough for even the most complicated of games and the busiest of players. At larger levels of granularity you start running the risk that not enough will happen in your game to keep players' interest.

Pace of Play: Game World

Likewise, your game world should have a *pace*. In some game situations, this pace should match that of the real world (for example, one week of real-world time equals one week of game-world time), but for other game situations, the game world should move faster or slower than the real world.

A good example of a turn-based game with a faster than real-world pace would be an empire-building game, in which a week of real-world time could equal a month or a year of game-world time to give players a more epic sense of scale. On the other hand, a turn-based gladiatorial combat game may choose to equate one day of real-world time to five minutes of game-world "fight" time.

World Geography, Organization and Size

In *Monopoly*, there are only 36 squares on the game board. How many "squares" does your game support? What does a "square" in your game look like? What features does it have?

These issues will be decided by the intended scope of your game. For instance, if you are designing what is essentially a board game that only eight people can play, then you probably do not want a million "squares"—rather, you will want only a few dozen, because you do not want your game world to appear to be too sparsely populated. After all, part of a game's fun is to quickly reach your opponents. Similarly, in a turn-based street-fighting game in which one turn represents a best-of-three fight in one of that world's most glamorous (or sleaziest) locales, your game world will probably have a relatively small number of locations, in which many players can coexist.

However, in an empire-building game, you will want many large territories for your players to explore and battle over. In this case, you can control the perception of sparseness by populating the game world with interesting objects, monsters, characters, and treasures that players can find in the early stages of the game.

Orders and Turn Submission

Most of the interaction between players and your game engine will pass through a turn-submission interface. This "interface" could be as simple as a free-form email message, or as detailed as a full-featured graphical application with plenty of support functionality.

Design your turn-submission interface according to the most common platform you will support. For example, because so many graphic possibilities are available via Web browsers, a purely text-based entry system is probably a bad idea–unless you are designing a game to be played on mobile phones, in which case you should optimize the interface to use the numeric keys as much as possible.

If you need to support multiple devices, such as Web browsers, wireless phones, and PDAs, plan to develop a flexible XML/XSL architecture, where the game data is presented in XML and the presentation is determined by the XSL. Discussion of this architecture is beyond the scope of this article, however (see [Holzner01] for a complete reference on XML/XSL).

Missed Deadlines

What can you do if some of your game's players have missed their deadline for turn submission? Here are three basic approaches to tackling this problem:

- **Take No Action:** Any units without explicit orders on file for the current turn do nothing, which makes these units particularly vulnerable. If you want to be a bit more lenient, allow the units to defend themselves from attack but nothing else that turn.
- **Repeat Last Orders:** Using this approach, the units without orders will repeat the movements of their previous turn, if possible. For instance, if unit 101 was heading west in the previous turn, it will continue its westward march, unless it reaches an obstacle such as an ocean or a vast canyon.
- **Use Default Orders:** This approach allows players to specify what all units, or even each unit, should do if no other orders are on file for the turn. For example, a dwarf mining unit might have default orders to "mine ore," while most army units might be "on guard" when not explicitly doing anything else.

You will probably find further ways to approach this issue, including using hybrids of the three approaches mentioned here.

Player Dropout and Churn

One of the critical issues you must contend with in turn-based games is the effect of players dropping out of the game. Sometimes players drop out for personal reasons, though all too frequently they leave because they are dissatisfied with their position in the game world.

Dropouts can affect the game in various ways. First, they can promote a "sucker effect" in which other players with less-than-stellar game positions will also drop out and rejoin the game from a new position. Second, a high *churn rate* (the percentage of players who drop and rejoin) can make your game world feel more like a ghost town than a thriving community. Third, those few players who drop out of a strong position might leave many loose ends your game administrators must fix in order to keep things flowing. Finally, at best, player dropouts can have a chaotic affect on your revenue streams; at worst, they can kill your business model.

Here are a few suggestions for handling player dropout:

- **Minimize or remove motivations for dropout:** Some players will drop out and rejoin simply because their current position is lower than that of a beginner. For instance, if a player starts your game with five units and plays himself down to a single unit, he would have a strong motivation to drop out and rejoin. Consider changing your game design to remove this motivation: have new positions start with a single unit; thus one motivation for dropping and rejoining is reduced.
- **Provide motivation for staying in the game:** Increasing motivation for players to stay in the game, even for those with weak positions is easy; simply provide them with game advantages that increase with seniority. For instance, in *Net League Baseball*, simulated baseball players generally feel more trust and goodwill toward well-established franchises. So, if your team has only existed for two seasons and another player's has been playing for 10, you must work harder to get ball players to take you seriously, because they will perceive the other franchise as more stable. However, you will already have more experience than another player's beginning franchise , and the longer you stay in the game, the more the ball players will trust you.
- **Develop procedures to minimize effects of dropout:** Players will drop out of even the best of games, so you will need some process for keeping the negative effects of such dropout to a minimum. If your game design includes provisions for players missing deadlines, you can also run dropped positions on "autopilot" as game-moderated positions. Or, dropped positions can be auctioned off. When all else fails, you can even remove the vanished player's units, although, for game balance and story reasons this is not a good idea.

Mid-Game Joins

Conversely, how do you handle new players in a world full of powerful players? New players generally mean new revenues, so it is in your best interest to make them feel welcome. Here are some approaches you can consider:

- **New Game Spawns:** Create new instances of your game world to accommodate new players, and give new players a choice of which game they can join.
- **Safe Haven Starts:** Your design could include "start areas" where new players are either relatively or completely safe until they go out to face the dangers of the game world. New players who join the popular play-by-email game *Atlantis* start out in Atlantis City, where a superior Town Guard enforces the law, coming to the defense of all inhabitants in case of attack. New players are free to practice entering turns and to learn about the game world before venturing out of city limits.

- **Newbie Flag:** Another way to protect new players is to have a "newbie" flag that marks them as protected from attack. Of course, such players would be forbidden to engage in such attacks, as well. Players can turn off their newbie flag when they feel comfortable doing so, or the game can turn it off for them after so many turns.

Bugs

Bugs in a turn-based game can seriously hinder the flow of gameplay. For example, let's say you run turn 264, and due to a bug in the latest version of the game software, all elven archers suddenly become godlike killing machines who can easily dispatch thousands of fighters of other races with a single arrow. As a result, a major battle goes horribly awry because five elves with 20 arrows manage to rout a dwarven army of 20,000 in seven seconds. What do you do?

One method of fixing the problem is to roll back the turn, fix the bug, and run the turn again. However, players who were not affected by the bug might get different, less satisfactory results when the turn is run again, and they might not be pleased. Another policy is never to rerun turns due to bugs, although this means that players who suffer from bugs must live with the consequences, and those the bug favored get to keep their sudden gains.

A compromise is to not rerun the turn but negate the effects of the bug. In the elven demigod example above, you might decide that the 20,000 dwarves should be resurrected due to godly intervention, thus setting everything back for proper resolution on the next turn.

Whatever you decide, make sure you post your policy clearly—as part of your game instructions, your terms of service, and anywhere else, in order to help prevent ill feelings.

Turn Resolution Loop

Once all your players have submitted their turns, you must process all the orders and calculate what happens. What types of orders should get resolved before others? Which players' turns should be resolved first?

The answer to the first question is resolved by the *Phased Order Resolution List*. Here is an example of a simple Phased Order Resolution List for a fantasy-based game: (1) Spying and Assassination, (2) Minor Magic, (3) Ranged Combat, (4) Close Combat, (5) Major Spells, (6) Movement, (7) Construction. In this game, I want to give players the ability to thwart major battles by sending an assassin into the region before the battle commences. Then, minor spells like magical armor or missiles are cast. Then, mundane ranged combat (crossbow, longbow, etc.) occurs. Next, close combat with swords, pikes, and so forth is carried out. Then, major spells such as fireballs, earthquakes, or demon summoning are used. Next, troop movements are allowed in the area; and finally, any ongoing construction is performed.

In what order should multiple actions of one type be resolved? In an empire-building game in which you want big battles to have more meaning than the activities of single scouting units, you might want to sort your world's locations by decreasing number of units, so that the areas with highest unit populations see their Phase 0 actions resolved first. Once all Phase 0 orders have been processed, go back to the top of the list and do all Phase 1 actions, etc., until turn resolution is complete.

Multi-Turn Actions

Some of the actions supported in your game can be completed in a single turn; for example, hunting for food will result in zero or more slabs of meat at the end of the turn. On the other hand, actions such as building a castle will probably take several turns to complete. You can simulate such complex activities by developing *multi-turn actions*.

Say you want to determine how long various construction projects will take in your game world. You could establish simple such rules as a hut takes one game turn, a barn takes two game turns, a castle takes five game turns. This solution is simple, but not very realistic: the number of qualified workers and the amount of resources available will certainly influence even the most straightforward building projects.

Revise the list to create something a little more realistic (and, hopefully, fun): building a hut requires 1 man-turn and 1 unit of wood, while a barn takes 2 man-turns and 3 wood, and a castle, 5 man-turns, 5 wood, and 10 stone. This solution looks a bit more realistic (although the numbers for constructing a castle seem very low), and we can see other aspects of the game that we will need to support. For example, if you include wood as a required resource, you must provide some way to create lumber, so you will need lumberjacks or foresters. Likewise, for stone you will need stonecutters. And unless all game regions are equally rich in unlimited resources, you must design a transport mechanism—wagons or possibly ships.

Friends and Enemies

Consider having your game design support various degrees of "like" and "dislike" among players and their units. For instance, if Player A is allied with Player B, A will defend B's units wherever the two players' units coexist. Likewise, if Player A is at war with Player C, their units will automatically whenever they find themselves within range of each other. Finally, Player A might want to adopt a position of neutrality with everyone else in the game, until he needs to decide who to trust and who to fight.

These kinds of rules allow your turn resolution mechanism to decide whether two units coexist peacefully in a single region, whether they will attack each other on sight, or whether they will lend a hand if some other position is attacked.

Rules for friends and enemies can also help you resolve more complicated issues. For instance, what happens if two parties attack a castle on the same turn? If they are allies, they will join forces. If they are neutral to each other, neither of them will be able to take the castle that turn; they must fight or conduct diplomacy next turn to decide who gets the spoils. If the players are enemies, they will attack each other after the castle is won to decide the issue on the spot.

Stacking Units

If your game will be massively detailed, with each player responsible for many units, you will want to design *stacking* or leadership rules to allow the players to merge units into more easily manageable groups. For instance, all units in a region could stack together under a single leader, and the player could issue orders to that group with a single command.

The term stacking *dates back to table-top war board games in which units were physically represented with cardboard tiles; players would stack these tiles in order to group units for easier movement, or to achieve greater group power than the units represented individually.*

Entertainment versus Realism

When entertainment and realism collide, which will you choose? Decide which route your game will take early in your design process, and be prepared to stick to your choice.

Some players prefer a game that errs on the side of realism. If wood must be moved from Crickley Forest to the Plains of Venz, then players will have an opportunity to specialize in supply chain management and to build service companies in that area. Many players, however, favor entertainment over realism: a real general might be forced to micromanage every detail of keeping his troops equipped and his horses fed every turn, but these players prefer fighting to logistics.

Scalability

If your game is successful, more and more people are going to want to join. How are you going to accommodate tens of thousands of people? Hundreds of thousands? Or even millions? The challenges may be technical, game-related, or both. For example:

- **Game World Scalability:** Can your game world enlarge to meet demand? For instance, if you are designing a space-opera game, can you provide new galaxies or quadrants that open up as needed? Can you tie this expansion to story events that make it believable and exciting?
- **Technical Infrastructure Scalability:** Can your game's technical architecture bring new servers (Web servers, email servers, application servers, etc.) online as needed? Is there a good load-balancing strategy in place?
- **Game Spawning:** Can you spawn multiple instances of your game? This approach to scalability produces some community-building challenges, but for

certain types of games (especially games with limited numbers of players) it is the best way to handle heavy traffic.

- **Resource Management:** If you produce email reports of turn resolution, or a game newsletter, can emails be sent when there is less demand for resources?

Game Balancing

No matter how good your game ideas may seem at first, testing them before release is the best way to find faulty game design and to avoid a multitude of post-release problems.

There are several ways you can test and balance your game designs before releasing them. The simplest and cheapest method is to walk through the design on paper with friends or fellow team members, in much the same way that you would play pen-and-paper *Dungeons and Dragons*.

For instance, if you were play-balancing the construction requirements discussed above, you might notice that it takes less than three times as long to build a castle as it does a barn. This seems low, so the playtesters will likely suggest a higher time cost. Other issues, such as whether it should be easier for elves to work with wood or dwarves with stone, might arise. Sometimes you will streamline the design in the interest of entertainment, and sometimes you will detail the design to make the game more realistic.

Another way to balance gameplay is to offer it to players as a beta release. For example, say version 1.5 of the game (i.e., original version 1.0 followed by five releases of bug fixes and minor enhancements) is in production, and you would like to replace it with version 2.0, which includes many exciting new features. However, you do not want to unbalance the existing game with any unforeseen side effects from the new code. You can set up version 2.0 on a new game server, and start a new game world from scratch, or copy the existing game world to that server. Better still, do both, a method that will allow you to test game balance from two different perspectives. When you are satisfied that the game is well balanced, simply upgrade the 1.5 game servers to 2.0 before running the next turn.

Community Building

Though turns are not resolved in real time, your game does not have disappear to a player until his next turn arrives. Rather, your game should promote much activity for your players between turns, using community building.

Obviously, a good way to start community building is to build your diplomatic channels first. Some games reveal (or allow the option to reveal) the players' email addresses so players can communicate with each other at any time. Other games create a "blind" diplomacy system so that players can contact each other, but without having access to players' email addresses, which is good privacy practice.

Another method of community building is through the publication of a "news wire" service to which your players can post. Players can write news articles, disinformation, even libel within the context of the game. You can even reward players for contributing to the news wire; for example, dropping some game-world currency into their virtual account each turn that they contribute to the publication.

Here is an exciting and compelling story my friend and colleague François-Dominic Laramée related to me about community building:

> *At its peak, my play-by-mail* World Electronic Hockey League *had been thoroughly co-opted by the players. Every bi-weekly turn report for a given 36-team league included 4 to 6 tightly-packed 8x14 pages of fake press releases, cartoons, and other creative material developed by the players themselves. I am sure that some of them spent 50 hours crafting their releases. And when we held a players' convention, about 100 people (over a third of our entire player base!) showed up, some of them driving 12 hours each way to spend a couple of hours with us. One of them even printed polo shirts in his fake team's colors!*

A third way to build community is to offer some limited real-time elements to your game, such as chat. For instance, in a fantasy-based exploration and empire-building game, you might want to put chat windows into each location in your game, so players with units in those areas can chat with other units in those areas.

Keep looking for ways to build community during the time between actual turns; it will keep your players coming back to the game universe for a long time.

Conclusion

Turn-based games provide natural support for gameplay mechanics such as diplomacy, flexible play schedules, and community building. And, given their technical simplicity, turn-based games allow developers to more easily create multiplayer experiences at less expense, which can handle large numbers of players at the same time.

Bibliography

[Holzner01] Holzner, S., *Inside XML*, New Riders Publishing, 2001.

4.2

Wireless Game Design

Stefan Pettersson

stefpet@algonet.se

Imagine yourself able to play a game wherever you are, whenever you want—against anyone. This scenario is a reality today with games for mobile phones, a reality that introduces new interesting kinds of gameplay and opens up entirely new dimensions in terms of game design.

The world of mobile games is growing rapidly, as telecom operators realize that providing games and entertainment services is becoming a more and more important factor in the consumer's decision to buy a specific brand or model of handset. The enormous growth of messaging traffic in Europe and the popularity of the i-Mode system in Japan have paved the way for mobile entertainment as a new frontier for the game industry. However, the infrastructure is still immature; new technologies are constantly being introduced as the development of networks, devices, and applications proceeds at a high pace.

Due to the rapid technology development in the wireless industry, this article will focus on the generic aspects, rather than the details, of the different wireless technologies and on their impact on game design.

Technologies

In order to understand the design limitations and possibilities offered by mobile games, we must take a look at the fundamental technologies underlying current and future wireless networks.

Messaging

Text-based messages are very simple, yet they are inarguably the most popular mobile service after regular voice calls. During the first quarter of 2001, more than 50 billion SMS text messages were sent worldwide, which represents a 500 percent increase over the same period in 2000, and the growth curve is showing no signs of leveling off [GSM Association01].

In general, a service based on wireless text messaging has to be very simple. An SMS datagram may consist of a maximum of 160 characters and supports no text formatting whatsoever. This limits gameplay to a dialog: the player sends a message, and then waits for a response. Further, because it is both difficult and tedious to enter more than a word or a short sentence on a phone's tiny keypad, the messages sent by the user to the game server should be limited to a short command, with maybe a handful of parameters.

When examining game types suitable for messaging, you might conclude that classic board games are an obvious choice. However, message-based games do not have to be this simple. The limitations in games based on messaging are actually somewhat similar to those of the once very popular turn-based play-by-mail (PBM) games. Strategy games like *Diplomacy* can easily be played by email; although the interface is plain and the technology is very limited, the underlying gameplay is complex and intriguing.

Markup Languages

HTML cousins like WML (which is part of the WAP standard) and HDML fall into the markup language category. Markup languages are based on content residing on a server. The content is requested by a browser on the mobile phone, just as if the user were surfing the Web on a PC, except that the mobile phone browser is very limited: in general, cellular phone browsers are limited to displaying plain text, static black-and-white images, and hypertext links.

Due to the nature of a browser, markup language gameplay is based on requests and responses: the user makes a request to the server by clicking a link, and the server responds with the content. The result is a turn-based architecture, where the server is unable to "push" a message to the user. If the game must communicate with users who are not currently involved in the game, or if it needs to send messages out of sequence, it must resort to SMS or similar messaging techniques.

The way to develop interactive and interesting games is to dynamically generate both the actual pages requested by the browser and the images to be displayed. Certainly, the fact that the phones are restricted to plain images and do not support animation may seem stifling. However, the fact that the device's display capabilities are limited does not mean that the image needs to be static on the server: in fact, the image may be dynamically generated for each request. The image may then be rendered to directly reflect the game state and be completely unique for that particular user and request.

For an example of a successfully executed game that takes advantage of the medium and is not crippled by the phone's limitations, let us examine the WAP-based golf game *On the Green.* Though it is a mobile phone game, *On the Green* is very similar to golf games on the PC, except that it has no animations. The player chooses a club, angle, and strength depending on the terrain, wind, and position on the course. After each stroke, a new image is dynamically generated, displaying the terrain, as a snapshot from a 3D view, with the exact position of the player and the player's view of the course.

Figure 4.2.1 shows dynamically generated graphics. On the left is an image seen from the player's perspective, while the middle and right images show a top view of the course, each from slightly different distances.

FIGURE 4.2.1   *On the Green screen shots.*

On the Green's use of a server-based 3D-engine, optimized to dynamically render golf courses on very small screens in only two colors, is an excellent example of how traditional game development technologies may be used in a clever way to deliver interesting gameplay on limited devices.

Local Execution

The ability to run custom software on a wireless phone is probably the most important step mobile phones need to take to become attractive to the mass market as a platform for gaming. As technologies such as Java 2 Micro Edition (J2ME) become more prevalent, phones will provide developers with an attractive platform for games far less limited than those based on browsing or messaging technologies.

Upgrading the phone's capabilities from those of a dumb client totally dependent on a server to being able to execute code locally greatly increases the opportunities for more interesting games. Obviously, local capture of keystrokes and real-time rendering make it possible to design games similar in scope to those available on other handheld devices, such as the Nintendo GameBoy, yet with a very important difference: the phone is connected to a network—the GameBoy is not.

Network

A number of wireless network standards for mobile communication exist in the marketplace. GSM—which is the most common system in Europe—is one example, and TDMA—more common in North and South America—is another. No matter what network system is used, its most significant features from a game development perspective are *bandwidth* and *latency*. With the introduction of third generation (3G) mobile networks, capable of packet-based data communication, latency and bandwidth are approaching levels acceptable for real-time multiplayer games.

Even more important from a game designer's point of view is how the network influences the way people use their phones. With technologies prior to General Packet Radio Service (GPRS) and 3G, the user connects to the network, which takes anything from 20 to 40 seconds, in order to access a WAP-based game or to let an application transfer data. GPRS and its brethren allow instantaneous connections without this tedious dial-up process, which makes game sessions of even a few minutes appealing to hurried players.

Device

The mobile phone itself introduces parameters that must be taken into account. In general, these devices have a very small display (often no larger than 90 by 40 pixels) and a limited keypad allowing the user to enter text and numbers.

As most mobile phone users have painfully discovered, entering large amounts of text with the numeric keypad is tedious, and typing errors are easy to make and difficult to correct. Because of this, games must be designed to require as little text input as possible from the user and be as forgiving as possible. In browser-based games, actual text entry should be avoided: the most common choices should be directly encoded into the markup as hyperlinks. Messaging-based games should let the user control the game with short commands (or even abbreviations) rather than complete sentences.

The small size of the mobile phone display means that little information may be shown to the user at any given time. Try to restrict the amount of text to display so that the user does not need to scroll up or down, and above all keep from splitting the text into multiple pages that the user has to request separately. In a browser-based game, each extra request that does not deliver a reward (e.g., a response to an action) is a possible source of user frustration because of the download delay involved.

Of course, images are just as affected by small screens as text, maybe more so. Using a tiny monochrome display does not only mean that the amount of information on an image is limited, it also means restrictions to game design. A game that relies on the user being able to view a large amount of information at the same time, such as a military simulation requiring a top-down view of a map, is therefore not a good idea. This does not mean that strategic military games are not good for mobile phones, but it does mean that it is necessary to design the gameplay in a way that works even if the user only sees a tiny bit of information at one time.

Note that some phones have some unique features that allow unusual types of gameplay. For example, Bluetooth-enabled phones may form a virtual local area network and be used for multiplayer games. Phones equipped with GPS devices allow treasure hunts and other city-wide contests, and they can transparently match users from the same city together in a virtual world or in a community dating game.

User Behaviour

The key to designing a commercially successful mobile phone game is to integrate it seamlessly into the typical subscriber's usage patterns. An otherwise perfectly good game can fail if it does not take into consideration the length and location of mobile game sessions, costs, and the playing environment.

Game Sessions

When you are at home and want to play a game, you will turn on your PC or console—there are few reasons to play on your phone when more elaborate solutions are available. However, when you are riding a bus or waiting for your order at a restaurant, your favourite game console is unavailable; this is when the phone becomes a viable gaming platform.

The result is vastly different usage patterns for mobile and traditional games. With a PC, you probably sit down to play for about an hour or more, while on your phone you play in short bursts of a few of minutes, scattered throughout the day.

Environment

Mobile phone games will rarely be played in ideal conditions. For example, picture yourself downtown waiting to meet a friend. If your friend calls and says he will be 10 minutes late, you may grab your phone to play a quick game because you have nothing else to do in the meantime.

Now, the last thing that you want in such a situation is to be forced to wait for downloads, because you only have a few minutes of idle time. If the game fails to deliver action rapidly, it wastes your time, and you will never come back to it again.

Instant feedback is essential and must be considered during the design of a mobile game. For example, consider multiplayer games. A standard Internet-style matchmaking lobby will not work, because by the time the user has joined the lobby, created a new game, waited for another user to join, and launched the game, he is already likely to be out of time. A better solution would be to design the game in such a way that it is natural for the user to automatically be coupled with an opponent of his skill level, so that the game session can start immediately.

Cost

The actual cost of playing a game is of concern for most people—if it is too expensive, people will not play. And while a PC game generally is paid for only once and then can be used an unlimited number of times, mobile games adopt the opposite business model: players pay by the move, the game, or the minute. (Browser games usually charge by the minute, like voice calls, because of the dial-up mechanism. SMS and other messaging systems charge by the message.)

The bottom line: design a game whose cost will be reasonable to the user. Among other things, this means that introductions and setup must be kept to a minimum: an SMS game requiring 15 messages and costing $0.15 per message will seem like a rip-off if the user is forced to spend the first $1.50 navigating a lobby.

The introduction of subscription-based services, as opposed to per-minute billing, is a positive change for mobile games, as the user no longer feels hurried by the need to control cost. Subscription-based billing is becoming more and more common with the introduction of packet-based networks such as GPRS, and will allow game designers to use a more flexible approach.

Technical Obstacles and Features

To use WAP over circuit-switched networks, such as GSM, a user must dial up to the WAP-gateway. It is not uncommon for this dial-up procedure to last 20 to 40 seconds or more, which, in combination with the short game sessions, makes the dial-up itself a significant obstacle. This may reduce the number of times that a user will play a game during a day. Games that allow the user to log on once per day and then do everything she wants, instead of requiring multiple daily accesses, is likely to be more successful.

For example, consider a soccer management game. The user logs in, checks her team's latest results, issues commands for the next round, and logs off. Then the matches are processed during the night, and the user repeats the procedure the next day with new results.

However, this type of gameplay is not as well-suited to networks that feature instant access without dial-up. In such a case, we want a game to promote and trigger repetitive gameplay as often as possible, no matter when—exactly the opposite of what we just did with the soccer game.

Business Model and Revenues

The stakeholders of the mobile gaming industry are slightly different from those of the PC and console entertainment business. And because everything finally comes down to earning money, the nature of the supply chain affects game design.

The Mobile Gaming Value Chain

The mobile telephony operator (or *carrier*) is, in general, responsible for billing the end users for airtime used or messages sent when playing a game. This naturally puts the operator in an important position, because he controls access to the consumer. Because most game developers are not themselves interested in the tedious process of setting up contracts with operators and performing billing integration, distributors have emerged in this market. A distributor aggregates content from a number of developers and makes it available to operators, usually on a revenue-sharing basis or on the basis of a fixed monthly fee. The revenue earned by the distributor is then finally shared with the developer.

Billing

Operators are interested in generating network traffic—users of the mobile network pay for the airtime used, amount of data transferred, or number of messages sent from their phone. Thus, the purpose of a game is to either generate network traffic or to make the user send as many messages as possible.

However, there are also costs to be considered. Operators do not charge for messages they send to users. Therefore, it is important to design message-based games that have a reasonable ratio of sent and received messages; otherwise, the operator will be losing money. Generally speaking, each message sent to a user should result in one or more messages sent by the user.

Conclusion: Wireless Design Principles

Developing games for mobile phones presents unique challenges. Mobile phones are very limited, they are not designed as gaming devices, and the underlying technologies are far from ideal for games. It seems as if the designer is at a great disadvantage when creating games for mobile phones compared to other platforms, and in some way he is. Therefore, it is extremely important to take advantage of the phone's unique capabilities.

Use the Strength of the Mobile Phone

Anywhere, anytime and *anyone* are what make mobile phones different from other platforms: you carry your mobile phone everywhere, you may use it at any time, and you can contact anyone through the mobile network.

A successful mobile phone game must take advantage of these strengths; otherwise, it is indistinguishable from a PC game, and the user has no reason to play it on the phone.

Target Audience

The gameplayer user base is very different on mobile phones than on other platforms. It is likely that a significant number of consumers who buy cell phones will have little or no previous experience of interactive entertainment of any form, let alone mobile phone games. This is especially true in countries where mobile phone penetration is higher than that of PCs and consoles.

In general, when it comes to games, users of mobile phones are more inexperienced than PC users. Therefore, extra care must be taken in order to ensure a very low learning curve of a game, especially given how difficult it is to provide help text on a mobile phone's screen.

Limitations and Possibilities—Future of Mobile Games

Mobile games are exploring uncharted territories, and the game design opportunities are numerous despite the technical limitations. The future of mobile gaming looks bright—the traditional PC gaming industry is getting more involved in mobile games, the mobile phones are growing in power, the market is expanding, and operators are eager to leverage their investments in new network technologies to generate revenues from games and other forms of entertainment. Mobile games will usher in a new era for our business—and it is innovative game design that will make it happen.

Bibliography

[GSM Association01] GSM Association, "50 Billion Global Text Messages in Q1!" Press release, May 25, 2001.

4.3

Designing Gameplay for Interactive Television

Bruce Onder

bonder@digitalarcana.com

While interactive television has achieved notable success in England and France, it has yet to obtain significant market penetration in North America. However, the high-profile failures of the 90s notwithstanding, many opportunities exist in this emerging market, with recent experiments such as WebTV, UltimateTV, and AOLTV only hinting at what is to come.

This article describes the specific issues that must be addressed when designing interactive television content.

An Overview

Interactive television (ITV) is a term that seems to have no universally accepted meaning. Some believe that ITV is synonymous with *enhanced television* (ETV), while others maintain a distinction between the two. For the purposes of this discussion, we will consider all forms of interaction with television-based content to be ITV. This includes:

- Interactive programming guides (Gemstar/TV Guide, etc.)
- Teletext/videotext (Minitel, etc.)
- Personal video recorders (TiVo, Replay, etc.)
- Video-on-demand services
- Pay per view services
- Integrated interactive television (WebTV, set-top boxes, etc.)
- Two-screen interactive television (Spiderdance, Gold Pocket Interactive, etc.)

Some of these forms of interactive television bear further discussion, notably Teletext/Videotext and two-screen interactive television.

Teletext and Videotext

Teletext/videotext systems represent the earliest text-based systems that display content on either television screens or dedicated terminals. Simple in design and functionality, they allow users to navigate standard menus to reach the desired information.

Videotext systems have been around in various forms since the 1970s. In the United States, Warner Amex's QUBE system, an early interactive cable television project, suffered both from technical problems (i.e., getting the data from the set-top box back to the cable system head-end) and economic ones (i.e., equipment that was too expensive to produce, and the cable system wars of the early 1980s).

France, however, had much more success with its Minitel system, which has been widely available since the early 1980s. Built on top of the French phone system instead of on its cable television distribution, Minitel has a very simple and effective paid model wherein consumers are charged by the minute of usage. Many hundreds of thousands of French citizens use Minitel every day.

Two-Screen Interactive Television

Two-screen interactive television simulcasts traditional, linear television shows and synchronized Web content streaming to a browser. The ideal two-screen setup is one in which the user has a laptop or mobile tablet device on her lap, and can interact with content while the show plays.

Currently, most of the two-screen interactive television success stories build upon the inherent interactive capabilities of game shows. MTV's *WebRiot* and Game Show Network's *Inquizition* are two prime examples.

Other Forms of ITV

Many of the ITV options listed above do not offer obvious gameplay options. For instance, how can you wrap game elements around the task of finding the next airing of *Hee Haw* using your interactive programming guide? And when you are trying to program your UltimateTV to record *Talk Soup*, you are probably not interested in playing a game so much as getting the job done.

Essentially, the budding interactive television designer has two main options currently open to him: Integrated interactive television along the lines of WebTV or any of the set-top boxes that cable and satellite companies are developing, or two-screen interactive television that strives to synchronize your television screen with your Web browser.

Integrated versus Two-Screen Interactive Television

Although they are similar in many ways, integrated and two-screen interactive television have some important differences that will affect how you design interactive gameplay experiences for each of them. Table 5.3.1 illustrates these differences.

Table 5.3.1 Comparison of Two-Screen and Integrated ITV.

Characteristic	Integrated ITV	Two-Screen ITV
Viewer Attention	Focused on the television screen.	Divided between television screen and computer monitor.
Design Surface	The design surface tends to be somewhat smaller than a 640x480 computer desktop, and both TV and ITV content must share this real estate.	Content can be designed to take advantage of whatever resolution the computer is set to.
Text Content	Because the typical television viewer is 9 feet from the television screen, font sizes must typically be 14 points or larger.	A computer user is typically less than 1 foot from the monitor.
Color Palette	Color elements should be adjusted to display well in the NTSC color palette.	Color elements should be adjusted to display well in the Web-safe color palette.
Screen Real Estate	All interactive elements must share space with the television signal.	Designer has a dedicated canvas in the form of the Web browser.
Control Devices	Typically, a remote control or wireless keyboard. Casual users will be more familiar with the remote's manipulation, while text entry is best achieved with the keyboard.	Standard PC mouse and keyboard, both of which will be familiar to the PC user.
Technology Choices	Limited to what ships with given set-top-box; likely to be HTML and Javascript, but more and more boxes are specified to support Macromedia Flash.	Not limited. Designer can take advantage of the most ubiquitous tools (Flash, Shockwave), or require the user to accept a custom plug-in.
Market Penetration	Varies; in the United States the current market leader is WebTV, with nearly 1 million users. In various other countries, some systems have several million users. Several more years of set-top box warfare are likely to elapse before clear winners are decided.	In the United States, more than 44 million people can take advantage of two-screen interactive experiences (meaning they can see their television while using their computer).
Industry Support	Set-top boxes are increasingly supported by various hardware manufacturers, cable/satellite/terrestrial broadcasters, Telcos, and other behemoths. Much fragmentation in the industry.	Two-screen interactive is not supported by any large manufacturers directly, but many networks and producers are interested in trying it.
Competitive Landscape	Many content developers, manufacturers, broadcasters, and other companies.	Relatively few companies competing in this space.
Job Opportunities	Greater due to large number of companies.	Limited due to small number of players.

Most of the existing media attention currently focuses on the integrated ITV land-scape, because it involves the usual big players, Microsoft, Sun, AT&T, AOL, etc. The two-screen ITV playing field is smaller, but many large corporations are looming on the sidelines.

What all this means is: Are you more comfortable being a small fish in the big pond of integrated ITV, where food is more plentiful but many predators are swimming around? Or, would you prefer to be one of the big fish in the water garden of two-screen interactive? Or, possibly, can you carve out a dual existence in both bodies of water?

Design Challenges for Interactive Television

The Show Is Supreme

Your job when designing interactive television content is not to take attention away from the broadcast, but to support it. First, the show should always be onscreen and never completely hidden from view. You can overlay interactive elements over the show, but you must take great care to make no negative impact on the broadcast signal. For example, it would be a very bad idea to overlay interactive elements on top of player statistics on a sports show. You can also embed the entire television signal in your interactive content, and frame it with your own game interface (much like picture-in-picture). A good practice is to use the overlay approach to get the viewer's attention, and offer some type of link (hyperlink, button, etc.) to get to the detailed content with an embedded television picture.

Second, your job is to enhance the show. If you ever find yourself designing content that could be considered an alternative to the show itself, stop immediately. For instance, it is probably a bad idea to offer a crossword puzzle for the audience to play with during *Law & Order*.

Design Beyond the Norm

If you look at existing interactive television offerings, you will find that the vast majority takes the form of trivia questions and surveys. However, there is room for much more.

Here is a short list of what should be considered trite and hackneyed ITV design conventions. You should *not* use these concepts in your work unless a client demands it, or unless you can come up with some novel spin on them.

- Trivia questions
- Audience surveys
- Behind-the scenes pieces
- Email
- Chat
- Banner ads

As the industry grows and matures, new items will be added to the list.

Design to the Audience

Tailoring ITV content to its target audience is a two-level challenge. At the higher level, make sure you design interactive content that will appeal to the typical television viewer. That does *not* mean that you should be condescending; rather, you should remember that people watching *The X-Files* will not be interested in playing a real-time strategy game at the same time. In fact, casual players will be familiar and comfortable with short, simple puzzle-based games that are related to the show they are watching.

Which brings us to the second level: make sure you are designing content that will appeal to the show's fans. For instance, if you are hired to create compelling ITV content for *The X-Files*, you might consider gameplay on the meta-story surrounding the alien invasion subplot that has been the focus of many episodes for the past several seasons. After all, this is why diehard fans tune in to the show.

Design for Convenience and Comfort

While the remote control is a wondrous product of human ingenuity, it makes a relatively poor navigation device for some kinds of interactive content. For example, fill-in forms that require users to type their names and addresses shows how inadequate the numeric keypad on the typical remote is for the task. Even if the form comes with a pop-up virtual keyboard, the result is not what most people would consider a user-friendly interface design.

If the viewer is sitting on the couch with remote in hand, he will give your ITV content a chance to entertain him *if he can do it with the buttons on his remote*. However, if he has to pop up a virtual keyboard or reach for his WebTV device, he just may pass. Do not put these kinds of roadblocks in your design. You will already have enough trouble with factors that you cannot control, such as low screen resolution.

Design for the Web

Both forms of ITV described above are very Web-centric. The ATVEF ITV standard is essentially Javascript-enhanced HTML with a handful of additional elements and attributes. And of course, two-screen interactive *is* standard HTML.

As a result, you will want to design good, scaled-down Web experiences. The normal Web design challenges are either completely relevant here, or take on additional importance: keep an eye on your page weights (try to stay under 25 KV per page); preload graphics wherever you can; and cache common client-side scripts.

A few special notes about caching and cookies: support for these features varies between set-top boxes. The ATVEF standard only requires a small amount of caching space, but many manufacturers are putting more caching memory and storage on board to improve performance. Cookies are supported to differing degrees as well. When in doubt, check the specs.

Design for Business Needs

Remember that interactive television still needs to support the entertainment industry. In the PC and console game industries, the designer has to think only about creating good game; if it is executed well, gamers will buy it.

However, in ITV, the design must consider how the broadcaster will make money. Here are some possible revenue streams that can be added to your ITV designs:

- **Banner advertising:** This item also appears on the hackneyed conventions list provided earlier in this article, but it needs to be included here as well. If nothing else, your ITV experience can possibly be paid for by banner advertising..
- **T-Commerce:** T Commerce consists of symbiotic marketing efforts that tie a product to an entertainment experience in multiple ways. For exmple: A big fan of *Survivor*? Then you will want the Doritos Survival Pack for just $19.99 plus shipping and handling! Order now!
- **Subscriptions:** Sell the ITV experience as a subscription-base service, for example, for $4.95 a season.
- **Sponsorship:** Find a single advertiser who will sponsor the entire ITV experience. This suggestion has actually been implemented for previous ITV experiments, but it remains to be seen if it can work on a larger scale.

Conclusion

Considering revenue models as part of ITV design may seem less invigorating than designing levels of a 3D shooter, but it is a necessary evil. You cannot expect broadcasters to open up the purse strings just to add interactive content to their linear broadcasts. To get the money, you will have to show them how to get more money.

4.4

Memory-Friendly Design for Small Platforms

Alexandre Ribeiro

alex@mind.pt

With today's powerful platforms, there are almost no limits to what game designers can include in a game. Fifteen years ago Pixar made a movie called *Luxo Jr.,* each frame of which took over three hours to render. Each second of animation (24 frames) required 72 hours of processor time. Today, animations of similar visual impact are rendered almost instantly. Given this, you might suppose that designers would never again have to worry about the size of a texture or the complexity of a model; however, it is not quite that simple yet.

While it is true that powerful platforms do indeed exist, a new generation of very popular small devices are beginning to emerge, including PDAs, mobile phones, and set-top boxes for interactive television. These devices were all created with a very specific purpose in mind and do not possess 3D hardware or any kind of special capabilities to enable a pleasant gaming experience. To develop games for these types of devices, you must go back to the "old school" of game programming, and optimize, optimize, and optimize!

And while these optimizations depend, to some extent, on the programmer of the game, a design that takes into consideration platform limitations is also very important. This article will describe ways in which to produce game concepts and art for small platforms that are both visually stunning and economical.

From Black and White to True Color

While a few alternative devices have an inherent limitation in their color depth, supporting only black and white, greyscale, or 8-bit color, others allow you to display images in 12-, 16-, or even 32-bit color.

For example, consider the Microsoft Web TV platform, which only supports a fixed resolution of 640×480 pixels in 32 bits. This means that the artists can (at least in theory) choose between 2^{32} possible colors to use in their images. This should not be seen as a limitation; it is a blessing! However, from a programmer's point of view it can be a nightmare: the CPUs on smaller platforms are usually not very powerful, and displaying a 640×480 32-bit image requires shuffling 1.2 MB of memory around.

This task is difficult work for a weak processor, but it is a task that must be done many times per second if you want your game to be interactive.

How can you overcome the limitation of a weak processor? The memory must be moved to the display memory anyway, right? Well, yes, but you should not forget about all the processing that is done behind the scenes before the image is displayed. This is where we can save a great deal of effort.

For example, most platforms support double-buffered graphics. Images are not manipulated directly over the front buffer (i.e., directly on screen), because that would mean the user would see every single operation being performed. Instead, an image is composed in a back buffer, off-screen, and when it is ready to be displayed, the back buffer is copied to the display memory. Now, if the graphical game objects are defined in a smaller color depth (such as 8 bits instead of 32), then all the processing behind the scenes will be inherently faster, because much smaller amounts of data will have to be moved internally.

So, what color depth should you choose? This choice is highly dependent on what kind of game you are developing. Card games do not require a high frame rate; thus, it is possible to spend more time building each frame, and you should choose a relatively high color depth. While 32-bit color is overkill (especially on a television screen), 16-bit color would seem to be a sensible compromise. On the other hand, if you are building an arcade game that requires a higher frame rate, you may have to make do with 8-bit color.

Color Palettes

8-bit color depth mode is also called *indexed mode,* because it involves a palette that defines the 256 available colors, and the colors of the pixels in the image are defined via an "index" to the palette.

To be able to use an indexed mode in a game, all the graphics that appear simultaneously on screen must share the same palette. However, you could have multiple palettes for different parts of your game and overcome the limitation of only having 256 colours; for example, a splash screen with its own palette.

Creating artwork in indexed mode is tedious. However, a number of applications, including Debabelizer Pro, Paintshop Pro, and even Photoshop can compile a "best match" palette from a set of true-color art files, and then modify the artwork to comply with this palette.

If you decide to develop the artwork in a color depth higher than that of the target platform, you must be careful. Avoid color gradients, unless you know that the final palette will include enough of the gradient's colors. Choose simple patterns over complicated ones: because many colors may be merged or deleted from the palette during the conversion to 8-bit depth, complex patterns may be altered beyond recognition.

Size Does Matter

Suppose that you are working on a platform that has a screen resolution of 640 × 480 pixels, at a color depth of 32 bits. If you read the previous section, you have drawn all of your art in a smaller color depth, but probably at the full resolution. Even at 8 bits, a 640 × 480 image still weighs around 300 KB. On many small platforms where memory is at a premium, this is too much: a 300 KB back buffer may not fit in the machine's limited RAM. And even if the memory footprint is not an issue, you may be interested in the extra performance provided by smaller graphics.

What should your graphic resolution be, then? There are only a few guidelines when it comes to a smaller back buffer:

- The ratio of the back buffer, that is, the width of the back buffer divided by its height, must be equal to that of the front buffer.
- The width of the display screen must be evenly divisible by the width of the back buffer, assuming the display screen is bigger or equal to the back buffer.

Thus, for a display size of 640 × 480 pixels, a reasonable back buffer could measure 320 × 240 pixels. There are, however, some drawbacks to this technique:

- Because the back buffer is smaller than your screen, you must either display it in its own size (and waste 75 percent of the screen's surface), or the programmer must write the code to resize the image to fill the display screen.
- You will effectively lose display resolution in your game. If you need to stretch the image contained in your 320 × 240 back buffer to fill a 640 × 480 screen, each back buffer pixel will be transformed into a little 4-pixel block on the display.

The smaller back buffer technique is highly efficient in the case of set-top boxes. The loss of resolution is hardly an issue, because the television's screen will blur everything anyway. (Many console games are, in fact, rendered at a resolution of 320 × 240. No one will complain if you can achieve the image quality of a console in your set-top box game!)

If you are considering the small back buffer technique because of memory requirements, be aware of the processor time required to resize the image before display. Unless, of course, the device can perform the resize with special-purpose hardware; if this is the case, then this option becomes one of the best.

3D Support

Some devices may provide support for 3D graphics, either via a 3D software engine or through specialized hardware. In the future, 3D support will become standard in PDAs, small devices and set-top boxes because of its potential for games and real-time effects. However, because these devices are designed to be built cheaply, it is probable that their 3D hardware will be inferior to current PC and console standards for a long time. When designing 3D content for these platforms, consider the following issues:

- **Carefully evaluate your polygon budget:** 50,000 polygons per second may seem like a large number, but if the game is to run at 60 frames per second it will only be able to display approximately 830 polygons per frame.
- **Choose the texture size judiciously:** When using cheap hardware (or cheap software 3D engines), texture-mapped polygons take substantially more time to render than flat polygons. This is particularly true if the texture size is large, and even more so if the texture size is not an exact power of two.
- **Try to pack several textures into a single image:** The ideal situation occurs when all of a model's textures can be combined into a single image, as seen in Figure 4.4.2 on next page; in this way "cache trashing" would be kept to a minimum.
- **Determine whether you really need textures in every polygon:** If you can get away with Gouraud shading in parts of the scene, do so. Carefully crafted models could make or break the game's speed.

Cache Trashing

Most 3D games need more textures than can fit into memory at any one time. Whenever a texture that is not already located in memory is needed, it must be loaded from a disk. In order to avoid loading the same textures repeatedly (loading from disk is slow), a *texture cache* is used.

A texture cache is a block of memory that holds the most recently used textures. This way, whenever a texture is needed, the game engine checks the cache to discover if the texture is available before trying to load it from the disk. Whenever a texture needs to be loaded and the cache does not have enough space for it, another texture is unloaded from the cache in order to load the new one. Usually, the *least recently used* (LRU) texture is the one that is unloaded.

Careless game object design can cause a situation in which all textures present in the cache must be evicted in order to allow new textures in. This is known as *cache trashing* and should be avoided at all costs because it causes significant frame rate degradation. Packing multiple textures into one, reusing the same texture in multiple objects, tiling textures, and so forth help minimize the number of files that must be

FIGURE 4.4.1 *Car model.* Courtesy of André Vieira and Filipe Dias.

FIGURE 4.4.2 *Tightly-packed textures.* Courtesy of André Vieira and Filipe Dias.

accessed to render a scene, and thus cut down on trashing. Figure 4.4.1 displays a 3D model of a car and 4.4.2 displays a single image file packing all of its textures.

Conclusion

Working with set-top boxes and other platforms not primarily designed with games in mind will force you to produce artwork using fewer colors (and probably in lower resolution) than you might in other computer game platforms. However, do not view this limitation only as a restraint; view it as a greater challenge. Designing for a small platform is one area where creativity and hard work can really make a difference.

4.5

Online Interaction Patterns

Markus Friedl

friedl.markus@onebox.com

How do we define interactivity? How do we design it into a game? This article unfolds some of the complexities of the concept of interactivity in game design, and suggests how to use a new model of interactivity as an analytical tool.

Establishing the Shot

The patterns introduced in this article focus on a special subset of computer games: *multiplayer online computer games* (MOCG). The challenge for the game designer of such games is that they add an additional dimension of interactivity to the playing process: interpersonal (human–human) interactivity. Thanks to the ubiquitous Internet, computer games are increasingly becoming a means of social interaction [Michael02].

For the purposes of this discussion, the concept of interactivity will be deconstructed into a number of easily manipulated parameters. This analysis will help us deal with interactivity in an abstract, formal way: these atomic parameters make up the pieces of a game's "interactivity-puzzle" and should therefore be the focus during development, testing, and research.

Three Dimensions

As shown in Figure 4.5.1, the suggested model approaches the concept of interactivity in MOCG from three different perspectives: Human–System Interactivity, Human–Human Interactivity, and Human–Content Interactivity. Each of these dimensions is defined and influenced by various key factors or patterns, of which the most important will now be discussed.

Human–System Interactivity

As suggested by Figure 4.5.1, the dimension of Human–System Interactivity should be viewed as a filter laid upon the other two rather than as a dimension of its own. To speak in terms of Human–Computer Interaction (HCI) research, the player is in continuous conversation with the computer system during the game. This process defines

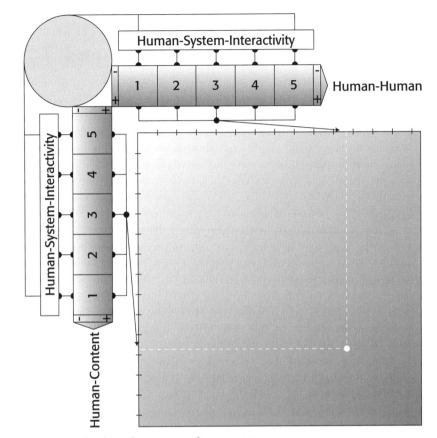

FIGURE 4.5.1　*The three dimensions of interactivity.*

a certain potential for the remaining interaction patterns, delineating what is potentially possible.

System Technology

Just as in real-life face-to-face communication, effective conversation with a computer system depends on immediate, synchronous response and feedback. Synchronicity is the key to a common understanding between the player and the system about their purposes and plans, and regular feedback is the only way to ensure evaluation of and adaptation to these purposes.

Further, enabling the system to present its responses to the player at the highest possible quality level, in order to avoid misinterpretations, is crucial. For games, this is mainly a matter of resolution, color-depth, shading, lighting, audio frequency, or spatial acoustics.

Controls

"Control" within this dimension is primarily a matter of how the player and the game can inform each other about their intentions and actions. Daily experience, education, and history teach us how to manipulate the real world, and how it tends to respond to human actions. Within a virtual world, however, player–system communication cannot (yet) rely on such a common ground.

For the game designer, the challenge is based on the fact that each type of intention is most easily communicated through a unique method that may not be easy to adapt to standard computer input devices. For example, the intention to steer one's car to the left is communicated better by rotating a wheel than by moving the mouse. Likewise, informing the player about the violence of a crash is easier and more intuitive to do with a force-feedback mechanism. Thus, in order to allow natural, effective, and convenient communication between users and systems, it is important to support the widest possible range of different I/O devices.

However, this is insufficient, as intuitive ways of communicating the same information may vary by user. Therefore, games need an ability to adjust and personalize control mechanisms. Do you want the Up key to trigger a jump or forward motion? Does moving the mouse upward mean a move along the positive or the negative y-axis? All controls used to communicate to the computer need to be freely mapped by the player according to his learned or preferred ways and be enforced neither by the designer nor the game. Most of today's shooters and real-time strategy games implement this idea very well by providing customizable keyboard and mouse layouts.

Commands

Commands are the player's mental controls. In real life, there are usually many ways to solve any given problem. Games should follow the same pattern: the ability for a player to identify what actions (or combinations of them) lead to an intended outcome means a freedom to act and interact, adapt, and react.

This freedom of choice should not be restricted to gameplay. Consider, for example, what happens when the player decides to quit the game. Must he press ESC, access a submenu item three levels deep and give positive answers to a pair of security questions? This may be appropriate when the player is in the middle of a crucial battle, but what about the end of a level? Are there specific points where it is "safe" and natural to log off, and where a quick-exit button would make more sense? Each of these possibilities should be available. Logging off is one example of a single player intention for which multiple alternatives should lead to the same outcome.

Focus

Interactivity with the system is different in nature from person-to-person communication, and each is better suited to specific demands and purposes. Within a game, however, all types of interactivity are intertwined and simultaneously experienced. It is thus essential to provide opportunities for the players to define the focus of their action at every moment in time, in order to meet their short- and long-term needs.

For example, in the typical fantasy role-playing town, a tavern where fighting is prohibited allows the player to focus on social interaction; training areas shift the focus to a study of the game's low-level mechanics; and letting the players select a game's difficulty level allows them to focus on learning high-level strategy and decide how much human interaction they desire.

Designed interactivity should be like every element in a well designed game—the player's actions must have, sooner or later, an obvious outcome and consequence. Only then will a single interaction process, like a player-to-player conversation, be experienced as a holistic entity.

Network

The underlying network, contains more for the designer to take into consideration than the obvious issues of bandwidth and latency. For example, the designer needs to be aware of the network's transparency as experienced by the player. User-specific network transparency means a simple and quick opportunity for the player to gain information about available, potential game environments (games, levels, maps), and information about what to expect within these environments and about other players within the network. Network-specific transparency can be understood as the possibility to gain information about the network's actual and potential condition and its security status.

Network transparency is implemented in practice by *GameSpy Arcade*, and seems to be one of the main design goals of Valve's *Game Master Server* technology [Bernier00]. *GameSpy Arcade* offers a vast amount of information about players, games, and network conditions; however, because it is a third-party "wrapper service" and not an integral part of the game, players must leave the game context to access all available information.

Artificial Intelligence

Advanced artificial intelligence (AI) is another way to allow adaptation, interpretation, and evaluation of others' actions and messages. Real-life face-to-face communication involves subconscious interpretation of another person's gestures, facial expressions, decisions, voice tone, and many other factors, in order to establish a common ground and understanding. The computer system needs the ability to do establish such understanding in its communication with the player as well. Lionhead's *Black & White*, in which the player's avatar makes decisions according to a continuously altered model of his master's personality, is a large step in this direction. The system interprets the player's messages, draws conclusions from these interpretations, and attempts to predict the player's intentions and decisions over the long term.

Degree of Real-Life Simulation

Interaction with the computer system is more intuitive and easier if the player can rely on already familiar and known experiences (most of them acquired in real-life events) during the process. It is thus the task of the system to simulate these real-life conditions in such a way that the player will recognize the pertinence of his experience. Through "direct manipulation" [Shneiderman98], the player should be able to translate the knowledge gained in real life into actions that are meaningful in the virtual game environment.

For example, a game's physics module should strive to represent friction, momentum, and gravity in sensible ways—unless, of course, the intent of the game's designer is to make the player experience unusual physical effects, such as weightlessness or a vacuum. Likewise, the volume button on an in-game radio, should increase and not decrease volume when turned to the right.

Human–Human Interactivity

Game design is a multilateral discipline. Designers must pay tribute to the meaningfulness of player–player interactivity, and study the results obtained by disciplines like psychology, sociology, cultural science, or anthropology. Knowledge about human–human interactivity patterns could make the difference between a good and a bad MOCG.

Range of Potential Partners

Within the dimension of human–human interactivity, *range* essentially represents the number and type of other players available on the network. A sparsely populated but friendly game world begets behavior patterns that have little in common with those of an overcrowded world filled with highly experienced player-killers.

Players need to know where they can find other people to talk with and play with, or at least how to search for these places. Game world locales such as marketplaces, main streets, and saloons are natural meeting places, so make them plentiful and easy to identify uniquely. Meeting points outside of the game world, such as a Web site or game service lobby, also work in certain cases. Give players reasons to visit these focal points of social interaction regularly, by organizing tournaments, meetings, discussions, auctions, and other special events.

Knowledge of Partners

Knowledge about a player's potential teammates and opponents–their personalities and goals and how they react to certain types of behavior–influences human–human interactivity in both real-life and virtual computer game environments. This knowledge could be an important basis for a player's decisions and further actions–her "way of interacting" with a specific other player.

Make this knowledge as obvious as possible, especially when it has the potential to disrupt gameplay for the unaware. For example, "innocent" *Ultima Online* players are warned of the impending arrival of a horde of evil player-killers by their unmistakable red screen-names.

Freedom to Define Range of Partners

It should be obvious that the nature of interaction depends upon knowledge of one's partner (or, to be more precise, one's interpretation of a virtual identity). Communicating with an old friend follows conventions that would seem out of place when dealing with a total stranger. Players should therefore have a possibility to define a potential audience for their actions according to their preferred interaction patterns. There should be a recognizable, definable difference between "macro community," "micro community," and "friends." The macro community could be defined as the entire range of potential partners (in extreme cases, the entire population of the Internet), and the micro community would be restricted to a game's active player audience. Micro communities, which meet on specific game-related Web sites, message-boards, and the like, are the target for certain intentions and patterns: discussions, exchanges of news and opinions, etc. "Friends" would mean players whose goals, personalities, and ways of playing the game are known and acceptable to the player; for example, members of a shared guild or clan, players on one's buddy-list, etc. Figure 4.5.2 illustrates this concept.

Persistence

The more a player can interact with others within the same context over time, and the more persistent an interaction pattern is, the more meaningful it can become. Actions and reactions are then not only based upon the immediate past, but can result from a shared history.

Persistent human–human interactivity allows players to establish reputations (and their consequences). It forms the basis for such complex behaviors as triumph, trust, competition, betrayal, and cooperation. Seen this way, a solid, well-supported and large game community is one way to make every MOCG a "persistent online world," regardless of whether it is actually intended as such.

Interaction Channels

Each type of human–human interaction is most appropriate, familiar, or effective in a specific context. Just as real-life people can choose from multiple methods of communication (telephone calls, letters, email, public forums, etc.), the player in a MOCG should be able to select how they wish to interact with others. Posting to a public message board satisfies other needs more than a private real-time player-to-player chat.

It is imperative that all of these channels be immediately accessible from within the game's context. Situations in which players must rely on outside tools to satisfy

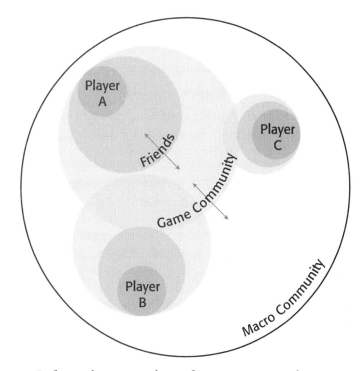

FIGURE 4.5.2 *Defining the range and size of communities according to certain interactivity patterns and purposes.*

these needs interrupt the interactivity flow, break suspension of disbelief, and make role-playing more awkward.

Besides the obvious technology-based channels, a game should provide ways to interact with other players in more subtle ways. A player should be able to initiate (consciously or unconsciously) feedback and reaction in the form of anxiety, happiness, feeling of safety, glory, shame, desire for revenge, and the like. These "higher levels of communication" can be implemented with body language and a multitude of other audio-visual cues (clothing changes, graffiti, etc.)

Game Environment

In real life, architecture and urban design are both predictors and sources of influence when it comes to the behavior of people. Entering a cathedral denotes a certain intention and defines the general parameters of what can be expected from other people within that environment. This holds true for "cyber-architecture" as well. It is thus important that players be able to establish connections between the "messages" given by the environment and the nature of human–human interactivity expected within.

Further, players need a way to communicate environmental cues to others. For example, if players need to define private areas within the virtual space for specific individual purposes, you may want to represent them as houses or guarded conference rooms. The more natural the association between real-world and game-world concepts, the more comfortable your players will be.

Interactivity through Game Characters

The player character (whether a simple screen name or a graphical avatar) is the most important communication "tool" within a game: it is the basis for the player's self-identification, as well as for other players' behavior. Remember that others will base their decisions upon a character's identification and the resulting interpretation. In order to allow such identification, a player should have opportunities to give and define cues through his game character. At the moment giving these cues is mainly dependent from a broad range of technology-driven design techniques, like character-specific graphics or audio a player can choose from and attach to the character.

Another way to do it is to provide a large number of stereotypical characters as a basis from which the player can build a unique persona. Such stereotypes immediately communicate not only appearance, but also an expectation of behavior as well. This enables players to quickly establish character-behavior connections, which are an important aspect of human–human interactivity.

A character seen as one's personal representative should further be as persistent as possible. Giving players reasons to play the game regularly with the same character could result in very unique and strong player character relationships. Persistent characters should establish their own virtual reputations within the community, which could further influence decision-making.

Human–Content Interactivity

The interaction patterns within the human–content dimension treat the players' interaction with the media, which in this case is the game, and with the contents that it presents.

Interactivity with Game Characters

A player's character is the very special part of a game's content that he can refer to over a long period of time, independent of any real-life temporal or spatial constraints. This unique game entity can evoke personal reactions toward the content, by means of emotional responses, internal associations, and experienced real-life correlations. Therefore, it should be stressed again how important it is to give players as much freedom as possible to define their game character, be it visually or behaviorally, according to how they want other players (and nonplayer characters [NPCs]) to perceive them.

Additionally, game characters can be seen as a very special type of interface element. As a continuous link between the game and the player, a character provides an effective way to direct certain commands and intentions, and it can also act as a mirror of the whole game and as a communication channel for the game to inform a player about changes in its state. For example, the hero's face in *Doom*'s user interface bar and the aspect of the player's creature in *Black and White* become a visual reference of the game's state as a result of the player's in-game actions.

Abstraction

Interactivity with the game and its content is absolutely impossible if the player does not "understand" the game. Understanding does not only mean knowledge of the rules: it also requires comprehension of the game's inner workings. What has to be done to reach this goal? What immediate and long-term consequences could such and such an action entail?

One way to provide understanding of complex systems is through *abstraction*. Again, a player's character, seen as a mirror of game-world conditions, provides much of this abstraction. NPC reactions to player actions, changes in lighting and music, and a host of other cues can also inform the player in subtle ways and allow a more diversified understanding of the game's underlying concepts.

Personalization

Besides visual or control personalization, a game should also provide players with ways to choose from a broad spectrum of goals, methods and purposes. Customizing the game according to playing styles creates tremendous replay value and allows vastly different players to enjoy the same game in their own unique ways. The fantasy role-playing game genre embodies this concept: a warrior must think and act differently from playing a wizard, and choosing one character type over the other leads to a different game experience. Other games, such as Bungie's *Halo*, combine totally different experiences even within a single action. While riding a military vehicle, for example, a player can either take over the controls and play the game like a simulator, or leave the driving to the machine (or a teammate) and handle the vehicle's cannons and rockets instead.

Game Atmosphere

It is obviously important to give players a clear idea of what they are expected to do within the game, and to do it immediately.

In MOCG, "content" is largely defined by the players dynamically, through their actions and behaviors, rather than by a fixed storyline. It is therefore the task of the game to communicate its purpose and nature to the player through atmospheric cues. These cues should address as many human senses as possible: visual, auditory, tactile, etc., and they must be both immediate and unmistakable. Peaceful areas where player-killing is forbidden should, for instance, clearly communicate their nature through appropriate colors, shapes, animations, sounds, and so on.

Atmospheric cues allow the players to understand interaction expectations within an environment. They are the basis for a player's decision to be part of the interaction process or to stay out.

Purpose of Play

We have already discussed the importance of a player's purpose and intentions. However, while some purposes are specific to a single game, game-playing style, or design, there is one global purpose that is always the same: the purpose of play.

Designing interactivity between a media and a user requires understanding *why* a person uses the media. Why in general do people play? Make sure that your game correlates to its users' intentions, whether they be learning, self-education, socialization, competition, self-actualization, or one of the many other reasons why human beings need to play.

Content Creation

Any discussion of human–content interactivity must also cover direct interaction with the game's content –visuals, sound, animation, AI, story, etc.

Players should be allowed to create new content, and modify or expand existing parts of the game, as easily and quickly as possible. In order to make the game truly their own, they need tools and interfaces to manifest their individual visions and intentions directly within the game. The popularity of public level editors, texturing tools, and public SDKs available for more and more games should demonstrate the importance of this collaborative content creation.

Further, it is essential to provide easy ways for players to share their content with each other, whether through server space to upload new content, or by giving active support to fan Web sites, or even by integrating player-submitted designs and creations into the game itself. This way, initial human–content interactivity could lead to further very unique subsets of human–human interactivity.

Conclusion

Interactivity in computer games is certainly a complex concept, and much more than the sum of all the patterns presented above. The list of what could influence a player's experience is endless, and new ideas, as well as any feedback or critique, would be highly appreciated by the author.

Hopefully, the approach presented in this article will provide a new perspective of interactivity and serve as a basis for a discussion of its role in computer games.

Bibliography

[Bartle90] Bartle, R., "Interactive Multi-User Computer Games." Available online: ftp://ftp.lambda.moo.mud.org/pub/MOO/papers/mudreport.txt, 1990.

[Bernier00] Bernier, Y.W., "Half-Life and Team Fortress Networking: Closing the Loop on Scalable Network Gaming Backend Services," *Proceedings of the 2000 Game Developers Conference*, May 2000.

[Bruckman92] Bruckman, A., "Identity Workshops: Emergent Social and Psychological Phenomena in Text-Based Virtual Reality." Available online: ftp://ftp.cc.gatech.edu/pub/people/asb/papers/identity-workshop.ps, 1992.

[Crawford00] Crawford, C., "Understanding Interactivity," n.p., 2000.

[Curtis92] Curtis, P., "Mudding: Social Phenomena in Text-Based Virtual Realities," *Proceedings of DIAC 1992*, Available online: ftp://parcftp.xerox.com/pub/M00/papers/DIAC92.txt, 1992.

[Evans01] Evans, R., "The Future of AI in Games: A Personal View," *Game Developer Magazine* (August 2001): pp. 46–49. [Huizinga50] Huizinga, J., *Homo Ludens: A Study of the Play-Element in Culture,* Beacon Press, 1950.

[Laurel93] Laurel, B., *Computers as Theatre,* Addison-Wesley, 1993.

[Michael02] Michael, D., "Designing for Online Community," *Game Design Perspectives*, Charles River Media, 2002.

[Shneiderman98] Shneiderman, B., *Designing the User Interface,* Addison-Wesley, 1998.

[Sims97] Sims, R., "Interactivity: A Forgotten Art?" *Computers in Human Behaviour,* no. 3 (1997).

[Turkle95] Turkle, S., *Life on the Screen,* Simon & Schuster, 1995.

[Watzlawick67] Watzlawick, P., et al, *Pragmatics of Human Communication: A Study of Interactional Patterns, Pathologies, and Paradoxes,* W.W. Norton, 1967.

[Wilson93] Wilson, S., "The Aesthetics and Practice of Designing Interactive Computer Events," *Visual Proceedings Art Show Catalog* (SIGGRAPH 1993).

Special Issues in Multiplayer Game Design

Joe Hitchens

joe@sleepless.com

If you choose to design a game in which two or more humans can play together, you will design what is commonly described in the computer game industry as a *multiplayer game*. In most cases, a multiplayer game also implies that the players will each have their own computer or console, and that the two machines are connected by way of a networking system: phone lines, a local-area network, the Internet, or wireless technology.

You will find a number of special issues that arise when you attempt multiplayer game design., The most obvious issue is that the project is much bigger, which means it will take longer to design and create,. more people to design and develop it, draw on many fields of expertise, and have more problems that must be dealt with. It will blossom before your eyes into something far, far bigger, grander and more complex than what you imagined.

This particular article, however, will avoid the technical issues that make a multiplayer game unique, and instead focus on some of the nontechnical issues, which are at least as important and can have as big an effect on the way your game works and is perceived by the player.

You might imagine a multiplayer game as similar to a single-player game, but with the added feature that two or more people can play at the same time and play against each other instead of an AI. The reality will probably be very different. When you put one human being with another, in any fashion, all sorts of wonderful and not so wonderful things begin to happen.

Chatting and Censorship

Put people together and they will communicate—in many different ways. Sometimes we speak, sometimes we act, sometimes we flee, and sometimes we behead and steal gold pieces. It all depends on who we are and what we want.

Most current multiplayer games will include some form of *chat* feature. Chat features are usually presented in the game in two rectangles: one a text entry box in which a player can type a message, and another, larger box that prints the text of message and those of the other players as they are entered. Some games modify this input mechanism by showing the messages that a player sends in a word balloon over the head of his avatar, if he has one. Some games even go so far as to digitize the player's actual voice and send it across the network to be played back on the other player's speakers.

Regardless of how it is done, the intent is the same; to allow players to interact verbally in addition to any other types of interaction that are provided in the game, such as armed combat (always an exciting form of communication).

Attempting Censorship

Chatting, however, means that a player uses words, and as we all know, the way words are perceived varies enormously based on the perceiver. What may be a common verb to some may be a repulsive obscenity to others. So what do you as the designer do if your game is intended for a wide audience?

You might think the answer is simple? You could censor everything that is said, but creating a list of undesirable words and replacing them with "****" whenever they are used

However, if a game is going to give a player the freedom to say anything to another player, you will find many people who do not care to have their words censored.

Let's say that you decide loss of freedom of speech is a small price to pay to avoid having some of your players offend others. Who is going to decide what is offensive and what is not? Remember, you will be dealing with real people, which means that this will be as difficult as it would if you were trying to compile a list of offensive words that should not be spoken at a business meeting. How large should the list be? Should you include every possible offensive word that everyone can think of?

Further, assume you managed to compile a list of undesirable words. If it is large, it can actually cause your game to slow, because the game's the engine now must look up every word each player uses each time they use it. And what about the time and money that will have to be spent to compile and maintain this list?

For the sake of argument, let's suppose that the word "macrohard" is universally recognized as unspeakable profanity. You could easily filter out that word and replace it with "****". But as soon as someone discovered what was happening to their chat entries, they would just type "macro-hard" instead. Or macrohaurd. Or macr0h@rd. Obviously, the problem of trying to truly eradicate a specific word is extremely difficult, arguably impossible.

Also, remember that there can be an infinite number of ways that one person can offend another without using any specific words that an ordinary person might consider offensive.

If the decision is made to attempt some form of censorship, consider implementing a voting mechanism, through which people who collect many "gag" votes are muted for 24 hours. Alternatively, you might choose to filter out a few of the most commonly accepted undesirable words, so that casual use would catch most of them. But beyond that, you cannot realistically much from a technical standpoint. Consider the problems of chats a social or community issue that is best handled in the same way you will handle other such issues.

Lobbies

A *lobby* is the part of a multiplayer game that facilitates the process of bringing two or more people together into a single game. The lobby mechanism is unique to multiplayer games, and so, for many, is a very new and unexplored territory.

A good lobby, or even a bad lobby for that matter, can easily account for a third of the game development effort. Do not dismiss the lobby as irrelevant. Not only does it demand a good design and much work, but it will be the first thing that players see of your game. In fact, they could be spending as much (or more) time in the lobby as in the actual game. The lobby is also the part of multiplayer games that is least understood, and most often overlooked or ignored until late in the project, even though it is poised to benefit the game greatly.

Most lobbies tend to be dull in comparison to the actual game. You might see a positively breathtaking real-time 3D world preceded by a drab, flat, quiet, boring, and business-like lobby. Why? Why must the lobby be dull, especially if it will unavoidably account for a lot of your development effort? If you are going to spend time and energy on that lobby, and people will spend much of the game time in it, then it seems perfectly sensible to make it as interesting and entertaining as the game. Granted, there may be some games in which the concept of the lobby is at odds with the experience itself, and so you may want to keep the two as separate as possible, but that is a very rare case.

Here is one idea. In a top-down real-time strategy game, why not use the game's own display engine to present a smaller world, perhaps a little town or clearing, where the players will appear when they connect to your game server? They can then mill about in the town, speak with each other, or challenge other players in full avatar form. If your lobby plans call for any player to be able to create a new game, then allow them to do so and have the new, unfilled game be represented by a glowing portal in the town square. If the new game has a limit of five players, then that portal can easily close once five people have crossed it, at which point the players are transported to the newly created game world.

At the very least, consider adding as much of the game's atmosphere as possible to the lobby, in the form of graphics, custom fonts, sound effects, and so forth, in order to ease the transition of the players into the game world.

Remember that the key function of a lobby is to provide players with a method of choosing who is going to play and on which teams. There should be endless imaginative ways that this can be accomplished without resorting to a dull list of nicknames with a scrollbar and a Shift-click interface.

Community

Any reasonably successful multiplayer game will develop a *community* around it. This is to be expected, because such games involve many people with common interests interact with one another. Also to be expected are the same challenges found in any other kind of community. People will do what all people do when they come together: talk, trade, fight, behave insensitively, flirt and fall in love, make friends, and develop an attachment and loyalty to their community.

Unfortunately, interacting with other people through a computer game possesses many drawbacks. Compared with the real world, a game world is a poor medium for communication. For example, in the game world, where players may never physically meet, they cannot read each other's facial expressions or body language, and so feelings inadvertently may be hurt. Unfortunately, this distancing also can bring out the worst in some people: the insulation via distance and technology invariably results in pointless abuse or base behavior. It is a good idea to provide players with the ability to *ignore* abusive players when necessary; this ability will allow them to tune out, at least to some extent, someone who might be ruining the experience for them.

In some ways, however, the insulation provided by the game medium can be beneficial. This distancing can allow players to more easily suspend disbelief and effectively become immersed in the game world. For example, it is much easier to believe that Sir Valiant DarkMoon is a towering figure with nerves of steel and a gallant manner if you do not know that in reality, he is small-statured Howard L. Obermuckle, balding mail clerk.

Protecting Community

One downside to anonymity in multiplayer games is the very real danger to innocent people, especially children. This issue is serious, and, if addressed properly, could mean an added operational cost for your game. You might have to hire people to monitor the game environment at all times and to use their judgment to ensure that vulnerable players are not abused or endangered.

The Ultimate Community

Cybersex is real, and, unfortunately, very common. Even if such a thing seems impossible, people will somehow find away around your game to participate in such activities.

If your game is a two-player game—even something as innocuous as checkers, for example—and provides a private chat room, where only the two players can read what is said, you have provided an opportunity for cybersex

Cybersex can be a serious issue for game developers—a private room can provide an effective way for online predators to search out victims, which is a good reason to consider avoiding private chat rooms. However, if your game is sex-related you absolutely must provide private rooms for the patrons.

User-Supplied Content

User-supplied content is another potential avenue of offense between players. For example, you might wish to allow your players to come up with their own icons, or 3D models of their characters, and allow them to upload them so that they can share their creativity. However, sooner or later, unfortunately, someone will decide they have to be outrageous. If nothing else, allowing user-supplied content will involve more development time to create the software to support it, and additional operation costs because you will probably have to require that all content be screened before being allowed into the game.

Persistence

In general, a multiplayer game will differ from a single-player game title by having the simultaneously good and bad quality of *persistence*. The game is absolutely fabulous—because it never really ends. It is also a nightmare—because it never really ends.

The game project itself may never end, either. Your team may look forward to the day when they can call the project complete, but usually, multiplayer gaming contains many ongoing operational costs and requirements. The game will probably run on a server, which must be constantly maintained and administered. And the user base will need to be taken care of: designers must handle complaints about other users' behavior, software failures, etc.

However, persistence can also be beneficial. Many large companies invest heavily in massively multiplayer, persistent worlds, with communities so large, rich, and vibrant, that people are willing to pay a high monthly fee for years so that they can live and play in these game worlds. There is limitless potential there from the marketing standpoint alone.

Cheating

Cheating is a very big issue in multiplayer games. Imagine that you have spent several months building a powerful character by conquering every obstacle, exploring every cave and castle, and building strong ties with neighboring kingdoms. Now, imagine that a 10-year-old who obtained a hacked copy of the game from his friend pops in and obliterates you and your war party with one swing of his multiply enchanted, 999,000,000th level Wand o' Death, after which the computer informs you that your character has been killed and can never be resurrected.

What can you as a designer do about such issues? There are several ways to make cheating virtually impossible, but they require careful planning in the game design stage, and even more care when the precautions are implemented by the programmers. There will, in most cases, be problems with anti-cheating methods that you will have to either design around or let go.

Server-Side and Client-Side Games

If the game world is run entirely on the server side, and the client program functions only as an input/output device (sending player input to the server, and displaying the results of their actions back to them), you will have an arrangement that is *potentially* cheat-proof. That does not mean it *will* be cheat-proof, only that it is theoretically possible to make it cheat-proof.

On the other hand, if your game functions as, in essence, multiple independent games, with a very small server side that functions only to transmit data between computers, and the client applications themselves are in charge of deciding the real state of the world, then you are probably going to have cheating problems.

Unfortunately, the server-side arrangement will be inherently less responsive to game changes. If every decision about the state of the world must be made on the server side, it will take time for actions to be transmitted to the server and the results returned. However, the amount of sluggishness in this system is largely dependent on your game design. For a turn-based game, such as a card game or board game, the server-side arrangement will likely pose no problems at all. But a 3D first-person shooter with flying bullets and rapid character direction change can be almost impossible to manage.

Designing Against Cheaters

If cheating is a big issue for your game, then consider your game's features very carefully. For example, always tyro avoid a game world in which things *accelerate* or *decelerate* rapidly. An object that moves fast but predictably is manageable, one that moves fast *and* changes velocity abruptly is not. Imagine a game in which a spaceship can move rapidly through space then collide with an asteroid and stop or bounce off in a new, random direction. The time scale on which these changes in velocity occur is much too close to the time scale on which updates about the ship's position travels from computer to computer. The result will be disagreement between the various computers as to where that ship really is at any given moment.

What often happens is that development will begin on a fast-action, real-time game that contains many of these *bad* features, and because the game must be completed somehow, the client software must be used to make certain decisions about the state of the world; otherwise, the game simply will not work. For example, if the client portion of a game tracks its own health level and simply transmits the information to the other players' machines, it might work well at first. But sooner or later, Hacker Jimmy will find out the location of that variable in the EXE file and modify the game so that his health level never decreases. This hack results in computers engaging in a "Bang! You're dead!"/"No, I'm not!" conversation.

A game such as a naval battle simulation is far more friendly to the anti-cheating designer. In this kind of game, ships move and change direction very slowly compared with the size of the game world, which allows the game server to detect discrepancies between what the client applications claim to do and what is actually feasible within the game rules.

The following is a simplistic list of genres, listing in descending order games that will be easiest to implement as multiplayer games.

- Turn-based card and board style games.
- Turn-based strategy games.
- Real-time strategy games
- Real-time action games.

The first games will have the fewest added costs and headaches, and will probably be the most successful or true to their designs when completed. The last genres are those that will have difficult and expensive technical problems and are least likely to be successful as multiplayer games.

Dealing with cheating can consume a tremendous amount of the development effort. Consider designing a different style of game if the genre you have chosen is one that is especially difficult to fit within the multiplayer paradigm; you will save yourself many headaches this way.

Conclusion

Consider carefully your decision to design a multiplayer game. Is your idea compatible with a multiplayer game? Do you have enough money in your budget to pay for the added development costs? Will the game be able to pay for itself and all the supporting infrastructure once it is published or deployed? Will the multiplayer feature improve your game, or could it be just as fun and profitable if it were a single-player game?

If you are just beginning to design multiplayer games, your first attempt should be kept very simple—problems can multiply quickly. Single-player game projects have the benefit (or drawback, depending on how you look at it), of *ending*. There is usually a point where everyone involved can stop detach themselves emotionally from it, and move onto something new. You will find that multiplayer games tend not to have such concrete closure.

On the other hand, a good multiplayer game will have a much longer lifespan than a typical single-player game. You can expect people to play your game for a very long time, if it is good. Eventually, they may even outlast *you*.

Last, if you can bring a good multiplayer game into the world, you will gain a certain deeper satisfaction than you might get from any other kind of game. When it is done, just log in from time to time and type: "Hello everyone. I created this game. Do you like it?"

4.7

Online Persistence in Game Design

Drew Sikora

gaiiden@hotmail.com

Now that the Internet has successfully permeated our society and brought high bandwidth with it, online gaming is quickly picking up speed. Whereas online functionality was once largely conceived as a mere add-on designed to extend value beyond the single-player experience, there are now many high-profile games that exist only in network space. These massively multiplayer online games are setting themselves up to be the future of gaming, and one of the major deciding factors of their ultimate success will be how well they handle the issue of *online persistence*: the fact that, while players come and go, the game world remains.

Online Persistence Explained

In the context of an online game world, *persistence* has two meanings. First, the *game world itself* is referred to as being persistent, meaning that even when the player is logged off, the world continues to exist. Obviously this must be true so that other players can occupy the game world, but even if no players are logged in at any given time, the world remains nonetheless and any actions (the passage of time, for instance) will continue with or without human intervention. This feature is one of the many attractions of massively multiplayer online gaming, but it can either enhance or hinder gameplay, depending on the genre of the game, which will be discussed later.

Second, persistence can refer to the ability of the *player* to remain active in the game world at all times. To date, there is no way for a human character to fully persist in an online game world–it simply is not feasible. People have lives to live, food to eat, jobs to go to, appointments to keep, etc, and cannot spend all of their time in front of their computers. Therefore, designers of an online game must take into account the fact that players will not always be active in the game world, and find ways to ensure that their characters, armies, castles, and countries will not be destroyed the moment they log off. However, while one can *realize* the existence of this problem, finding an appropriate way to solve it is far from obvious.

Online persistence (which, from here on will refer to the player) presents many design issues that need to be overcome. What will become of the player's avatar when she is offline? Will the absence of the player affect the game? Will the absence of the player affect other players? Can the player lose anything while offline? Can the player *die* while offline? These are just a few examples; depending on the type of game there can be many more, and all must be answered in order to maintain clean gameplay.

Online Persistence and the Genres

Online persistence directly influences every aspect of a game, including its most basic design issues. For example, an action game should be fast-paced with little puzzle solving and many targets to shoot at. A strategy game must be well balanced and contain a good mix of manageable units. A role-playing game (RPG) needs a robust skill system and engaging storyline. These are the normal design issues. If we take one, say *story*, and add online persistence, the usual solutions fall apart, as we will discuss in the next section.

Role-Playing Games

The role-playing genre is the one least affected by online persistence. Players come and go, but this fact affects the game world very little. Community interaction, while valuable, is also not an absolute requirement in role-playing games: players can just as easily play on their own as they can team up with others.

Because the role-playing genre relies mainly on skill-based systems, a character does not have to be constantly online. Skills are intangible, and cannot be stolen. A player can log off for a while, and her character will not have changed by the time she returns. This is not to say that nothing *can* happen to the player's character while the player is offline, as we will discuss later.

Also, most role-playing games rely on *quests* that send the player off to some far corner of the world in order to defeat a monster or recover a mythical item. These quests, which the player can use to enhance existing skills and gain new ones, do not require the player to complete them in a set period of time. True, if other players are aiming for the same goal and the quest's objective is one that does not "re-spawn" after a certain time, then, of course, time is of the essence. However, solitary quests usually do not depend on whether the player is there or not. The player logs off, logs back on, and continues. Other players may not notice or even care–they do not require other people to remain online. In role-playing there is no real "opponent," except for players who like to fight other people's characters to gain experience points. This changes, however, when we look at action games.

Action Games

Action games, relative to our discussion, fall between strategy games and RPGs. Action-based massively multiplayer online games today consist of team environments, which usually do not require a large number of people to be online at the same time. However, the scalability of the game relies on its design.

In the subscription-based version of Microsoft's *Allegiance*, players form teams that exist in a persistent world. There is never any guarantee that the entire team will be assembled at any given time; however, an outnumbered team is clearly vulnerable. This problem can be countered in two ways, only one of which is a desirable solution.

The wrong way for players to solve this problem is to create huge teams so that their side will always have enough players online at any given time, no matter what happens. Diversity is lost as players crowd to one team or the other. Also, many people are against the idea of forming overly large groups, because getting to know everyone and working together becomes increasingly difficult as the team grows. Finally, the responsibility for working around design issues should never come to rest on the players, as it does in this case.

The correct way to handle such a problem is to provide scalable targets. Let us suppose that, on a certain day, only six members of a team of 12 are online. Instead of attacking a space station or other large object, they could choose to harass the enemy's mining operations or disrupt a small outpost. The point here is that the game provides smaller targets for smaller groups, while rewarding larger groups with the ability to take on larger targets. This means that, whatever the size of the group, there will always be something for them to do. This is good game design with relation to online persistence.

Strategy Games

Strategy games are definitely the games most affected by online persistence. This is simply because strategy games consist of warfare, and each player has a defined opponent. Whether or not there is more than one opponent does not matter. The point is that only *one* person is in charge of his or her units, and when that player leaves, then what?

Strategy games is the only genre in which the absence of a player will affect everyone else in the game. All other players will know that the player has gone, and this information is important because other players may now be allowed access to her base or have relief from constant bombardment from her units. And what is to be done with the player's resources when she is not there?

Planning for a player's discontinued existence, however temporary, is not easy. Will the computer control his assets and defend his bases against an onslaught? Will all his units return to his main base and all his resources go into a lockdown that cannot be broken by other players? Will the game allow the player to turn control over to an ally?

Many people would argue against the computer-controlled solution, saying it would take up server resources. True, but this is not really an issue if the game world is sized to handle it. The lockdown solution also has its downside. Not only will the game flow seem interrupted by inert bases, but it may prompt other users to go offline and return later, still fresh and new, at a time when everyone else has suffered debilitating casualties. This problem can be solved by allowing bases to be attacked (and defended automatically), or by a time-based unit and structure deterioration mechanism, perhaps as an effect of the lockdown shield. Finally, turning control over to another player has its benefits, such as having a human in command, but this solution does not prevent that player from logging off as well.

Perhaps the best solution to the problem of persistence in a strategy game would be to permit some sort of unofficial team play, for example by houses, tribes, or factions. Factions can allow for the sharing of resources between members; if each member of the faction contributes a certain share of the resources she gains (possibly even all of them) to a central pool, then the absence of players for an extended period of time would have a considerable affect on the faction's economy. Furthermore, when a player is offline, the rest of the faction can contribute resources to defend the base of that player, as well as controlling any units that player may have. Factions also create a much broader definition of the term "enemy." Instead of player against player, it is faction against faction, which means that a few players logged off still leaves others to fight groups of similar size.

Strategy games may have to go the way of the action genre in promoting team-based play in order to provide a viable long-term multiplayer gaming experience. We must also keep in mind the other ways a faction-based game can help us: for example, by allowing people to become double-agents and work for an enemy, turn coat and side with a new faction, or break off and form a whole new faction of their own. Such elements would provide a richer gameplay and still maintain the structure that would allow the game to work online.

Online Persistence and the Story

Although strategy games suffer from online persistence, at least they have a chance. However, the massively multiplayer online adventure game may not have as much hope.

The adventure game possesses one unique aspect not shared by any other genre—whether online or offline, it must have a story. The *story* is the backbone of the adventure game. Unlike the role-playing game, which can fall back on its skill system and promote character improvement over plot, the adventure game is not so lucky. Probably the closest thing to an alternative to story as a gameplay driver in the adventure game (where the character is more or less static) is item trading. However, it is difficult to imagine how a game based exclusively on item trading could still qualify as an adventure.

Is it impossible to create a story because of online persistence? The answer is no, but a classic linear story clearly will not work. First, it would seem awkward to the player for a story to advance while he or she is not there to witness it. A news system would have to be created to inform players who have been away of the latest happenings in the game world. Then, you must to determine what advantages go to the players who are actually advancing the story, while others sit by and watch, waiting to pounce on the treasure once the enemy is defeated. In short, not only must the designer worry about the *way* the story is carried out, but he must also monitor *who* carries it out. In other words: who is the story's main character? And who is the villain?

Obviously, these activities would overwhelm even the most ambitious design team, so any form of online storytelling would have to seriously branch away from the norm. One solution would be to make both the main character and the villain into nonplayer characters (NPCs), and have the players take on supporting roles on either side. The overall story would then advance according to an aggregate of the players' performances.

Let's look at a quick illustration of this solution. Suppose we have a game set in a solar system with about six to nine planets. Each planet has its own tribal race, and each tribe has its own superweapon that has been hidden since time immemorial, when the races threatened to destroy each other until a group of extra-solar aliens imposed a peaceful solution. Millennia later the sparks flame again and the race is on to recover the superweapons and wipe everyone else out. The game is already shaping up to be a great squad-based shooter, but then we throw in the story, which is the history of each tribe and how they are intertwined with the other tribes. This element of story will mean that tribes must explore the planets of other tribes to find the answers they seek, which leads to the game's fighting.

Our task here is much easier thanks to the squad-based gameplay, which means that every member of a tribe will be after the same goal. Greedy bystanders will not be an issue, as the entire tribe will benefit from any discoveries. The story also rids the game of bystanders on the grand scale, meaning no tribe can watch and wait for the other tribes to uncover new information, because each tribe has their own story to follow (finding the weapon) within the larger overall story (the past of all the tribes together and the use of the weapons). There is also no main character to the story, or a villain—just tribal warfare. So already we have simplified the problems down to one: informing offline players of what they missed while they were away. This is easy to solve with a tribal newsletter or other information source somewhere in the tribe headquarters.

Thus, we have shown that a multiplayer adventure game is possible, even if it cannot be done with traditional storytelling where there is a main character, villain, etc.

Online Persistence As Gameplay

So far, we have been discussing the negative aspects online persistence and ways in which it hinders gameplay. Now, let's see how it could be used to complement the gameplay. Instead of planning against the player's absence, we will be looking at ways to take advantage of it.

Role-Playing Games

A persistent RPG may allow characters to rest and slowly regain any drained powers or health while the players are offline. Of course, some restrictions would have to apply: otherwise, players who are in the process of getting injured by monsters will simply log off, heal while the battle is put on hold, then log back in to finish the job. Two obvious ways to combat this perverse strategy: make the healing process rather slow, so that it would take at least a day or two of inactivity for the player to regain all health and power, or force the player to travel to the closest inn or tavern and pay a fee for a bed. Both options are valid; however, the second is reminiscent of the save points in console games, which not all players appreciate.

Strategy Games

A persistent strategy game could allow people to try to sneak into the bases of opponents and steal technology while they are logged off. These stealth commando raids would cost a lot, but while they could take place at any time, they would have a slightly better chance of succeeding when the victim is logged off.

To protect himself against raids, a player could buy secure installations and automated defenses, or hire guards or mercenaries to protect his bases. (An interesting side effect of the mercenary option is that their salaries will drain the treasuries of absent players faster.)

Few games focus on defense or the guarding of secrets, instead relying on constant attacks. That may work well for traditional online games, but the point of a persistent world is that games are able to last longer. Therefore, the guarding of researched technology and other assets with long-term value would be an interesting addition to gameplay.

Action Games

Using online persistence as a gameplay element in action games could provide an alternative to the scalable targets we proposed for smaller teams.

If, for whatever reason, a game concept could not support scalable targets, we could give each team a central power source from which each player could draw as required. This power would help them shoot better, run faster, protect themselves more effectively, and so forth. The more players who are online, the more the power source must divide its energy, and the less power boost each individual player on the team gets. On the other hand, if only one player from the team is online, then he gets the full boost from the power source, allowing this one person to take on many opponents.

With further checks and balances, this power source could be designed as a workable game element, and allow an even confrontation between teams of differing sizes.

Overall

Using online persistence as a gameplay element has its pros and cons and works better in some genres than others. This brief section has skimmed the surface of what might work using the benefits of online persistence for several gameplay genres. Remember that online persistence is not a total hindrance, and can be utilized as part of the game itself.

Solution to Online Persistence

Even if we cannot do away with online persistence altogether , we can strive to tone it down, and make it less of an issue. Fortunately, wireless devices may provide us with an attractive solution.

Slowly but surely, the Internet is becoming more and more important to daily life, and the number of online-enabled devices is quickly growing. Today, Internet access is available through cell phones, laptop computers, and personal digital assistants (PDAs), to name but a few. Who knows what else we will have at our disposal in the future? Sooner or later, it will be a trivial matter to connect to the Internet anywhere, anytime.

Computing power is increasing rapidly, but today most PDAs and cell phones are weak when compared to laptops and desktops. Therefore, functionality on these devices will likely be more limited.

For example, when a player logs off from his desktop computer, an AI routine takes over his avatar. The player then accesses a simpler game client on his cell phone, and uses it to send high-level commands to the AI. In a role-playing environment, the player can still walk around and chat with other players, but the AI will take care of the intricacies of battle if the need arises. In a strategy game, the AI could simply warn the player that he is under attack and give him time to take log back in with his computer (or ask an ally for help) before the battle begins.

As the power of portable devices increases, players will no doubt be able to do more than what we have outlined above. Further, in addition to regular handhelds, other common household appliances such as telephones, fax machines, and wireless email machines are all viable methods of informing the player of something happening to him while he is not in the game. *Majestic*, a game wrought in conspiracy that calls you, talks to you on instant messenger, faxes you, emails you, and uses Internet sites to move the story along, broke new ground in this direction. Imagine waking up in the middle of the night to a phone call from a shaky voice saying: "They're on to me!" and asking for help?

Conclusion

We have discussed the many aspects of online persistence, as well as the fact that, although the problems of online persistence can be somewhat negated, it will always be an issue in the design of massively multiplayer online games. We have also realized that, while it is easy to diagnose the problems associated with online persistence, it is far more difficult to solve them. And when it comes to solving them, you must remember that the solutions must fit the gameplay.

The world of massively multiplayer online persistent games is definitely one worth exploring, and solving the problems of online persistence is like stamping your ticket to this intriguing frontier.

P A R T

5

CHARACTERS AND STORYTELLING

5.0

Introduction

Since the dawn of time, human beings have entertained each other, transmitted their knowledge and culture, and immortalized their accomplishments in stories. Storytelling may even predate the invention of language, as hinted by prehistoric paintings found on cave walls in Western Europe.

In the game industry, however, a sometimes acrimonious debate rages as to whether storytelling enhances—or is even compatible with—gameplay. This is a futile controversy: even if a game does not feature an explicit plot line, nothing prevents players from anthropomorphizing events and making up their own implicit story to describe their experiences. An example of this is post-mission chat sessions, often lasting much longer than the gameplay itself, that regularly follow death-matches. And of course, the opposite is just as true: in many cases, players can ignore a game's story line without detracting from their enjoyment.

This section of the book focuses on techniques to enhance explicit stories; for the implicit kind, rich gameplay and a lively player are the only prerequisites.

Stories for Games and Linear Media

Make no mistake: writers who create traditional linear entertainment and writer/designers who plot stories for their games have very different jobs on their hands. As the many Hollywood studios that tried (and failed) in the mid 1990s to make interactive stories out of screenplays deemed too weak for direct-to-video movies discovered, there is more to interactive entertainment than a few branching story lines.

The key differences between linear and non-linear media, from a storytelling standpoint, include ownership of the main character, point of view, and structure.

Character Ownership

In linear media, the viewer watches the main character from outside. While the writer may try to instill a sense of identification with his hero in the customer, the protagonist's decisions are still his or her own. In fact, one of the most important characterization devices in the writer's toolbox is the moment of enlightenment, where the hero changes in fundamental ways as a result of a life-changing event.

In a game, however, this is not possible, because the player *is* the main character. If Anakin Skywalker had been a game character, he could never have decided to surrender to the Dark Side and become the evil Darth Vader, because the majority of players would have rebelled at the thought of being forced to switch sides in the middle of a battle.

For similar reasons, game characters can never be saddled with tragic flaws that seal their doom. Giving a character limitations ranging in severity from ingrown toenails to a fatal reaction to kryptonite is perfectly acceptable, and should be done more often, but there must always be a way to overcome or sidestep them if the player performs admirably. That does not mean that a game with tragic undertones is impossible; secondary characters have sacrificed their lives to save the player or avenge a grievous loss in *Planetfall* and *Wing Commander II*. However, should the main character make the ultimate sacrifice to achieve resolution, it must be at the player's behest, and it should never be the only way to win.

Point of View

Because game players become their characters, game writers should confine themselves to single-person, limited point of view. This means that the player should never be shown or told anything that the character has not experienced directly.

As a consequence of this axiom, such common devices as cut-scenes in which the villain explains his devilish plans to his henchmen ought to be banned from the interactive entertainment landscape. In movies, scenes like this create dramatic tension, because *we* know that the hero *does not* know what is about to befall him. In games, no such payoff is possible, because there is no distance between player and character. It is far more effective to let the player be shocked by events as they happen to his avatar. For example, consider the reaction of the movie viewer who learns that John Nash's college roommate and secret service employment in *A Beautiful Mind* were figments of his schizophrenic imagination, or that Bruce Willis's character has been dead all along in *The Sixth Sense*.

As a rule, players should never receive any information before their characters do. This does not mean that nothing should ever happen off-camera; in fact, a friendly NPC can very well be abducted, brainwashed, and coerced into serving the evil overlord while the players wonder why their buddy has missed their appointment. Simply do not tell the players what has occurred until the friend stabs them in the back.

Beginning the Story

Contemporary commercial fiction usually begins right in the middle of the action: the hero is being chased by police, receives a crucial visitor, etc. This is necessary to hook the attention of the reader (and especially of the editor deciding whether to publish the story) at a moment's notice.

In a game, however, the player must be given a chance to learn the controls and bond with the main character before trouble begins; otherwise, the player will not care as much about what happens, and dramatic tension will be weaker than it could be.

The Middle

In linear fiction, making every scene count is a cardinal rule: anything that does not advance the plot or reveal an important aspect of a character's personality should be thrown out. However, in a game, secondary quests, red herrings, and other side issues that do not relate directly to the main plot are the best way to create the illusion of freedom and vastness.

Resolving the Story

The linear story writer's toolbox includes tragic endings, compromises, non-endings that leave the reader guessing the characters' fates, and any number of other shades of gray on the scale between total success and total failure. The writer selects the outcome that feels the most satisfactory given the situation, even if it spells disaster for the hero.

Game writers must create numerous endings, because the story's outcome will depend on player actions. Each of these endings should be equally satisfying, in the sense that the player must be able to understand the causal relationships between in-game actions and events and the ultimate result being presented. Most important, one of these alternate endings must represent total success; thus, the game writer must build a story that can logically result in both highly positive and highly negative consequences.

Settings

Many stories arise from the world in which they take place. One way to create a compelling plot line for a game is to design a world, develop its history and geography, and look at the kinds of dramatic events that could happen there—and *only* there.

For example, suppose that you are asked to design a science-fiction hunting game taking place on another planet. A serviceable design would require little more than strange animals and sophisticated weapons to capture them with. However, you could also decide to take advantage of the setting by creating a high-gravity world with a dense atmosphere—one too dense, in fact, for human lungs. Human colonies on this planet would be limited to high plateaus and mountaintops, where the thinner air would be perfect for Earthlings but insufficient for local wildlife. A hunter whose vehicle breaks down in a valley would be in jeopardy: the high gravity would cause her to tire quickly, and the slightest puncture in her protective gear would lead to oxygen poisoning. Sounds like a good premise for a game to me!

Also, make sure to exploit the setting you choose to the fullest. On a high-G planet, life forms will be sturdy, low-set, and may have many legs; your hunters will not be able to seek giraffes and giant spiders. An alien race that communicates telepathically will likely be unable to understand the concept of the radio; talking to them in outer space will pose an enormous challenge. And if nanotech allows any material to be transformed into any other, what happens to a society's economic structure?

Character Design

In many genres, the character makes the game. For example, *Tomb Raider* would not be *Tomb Raider* without Lara Croft, while extreme sports games would be much less appealing without star athletes' signature moves. The relationship is even more intimate when it comes to industry staples such as Leisure Suit Larry, Mario, and Donkey Kong.

Of course, game writers cannot spend a large amount of time exploring the depths of their characters' souls. However, it is possible to make a game character stand out in a way that is easy for the player to relate to.

Mannerisms

Consider giving your character revealing gestures, special clothing, interesting habits, or memorable sayings. Here are a few examples:

- Montgomery Burns, the evil centenarian boss on *The Simpsons*, would be much less creepy without his curved skull and characteristic hand posture.
- Rubeus Hagrid, the gamekeeper in the *Harry Potter* novels, is not average in any way at all. He is huge, has a spectacular head of hair, carries everything from magical keys to live poultry in the many pockets of his cloak, and has a tendency to speak too much, especially when he is trying to hide a secret.
- The Rock, wrestling star and actor, has built his tremendous following on a raised eyebrow and a handful of catch phrases.

For game designers, ideal ways to add depth and color to characters include:

- **Special moves:** El Kabong, equine cartoon superstar Quick Draw McGraw's swashbuckling alter ego, attacks his opponents by smashing them over the head with a guitar. Sonic, being a hedgehog, becomes invulnerable when he rolls himself into a ball.
- **Amusing idle moves:** When he is bored because the player is doing nothing, Wario juggles bombs to pass the time, while Leisure Suit Larry liked to hold his breath (and change colors accordingly) during pauses.
- **The walking cycle:** This most basic of all character actions reveals much about the underlying personalities, from the take-charge attitude of Solid Snake in *Metal Gear Solid*, to the happy-go-lucky Mario, to the quietly confident Terminator, to the not-so-quiet and not at all confident Sammy in the *Scooby Doo* cartoons.
- **Conversation styles:** This technique is easier to apply to secondary characters: a cocky villain may describe his plans in detail, with a calm and cool voice, while others may try to defuse questions with humor or irrelevant trivia. In *Star Control II*, the first alien that greets the player is a cowardly Spathi, who reveals the secret password giving access to his home world without even being questioned. By the time the conversation is over, the player knows exactly what to expect from other individuals of the same species.

Stereotypes

Make sure not to overuse characterization, though. In his famous novel *Les Misérables*, Victor Hugo recounts the life stories of several revolutionaries in great detail, over the course of several pages—and then blows them all up in an instant, without letting them do anything worthwhile. Obviously, no writer could get away with a trick like this today, much less a game designer.

With henchmen and extras, characterization is largely a waste of effort. Use stereotypes that players can recognize immediately: brawny bodyguards, ninjas dressed in black, putrefying zombies, etc. Only the characters that will interact with the player in significant, unusual fashion require any more.

Using stereotypes for your masses also reinforces, by contrast, the uniqueness of your important characters. Darth Vader is dressed in black to stand out among the hordes of white armored imperial stormtroopers, and he wears a mask and a cloak to mark his difference from the Emperor's regular officers in their classic military uniforms.

Symbolism

On occasion, a well-placed symbol can generate cognitive resonance in the player. F. Scott Fitzgerald was one of the great masters of symbolism; for example, in *The Great Gatsby*, the title character's unrequited love for the socialite Daisy is represented by a green light suspended over her mansion's dock—across the bay from Gatsby's home.

To use symbolism in your games, you might want to employ the same device in a variety of contexts. For example, the gameplay concept of "breaking a ring" might mean destroying a piece of jewelry, sacrificing one member of a company of friends, removing one of the mirrors forming a circle of light, lifting the curse forcing a fallen warrior to relive the battle that killed him every night, etc.

Character Creation Checklist

When designing a major character, err on the side of excess instead of paucity. Write down the character's life story, pet peeves, favorite activities, etc. You may not use all (or even most) of this material in the game, but the added layers of hidden detail will help you maintain self-consistency.

Here are a few questions you will want to answer for your protagonist, your antagonist, and the most important secondary characters:

- What is the first thing that people will notice when meeting this character for the first time? An unusual physical trait? An eerie laugh? A missing limb?
- What is the driving force in this character's life? A thirst for justice? Revenge? Greed? Laziness? Lechery?
- Is there anything that really, really annoys this character? Why?
- What kinds of trouble does this character tend to get into? Fights with much stronger opponents? Streaks of bad luck?
- What is this character deathly afraid of? Spiders? Light? Flying?
- How is this character atypical of its species, gender, or profession? Is he a bio-chemist with a bodybuilder's physique? A Native American shaman running for President? How is this difference justified?

As I wrote this list of questions, the following characters popped into my mind: a dragon who is afraid of flying and who must take nerve pills every few seconds or start losing control of his wings; a lazy bum who scores highest when he does as little as possible to solve a level; a blind police officer solving crimes in light-deprived environments; and a demon who speaks in iambic pentameter. Will any of them ever find their ways into games or short stories? Who knows? But if they do not, some of their spiritual siblings will.

Plausibility

A final thought: make your characters stand out, but not so much that they become implausible. Of course, the definition of plausibility depends on the setting: you can get away with far more in a comic book superhero environment than in a World War II scenario.

If your game requires a character that clashes heavily with expectations, you will have to work a little harder to justify its presence. However, a crafty writer can make even the most dubious premise plausible with a little effort. An example is found in the *Harry Potter* stories: the author explains the presence of a hidden culture of wizards in the midst of contemporary society by the tireless cover-up efforts of a Ministry of Magic. Needless to say, given the series' staggering sales numbers, readers were more than willing to accept this piece of mental trickery!

Plotting

Sadly, game plots have rarely risen above the level of the B movies of the 1940s and 1950s. There is a widespread sentiment within the game development community that this mediocrity is not much of an issue; after all, we are "making games, not stories" and players do not care much either way. While this might be true, up to a point, for gaming's traditional teenage male audience, the lack of effective plots is one of the factors contributing to interactive entertainment's limited appeal among older consumers.

Let us now take a look at some simple plotting tricks that can improve a game's appeal at little cost in time or effort.

Balancing Conflict

An even fight is always more interesting than a lopsided one, whether we are watching a heavyweight championship match or playing a first-person shooter. For the twelfth-level warrior, facing wave after wave of lowly skeletons may provide easy treasure, but little challenge and no tension whatsoever. A tenth-level wizard, on the other hand, is a formidable opponent with a reasonable chance of victory; the warrior will have to draw on his full array of skills to survive.

Dramatic tension is optimized when the player is perpetually on the brink of disaster, repeatedly escaping by the narrowest of margins. However, if a fair fight is impossible or undesirable, make the player stronger than his opposition. An easy victory may be less thrilling than a hard-fought one, but getting killed constantly is far worse.

Increasing Motivation

The single greatest weakness of the average game plot is a villain with no reason for being a villain, other than a thirst for blood or a desire to destroy the world for the thrill of it.

The mad scientist, the evil overlord, and the devil-worshipping undead monster all but disappeared from movies half a century ago. It is time we game designers put them to rest, as well. Not only have these character types been grossly overused, they are *boring*. An opponent who, deep inside his warped mind, believes that what he does is right, is far scarier than one who pursues evil for no good reason. The worst villains of twentieth-century history inspired sometimes fanatical loyalty in their followers because they convinced them that they were on missions from higher powers or ensuring the survival of their races; evil for its own sake could never hold this much power over people's souls.

Effective antagonist motivations include:

- **A common desire:** The hero and his opponent covet the same treasure, the same throne, or the same love interest.
- **A stereotypical enmity:** Cop vs. robber, usurper vs. rightful heir, etc.
- **A grudge:** The hero and the villain share a past history; this motivation is more difficult to implement into a game—because the player was not the hero at the time the grudge began, identification is harder to achieve.

Note that the players do not have to know their enemies' motivations right away; in fact, learning them as the game unfolds provides more dramatic tension than a long cut-scene.

Shifting Focus

While game designers strive to create the illusion of freedom for their players, they must eventually draw them back into the main story line. An effective way to do both at the same time is to keep shifting the player's focus: introduce new characters to widen the scope of the game (for example, by presenting a secondary quest), and then do the same to return the main story to prominence.

The key is to pique the player's interest with each shift in focus. For example, in a hostage rescue game, a child who runs toward the player could be assumed to be looking for protection. But what if the child stops a few feet away as she recognizes the hero, gets a horrified look on her face, and runs away screaming? This unexpected behavior deserves investigation—and the player's focus shifts.

Other Perspectives

The authors who contributed to this section agree that storytelling, whether explicit or implicit, is an integral part of interactive entertainment:

- Drew Sikora explains the three basic types of stories and how they can apply to games.
- Sean Timarco Baggaley looks at some of the techniques used by screenwriters to tell their stories, and tells us how to use them to our benefit.
- I, as a sometimes-professional comedy writer, analyze the tricks of that particular trade and discuss ways to make our games as funny as they are fun to play.
- And finally, Bruce Onder looks at the storytelling aspects of level design.

Oral tradition, theatre, literature, television, and movies have all come to use stories and characters as the vehicles for the wisdom and entertainment they carried. Games are no exception—or at least, they do not have to be. Whereas some genres can live quite well without any sort of personification or linear plot, others are intimately linked to their storylines. And that being the case, why should game designers settle for stories that would not make the grade in other media?

5.1

Storytelling in Computer Games

Drew Sikora

gaiiden@hotmail.com

When gaming was young, the king of the crop was the adventure game. The main reason for its popularity was that an adventure game could be enrapturing even if it was only text-based with no graphics at all. Of course, when graphics began to become more than just "eye candy," then the adventure genre began to not only tell stories but provide visual cues as well. And although the adventure genre is the one most notable for its storytelling, it should be mentioned that role-playing games (RPGs), strategy games, action games, and almost every other game genre has at some time had representative titles that became famous for their inspired storytelling.

Recently, however, storytelling in games appears to have taken a rather sharp decline. With the advent of massively multiplayer online games (MMOGs) and improved graphics, storytelling seems to have taken a back seat to other gameplay elements. Of course, this does not mean that storytelling is dead—MMOG developers are inventing ways in which they can include vast storylines in their games, and a few designers out there still are dedicated to writing games that follow strong storylines.

The future holds much promise for story-driven games. Improved artificial intelligence (AI) means more interesting and informative nonplayer characters (NPCs) with which the player will interact. Improved graphics means improved visual cues through facial and skeletal animation. And while the keyboard and mouse still reign supreme, a better input device may come along as well—voice-recognition software, for instance.

Indeed, it appears that games featuring strong stories will not be leaving soon. Thus, this article will give you an overview of storytelling methods and how they can be applied to games.

Storytelling

It is one thing to come up with an idea for a story, but quite another to project that story idea into the minds of the people listening to it. Communication is difficult enough when the receiver is actively participating; it becomes even more so when only one side of the discussion provides input.

For example, say you want to tell a friend about a recent event in your life. You know what happened—it is all in your head—but your friend starts out with no knowledge of the event at all. As you proceed with your story, you may miss a few facts and have to back up and start over, which confuses him further. If, at your conclusion, he stares blankly at you, you know you have done something wrong. Misinformation, wrong event ordering, not enough background information—all can lead to a rather confusing and even boring experience for the person on the receiving end of the story.

This is why your friend will likely interrupt you and ask questions when he becomes lost or confused. A game player, however, does not have that luxury; therefore, game storytelling must be clear, precise, and unambiguous.

Plot-Based Storytelling

One method of storytelling is through the plot. This method is a good choice for a story that involves a complicated scenario with many characters and settings and a scope too broad to allow description of every detail.

For example, say you are telling an epic science-fiction tale of a new Earth colony in some faraway galaxy. Players take on the roles of leaders of the human fleets who must battle hordes of aliens and hostile environments to reach their new home. Your story will be told in terms of momentous events; you know all the steps that the game will take as the player progresses. Now, you must invent the generic, shallow, easy-to-understand nonplayer characters that would best move the plot along: because each of them will receive limited screen time, you cannot afford to go into details.

You will probably want to start with a fleet commander, or with someone who will narrate the journey. Then, you will add various spokespeople for any alien races that will be encountered in order to provide dialog. All of these characters have no real personality, or any purpose other than to move the story along—they do not affect the story themselves.

In other words, plot-driven stories usually involve shallow, stereotypical main characters, as well as huge casts of generic supporting players such as stormtroopers, alien bugs, and spear-carriers. Plot-driven games also involve much action, leaving little time to develop characters into anything more substantial than the "gun-toter" or the "damsel-rescuer" or the super action hero. If you wish to focus on a large, expansive story that moves at a brisk pace, and for which you do not need the player to identify deeply with the character(s), then plot-based storytelling is the way to go.

For example, the game *Homeworld* has a story much like the one described above—an exiled race are trying to reach their homeworld, which is now under the control of a galaxy-wide empire. The term *galaxy-wide* should be enough to imply plot-based storytelling, as well as the fact that the distance the characters must travel is over half the size of the galaxy. We are also involved with an entire *race* of people, not just a few hundred, but many thousand. So we already have the three points that define a plot-based game: the large scale of the game world, the large scale of the story, and the multitude of possible characters.

Because no hero exists in this game, it has no main character, and all in-game dialog is carried out by generic characters such as the Fleet Commander and the Bentusi—a name that, by itself, represents another entire race. Returning to the discussion above, again, these characters have no personalities or purpose other than to move the plot forward—they cannot affect the story themselves—which is another distinctive mark of plot-based storytelling.

Character-Based Storytelling

Directly contrasting plot-based storytelling, *character-based* storytelling involves the creation of a deeply detailed character (or, in some case, multiple detailed characters). This character-based method is best used when you begin with a shallow plot. The first thing to do is to build up the characters: decide their strengths, their weaknesses, their physical attributes, and so forth. Here are some good rules for constructing characters:

- The main character and villain should share strengths and weaknesses.
- Supporting characters should either add or detract from a main character, depending on their roles in the story.
- Each character should be unique in some way, so that they can each stand alone and not be dependent on one or more other characters.
- Do not skimp on character back stories. Constructing past lives in detail gives characters depth and makes them more believable. Character histories can also be used to explain events and decisions in the story.
- Using Achilles' heels is cheating. Never take the easy way out by providing a character a lethal and very obvious vulnerability that others can take advantage of in the story.

After you have created the characters, you can start developing a story. Examine the characters and their backgrounds. How did they get where they are? What sort of problems do they tend to run into? Answers to such questions will provide you with the beginning of the game and of your story. From there, go straight to the conclusion, skipping everything else in between, and decide how the story will end.

After deciding the story's conclusion, go back to the beginning and start fleshing out the major plot twists—such as a death here, a major victory there, a moral decision here. Finally, start connecting the major events using the character models. Ask yourself: "What would this character do or say in this situation? How would he or she react?"

As you can see, character-based storytelling is excellent for a dynamic storyline in which all the major plot points are branches of the story—similar to a "choose your own adventure" book.

In a character-based game, you must allow the character to slowly change and evolve throughout the course of the story. For example, in *Deus Ex,* the main character starts out as a highly enthusiastic employee of a government peacekeeping agency, ready to defend justice; by the end, he has been embittered by discoveries of endless lies and corruption. However, to evolve your character's beliefs, you need a catalyst, which should be on hand if you did a good job creating a history for your character. Batman's change in beliefs stemmed from the murder of his parents; in *Deus Ex,* J.C. Denton's beliefs changed when he learned the truth about his agency, and his dreams of righteousness were shattered.

Idea-Based Storytelling

Now that we have covered storytelling that focuses on events and characters, we can look at the last type: stories based on ideas. If you have ever read a novel based on an alternate history (such as those by Harry Turtledove) or seen the movie *Planet of the Apes*, then you have experienced this type of storytelling, which is based on a single question: "What if?" For example, What if there was a galactic empire? What if Spain had lost to the Aztecs? What if Atlantis really existed? These are all ideas that you can turn into fodder for stories.

Idea stories do not necessarily need to be grounded in facts. However, if you do plan to create a story based on a real-world event, it can be beneficial to remain true to the setting. For instance, if you imagined the Aztecs defeating the Spanish, you might want to posit that they won by using advanced ramps and catapults to drop boulders on the enemy and channeling water to flood out Spanish camps. The Aztecs were actually quite advanced in many ways, a fact that can give you the freedom to create imaginative weapons that still remain primitive enough to have been real. On the flip side, of course, you could conjecture that the Aztecs won through use of spiritual and alien powers, beaming down bolts from the heavens using their massive stone ziggurats and wearing futuristic armor. (And who is to say that is wrong?)

Character development in an idea-driven story depends on the idea you are trying to convey to your audience. An idea such as a galactic empire would require many shallow characters for the player to encounter throughout the empire, whereas the Aztec scenario is local enough that several important characters could exist and actively participate in the flow of the story. In this way, idea-based storytelling is the most versatile of them all, because it can handle such a variety of character types.

Not Just Pretty Graphics

So, you have crafted a storyline that is deep, enriching, and captivating. Congratulations. But your work does not stop there (it might have years ago when graphics were little more than lines and 2D shapes incapable of conveying human movements or emotion). With new technologies that have arisen in only the last few years, graphics now offer many more options to game developers, and many of those options can be applied to storytelling, or to an aspect of storytelling known as *character interaction*.

Deus Ex provides a good example of character interaction in a game; the game's characters seem to come alive. Although they do not form facial expressions, the characters' mouths open and close in sync to the dialog. This simple effect makes a character seem more like a real person, and less like a mere collection of textured polygons. Furthermore, *Deus Ex*'s characters exhibit body language. Characters nod, shrug helplessly, and spread their arms slightly. Whether through design or luck, most of the time the body language coincides perfectly with the ongoing dialog. This feature may not seem very impressive, but the simple fact that the character is *moving* and not just standing like a wax figure adds life and creates a more believable experience.

Visual cues such as facial expressions, hand movements, and walking styles—in effect, all body language—can help you tell a story. A character grieving for his dead wife is more believable when tears stream down his face. When a character is angry, he should be waving his arms instead of just yelling. It would be strange to watch a person verbally abusing you while standing still and not moving a muscle. Can you imagine that? Of course not; no human being would behave that way. The fact that you cannot believe in such a scenario is proof that experiencing it in a game will not create a believable atmosphere for the player.

The way a character appears is also very important. *Deus Ex* featured characters in trench coats and dark glasses, *Matrix*-style, which fit its gloomy atmosphere and futuristic setting. *No One Lives Forever* had its main character decked out in a tight 60s-style outfit to match the setting. It has become increasingly obvious that you can style a character for success. In short, graphics in games today are no longer used merely for "eye candy," but as visual effects to help tell a story that the player can internalize and enjoy.

Conclusion

This brief overview should inspire you to think about different ways in which you can integrate stories into your games, and how to enhance stories using modern graphics technologies. Storytelling can become a complex beast, and it is very important that you choose the type of storytelling that will best fit the kind of gameplay you have in mind, otherwise you could merely compound the problem.

Finally, remember that a game cannot survive on a good story alone—focusing too much on the story and failing to see how it integrates with the rest of the game mechanics will lead to a poor experience for players—and for you.

5.2

Show and Tell: Applying Screenwriting Techniques to Computer Games

Sean Timarco Baggaley

stimarco@bangbangclick.com

Computer games are always a linear experience. When controlling a character in a game, the player cannot turn both left and right at the same time. Instead, he must make a choice, determining which path this particular instance of the game's story is going to follow.

If we play a computer game all the way through once, then look back on the experience and write down what we did, the end result will be a linear story. Depending on how the game was designed and implemented, that story may not necessarily be one the designer anticipated, but it will be a story nevertheless. It is only when replaying the game several times, taking different choices each time, that the true nature of the computer game as an interactive medium becomes obvious.

One of the advantages of the essentially linear user experience of computer games is that we can take advantage of some traditional techniques from fully linear media, such as novels, movies, and other dramatic forms when designing our games.

The Art and Craft of Storytelling

The tradition of oral storytelling dates right back to the earliest beginnings of language—a period which has allowed the art and craft of telling a story to become steeped in cultural traditions. Over the millennia, the art and craft of storytelling has built up a set of symbols and structural techniques. Together, these techniques form a framework within which the story itself sits—every language teacher tells us, for instance, that every story must have a beginning, a middle, and an end. This is merely one small component in the overall structure of a story.

Most of a storyteller's audience will be completely unaware of this framework, but you do not need to know how to program a computer in order to spot a bug. People can smell an ill-structured story just as easily without knowing *why*—which is why we have critics!

Over time, traditional storytelling has embraced each new medium, be it the written and printed word, stage plays, or more recently, movies, television, and even computer games. The sophistication and depth of the craft of storytelling—a craft that has been refined over millennia—means that today's writers, movie directors, and even games designers have an array of tools available to adapt to our own stories.

In video games, designers are a little more limited in how these tools can be used. Often, we have to invent tools, or at least heavily redesign existing tools to fit our new medium. After all, we do not usually have the luxury of knowing exactly which path the player will take through our simulated worlds.

Instead, our job, as with any other craft, is to determine which tools are the best suited to the task at hand. In some cases, the very program code itself will need to wield such tools to ensure the player experiences a good story. In other cases, we can use storytelling tools at the content creation stages.

It is important to understand that the story experience is not simply a feature we can tack on once the core gameplay is defined. It must be designed from the beginning as an *emergent feature* of the gameplay itself.

A thorough exploration of storytelling techniques and how to apply them to computer game design would fill an entire book, so this article will examine only a couple of common storytelling techniques and their applications to interactive entertainment. In particular, I have chosen one of the bluntest of instruments within the storyteller's toolkit—an instrument that has been used in many successful stories, movies, and even wildlife documentaries.

"Show, Don't Tell"

The phrase "show, don't tell" is a common storytelling tenet. It boils down to avoiding blatant exposition and instead, keeping the information necessary to follow the story within the context of the story itself.

Blatant "telling" occurs in those scenes in which a character's sole objective is to tell the hero something he already knows. (In fact, most writers actually name this storytelling fault, calling it an *"As you know, Bob…"* scene.) The justification for the entire scene is to give the reader necessary information, but as the hero clearly already knows the information, the audience is bound to ask: "If Bob already knows this, why are you telling him?"

Such lazy writing is depressingly common in Hollywood science-fiction stories, where the impossible "science" must be explained to the audience so they can understand the characters' motivations. A science-fiction setting is not a prerequisite however; other examples can be seen in many B-movies and bad novels.

Good writers might instead use a hero who has a good reason not to know this information, and who learns it as the audience does. A good storyteller would include scenes where the hero is *seen* to discover the information for himself, picking it up the same way a detective would track down and interpret clues.

Unsurprisingly, good murder/mystery stories provide excellent examples of this storytelling tool in action. Similarly, the better science-fiction movies usually take the route of having a layperson, such as a journalist, for the main protagonist.

The Value of Foreshadowing

One of the most effective ways to show information instead of telling it is a technique known as *foreshadowing*.

In writing, foreshadowing is the insertion of an event or plot device that hints at later events in the story. This technique can be found in practically all drama. It is certainly the most common—and visible—form of implicit communication found in Hollywood movies and most television entertainment, and it is starting to trickle into computer games, although the technique is still comparatively rare outside of level design.

For example, imagine the heroine of a movie who needs to locate a mobster's hidden safe and steal some documents that the villain is using to extort money from her husband. If the heroine does not know where the safe is, both she and the audience will somehow need to find out. A bad screenplay would use blatant exposition, similar to the *"As you know, Bob..."* technique mentioned earlier—an interrogation scene with a henchman who simply blabs the necessary information would be a typical example.

A better writer would be subtler. If the finding and opening of the safe is not important to the overall storyline, our heroine herself might find out about it in a relatively simple way, such as overhearing a conversation between two henchmen or finding a plan of the room.

If, on the other hand, the finding, opening, and emptying of the safe is a really important part of the plot, a good writer would increase the tension by requiring the heroine—and, by association, the audience—to do some work to discover it. To achieve this, the writer needs to show the audience both where the safe is and how the heroine can open it.

Without this information, when the heroine bounds into the room and immediately pushes aside the painting to open the safe, the story's continuity is violently shattered because the audience is left to wonder how she knew about it.

Most classic mystery stories, of the sort Agatha Christie was famous for, have an explanation scene at the end, where the intrepid detective gathers all the suspects into a room and tells them how they solved the mystery. However, in all cases, the reader is always given the exact same clues. The audience *expects* to slap their forehead and wonder aloud: "Of course! Why didn't *I* see that?"

This technique of placing clues within the main body of the story is what foreshadowing is all about, and examples can be found not only in detective stories and cop shows, but in all genres,. A highly visible example of foreshadowing can be found in most James Bond movies in the ubiquitous scene between the hero and the character Q. In these scenes, Q doles out gadgets and weapons like Santa Claus giving presents to a child; the audience expects these items to be used in later scenes. The first scene foreshadows the later scenes and also performs the necessary task of giving the audience a hint as to what is to come.

It is also possible to use foreshadowing to place red herrings into the story. James Bond may be given a super-powerful weapon that the audience assumes will be used in a later shoot-out, but the hero's antagonist might take it from him before he even gets a chance to switch it on.

Imparting Knowledge

A common mistake when working with foreshadowing is to forget that while the audience needs to be given the same information as the protagonist, the protagonist must also be *seen* to find the same information. Returning to our example with the heroine and the safe, it is not enough that we know where the safe is. We must also know that our heroine knows.

For example, if the picture covering the safe is a portrait, the villain might spend a scene worshipping the subject of the picture, possibly implying that the subject is protecting precious information, to give us the link between the picture and the safe. ("Ah, my dear departed mother, I do hope you're keeping an eye on our little . . . secret!") However, this technique fulfills only part of our requirement. The audience has been given information, but unless our heroine was present, the audience knows that she does not have that information.

Thus, the information needs to be imparted twice. Perhaps a henchman might steal a surreptitious glance at the portrait when our heroine questions him about the blackmail documents. Often, this is all the audience needs to see to feel in sync with the story's protagonist.

Audiences expect to identify with the lead character. In many ways, the audience *becomes* the lead character, so any secrets our hypothetical heroine knows, the audience must also be able to learn before those secrets are thrust into the limelight. It is therefore important that the audience knows what the heroine knows. An important piece of information must be synchronized between the audience and the protagonist before it is used.

Applying the Theory

The "show, don't tell" philosophy is regularly violated in the computer role-playing game (CRPG) genre. In almost every such game, we find non-player characters (NPCs) who exist solely to regurgitate some expository text. You could argue that, because the character is in context, this is a perfectly valid application. However, this technique means the game wrests control from the player and plays a one-sided conversation—usually with subtitles.

The game is *telling* information, instead of *showing* it. It throws the player's suspension of disbelief out of the window and turns him into a passive audience, rather than an active participant. This is not to say that conversation within the game is inappropriate, but when such techniques become the primary means of advancing the story, playing the game becomes a very monotonous, linear experience.

To ensure that the player remains immersed in the experience, the designer must keep as much of the needed exposition as possible *within the interactive game world*.

Look at the silent, wordless travels of CRPG characters as they roam the world from encounter to encounter. Contrast this with the character development of action-adventure movies. Action-adventure movies develop the plot and characterization during the action itself. If we were to translate a traditional CRPG literally to movie form, we would see the lead characters running from point A to point B without uttering a word, speaking only when they meet someone else. Worse still, when they did meet another character, the action would stop completely while the conversation took place.

Using the Tools

As with traditional storytelling, the best exposition is completely implicit. Instead of an NPC telling characters that the Irritated Dragon is extremely hard to kill and has wiped out countless armies and heroes, the environment could instead be dotted with clues. Villages might boast notices reading: "Rewarde of One Halfe of Kingdom & Hande of Princess In Returne for HEAD of Dragonne!" As the players approach the dragon's lair, masses of corpses, skeletons, and other detritus of its previous kills would strike the necessary fear into the player.

If you really want to show off your design skills, give the player and his team a close call with the dragon—maybe have it capture a key member of the team, so that the player has an even better reason to go after it.

If this option is too difficult to engineer, you could go for a more explicit exposition. Why not, for example, have an NPC join the adventuring party, chatting to the team and helping them as they travel to the NPC's ultimate destination. The NPC could even double as a commentator during action sequences and make wisecracks about the hero's fighting skills—or lack thereof. The NPC could also act as a mentor to the player's own character, perhaps teaching him new skills as they travel. Alternatively, the NPC could be a cynical type whose conversation reveals what the dragons in your game's fantasyland actually do with all those gold coins!

Conclusion

You should find little difficulty in embracing traditional storytelling techniques in the design of games, and many game designers are already moving in this direction. Today's advanced platforms should completely eliminate the need for old design philosophies and techniques that were developed solely to avoid problems such as limited memory and backing storage. It is high time we developed our own language—our own traditions. But before we can do that, we need to embrace those traditions that have kept humans enthralled for countless millennia.

The tools of traditional storytelling are powerful, but the art is in knowing how to wield them to best effect. With care, they can help us take our chosen medium to new heights.

This article has touched only the very tip of a truly massive iceberg. There is far more to storytelling techniques than the few examples I have given here. The ancient tradition of storytelling has much to teach us. After all, why else would you be reading this book?

Comedy in Games

François Dominic Laramée

francoislaramee@videotron.ca

Let's face it: our games may be *fun*, but not many of them are *funny*. Sometimes, games contain no humor because their subject matter: after all, how can you laugh at civilization-building or violent alien invaders? The difficulty inherent in comedy is another reason designers might avoid it: writing effective comedy is very, very hard work. However, if we choose, we can write comedy into a wide variety of games.

As regular readers of my online columns know, I like to spice up my writing with humor. In fact, I also regularly write comedy material for professionals.

In my own mind, this qualifies me to pontificate on the topic of humor in front of a worldwide audience. So let's get started learning how you can make your games funny.

Why Comedy?

Why bother trying to develop funny games? Because, usually, comedy sells. Movie ticket sales provide a good example: the three films that grossed over $200 million in North America in the first nine months of 2001 were *Shrek, Rush Hour 2,* and *The Mummy Returns*. In television, sitcoms account for over half of the prime-time schedules on all major networks. If you look at the annual lists of the highest-paid entertainers in the world, at your local club listings, and the best-seller lists, you will see that comedians are everywhere.

Now, think long and hard: when was the last time a game made you laugh? Intentionally?

Where Comedy?

Building comedy into a game is no easy task, and it is even more difficult when the humor moves from a supporting role to the main focus of the player experience. In increasing order of difficulty, the four major ways in which you can introduce comedy in your game are: the *incidental character*, the *setting*, the *sidekick*, and the *main theme*.

Incidental Comedy Characters

Sometimes, players just need a break. Finally killing an enemy after a half-hour fight, completing a major quest, or escaping from an exploding cathedral at the last second, all require an incredible amount of concentration and adrenaline. Few people can withstand a sustained level of high tension for more than 30 minutes, after which they require a change of pace. And nothing helps change pace quite like a comic interlude.

The easiest way to implement such a break is through a meeting with a transient comic character who appears, delivers his lines, and goes away without further involvement in the story. For example:

- In Greg Costikyan's fantasy novel, *One Quest, Hold the Dragons,* one of the major characters spends a few pages in a dungeon in the care of a hardcore nonviolent pacifist—who happens to be the city executioner. The scene in which the jailor rationalizes the need for professional, high-quality torture services in a civilized society has to be seen to be believed. The author repeats the pattern throughout the novel, turning an otherwise "serious" plot into a very funny book.
- In *Star Control II*, the player is constantly harassed by an ever-increasing tide of aggressive, self-replicating space probes. When he visits a gas giant inhabited by the Slylandro, a race of friendly sentient sacks of plasma, he learns that the probes are actually harmless mail-order items that went berserk because a novice Slylandro hacker introduced a bug into their programming. To get rid of the menace, the player must debug the source code with a painfully dense alien, to hilarious effect.
- In the classic *Starflight*, the Spemin are a race of overly aggressive blobs who try to intimidate the player. However, their technology is so primitive that, once the player has been coerced into a fight, he always wins it with a single shot. And then, the Spemin worship him as a god.

In each of these examples, the comedy element is, at most, a side dish to the game's main course. This is "safe" comedy: some players will laugh, and those who do not will not be deprived of anything important.

Comic Settings

If the occasional interlude is not enough, the entire setting (including any number of secondary characters and enemies) can be made a funny element itself.

This is the case in *Lemmings*, a real-time strategy game in which the player must use a variety of tools to prevent hordes of cute little rodents from plunging to their deaths in gruesome fashion. *Lemmings* is not a comedy game per se, because the core of the gameplay lies in puzzle-solving and not in reaching punch lines. However, everything that *surrounds* the gameplay is at least tainted with funny overtones.

Comic Sidekicks

A funny sidekick character who tags along with the hero throughout the game is a dicey proposition. The sidekick's presence is more invasive than that of a funny setting, because a sidekick *talks*, and he is there *all the time*. Thus, he had better be *really funny*, or else he will quickly turn into a major nuisance.

At best, a comic sidekick can deliver effective punch lines while the player is otherwise occupied, resulting in a classic "straight man, comic" routine. At worst, he is an unwelcome, infuriating distraction; for example, look at the horrendous backlash against the character Jar Jar Binks in *Star Wars Episode 1: The Phantom Menace.*

Full-Fledged Comedy Games

Games in which comedy becomes the theme and core of the gameplay are few and far between. They are the interactive equivalent of a Zucker Brothers or Leslie Nielsen movie: the plot is light, acting is approximate, but no one cares because the jokes are so good.

The prime example of a comedy game is *Leisure Suit Larry*, where a balding, pot-bellied 70s castaway attempts to seduce women and is thwarted in ever more creative fashion each time. Certainly the *Leisure Suit Larry* games are adventures, but only in the technical sense. The puzzles are complicated enough to justify calling the game an adventure and to require a guide book—but the puzzle-solving is just an excuse to delay the inevitable. Players really stick with the game to see how Larry will mess up next time.

Of course, in a game based on comedy, the comedy needs to be very, very effective, because otherwise the game collapses. It is unfair but true: while players will happily ignore a below-average dramatic storyline if the gameplay is compelling enough, failed comedy will overshadow everything else.

The Big Book of Recipes

Many well-established comedy formats exist that can be exploited in games as well as in linear media. Here are a handful, with examples.

Running Gags

The running gag is a joke that is repeated again, and again, and again. And again.

For example, in the movie *Pure Luck*, Martin Short's character is the unluckiest man alive. No matter what he does, no matter where he goes, disaster strikes in increasingly improbable ways. If he is invited to sit down in a huge conference room, he will choose the one seat with a broken leg. He will be stung by a bee (and undergo a grotesque allergic reaction) while riding an airplane. He will be struck by lightning while sitting in a movie theater. And his task in the movie is to search for his boss' missing daughter, who is afflicted with the same bad-luck disease.

There are three major classes of running gags:

- **Repetitive:** The same thing happens many times, in an identical or slightly different fashion. Wile E. Coyote's obstinate reliance on ACME products in his quest to catch the Road Runner is a repetitive running gag: we all know the mail-order junk will fail, we just do not know how.

- **Looping:** This type of running gag uses the same device as a setup for several punch lines. For example, let's say a comedian is railing against the drawbacks of car safety belts. He may go on to discuss a trip during which he drove his car into a lake, and come back to his original topic with a line such as: "Luckily, I was wearing a safety belt, which got stuck so it could keep me inside the car where I belonged, and I almost drowned."
- **Crescendo:** When the same joke will not work more than once, running gags require increasingly outrageous punch lines. For example: "Last night, I was really drunk, and I got sick in front of hundreds of people. My wife laughed a little. The priest, not so much. The family of the deceased, not at all. The nationwide TV audience wasn't pleased either."

Reversal

This is the funny version of the shootout at the OK Corral: a comedic reversal occurs when a bully, a bad guy, or a loudmouth get shot down by the perfect comeback. Here is a joke built on reversal:

> *A guy approaches a gorgeous lady in a bar. "Hey, babe," he says, "my locker room buddies call me The Eel. Wanna guess why?" And the woman replies: "Because you're too soft, slimy, and you smell like fish?"*

The key to a successful reversal is to lead the audience to believe that one character is getting the upper hand, when in fact he is merely setting himself up for disaster. Leisure Suit Larry made a comfortable living of being on the wrong end of these things!

Divergent Thinking

Remember Yogi Berra's admonition that, when coming to a fork in a road, you should take it? This is what divergent thinking is all about: start with a set of reasonable assumptions, and draw an absurd (but still, somehow, appropriate) conclusion. For example:

- **Fact:** More than half of the Earth's population still lives at least two hours' travel from the nearest phone. **Divergent conclusion:** They must really get annoyed when they receive a call and it is a wrong number.
- **Fact:** Mr. X has just suffered his sixth heart attack. **Divergent conclusion:** He is really happy, because thanks to his HMO's frequent-customer program, his next quadruple-bypass will be free.

In games, divergent thinking is safe when used in dialog, but potentially dangerous in gameplay. The puzzles in old-school adventure games often required extremely divergent analysis, so much so that they became intractable without a hint book. Be careful: the reason this technique is so effective in verbal comedy is that most people *will not* think of the divergent conclusion, at least not right away.

Personification

Comedians use personification to illustrate human characteristics by giving them to animals or inanimate objects. The carnivorous cartoon potted plant licking its chops and baring razor-sharp teeth while hopping toward its terrified prey, Eddie the dog on the sitcom *Frasier*, and just about every "appliance" on *The Flintstones*, are perfect examples of this comedic device.

Transposition

This is an age old trick: put someone, usually an expert and/or overconfident character, in a situation for which he is not prepared at all, and let him try to fix the problem using his grossly inappropriate skills.

Sitcoms and movies use transposition as a basic tenet all the time. Picture a hostage negotiator, caught in an elevator with a woman who is about to give birth. How will he deal with the situation? ("Ok, little baby. You're surrounded. You can come out now, hands behind your head. Nice and slow. No one will hurt you.") Or take Arnold Schwarzenegger's take-charge, no-nonsense police officer forced to go undercover among preschool children in *Kindergarten Cop*. In both cases, transposition is the setup, and comedy, the consequence.

In a game, transposition is relatively easy to implement: just create a player character that does not follow the stereotypes of the genre. The boxing game *Ready to Rumble*, which features politicians and pop musicians as fighters, is itself one big transposition.

Exaggerations and Understatements

We have all seen the skinny cartoon characters who suddenly sprout 26-inch biceps after lifting weights for five seconds. And who will ever forget the tiny dog who turns into a human-wrecking machine in *There's Something about Mary?* Heaping portions of overkill is a superb way to make people laugh.

The members of Monty Python were masters of the exaggeration. One of the sketches in the movie *The Meaning of Life* features an enormously overweight man who goes to a restaurant, gobbles mountains of food until he is completely full, and then literally explodes, showering the entire room with bucketfuls of disgusting goo, when the waiter convinces him to swallow one little mint. Trust me: this is not a scene that you can easily forget.

Exaggerations and understatements are among the easiest techniques to use in games, because they can be applied to gameplay elements as well as to dialog. A simple example: the last weapon acquired by the player in a shooter could be a tiny pink plastic water pistol—which packs more punch than the 82nd Airborne. Just let your imagination flow.

Face Value

This very effective technique consists of taking a worn-out cliché, figure of speech or proverb, making an inappropriate literal interpretation of it, and acting accordingly.

In my favorite *Dilbert* cartoon of all time, the pointy-haired boss introduces a new employee and asks our nerdy hero to show her the ropes. Dilbert, without a word, pulls out a hangman's noose. In Isaac Asimov's short story, *Little Lost Robot*, a very annoyed technician tells a meddling but valuable (and potentially dangerous) prototype robot to go lose itself. Eager to obey, the robot first hides among a crateful of similar-looking but far less valuable androids, and then tries to steal a spaceship to hide in outer space.

Puzzle design is one of the possible game applications for this technique. Suppose the entrance to a treasure room is guarded by a vicious fire-breathing camel, clad in +12 plate armor from hump to toe. None of the player's spells and weapons have any effect. Will he have to go home empty-handed? Not if he notices the straw hat hanging on the wall, and throws it at the animal. ("The straw hat that broke the camel's back.") Or maybe the arrows he picked up in the previous room had straw shafts. You get the idea.

Visual Humor

Games are a visual medium, and therefore natural vehicles for sight gags. Game designers can benefit from an enormous variety of visual humor techniques, including:

- **Passive humor:** *Powerslave*, an album by the heavy metal band Iron Maiden, features an incredibly complicated jacket. The Egyptian-style pyramid dominating the scene is covered with hieroglyphics—which include a picture of Mickey Mouse and a couple of written graffiti. The funny stuff is hidden in plain sight, so that viewers have to search for it.
- **Contrasts:** The enormously popular French film *Les Visiteurs* (remade in Hollywood as *Just Visiting*) tells the story of a medieval knight and his smelly servant, who are caught in a time warp and forced to live among their twentieth-century descendants. When they walk across a country road and almost get run over by a speeding car, they mistake the vehicle for a fire-breathing, honking, Devil-worshipping dragon—and proceed to destroy it with sword, mace, and fierce battle cries. And of course, the movie *Twins* is based on the obvious differences between the genetically engineered, super-genius hunk Arnold Schwarzenegger and his crooked, pudgy, side-effect twin brother Danny DeVito.
- **Silent film humor:** Imagine an enemy character who is a drunken skeletal custodian. You give him a beer, he drinks it, the beer spills all over the floor (because he is a skeleton and does not have a stomach), he picks up a mop and cleans up the mess, and you go on your merry way because he is now too busy to deal with you.

And Finally, a Couple of Quickies

There are many, many other recipes for comedy, but their applicability to games is less obvious. For example:

- **Misunderstandings:** This method is a staple of television sitcoms: one character walks in on an ongoing conversation, but because he has not heard the first part, he lacks the proper context information and misinterprets what he hears.
- **Stupidity:** Characters happily ignore the blatantly obvious, or devote inordinate amounts of effort to straightening pictures on the bathroom wall while the kitchen is on fire. The easily-manipulated Homer Simpson is a prime example of the comic power of stupidity.
- **The Blind Watchman:** This is a joke with a punch line that depends on hidden information. A classic example: a six-year old comes home in tears because he was expelled from a public swimming pool for peeing in it. Sounds like the life guards overreacted—until we learn that the kid did it from the diving board.

Of course, you can use any of these techniques in dialog, but inclusion in gameplay is more difficult.

Conclusion

If you are prepared to devote the appropriate amount of talent and craftsmanship, any game genre can benefit from comedy. After all, *Lemmings* is a real-time strategy game in which players must prevent mass suicide, while *Duke Nukem* is an ultra-violent shooting game, and they are both hilarious.

However, be wary of comedy's inherent invasiveness. In the eyes of the average viewer, a dramatic action flick is an action flick first and a dramatic experience second. If the explosions are pretty and the damsels in distress even prettier, the audience will forgive any number of plot weaknesses. But a funny action flick *is a comedy first*, and no amount of stunts or special effects will be able to make up for a series of jokes that fall flat. It is unfair, but true, for games as well as movies.

Not that I would know about jokes that fall *flat*, of course.

5.4

Storytelling in Level-Based Game Design

Bruce Onder

bonder@digitalarcana.com

Storytelling in a level-based game design usually invokes images of cut-scenes of various levels of quality—everyone has a favorite example of the stereotypical bad cut-scene, in which the characters drone on and on, expositing mechanically all story elements that must be dumped onto the disinterested player before he can commence to the next level. What was the escape sequence to get out of this movie, again?

Game design does not have to be this way. In this article, we will look at some of the things that movies and television shows have learned to do very well over several decades of craft-honing, and see how they can apply to twenty-first–century level-based game design. We will also look at some tools we can develop to help us integrate these storytelling techniques into our work as game designers.

The Hollywood Formula

Over the years, the movie industry has developed a set of rules to govern screenwriting. These rules include the three-act structure, the 120-page ideal, and the so-called "car chase rule."

Three-Act Story Structure

Every screenwriter chafes at the idea of writing to a formula, and yet its formula is the foundation of storytelling in Hollywood. The basic idea of three-act structure is extremely basic indeed: each story has a beginning, middle, and end—three "acts" that tell the story. Fiction writers have created a more useful, dramatic variation of this model: chase your main character up a tree; throw rocks at him; get him down again.

This variation is more useful for the aspiring screenwriter, author, or level designer, because it hints at purpose instead of structure alone. In the beginning, or first act, your job is to get your hero stuck in a tree (introduce the problem); in the middle, or second act, your job is to throw rocks and other plot devices at him (raise the stakes); and in the end, or third act, you must bring him back down again (resolve the story).

The 120-page Ideal

Another Hollywood formula states that a feature-length screenplay should be 120 pages long. One minute of screen time per page of script works out to the typical two-hour movie. Act One should average 30 pages, Act Two, 60 pages, and Act Three should round out the last 30 pages. Expressed in percentages, the writer should spend the first 25 percent of the story getting his hero stuck up a tree, 50 percent of the middle throwing rocks, and the final 25 percent getting him back down.

The Car Chase Rule

Yet another Hollywood dictum states: action scenes stop the storytelling dead in its tracks. Put another way, anytime a car chase occurs, the story is put on hold until someone crashes, is captured, or gets away. This dictum applies to all action sequences—chases, fights, explosions, etc.

In a level-based game, the rule is simply reversed: storytelling scenes stop the action dead in its tracks. Put another way: do not tell so much story that you forget the game is about the chasing, the shooting, and the exploding.

Applying Hollywood Formulae to Level Design

If you know that a Hollywood screenplay breaks a story down into 25 percent–50 percent–25percent for the three acts, you could then apply these percentages for any level-based project you are working on. Have 12 levels? Then spend the first three setting up the problem. Spend the middle six raising the stakes and telling more of the story. Spend the last three building up to the final explosive confrontation and final wrap-up.

The three-act structure can be applied within each level as well. Each level needs to set up the mission, quest, or other objective. You can pepper the setup throughout the first part of the mission using traditional (and/or more original) level-design constructs. The middle section of the episode contains the player navigating the obstacles between him and the established objective. Then, finally, in the last third or so of the level, you present the biggest challenge, give the player a way to succeed, and when he does, end the level.

Why, however, would you want to mimic Hollywood screenplay structure?

One reason to consider doing so is to appeal to a wider audience. If you are interested in bringing more mainstream players to your productions, you may want to consider adopting and adapting tactics and techniques that work for the masses. People in general like a well-told story filled with unforgettable characters (mind-blowing special effects do not always hurt, either).

Borrowing from Television

Level- or mission-based game designs actually have more in common with the modern television series than they do with movies; therefore, we will look at the specific story structures used in that industry.

If you examine a long-running episodic television series like *Star-Trek: Voyager*, or *The X-Files*, or even *Quantum Leap*, you will see that the writers of these shows are actually telling two stories in each episode: first, the episode's story, and at the same time, the series' overarching story.

The best example of the two-story structure can be found in *The X-Files*. The series story is that the main characters, Mulder and Scully, are trying to investigate and penetrate the alien invasion conspiracy. Each episode also tells its own story, which is sometimes directly related to the overarching story, sometimes tangentially related to it, and sometimes completely unrelated to it. In episodes that tie to the series' main story, however, great care must be taken with consistency while letting the episode slowly "peels back more layers of the onion" to keep fans wondering how everything is going to come out in the end.

The level designer has the same responsibility: he or she must create not only an interesting individual level or mission, but one that fits seamlessly into a greater story. That means that plot elements from both stories must be developed and/or advanced during the course of the level's story.

Conceptually, the level or mission is the equivalent of a television episode, and the game is the equivalent of the television series. The only difference is that, in general, you probably do not want any levels that are not connected closely to the game.

For the levels in Act Three, all story threads must begin to be tied together, and nothing must be dropped. For example, do not introduce an assassin in Mission 4, have him spend the majority of the second act trying to kill the player and then suddenly forget about him in Act Three..

Interactive Story Elements

Of course, one crucial difference separates computer games from television shows and movies (at least for now)—movies and television shows must tell their story sequentially and statically (meaning that every viewing of *Alien* begins and ends in the same way). In a computer game, we have the ability to tell the story in a completely different sequence each time. We can choose to tell or not to tell a part of the story based on what objects the player picks up.

Of course, in reality we cannot simply do whatever we want and still hope to have a good story. For instance, we cannot specify that the story elements be dropped into each level completely randomly from play to play—that would produce a chaotic mess.

While we have the ability to create whatever literary monster we choose, we will more than likely want to rein in our creative impulses and continue to produce good stories that engage the player and involve them viscerally and emotionally in our creations.

However, within reason, the techniques discussed in Article 1.3 in this book apply to level-based games as well.

Plot Devices

Here are a few techniques that you can apply to solidify your levels' dramatic structures:

Through-line

Your game's story must have a consistent *through-line*, meaning that the main character's desire ' does not change from beginning to end. For instance, if your hero's motivation at the beginning of the game 'is his desire for revenge against the crime lord who caused the death of his wife and children, it should remain his motivation throughout the story. He should never veer from that desire until the very end, when the hero either obtains his revenge, or fails to, or realizes that his desire was not what he really wanted or needed, and changes it.

Need versus Desire

There is a crucial but subtle difference between the literary concepts of *need* and *desire* with respect to character growth. A character's *desire* is closely linked to the story's through-line, and serves to drive the story from page one to the closing credits. For example, your hero, a reformed terrorist, *desires* to bring an international terrorist (his ex-boss) to justice.

On the other hand, your character's *need* is an underlying character flaw that he must address in order to succeed at his desire. For example, you hero *needs* to redeem himself in both his own eyes and the eyes of the world, and overcome his self-doubts about being able to capture his former superior.

Character Arcs

By the end of the game, your hero should either have grown as a character, or have actually regressed. For example, your terrorist from the above example could change from a villain into a hero if the game is completed successfully. Or, he could topple his former boss and take the throne of evil, essentially degenerating into a worse monster than before. Either way, your main character will not end up exactly as he started out.

Backstory

Backstory is what happened before your story begins. Every story has a backstory, even if it is never told: the main characters' backstories are what makes them characters as opposed to faces on your control panel.

Backstory can be used most effectively when peppered throughout the story to reveal interesting tidbits about characters, events, and objects in the story. Even if it is not used directly, backstory helps the writer write a richer story.

Callbacks

A *callback* is a reference to a previous event in the story, and helps the player associate meaning between elements of the story: a good callback always elicits an audible "ah!" of realization from the player.

For instance, say that one level of your game, the player finds a gold-plated gun. In another level, he enters a mansion in which he finds gold-plating equipment. The player remembers the gun and draws an association between the gun and the owner of the mansion.

Flashbacks

A *flashback* differs from a callback in two ways. First, a callback happens in the player's head, whereas a flashback takes place in the game. Additionally, in general a callback refers to a previous scene, whereas a flashback tells part of the backstory (that which the player 'has not experienced before).

Flashbacks tend to be overused by writers of all skill levels, but when done well, they can add tremendous value to the game. For action games, flashbacks should be short and sweet—they are even better if your player can continue to shoot things in them!

Foreshadowing

Foreshadowing is the opposite of a callback—'foreshadowing refers to future story elements before they have happened. Foreshadowing can range from the simplistic (a wild-eyed fortune teller who predicts the main character's death by scene 21) to the skilled (an early scene in which the player ascends a staircase soaked with his comrades' blood foreshadowing a scene in the last level in which he must ascend the stairs again to do battle one last time).

Cliffhangers

Almost everyone remembers *cliffhangers*, suspenseful endings to episodic serial adventures such as *Flash Gordon* in which the hero is caught in some deadly trap or is about to plunge into hot lava, only to save himself miraculously (sometimes only by rewriting the setup to be less deadly that previously perceived) at the beginning of the next level.

As with flashbacks, cliffhangers can add value to your story, but you should be careful not to use them unless you are convinced that what you come up with works well and adds value to your story.

A novel use of a cliffhanger could be in a secret or bonus level that foreshadows a sequel—you could consider such a cliffhanger the equivalent of sticking your hero up the tree of the sequel.

Red Herrings

Red herrings are false clues. Although a number of famous storytellers, including Alfred Hitchcock, use red herrings on a routine basis, you should avoid simply tossing red herrings into the story to add filler.

Done well, a red herring will lead to a dead end story-wise, but will instead lead the player further into the story. A good example of this would be to have a plea for help from an old friend of the hero turn out to be a trap laid by the villains. The hero dispatches the ambushers, which seems 'like the end of the story—until it turns out that the old friend is really the master villain trying to kill the hero. Make sure your red herrings fit naturally into the story, and that they are only red herrings (false clues) on the surface level—there should always be some meat on their bones the player does not see at first, but will come to appreciate later.

Keeping It All Together

Let's assume that you are sold on the idea of adapting Hollywood's storytelling techniques to your title. However, it sounds like telling two levels of story across three acts while creating all the things a good level needs (environment layout, triggers, enemy and object placement, etc.) will be a lot of work. How will you accomplish all these tasks?

One way to track all your level elements is with the "Story Matrix," as shown in Table 5.4.1. Using a spreadsheet (or a table, if you do not have access to a spreadsheet program) name one column "Story Element" followed by a column for each level/ mission/episode in your story. If you like, color-code the episode columns that fall under each act in your story.

Each row under "Story Element" will contain the name of an entity. Each cell under a level column will contain a describe how the story element should be advanced in that level. Cells that are left empty indicate the story element is not developed during that level.

The Story Matrix can help you track the various story elements you weave throughout your game levels, and helps you ensure that each gets resolved. I find it helpful to mark story element resolutions in boldface so that it is clear they have been resolved.

Additionally, the Story Matrix can point out problems with your story element development in two ways: First, the Story Matrix provides you with a bird's-eye view of how much storytelling happens in each level or mission. A single level with too many developments will produce problems on different levels. Story-wise, the dramatic pace of the level will seem too rushed because you have too many different things going on, which will confuse the player. Gameplay-wise, the action must stop or slow significantly while you develop all these threads. The Story Matrix helps you see this and helps you juggle elements to balance things better.

Second, all of your major story threads should be wrapped up in the third act. The most important story elements (especially your character's main motivation)

Table 5.4.1 Story Matrix

Story Element	Level 1 (Act I)	Level 2 (Act II)	Level 3 (Act II)	Level 4 (Act III)
London is Under Attack! (Through Line)	"Our hero, Dirk Manly, is dispatched to a remote country-side village."	Dirk uncovers Bug-Eyed Monsters who prey upon hapless villagers.	Dirk chases the Evil Alien Overlord.	"Dirk and the Over-lord go at it aboard the Big Alien Spaceship. Dirk wins the day, but is trapped on the spaceship. Where is it headed? To be continued…"
Bug-Eyed Monsters!	Dirk is ambushed by bug-eyed monsters.	Bug-Eyed Monsters use flanking maneuvers to try to nail Dirk.	"Overlord mutates all of the Bug-Eyed Monsters into Bug-Eyed, Lobster-Clawed, Fire-Spitting Behemoths, and sends them at Dirk."	"Behemoths board the spaceship, chasing Dirk."
Secret Lab		Dirk uncovers a secret underground alien laboratory filled with bug eyed monsters and hap-less villagers.	Dirk can destroy the laboratory in this level.	
Evil Alien Overlord	Drop some fore-shadowing here about the overlord.	"Overlord makes an appearance, but slinks into the deep caves."	"Overlord narrowly escapes from Dirk, and boards the spaceship."	"Overlord takes off in the spaceship, trying to escape Dirk."
Spaceship			The gigantic alien spaceship can be seen in the distance. It's huge and menacing.	"Spaceship is on auto-pilot, with only Dirk on board…"
Hapless Villagers	Villagers beg for Dirk's help and generally run around in a panic.	Villagers beg for Dirk's help and generally run around in a panic.	Villagers may actually band together and help Dirk in this	

should be resolved as dramatically as possible, and as late in Act Three as possible (otherwise, you might have the player twiddling his thumbs well before the end credits start to roll). If you can see that too many important story elements are finishing in Act Two or early Act Three, you will know you need to rebalance your third act.

Conclusion

With an army of plot devices and formulae, and the support of a Story Matrix to keep you on course, you should find it relatively easy to add rich, deep, and rewarding stories to your level-based game designs.

If you are still a bit overwhelmed, begin simply—limit yourself to only half a dozen fairly straightforward story elements and observe how they work for your current title. If you like the results, become a little more ambitious with your next effort.

Most of all, add story elements only if two criteria can be met: that doing so enhances the game and that you enjoy the process. After all, if you do not enjoy designing the game and your audience does not like playing it, it was not worth doing.

THE USER
COMMUNITY

6.0

Introduction

Designers do not work in a vacuum. Increasingly, users are building communities around the games they love: they create new levels and missions and even bring favorite characters out of the game world and into the universe of fan art and fiction. Thus, not only are players our bread and butter, they are fast becoming our equal partners in the creative process.

A Growing Symbiosis

The first step in the evolution of a true partnership between developers and players took place as soon as games and personal computers entered the home. During informal gatherings, which began in local stores and computer clubs and soon migrated to the online networks of the time, the makers of entertainment software and their customers discussed the games they loved and ideas for improving them. Sometimes, the results were immediate: amateur developers would go home, code feverishly, and come to the next meeting with new versions of their games. When shrink-wrapped software was involved, the users' input would influence the next title created by the developer.

The next step emerged with the introduction of service Web sites, where players could learn about the developers, download patches, and obtain additional game levels. Catering to the needs of the player community this way enhanced sales and kept games alive, but the users' involvement remained passive: they would take what the developers gave them, but could contribute little content of their own.

Concurrently, online communities evolved around a few games. Some had actually been in existence since the days of the commercial online services, when multiplayer worlds like *Isle of Kesmai*, *Gemstone III*, and *Air Warrior* drew paying customers at $3 to $6 an hour, sometimes for years. However, the phenomenon exploded with Blizzard's *battle.net*, the massively multiplayer fantasy worlds, and the ubiquitous *Quake* servers: now, players became active contributors by building a culture around (or even within) the game.

The final step (thus far) came with the appearance of freely distributed level design tools. Now, a game is a shared creation: the developers build a world, a framework for the collective imagination of the community; then, thanks to the efforts of many, the world grows and evolves into far more than the designers themselves could have intended. What fan fiction did for *Star Trek*, fan levels did for *Quake*: transform the creation of a few into the focus of a collective sense of pride, loyalty, and emotional ownership.

Important Partners

People talk, or email, or chat; gamers more than most. Developers who take the time to open a prelaunch Web site, write an online diary, participate in fan activities, release patches promptly, or simply respond to fan email, buy themselves goodwill and trust, which may later translate into sales. However, establishing an equal partnership between developers, publishers, and customers does far more than increase short-term revenues. It creates brand loyalty—and better products.

Not only do people like to talk: they want to be heard. A developer who trades email with a fan a few times is no longer a faceless stranger; the player will look for the developer's upcoming projects and tell friends about them.

Players may also have some very good ideas about what could have made a game better. (They may also have very *bad* ideas; you, as the professional in the conversation, will have to discern between the two.) The best player input can find its way into a sequel, but be careful: this is a litigious society, and while most players will cheerfully discuss games just because they like them, the risk of a "stolen idea" nuisance lawsuit always exists. Talk to your company's counsel to determine how to proceed in this area.

Finally, some companies may find tomorrow's developers among today's players. The creators of great freeware levels for the game you released last year may be just the kind of people your team will need next month.

The Ones That Got Away (Again and Again)

As an industry, we have hardly even begun to reach out beyond the young male hobbyist audience of our beginnings. There is an enormous, largely untapped market of female, middle-aged, and/or elderly people who are passionate about entertainment—but have yet to find much that is entertaining *to them* in what we offer.

Contrary to popular belief, games targeted to atypical audiences do exist, and sometimes achieve significant success:

- Middle-aged women, not male teenagers, are the most active online gaming demographic slice—but they play Bridge, not shooters.
- Casino games consistently rank among the annual best sellers on the PC platform.
- The industry's breakaway hits, like *Tetris* and *Myst*, reach across all social divides.

Some years ago, the company I worked for developed simple arcade, puzzle, and card games for an interactive television service. Not only did the elderly constitute a significant subset of our customer base, they were among the most loyal. In fact, some of them called to thank us for making games they could relate to, because spending so much time manipulating the controllers alleviated the arthritis in their hands!

Sadly, these achievements have been relegated—by us professionals, not by the consumers—to the disreputable fringes of the industry, like an ugly family secret.

When we discuss these types of games at all, it is to deride their lack of sexy special effects or dismiss their developers as untalented hacks who could not cut it in the "real" game industry. Well, it is true that so-called mass market games usually involve less technical wizardry than hardcore gamer flagships, but it is fairly safe to assume that the publishers of *Deer Hunter* stopped fretting over the game's low-tech look and feel once the checks started piling in.

Gaming is already a huge business, but certainly not so huge that it can afford to ignore four-fifths of the buying public.

Other Perspectives

The articles included in this section look at ways to reach out to audiences beyond the archetypical teenaged male gamer, and discuss how to take advantage of the tremendous vitality of the player community to make better games than we could on our own:

- Sheri Graner Ray asks what must be done to make games appealing to females—and the answer is surprisingly simple.
- David Michael explains how to create games that support and nurture player communities, thus ensuring their long-term success.
- Ben Carter reports on the growing phenomenon of fan appropriation of game characters, stories, and content, in Asia and elsewhere.
- Wayne Imlach discusses ways to use player-made modifications to a game as a design tool.
- Tom Sloper explains how taking an active role in supporting the player community after a game is released can help build loyalty—and obtain good advice for sequels.
- And finally, Ruud van de Moosdjik discusses the peculiar challenges involved in designing games for very young children.

Artists in other fields make a living by building a fan base and maintaining it for many years. With a few notable exceptions, this phenomenon has been curiously lacking in our business. It is time to rectify the situation.

6.1

But What If the Player Is Female?

Sheri Graner-Ray

sheri@silvar.com

Thousands upon thousands of computer and console games are sold each year, each title bigger, better, and faster than the last. The market, once considered a small niche, is gaining mainstream acceptance, and the average American home now owns at least one game system—and probably a computer or two as well.

With the wild popularity of such games as *Deer Hunter* and *You Don't Know Jack*, game publishers began to push their developers to produce games that target this new "non-gamer" market. Designers began to look at new genres and special interest markets outside the traditional game field in an attempt to find the next blockbuster. However, in this frantic quest for new market share, one question remains overlooked: "But what if the player is female?"

The topic of designing games with females in mind immediately makes developers think of the Mattel® line of Barbie™ titles. They envision makeup- or fashion-oriented games, shudder, and immediately drop the idea. But designing with females in mind is about much more than a pink box. Simply by considering the question of whether the player is female, the designer opens up his or her product to a whole new market and may actually design a better game while doing so!

Taking the female player into consideration can be as simple as making sure the avatars of both genders are equally represented, or offering additional solutions to problems. However, before the designer can introduce these concepts into their game, they must understand some of the differences between males and females, and how each approaches games.

It is obvious that entertainment for men can be very different than entertainment for women. Through my research, I have identified several physiological and psychological differences that have an effect on what each gender considers "fun." Three of these key differences are: stimulation, how each gender handles conflict and the associated rewards, and the differences in each gender's learning style.

Stimulus Response

One of the most profound differences to observe between the genders is the difference in stimulus response. Males are visually stimulated, meaning that when given visual stimuli they have a physiological reaction. They experience an "adrenalin rush" of increased perspiration, pulse, and respiration. These responses result from any intense visual stimulus, such as a fast-moving object or vivid colors.

This reaction to visual stimuli can be traced back to one of the earliest forms of human culture, the hunter-gatherer society, where males served as the hunters and females as the gatherers. This arrangement made sense because the adult females spent a very large portion of their lives either pregnant or lactating; either condition renders chasing a wildebeest a bit difficult. Also, the female was vital to the survival of the tribe because her offspring relied upon her for sustenance. So, the male could take the much more risky job of hunting because if he died, it was only one loss. If the female died, it often meant the loss of two—the woman and the child that was dependent upon her.

Additionally, human eyes are set forward in the front of their head. This is an eye configuration seen particularly in predators that hunt by sight, because this configuration results in good depth perception and the ability to quickly perceive movement. The more successful hunters were the ones that saw the prey first and reacted to it quickest. To react quickly to the prey required a body that was prepared by an increased heart rate and respiration rate–all the result of an adrenaline surge that was spurred by the visual stimulus. The successful hunters were the ones that survived to pass on their traits—classic Darwinian evolution.

Females, on the other hand, do not receive this sort of physiological response from visual stimuli. This does not mean females do not appreciate them; in fact, females can be just as passionate about visual images as males are. They simply do not receive the physiological response that their male counterparts do.

What does elicit a similar physiological response in females is emotional and/or tactile input. A perfect example of the effect of tactile input can be seen in the arcades of today verse those of 10 to 20 years ago. Ten years ago, video arcades were dark places filled with rows of machines where males hung out. If females were there, they were usually standing around watching the boys play.

As game technology advanced, the arcade game manufacturers began to integrate tactile stimuli into their products through the introduction of forced-feedback components. A surprising thing began to happen: arcades found their revenues increasing beyond what new games usually generated, because tactile feedback devices were more than just new technologies, they were the right new technologies to attract a female audience. Arcade owners invested more in these types of games, and they are now one of the predominant features in arcades today. This phenomenon can be directly related to the effect of tactile stimuli on female entertainment.

Emotional stimulation is just as important for female entertainment. The romance novel industry is built on this: publishers know that when you give a female an emotional stimulus, she experiences a rush of increased heart and respiration rate and will seek to repeat the response. This explains why thousands of young women watched *Titanic* 16 times. Likewise, males will return again and again to a flight simulator or first person shooter to "feel the rush" of the visual stimuli, as his guns blow up his opponent into millions of tiny particles. Each response serves as a "reward" for the person engaging in the entertainment and encourages them to return to it repeatedly.

Conflict Resolution

Another area where males and females differ is in response to conflict situations.

Males, when presented with a conflict, will seek to push the outcome into a confrontational situation with results that can be measured by victory or defeat. That is, males will prefer to resolve a conflict with a clear knowledge of who won and who lost.

However, given the same situation, females will choose to use diplomacy, compromise, negotiation, and even manipulation to resolve it. Hence the result is not measured by who won and who lost, but rather by the quality of the emotional resolution/solution reached.

This, again, can be taken back to human beginnings. Being pregnant or having a nursing child would make the female less able to defend herself in battle. Therefore, any physical confrontation that might result in harm would be something to avoid, and she would favor nonphysical conflict resolution methods. It would also benefit her to not repeat the situation that led to conflict, thus the focus on coming to a satisfactory resolution rather than a victory.

Because we also know, through various sociological studies, that patriarchal societies arise when there is conflict over resources, the desire to win would be an asset to the gender whose job it was to defend the home territories. It would also benefit the gender whose job it was to hunt and kill prey. The desire to negotiate a settlement rather than to fight to win would have been beneficial to the gender who was constrained by the physical demands of pregnancy and lactation.

Learning Styles

Men and women also have very different learning styles. There are numerous books dedicated to this particular subject; however, I am going to focus on one specific point: males learn by doing, while females want to know how something works before they put their hands on it.

Go into any arcade to see this premise in action. Young males will rush to a machine, glance at the attract loop, shove their tokens into the slots, and begin to pound excitely on the controls while hollering to their friends, "How does this work?"

Now watch the young females at the arcade. They will walk slowly through the aisles of machines, stopping to study attract loops or to watch others play. They will remain until they either understand the game's mechanics, or decide it is not worth trying to figure out. They will not put their tokens into the machines until they are comfortable with their understanding of how it works. Because the attract loops are most often designed with fast action and bright colors (visual stimuli) to attract males, they do not often show how the game actually is played. The manufacturer relies on the masculine inclination to learn by doing. The result of this is an attract loop which does not attract females, and thus girls very often walk off without putting their money into the machine.

Avatar Choices

Men and women also differ in how they feel about the character or "avatar" they are watching on the screen.

It is very important for females to have a character or avatar that is female and is not hyper-sexualized. There is quite a bit of misunderstanding about this issue. Male developers have often told me they do not understand why females "have to make such a big fuss" about it; after all, they (the males) are comfortable playing a female avatar. Unfortunately, there are societal reasons why males and females have different reactions to the character they are being asked to identify with.

In most sociology courses, a student will be introduced to the concept of the *pyramid of power*. This is a model that represents the power level of people within the strata of society. Everyone falls somewhere into this pyramid, with those holding more societal power placed above those holding less power.

One of the concepts taught about the pyramid of power is that everyone is comfortable operating within their own strata. They understand the societal rules involved with that level, and move easily within it. They are also comfortable moving in the levels *below* their own strata. However, when asked to move into a level above their own, they become uncomfortable. This discomfort continues to increase the further the person moves up the pyramid, away from their own level.

In the majority of today's cultures, the upper levels of the pyramid are populated with males. Thus, it begins to become clear why a female is not comfortable moving "up" a level to take the role of a male: it is above her strata and is simply not a comfortable role for her. At the same time, it explains why males have little difficultly stepping "down" the pyramid to take the role of the female.

Hyper-sexualized vs. Hyper-masculine/feminine

This separation between the genders is exacerbated when the female avatar is hyper-sexualized. To understand this point, it is important to understand the difference between the terms *hyper-masculine/feminine* and *hyper-sexualized*.

Hyper-masculine or *hyper-feminine* means an emphasis is placed on those qualities beyond the physical that make a character male or female. Perfect examples of this idea are the characters of Blanche and Stan in Tennessee Williams' play *A Streetcar*

Named Desire. Both characters are ugly exaggerations of their genders. Blanche is purposefully helpless and shallow, while Stan is animalistic and brutish. And, while they are both quite sexual, neither is hyper-sexualized.

Hyper-sexualized on the other hand means having exaggerated physical gender traits. We see this regularly in the case of female avatars in computer games today. They have enormous breasts, tiny waists, well-rounded derrieres, and are shown in provocative clothing meant to enhance these exaggerated features. This makes it apparent that rather than a character, they are "eye-candy" or something designed to titillate the male players. Males will claim that the male characters are also hyper-sexualized, because they look like body builders or Conan the Barbarian. This, however, is not a hyper-sexualization; rather, it is simply caricature. If the male character were hyper-sexualized, he would be wearing a tight swimsuit and presenting a huge, erect phallus.

It is no wonder females are not comfortable with the majority of avatars they are presented with today. At best, they are being asked to step up to a character whose role they are not comfortable with or, at worst, they are being asked to take on a role that is sexually objectified by the members of a higher strata. This does not mean you cannot make female avatars sexy. It just means there is a big difference between Xena and a character wearing only pasties and a chainmail g-string.

We know that males like win/lose outcomes to conflict. They are visually stimulated and seek out the rush it produces as a reward. They also learn by doing. Now think about the average "fighting" game. The player takes on an opponent, one on one, finds secret moves through trial and error key strokes, and receives visual stimuli of flying blows and blood, until he wins with a triumphant explosion of body parts. It is no wonder males are attracted to this sort of game. Furthermore, because of the visual stimuli and the ability to win, they may seek this entertainment over and over again.

Females and Violence

At this point I would like to address the common myth that females do not like games that are violent or gory. Nothing could be further from the truth. A study *Her Interactive* conducted with junior high school girls in Albuquerque, New Mexico, found that girls had no problem with violence. They did not find fighting or shooting games too "gory" or "icky." What they did say was that those types of games were *boring*. They did not see the attraction of fighting repeatedly with no purpose other than to defeat the other character.

However, when some of the components that engage females were added to the mix, their attitude immediately changed. For instance, when a compelling reason for the girls to fight (such as a reason to hate the opponent, or something to fight for) was included, they were immediately more engaged.

Conclusion

Armed with the knowledge that females prefer emotional resolution to conflict situations, tactile or emotional stimulus as reward, have a "want to know how it works first" style of learning, and want an avatar they can identify with, it is possible for the game designer to begin to have answers when asked that fateful question, "But what if the player is female?"

The answers can be as simple as providing equal representation of genders in a fantasy role-playing game's avatar selection, or as complicated as providing alternative solutions to combat situations in flight sims. It can be as involved as providing deep story background for the characters in fighting games or shooters, or as easy as providing a male love interest as well as a female. While all of these things may take more time to design or implement, none of them would ruin any genre. In fact, all of them provide the player with the choice to become involved with them or not—regardless of gender.

And giving the players more choices and more control over the game is *always* the best design decision.

6.2

Designing for Online Community

David Michael

davidrm@samugames.com

Today's online games attract growing communities of players that come together not just to compete, but to get to know each other. Friendships are being made, alliances forged, and histories passed on to new generations of players.

Strong communities of players can often keep a multiplayer game growing—and profitable—long after a traditional single-player game has been dredged from the bottom of the bargain bin. With that kind of potential, it makes sense to design your game from the beginning to promote a sense of community.

But how do you create a "sense of community" among your players? The answer is easier than you might think.

Defining Online Community

Community is a powerful social concept. But what is *community*? And how does it translate into the online world of the Internet?

The simplest definition of *community* is a group of people who share an interest, whether one as narrow as home gardening, or one as broad as a political affiliation. People identify themselves and others by their participation—or lack of participation—in particular communities. But this definition overlooks the more social aspects of community, and turns an important human institution into a filing system.

An expanded definition of community, which better emphasizes the social nature of the term, is ". . . a group of people with a shared interest, purpose, or goal, who get to know each other better over time." [Kim00] This definition moves beyond the simple beginning of "something in common," and portrays communities as a dynamic collection of people interacting and developing relationships with one another.

This is the definition we are interested in. We want our players to be more than the collection of people who bought the game. We want them to know that they are part of something bigger. The game provides the context for the community by existing. But by letting the players "get to know each other better over time," the game also provides and promotes a sense of community.

This sense of "online community" encompasses more than just playing the game. It also includes preparing to play the game, discussing the game, retelling experiences from the game, and, ultimately, *living* the game. In other words, through its online community, the game becomes a part of the player's *life*—not just an experience that lasts some number of hours before the player "beats the game" and moves on to other things. Online community provides a sense of belonging, which can become powerfully addictive.

So how does a designer "design for online community"? The answer is simple: Let your players talk to each other.

Let Them Talk

People like talking to each other; therefore, it only makes sense to let them.

The simple urge to talk to other people, to relate and share experiences, is a powerful draw, evidenced by the continued popularity of "talker" MU*s and Internet Relay Chat (IRC). These venues survive and even flourish in the face of such technological *tours de force* as *EverQuest* and *Ultima Online*.

Most talkers MU*s are entirely text-based, using technology older than most game developers. The gameplay is driven by the role-playing descriptions (and out-of-character chatter) of the different players as they interact within the loose framework of the MU*. IRC works very much the same way, but without even the minimal structure of a talker MU*. A community develops simply because people talk to each other. The game (or chat channel) serves only as a catalyst for the interaction.

Because the players talk to each other, they meet, they swap secrets, they exchange tips and tricks, and, in the process, they develop ties of familiarity and even friendship. And because of these ties and relationships *they come back!* Even if they stop playing the game, they will continue visiting to see how the game is developing and to catch up with their friends.

The players keep coming back because they *know* the people there. Remember the sitcom *Cheers*? Certainly, there were other, possibly better, bars in Boston, but the regulars kept coming back because Cheers is where they could meet the people they knew. This was their extended family, their home away from home.

Never underestimate the social and psychological benefits inherent in being where "everybody knows your name."

Implementing Online Community

In the online world, the primary method of socialization is chatting, specifically text chat. A holdover from the early, low-bandwidth days of the Internet, text chat continues to be popular because of its simplicity and its flexibility. The proliferation of microphones and Web cams has made voice chat and face-to-face chat possible, but plain text still rules the Web.

Even within the constraints of text chat, however, there are still many different kinds of communication: general (large-group) chat, small-group chat, player-to-player chat, notes, and more. Not all are viable for all games and some are more effective for building community among players.

General Chat

General chat refers to a small number of large forums that are visible (possibly as an option) to all players logged into the game. All chatter is made of scrolling text, shown in chronological order of arrival at the player's PC. Whatever a particular player says is identified by his name or in-game persona. Sometimes the player is able to embellish the chat with small graphical emoticons.

Zone chat is a form of general chat. All players in a particular zone or region of the online world can participate in zone chat. Zone chat is not global because it is limited to the zone, but as online games become larger, the number of players in a single game zone also gets larger.

There is no such thing as privacy in the general chat forum. Anything said is open to comment from anyone else also logged in (and paying attention). This can make for some interesting, amusing, or annoying banter. It can also be infuriating to players who simply want to play the game and be left alone, so participation in a general chat forum should be optional. In the same vein, if it is important that the chatter in a game be in character, then it is a good idea to provide a separate general forum for out of character discussions.

More than any other chat type, general chat sets the tone for the game's community. The topics that are discussed (and the level of civility that is displayed) in a general chat are often the first impression a new player will receive of the community. Thus, it is important that all general chat forums be monitored and moderated.

Small-Group Chat

The *small-group chat* is a more condensed version of the general chat forum. Usually limited to a small number of participants (5-20 players), the small group allows for both general discussion and semi-private conversation. Small-group chat expands the intimacy of private conversation to include a select number of others.

Generally, the only relevant small-group chatting that is likely to occur in a game is between teammates, but even "sworn enemies" in the game may join the same discussion if it interests them. A small number of topical conversations about aspects of the game world may also erupt outside of the game environment itself, for example in a general lobby area.

Person-to-Person Private Conversation

Person-to-person conversation is the exact opposite of general chat. Two players swap messages in a private conversation, whether through a scrolling chat system like IRC or via instant messages. This is the most private communication option.

While general chat introduces players to each other, private conversation allows them to get to know each other. It also allows for private planning sessions between two players.

Buddy Lists

When the number of players online at any time is large (more than 100), it can be difficult for players to discover whether the other player or players they wish to talk to are also online. If the game world is divided into zones, then this becomes even more problematic because there is a good chance that the players are in different zones. Allowing the player to set up a "buddy list" can alleviate this problem. The player immediately knows if her "buddies" are online or offline, and can easily talk to one or more of them if she wants.

Because the buddy list applies only within the game, the implementation can be kept simple. Displaying the names of the buddies with an online/offline flag, and giving the player the option to open a person-to-person chat session and/or send simple messages, is usually enough. The buddy list's feature set does not need to compete with ICQ or MSN Messenger to be extremely useful within the game.

Buddy lists keep the player from being overwhelmed by the number of other players also in the game community. By making it easy to find the people she knows, you help the player create a community within a community.

Note System

Not all communication must be immediate. Players might want to leave messages for other players who are not online at the moment. So, give them access to a global note forum, similar to a Usenet newsgroup or a bulletin board. Of course, players will often "pollute the airwaves" when they engage in long discussions of dubious worth, but there will also be some legitimate use made of the facility. And both kinds of notes ultimately help shape the community of the game.

Unlike the various chat communication options, the note system does not need to claim screen real estate all (or even most) of the time. A separate form or screen can handle the note functions. If the player wants to check the notes, she opens the form and does so. If not, she will not.

And if you do not want to support the note system within your game, you are not required to. There are a number of packages now available, both free and pay, that you can use to setup a "message board" Web page. Ezboard (*http://www.ezboard.com*) and Ultimate Bulletin Board (UBB) (*http://www.infopop.com*) are popular options.

Voice Chat

Voice chat offers a new level of interaction above and beyond normal text chat. Because the human voice is so expressive, it is possible to convey significantly more meaning than is possible when typing in questions and responses.

Voice chat provides an excellent in-game team-coordination feature. Rather than having to stop what you are doing to type in a call for help or provide information, team members can "just talk" and achieve a high level of coordination.

Voice chat is becoming more and more viable, but its bandwidth requirements are still high. Also, the nature of voice communication limits it to only a small number of participants. If you have more than four or five people in a group talking at the same time, it ceases to be a conversation and becomes a conference call. Contrast that with a scrolling text scenario, where it is not uncommon to have hundreds of people conversing on a variety of topics and even engaging in side conversations, all at the same time in the same channel.

Although arguably the best small-team communication option possible, voice communication is, unfortunately, not a method of meeting and interacting with many of new people. So while voice chat can augment an online community, it generally does not create it.

Integrating Chat

You have many players online and they are all talking at once. How do you present all that chatter in a way that is both easy to read when the player is interested, and easy to ignore when she is not? How do you make it obvious who is talking? How do you differentiate general conversation from private messages?

The simplest method of presenting text chat is a scrolling display, with each line attributed to the player who said it. New chat follows old, and when the scrolling area is filled, newest pushes oldest off the top. It is easy to implement, and easy for the players to understand. Unfortunately, such a method can take up a lot of screen real estate. Even if the text transparently "overlays" the main game display, it can become difficult to see real game information through the clutter of text.

If you can afford to make in-game chat less convenient, then you can minimize the space it requires and force the players to take extra steps if they want to converse. If instead you want chat to be a vital part of the experience of the game, then you will want it to be as easy to use and understand as possible. It is even possible to support both, by allowing the player to toggle back and forth between chat interface and the game. During a heads-down, high concentration period, the player can switch off all conversation, or reduce it to a minimal space on his display. Afterward, when the situation has eased, he can bring back the normal chat interface.

There is no one-size-fits-all solution that a game designer or user interface specialist can apply. Every game is different, and user interfaces for games are still evolving. It is important, though, that the communication interfaces in the game be considered from the beginning.

Protecting Online Community

Having explored the ways in which you can allow your players to talk to each other, we must now consider that not everything that a player says is going to be appreciated by all other players. The competitive nature of most games, pitting the players against each other, guarantees that flare-ups will occur. But beyond the obvious cases of in-your-face trash-talking and sour grapes, there are more insidious uses of communication to intimidate and harass.

"Community Guidelines" and "Terms of Service" must be posted and agreed to by all players. These help protect the players, but also help protect the company providing the service. A full description of how these should be created, however, is beyond the scope of this article.

There are features that can be built into the game to provide players with the means of protecting themselves. An example of such a feature is an "ignore player" option. This option allows the player to choose whom she will and will not talk to by suppressing all communication (text chat, notes, voice chat, *et al*) from the ignored player.

Another feature the game might provide, depending on the nature of the game and its players, is a language filter. This would be an optional feature that the players themselves would turn off or on. Like the ignore flag, this is a player-empowerment feature.

In addition to posted "Community Guidelines" and the built-in protections discussed above, the online community will need moderators and mentors. Whether volunteers who have accepted the added responsibility or paid employees, these moderators and mentors assist new players in learning the ropes, ensure that the posted guidelines are adhered to, and keep disruptions and "bad blood" from overwhelming the atmosphere of the game.

This solution may seem more of a post-production issue than a design issue, because it only comes into play when the game is actually online. To properly support the administrative functions of these community leadership roles, however, the game must have the appropriate hooks designed into it from the beginning.

Promoting Online Community

Promoting the development of a group of players into a community begins with letting them talk to each other. But what comes next?

Obviously, you want your online community to be as friendly and open as possible. A community in which players feel welcome—and wanted!—is not something that can be handled with a "fire-and-forget" solution.

Discussing all the ways to promote online community is beyond the scope of this article. However, each path begins with taking an active part in the community, and being a continued presence as the game grows and changes.

Players enjoy interacting with the people who designed and developed the game. The people who maintain the game do not have as much "star power," but are still important to the players, and are looked up to. Take advantage of that fact. Interact with your players, and they will make sure you know about the bugs in the game, they will suggest features that will make the game more enjoyable, and they will give you a good "feel" for how the game is doing.

There is no substitute for active participation. No community can thrive without direction. You must plan for community from the beginning, and you must provide leadership as the community grows.

For more on this topic, see [Sloper02] later in this section.

Conclusion

As more and more massively multiplayer online games are released, the competition for players will only increase. With so many games to choose from, player loyalty will be difficult to capture. But by promoting a sense of community among the players of your game, you can keep them involved indefinitely.

Communication is the heart of a community. People who talk to each other become friends and/or rivals. They are a recognized presence.

And *that* will keep them coming back.

Bibliography

[Kim00] Kim, A.J., *Community Building on the Web,* Peachpit Press, 2000.

[Sloper02] Sloper, T., "Following Up after the Game Is Released: It's Not over When It's Over," *Game Design Perspectives*, Charles River Media, 2002.

6.3

Character Interaction Outside the Game World

Ben Carter

ben@gunk.demon.co.uk

It is a commonly held belief that the sole factor determining the "worth" of a video game is the quality of its gameplay. While this is certainly true in some cases—*Tetris,* for example—in others it is more accurate to say that a multitude of elements make up the player's experience of the game, and hence define how they feel about it. A large part of this experience depends on the game world and on characters therein—and if done well, these act as the most readily recognizable image by which the game is known.

While it is natural for marketing departments to make use of characters to promote the game, what is more interesting is the promotion that the fans will do themselves if they enjoy the game—and how encouraging this behavior can benefit the developer enormously.

Missed Opportunities

In the Western world, many game companies regard character personalities and storylines as incidental extras to be added at the end of the project, in order to flesh out the manual text, justifying this approach with the statement that it is the gameplay that counts, not the incidental "fluff."

Japanese companies, on the other hand, tend to take a very different view: they see that characters are important, sometimes more so than the gameplay. While this thought does generate some games that are little more than digital stories (and in fact, there is an entire genre of Japanese games that are just that), a happy medium can be reached in which gameplay and characterization are in balance.

And then something wonderful happens. The player will happily overlook the odd bit of substandard gameplay or design because they like the characters and story (even if the story has little to do with the gameplay itself), and likewise because they are enjoying playing the game, they will not mind or much if the odd cliché or bit of poor dialogue creeps in. The whole, in this case, is more definitely greater than the sum of its parts.

Better still: the benefits of this balanced approach to game design extend beyond improving the game experience directly, because the players will think of beloved characters and world even when they are not playing.

Character Appeal

So where do the fans fit into all this? Simple: people relate well to other people, even if those other people are just characters in a video game. This personal connection, once established in the players' minds, gives them a handle on the game world *that they can build on themselves.*

This phenomenon also happens, to some extent, with gameplay. Dedicated players build homemade extensions that extend or tweak the mechanics of popular games, sometimes with great success. But the range of possibilities with game characters is much wider: stories, artwork, music, poems—even other games!

In Japan, this type of fan activity is enormously pervasive. Much of it has grown out of similar fan productions based on popular *anime* or *manga* series, leading to the two intermingling freely, which is hardly surprising given how frequently successful *anime* series spawn spin-off games, and vice versa.

Japanese fans of every genre of game produce massive quantities of material, a large proportion of which is in the form of *doujinshi*, fan-produced books containing stories, artwork, and similar materials. Somewhat akin to Western fanzines, these doujinshi are usually produced in small quantities at print shops, and sold to other fans at conventions, by mail, or through the various specialist shops that stock them.

The Doujinshi Subculture

One of the largest of the doujinshi conventions, *Comiket* (short for "Comic Market"), is held twice a year, and over the course of three days is attended by 20,000 "circles" (doujinshi groups), each with a stand for their latest creations, and over 300,000 visitors. A large percentage of the material offered is based on videogames, and popular games are particularly well represented. Indeed, the phone-book sized catalogue for Comiket #60, held in the summer of 2001, reveals that around 720 circles were devoted almost exclusively to material based on games from just two companies—*Leaf* and *Key*. And of those, the vast majority were focused on a mere four games, *Kanon, One, Air,* and *To Heart,* all four of which are highly character-centric adventures and/or dating simulations. These games' massive popularity has, in turn, pushed their expansion into other media, such as anime, novels, and manga.

There are two ways of viewing this phenomenon. On one hand, this activity is obviously at the very least legally dubious, because the doujinshi are based on copyrighted characters and, in some cases, compete directly with official merchandise. (However, Japanese law regarding this matter is somewhat different from Western convention.) On the other, this grassroots activity provides the best promotion a game company could hope for, and can often expand the market for its games and official merchandise significantly, and at no cost whatsoever. Most Japanese companies seem to be of the latter opinion—almost no legal action (or even threats of such) has been taken against doujinshi creators.

Fan-Produced Games

Certain games have achieved cult status amongst Japanese fans. The characters in the dating sim *To Heart* are so popular that, in addition to innumerable doujinshi, they have also appeared in several fan-produced games, the most notable of these is the *Queen of Heart* series of fighting games starring the *To Heart* characters.

The production values of these fan games are remarkably high; while not particularly hi-tech, they have been designed and tuned very well, and their artwork is superb. And while they may seem to be treading dangerously close to competing with the original product, the original *To Heart* games are dating sims (about as far from a fighting game as you can get), so there is little real economic conflict—and because the fans almost always distribute their work for free or a token cost, they cannot be easily accused of profiting by stealing the companies' hard work.

Ubiquitous Characters

One of the most striking facts regarding the popularity of game characters is that it is almost irrelevant what game they actually appear in. Many of the most famous characters have sprung from genres that are typically devoid of any story or personality: the original *Donkey Kong* and *Mario Bros* were both platform games with minimal relationship to the story, yet their star characters remain popular even today. Konami's *Twinbee* shoot-em-up spawned a long-running radio series, anime, and masses of merchandising, despite the characters not actually even appearing on screen during the original game!

Another (Western-developed) example of this phenomenon is *Lemmings*, the success of which was undoubtedly aided significantly by the uniqueness and appeal of the central characters, despite their irrelevance to the gameplay and their minute size.

Doujinshi as Job Training

Another (admittedly minor) consideration is that it is not uncommon for doujinshi or mod-making (i.e., the production of extra levels by amateurs, often using tools provided by the developers) to lead to "real" professional work for some fans. There have been many cases of mod-makers demonstrating their skills on a fan production, and subsequently getting a job with a company working on a similar type of game or technology. It is very much the case that, while the days of "bedroom coding" in the professional game industry have all but vanished, in the amateur domain it is alive and well—and the fan of your game today may well be the employee you hire tomorrow.

Target Your Fans

So how is all this relevant to games that are developed for Western audiences? After all, outside Japan, there is no massive base of fan talent just waiting for you to give them something to work with, right?

First, while they are by no means as common or well-organised as in Japan, there are dedicated fans who become devoted to games and produce spin-off works in the Western world. A simple Internet search for "fanart" or "fanfic" (short for "fan fiction") based on the *Final Fantasy* series will prove it. In fact, in comparison with their Japanese counterparts, these fans are practically starved of material to work from—so much so that the vast majority of their efforts are derived from translated Japanese titles rather than Western-developed ones.

Second, the size of this segment of the audience (and its effect on the market) is growing. With the continued growth of the Internet's use as a communications medium, and more and more people getting into gaming as a hobby, we can expect to see a dramatic increase in this sort of activity. Already, game-related Web sites like *Penny Arcade* (a comic strip about games and gamers) are receiving massive numbers of hits, and more gamers are obtaining their information and opinions on games from *other fans* than from traditional channels such as magazines or advertisement. Anything you as a developer can do to get more of these people interested in your game is a good thing—and if they are actively helping you promote the game, then that is a *great* thing.

Third, this is something you should be doing anyway. While it certainly takes effort to create good characters and a coherent "theme" for your world, it cannot be argued that the time taken does not noticeably improve the end product, and if nothing else, good characters can be a focus for your own marketing efforts.

Why You Should Encourage Fan Activity

Of course, you may feel that you do not want such dedicated fan activity, and that while the publicity would be nice, having fans ripping off your ideas and twisting your characters to fit their own concepts would be disastrous. Many Western companies seem to believe that the proper response to fan creations is to send a "cease and desist" order—after all, if these fans are so talented, why are they not creating their own characters?

This strategy can be self-defeating. First, stamping out fan activity eliminates any free publicity you may have been getting, in exchange for very little gain. Most of the time, there is absolutely no conflict between what the fans are producing and your interests. And even in cases in which conflict might exist (for example, if both you and fans are producing posters or similar merchandise), chances are the fans will buy the official items as well—after all, that is practically what defines them as fans.

Second, threatening your fans will only create bad feelings between them and your company, not only ruining any chance you had at acquiring free publicity through word of mouth, but probably also giving you some bad press as well. Fans do not take kindly to companies rewarding their dedication with threats, and will almost undoubtedly do their best to ensure that other fans know how they have been treated. While you may feel that you can live without these copyright-infringing villains buying your product, it is best not to forget that these are the same people who will be recommending games to all their friends, writing news and reviews for Web sites, and making their views known in public forums—and they can have very long memories.

If you do believe it necessary to curb the activities of some fans, then a polite letter explaining your reasons is much more likely to have the desired effect than sending in the lawyers.

A second issue, however, goes beyond the question of legalities: there is also the problem of the "artistic integrity" of the game. Many developers and publishers believe that they should have the final approval about where and how their characters appear, and the concept of fans being free to produce works that run contrary to the original "vision" (or marketing plan) goes against the grain. This is a much trickier issue. Chances are, if you have done your job well, and your fans actually do feel they can relate to the characters, they too will be very protective of them—regarding them as "common property," both in terms of wanting to be able to use them in their own works, and in terms of not wanting to see them "abused" at the hands of the company that created them (if, for example, a sequel is poorly scripted or designed). Issues in this area have no easy answers, and they are probably the most problematic for companies who would like to nurture fan support for their games.

Conclusion

The best place to look for answers, and for the future of game worlds, is in the Far East. Japanese developers have been building plot- and character-driven games since the origins of the computer game industry, and their fans (whose actions and attitudes are increasingly being mirrored by their counterparts in the Western world) have been the driving force behind many successes. So much so, in fact, that the phenomena has come full circle with the recent release of *Comic Party*—a game in which the player must guide their character through the trials and tribulations of producing a popular doujinshi book. As you might expect, the 2001 summer Comiket featured many, many *Comic Party* doujinshi!

Every game developer should look very seriously at how they are creating their characters and worlds, and asking themselves if they are up to the standards they would expect from other areas of their game design. After all, no one would ship a first-person shooter without at least a reasonably up-to-date graphics engine behind it, so why should they ship a game with a trite plot and boring characters?

It is easy to claim that the player should not be concerned with these details, but can you really state, with a straight face and without a shadow of a doubt, that your gameplay is so compelling that the player will not have time to notice the plot?

Bibliography

[Comiket2001] *Comiket* Web site: *www.comiket.co.jp/*
[Penny Arcade] *Penny Arcade* online comic: *www.penny-arcade.com/*

6.4

Utilizing the Consumer— Making the Most of Modding

Wayne Imlach

wimlach@hotmail.com

This article explains the advantages of allowing the consumer to modify and expand on the content of your game (*modding*), details the ways in which modding can be used to promote the game, suggests possible areas where modding can be implemented, and discusses the additional planning that modding requires.

Advantages of Modding

Allowing the consumer to participate in modding has several advantages.

Longevity and Value

New missions, models, and settings for a game can extend its lifespan. In effect, the consumer is receiving a game with the potential to offer far more content and enjoyment than what was originally provided, normally at little expense to the developer. In this way, a lively modding community can help sustain sales of a title well beyond its initial release.

License Workarounds

Modifications to commercial games may well be based on popular licences and intellectual properties that the developer would not normally be allowed to use himself. For example, a space combat game could be modified by consumers to include elements from a popular science fiction film. This change immediately makes the game more attractive to fans of that film, who might not have been interested in the game's original setting.

While legally questionable, this type of fan-driven workaround is unquestionably beneficial for developers. It has been used quite extensively in recent first-person shooting games, in which characters from popular films and comics have been modeled and animated to replace the default game characters.

Levels of Modification

It is possible to support modding of most of a game's assets and components, and commericial utilities such as Discreet's *gmax* are now available to support this in games that license it

Variables

Providing players with access to the attributes that define the behavior of game objects (such as hit points, damage values, costs, etc.) is one of the easiest methods you can use to allow players to tinker with your game. Players can use a variable-tweaking utility to create custom difficulty settings for your game. This tweaking ability is generally favored by either hardcore players who find even the highest difficulty setting easy, or extreme novices who are having trouble with the lowest settings. Depending on the importance of the targeted variables in your game, these adjustments can radically change the game's style , adding replay value once the player is bored with the default content.

If you plan to allow the player access to these values, ensure the values are stored in an easily read format (such as a plain text document) in the case of PC titles, or that they can be accessed from an editing screen in the case of console games. Variables usually use only a small amount of memory, and so the variable-tweaking flavor of modding is ideal for consoles that rely on limited memory card storage.

Scripting

When game events trigger the execution of customizable behaviors through a scripting language, allowing the player to create their own scripts can increase the longevity of a game considerably. Using scripts, consumers can create their own scenarios and levels easily by redefining the ways in which characters react to game events. For re-scripting to be feasible, the developer must ensure that all game events are accessible via script commands rather than hard-coded as special cases in the engine.

This kind of consumer input is generally limited to PC titles, because both script command documentation and the ability to generate a typed script is required. However, with the increase in new Internet-enabled consoles that accept keyboard peripherals, this limit may not remain for long. Like variables, scripts are storage-friendly and well-suited to consoles.

Textures

Modifying the textures placed on game objects is another one of the easiest and one of most spectacular ways of customizing a game. The most common use of this technique is in the generation of custom skins, which are wrapped around the 3D models in first-person shooters.

To facilitate this texture modification process, ensure that game textures are stored in a common file format understood by freely available graphics packages, and that they are suitably labelled in the game directory.

The visual content of console titles is less readily customized due to the general lack of storage space. However, you can provide a simple graphics editor for adjusting a small number of game textures—for example, the tattoos worn by in-game characters, logos on vehicles, and banners displayed by factions.

Sounds

Sound effects are another area that attracts the attention of the modding community, although changing sound effects requires greater access to additional hardware and, as such, is not easy to implement, especially for non-PC titles.

Given the appropriate sound editing software and/or hardware, consumers can modify game sound with a labelling scheme similar to the one used for textures and a standard file format accessible with common editing packages.

Modeling

Allowing the consumer to modify the 3D models used in the game is the next step in customization. Modifying models is normally much more difficult than the modifications discussed above, because the software used by industry professionals to create these models is not cheap and requires significant training. Creation of a custom editor to build game models is an alternative, but it can be a time-consuming task, especially if the editor is required to be robust enough for public use. However, modeling is still one area in which consumer support can really expand and improve the content of a game.

Animation

You must provide a means for custom animations if you want the consumer to create not only new variations on existing game characters or objects, but entirely new items that each have a unique look and behavior. Custom animation is a highly specialized area of modification, and most consumers who are courageous enough to attempt it are semi-professional or amateur animators who have already received some animation training. Thus, providing a custom editor is superfluous—ensuring that the models can be manipulated in commercial 3D modeling and animation software should suffice, because most amateur animators will already have access to these products.

Level Design

Level design is the area where consumers can add the most value to a game, though at the greatest cost to the developer. There are two ways to allow customers to develop entire levels for a game: invest in the development of a custom editor that will be released with the game, or ensure that the game levels are constructed using an existing public level editor. The approach chosen depends very much on how far the game strays from current technology, the complexity of the levels, and whether a licensed game engine is used. 3D titles will have the most complex architecture, though custom editors are often provided with licensed technology. Games based on tile maps are simple enough to construct that they can be packaged with a custom editor, as such software (required by the game developers themselves anyway) is no great burden to create.

Planning for Mods

Consumer input and editing should not be ignored during the design stage of the game. In fact, it should be considered an important aspect of its financial success. This consideration can even extend to the choice of the technology used to develop the game: what support does the technology provide for third-party modification?

In addition, ensure that adequate time is scheduled for the development and testing of editing software. While in-house developers might be able to forgive quirky and buggy editing software, the consumer will be less charitable. Documentation will also be required for any editors that are released with the game, so make sure that this information is collated and refined during the development process rather than at the end of the project.

Multi-User Issues of Modding

Where a game has the capability to support multiple players in an online environment, ensure that suitable provision has been taken to avoid manipulation of game elements for cheating purposes.

Ideally, any modifications made to a game should be stored in their own directory, and kept separate from the original game data (which should be preserved). Mods should be accessible as an alternative to existing data, rather than as an absolute replacement. This way, online games can be restricted to the original data, unless all players agree to the use of the same modified version of the game.

Finally, the game should provide the players with the ability to download mod files from other users, so that they can also take part in a custom session.

Conclusion

With the Internet providing most gamers with easy access to shared resources, the advantages of allowing your game to be expanded upon should not be ignored. Consider the top 10 best-selling games of any recent year and study the level of customizing support they offer. If you provide a great game with the framework for modification, the consumer will take it to levels you might never have imagined.

6.5

Following Up after the Game Is Released: It's Not over When It's Over

Tom Sloper

tomster@sloperama.com

The most successful games are sequels, prequels, and spinoffs-part of a series or successful franchise. The AAA game is not an island, it is an archipelago! After people have visited and enjoyed the first one, they will want to visit the next one. And the next, and the next.

For the type of game that begets more games, it is vital that one or more members of the production team stay involved after the game's release. This article relates experiences producing the *Shanghai* series of games and reveals simple steps for learning everything you can about your audience : find out what they love; find out what they hate; and find out how to keep them happy and get them to buy the next game.

Case #1: *Shanghai Great Moments*

In 1993, Activision had been through some bad financial times, but was on its way to recovery . They were working on *Return to Zork*, a project that used what was then a revolutionary new technique: live actors filmed against a blue screen and superimposed over computer-generated backgrounds. They wanted to use this "Siliwood" approach in creating new updated versions of several classic Activision properties. One of those was *Shanghai*, the tile-matching game played with mah-jongg tiles.

The assignment was to make a "multimedia extravaganza" version of the *Shanghai* game for personal computers. We knew that we wanted to use the live action blue screen technique but did not know what features and tile set themes would most please the audience and thus garner the most sales.

Two questions in particular were much in contention:

- **Gameplay features:** We wanted to include the actual game of mah-jongg, playable as a multiplayer online game. Others were skeptical; they believed actual mah-jongg was irrelevant, and insisted that we should stick with solitaire tile-matching.

- **Graphic themes for the non-mah-jongg tile sets:** Suggestions ranged from "Great Works of Art" to "Designer Logos" to "Retro" (whatever that meant). Creating hundreds of tiny animated graphics would be expensive, so only a few themes could be used. Achieving consensus on *which* themes to create was proving difficult.

Internal committee meetings having failed to resolve these main questions, it was decided that the players themselves would be asked. A questionnaire was written and posted on America Online and some other online venues, and sent to every *Shanghai* player available. 125 replies were returned— not as many as one might hope for, but enough to reveal trends and answer questions.

With regard to the mah-jongg question, the questionnaire showed that 100 percent of the respondents agreed with the idea of an online mah-jongg game. But the feature was still rejected by the company, and in hindsight, it made sense: not every *Shanghai* gamer had an Internet connection or even a modem in 1993. (We will revisit this discussion later in this article.).

The respondents gave us much good feedback about tile set themes. The results were surprising—and revealed that a lot of *Shanghai* fans are Trekkies and sci-fi aficionados.

There was also an unexpected benefit from the questionnaire. We learned that *Shanghai* is played by males and females in equal proportions—, which was a surprise. This-demographic information proved very useful in helping determine which graphic themes to use.

In the end, the questionnaire helped in making some important decisions about the *Shanghai* brand, not only in making *Shanghai Great Moments* but also the next version, *Shanghai Dynasty,* as well. Therefore, we highly recommend polling players of your game when faced with difficult and important decisions about subsequent versions and sequels.

TIP

Take care when you write a questionnaire: do not slant the questions. It is tempting to write the questions so that the result will match your desires. But you need genuine facts.

America Online

After *Shanghai Great Moments* was released, the associate producer informed us of a problem: customers were posting customer support questions or complaints on America Online (on a bulletin board, now defunct, that was devoted to *Shanghai*), and were unhappy because they were not getting answers. A typical post read:

> *Subject: WHAT'S THE DEAL*
> *hey i just bought this game and it doesn't work HELP!!!!*

The company was going through difficulties at this time and the customer support department was small and understaffed, and some of the CS representatives were new and under-trained. Therefore, the responses to customer problems were not as helpful as one might have hoped.

In addition, because of the way the AOL bulletin board was configured, replies to posts could not be seen easily in the bulletin board list, unless you were completely AOL-literate. For instance, you might see that there was a post entitled, "What's the Deal" if you were very knowledgeable about how the board worked, that little number "2" to the right would indicate that there were two posts under that heading: the original, and a reply. But someone who careless enough to simply post "it doesn't work" (without providing any specifics) was unlikely to realize that that little "2" had any kind of significance.

It did not take long to realize that the problem needed to be addressed. We began replying to each post on the *Shanghai* board, and posted the reply on the bulletin board (so that someone who was reading the posts would realize that the company was being responsive) and send by direct email to the person who had written the post (so that he would get the help they needed). Responding to this bulletin board became a regular procedure.

As time went on, we began to collect frequently given replies, so that when a question was asked again the answer could simply be pasted in. Some replies worked and some did not; those that did were used again. . It was a lot of work, but here are the rewards:

- The actions made the company look good.
- We developed a reputation among the customers as someone who cared about their enjoyment of the game.
- We developed a reputation in customer support as people who had the answers they needed to help our customers.

This experience taught much about what customers like and dislike, and what to do and what not to do in the next version of the game.

Case #2: Shanghai Dynasty

Remember the questionnaire used to poll the *Shanghai* fans to settle some design questions for *Shanghai Great Moments?* Including mah-jongg in *Shanghai Great Moments* had been suggested, and the questionnaire results agreed, but in the end that feature was omitted. The market had not been ready for multiplayer online gaming in 1993 (nor was it in 1995 when the game was finally released).

But in the spring of 1997 in the next version, *Shanghai Dynasty*, and the fruit of that old questionnaire finally ripened. The market was *clamoring* now for online games. *Shanghai Dynasty* would at last include mah-jongg, playable on the Internet.

Newsgroups

Because we worked on a mah-jongg feature, competitive online mah-jongg games were being researched, and when the mah-jongg newsgroup (news:rec.games.mahjong) was created, we immediately joined, lurking at first mainly to learn about mah-jongg, and second, to be on the lookout for posts from *Shanghai* customers. In time, the newsgroups proved to need a set of FAQs, and we provided them. They were refined over time with input from newsgroup regulars and visitors, and we still maintain those FAQs today.

In your campaign to support and nurture the players of your game, find out if they favor any particular newsgroups. Participate, instead of just lurking. Lurking is a good way to ease into the group slowly, but after you have gotten the feel of the group, participate fully. However, do not try to create topics because threads initiated by you will likely be perceived as promotional efforts. Simply participate in discussions, and be forthright about who you are and what work you do on that game. Be helpful and openly interested in learning how to make the next game better, which will work much more effectively than any proactive promotional efforts. The game customers will be impressed that the company cares about them.

Online Gaming—Team Participation

After *Shanghai Dynasty* was released, as before, this meant merely that one phase was finished and another begun. Now it was time for customer relations.

A weekly routine of playing the game every Friday night was established, so that we could give real-time tutorials to newcomers and play with regulars.

Through weekly play sessions, we learned which aspects of our online interface worked and which did not, and learned about the people who bought and played the game: how they thought and what they liked.

If your game is an online game, you simply *must* join the game's playing community, and play it after it has been released.

Company Web site and Bulletin Boards

Another aspect of supporting your game after release that you must consider is the way in which the game is presented to the public on the company's Web site. Get involved in the site design and stay involved. Get to know the Webmaster, and make sure the site presents the game factually and in an easy-to-use manner.

Enter the Web site as if you were a customer of your own game. Take notes: specifically, record the navigation clicks required to get to your game's page, to access the FAQs, to find downloads, or to buy the game. Is it easy, friendly, and intuitive? Write down the steps in case you need to tell a customer how to do it.

In the case of *Shanghai*, the Webmaster went so far as to create a bulletin board on which users could discuss the game. But as usual, most of the posts were by computer users who were experiencing installation or configuration problems with one

Shanghai game or another. And as usual, customer support was not monitoring the posts (their hands being full enough with user queries coming in through normal channels). So we monitored the board, posting replies and (whenever possible) emailing posters directly.

Customer Support

Work with your customer support group; share all known workarounds and frequent answers with them and find out how CS representatives work. Help fill in the gaps.

Frequently, a customer would complain in a public post that it was impossible to get through to customer support. Whenever this happened, we would call the support number. When someone answered and went into the very professional support routine, we explained we were just checking the service. Then we would talk to the customer service representative face to face, engaging in a little "management by wandering around."

Most of the time when a customer has a problem, they are very upset and have little or no patience for dealing with the automated system that must be endured before speaking with a live representative. We recommend that when one of your customers complains publicly about your company's customer support,. that you investigate the problem and respond accordingly. If a problem really exists, talk to the CS manager about your findings (add him/her to your management wanderings). At times, however, customer complaint can be attributed to sour grapes.

Emails, Letters, and Telephone Calls

When your name is in the credits as designer or producer, you may well find yourself on the receiving end of communications from users who approach you directly with suggestions or comments on the game. Or customer support will receive a communication that they do not handle normally (suggestions, comments, or non-bug-related questions), and will forward them to you.

Respond to these; do not simply file them away. If you want customers to be good to you (and continue buying new versions of your game), you must be good to the customers. Answer their mail personally, politely, and helpfully.

Good Ideas Are Good Ideas, No Matter What the Source

You have probably heard of *NIH syndrome*—"Not Invented Here." Do not allow ego to infect you with it. While working in *Shanghai,* we maintained a file on "ideas for the next version of *Shanghai*"; when customers sent with their suggestions, and if they were good ones, the suggestions were added to the file.

Once a few friends showed us how they liked to play it together. They had invented their own terminology, which added a fun element to the game—the idea was adapted and added to the list, and it went into the next game, *Shanghai: Second*

Dynasty. Another time a fellow employee related how he and his wife wanted to be able to play the game—the suggestion went on the list, and into *Second Dynasty*.

Finally, get to know the legal counsel of your company. If you discuss the legalities of using player suggestions in your games, they might warn you off—it is a lawyer's job to be careful, after all. But no one whose idea was used on our games has asked for a royalty. On the contrary, they are thrilled that their idea was implemented, because now they can play the game the way they like—and they helped make it happen! (But remember this is a litigious society, so use your best judgment.)

Conclusion

When the game is released, your job is not finished—it just enters another phase.

Poll the player base to get answers to questions about how best to design sequels. Frequent bulletin boards and newsgroups where your customers are likely to post. Answer each post forthrightly, both on the public forum and (assuming you can and that it is not bad manners) with a direct communication. Do not try to proactively promote the game in public bulletin boards and forums—only respond to posts, and help the users. In the case of a multiplayer online game, play the game with your customers and help newbies.

Put yourself in the customer's shoes. Try to get online information about the game; try to buy the game online; download the demo or patch; try to get online support. Call your company's customer support line to see for yourself how the customer interaction takes place.

Personally answer every customer letter, email, or phone call that comes to your desk. Be helpful, pleasant, and supportive. And be receptive to player ideas.

All of these steps will ensure a well-received game and assist you in choices for the next release, sequel, or spinoff.

6.6

Games for Young Children

Ruud van de Moosdjik

ruud@engine-software.nl

Anyone involved in game development will easily agree that many factors influence the design of a game. Target audience, platform, input devices, genre, and technical limitations all must be taken into account and may force the designer to forego his or her own preferences.

However, there is nothing that comes close to the design issues raised when developing games for young children. When designing entertainment or edutainment for children of 4 to 8 years of age, even axioms that would be taken for granted in 99 percent of projects for other audiences—for example, that fact that the player can read—will have to be discarded.

The Design Issues

The most difficult thing when designing games for the 4- to 8-year-old age group is to put yourself into the mind of a young child. While actual development of a game for preschoolers and elementary school children rarely poses difficult technical challenges, it is a far trickier job to keep it simple enough that it is immediately appealing and fun for your target audience, but also varied enough to retain their attention for a long time.

Difficulty Level

Selecting and implementing an appropriate difficulty level is among the most challenging tasks of any designer, especially so when dealing with an audience of young children. What makes this issue so difficult in our case? Young children's tastes and abilities change very quickly as they grow, and if a game is to have an economically reasonable audience to target, it must adapt to this factor and provide a variety of difficulty levels for 4-, 6-, and 7-year olds.

First, the core of the game should be easy to understand and easy to win. Children need constant positive reinforcement, with something interesting happening on screen every 30 seconds or so, or they will quickly grow bored or frustrated.

However, the game should also provide a fair challenge, and stay challenging even as the child grows and learns. Of course, there is no universal solution to this quandary, but an activity-based game, for example, gives designers the opportunity to provide appealing content for children of all ages within the same product. In short, an activity-based game offers the player a choice between several different activities, through a menu or by moving around in a selection environment. The key advantage is that each activity can implement a completely different type of game: for example, a game based on popular characters from Saturday-morning television could include thought puzzles for 7 to 8-year olds, musical activities for younger kids, and a virtual coloring book for everyone. Thus, kids would be able to return to the game over the years, and shift their focus to different activities as they grow older. Logically, a decent build up of difficulty is far easier to implement in such a case, in comparison to a linear game design.

Consistency

Consistency of controls, of language, and of naming conventions plays an important role when designing a game for young children. Every aspect of the game should be easy to learn, preferably without the help of a parent (unless the goal of the game is to persuade families to play together), and the controls should be easy to memorize so that players can repeatedly return to the game. For example, if button A controls character jumping in one part of your game, it should do so everywhere that jumping is required to avoid confusion and frustration—and, if possible never be used for anything but jumping. Also be careful to use a small, simple, and consistent vocabulary in your naming conventions: if there is an item in the game that is referred to as a *stick* when it is first picked up, and then a character later asks the player to give him a *rod*, most kids will go look for a new item, instead of handing over the stick.

Visualization

Visualization is one of the more obvious issues: anyone who has ever viewed a game designed for children will have noticed a major difference in graphics between such a game and an "adult" game.

Children-oriented graphics must be bright, colorful, clear, and recognizable. Very young children may have trouble perceiving depth and slow color gradients; highly detailed graphics will confuse them and increase the danger that certain assets will be overlooked.

The visual aspect of a game for young children is especially important because reading abilities cannot be taken for granted. Showing objects, using voice-overs, and having characters demonstrate what the player is expected to do instead of using text will make the game easily accessible and more appealing to young gamers.

Content

There are several issues you must keep in mind when determining content for children's games. The most obvious issue is, of course, what you must censor: nudity, sexual content, and foul language. Violence or the death of a beloved character are also inappropriate. Further, complicated words and relationships may confuse the players.

On the positive side, educational content in children's game is highly appealing, both to the children themselves and to their parents. While the game mechanics themselves already teach children—for example by training memory, cognitive abilities, and language skills—many of the most successful games targeting this audience also provide explicit educational value. The nature of this content and how it is implemented is highly dependant on the type of game. Educational value is always a big plus for parents, and because the parents are the customers who actually buy the game, educational value is certainly worth considering.

Conclusion

Of course, there is more to children's game development than we have mentioned in this short article, but these key issues can make the difference between an "average" game and a high-quality, educational, and fun one for very young audiences.

MANAGING A GAME DEVELOPMENT BUSINESS

7.0

Introduction

Game development is not merely about cool jobs and cooler products: it is a huge business. As the initiators of new products, designers play a strategic role in their companies' ultimate success; therefore, their creative efforts will always be constrained by marketing, financial, and technical considerations.

Whether you are an independent developer building the entire game essentially on your own, an employee of a large studio, or a freelancer, you as designer must assume an active role in the development process once the true design phase is over, to ensure that the finished product faithfully represents your vision. Even more so, obviously, if you also take on the role of producer or project manager. But whether or not your job description expands beyond "just" design, you need to know as much as you can about the development team's strengths and weaknesses, the studio's business plans, the publisher's intent, and the market's conditions if your creations are to achieve acceptance among players—and financial success.

The Big Picture

The game development business maintains an aura of rebelliousness; of big money earned and spent by the bucketfuls; of disregard for the tired models of financial forecasts and market research and gray flannel suits and haggling over contracts.

If this popular perception of our industry as the mythological hacker heaven was ever accurate, it certainly has not been since I started working in it.

A Real Business

Many new developers are shocked when they realize that the game development business is just that: a business, sometimes less stuffy than others, perhaps, but a business nonetheless.

As with any other business, game development has its dark sides. Game developers often work long hours, earning less than their counterparts in other industries. Studios are notoriously short-lived, and the pace of mergers, acquisitions, and closings shows no sign of decelerating. And one of the reasons why the average developer is so young is that many seasoned veterans leave the industry after a few years, never to return, because the lifestyle that accompanies our collective corporate culture is often incompatible with the needs of a family.

A Tough Business

Financially, the game design business picture is hardly rosy. According to numbers quoted by a publishing executive at the 2000 Game Developers' Conference, fewer than 3 percent of the PC games and 13 percent of the console games available on the North American market in 1999 sold more than 100,000 copies. As a result, the overwhelming majority of games lose money, whether for their developers, their publishers, or both. The retail channel for games is partly to blame for this situation: few stores carry more than 100 titles at any given time, including a mere handful of products older than six months, a state of affairs that would be considered intolerable in the music or movie-rental markets.

Meanwhile, the upward pressure on development and marketing budgets is increasing. Japanese console role-playing games, for example, are notoriously expensive to create: published reports placed the production costs of some recent popular releases at over $40,000,000.

An Attractive Business

Still, new game development teams break into the field with enormous hits on occasion, and there are few other industries in which 20-somethings without Harvard MBAs or MIT Ph.D.s can reach leadership positions if they have inclination and ability. This (and the fact that games are, well, games) is why so many young people are attracted to our field.

Doing It Right

Managing a profitable game development business being inherently difficult, it stands to reason that every reasonable effort should be made to alleviate the risks wherever possible. Adopting effective business practices is crucial to a studio's long-term success.

Over the years, I have often written about the mistakes that game studio managers make. The rest of this article will describe a number of positive business practices that will make your team's life and work easier.

Market Awareness

With so many studios competing for so few slots on publishers' release schedules (not to mention precious shelf space), it is all too easy for a title to get lost in the shuffle. For this reason, designers should talk to their company's business development staff and/or agents early and often.

Each publisher has its specialties in terms of platform, genre, or distribution network; signing with the wrong one can seriously damage a game's sales potential. Similarly, a product that is slightly off-target with regard to its intended audience may fail to sell as well as a competitor's, whatever its good qualities. And once a publisher has been selected, a lawyer who knows the ins and outs of the game industry will be able to protect your interests by identifying potentially damaging clauses in proposed contracts.

Team Building

Game development is a labor-intensive business. Nowhere is a company's success more dependent on the quality of the people it employs. Thus, assembling the right team and keeping its members happy are the studio manager's most important jobs, especially for long projects, which can be seriously hurt by employee turnover.

To build an effective team, companies should look not only for talent, but also for people who get along and work effectively together. No one is smart enough to deserve to keep a job when they are making their coworkers' lives miserable, because the global loss in productivity greatly outweighs their own contribution.

Ideally, team members should also share the same values. If the company has a policy of long hours, it should hire career-driven people who are willing to work those long hours. Promising a 35-hour work week during interviews and then demanding a 60-hour one once the employee is on the job is counterproductive, because the new recruit will leave—or worse, he will stay and transmit his frustration to others. Hiring people with similar values will also help the company choose rewards for high performance (i.e., extra vacation time, stock ownership, monetary bonuses, or paid trips to conferences) that will be equally appealing to everyone.

Effective Growth Management

As a company grows, job descriptions tend to specialize. In a team of six, the same person may act as designer, producer, part-time programmer, and PC service technician. Once the team grows to 15 people, project management will become a full-time job. In a company employing 100, there may be several managers who never even work on the game itself at all.

Know yourself and your team. No matter what the business press may say, growing your company might not be the best idea—at least, not by forcing your teammates into roles that they do not want to take on. If they are happier as jacks-of-all-trades than they would be as specialists or as department heads, stay small.

Realistic Self-Assessment

Before signing a contract with a publisher, studio managers need to answer a few questions:

- Can this team deliver a product within the parameters of this contract?
- If new people need to be brought on board, are they available, and is the company in a position to make them a competitive offer?
- Do we *want* to work on this project?

There really is no point in signing a contract for a project that no one in the company cares about, or that would require the team to go into crunch mode from day one, or that will fail unless every single detail works out perfectly.

Middleware

It is often difficult for developers (especially programmers) to accept the fact that building every component of a game in house is unnecessary. Worse, doing so may even be detrimental to the overall effort, because it forces the team to spend time working on elements that they are ill-equipped to produce and that could be acquired cheaper on the open market.

Middleware has many virtues, the most important being that it allows teams to concentrate on their own strengths. If your company employs a trio of 3D graphics wizards who know little about networking, buy a multiplayer library layer and focus on imagery, and vice-versa.

As a rule, game studios should buy everything that they can buy, whether technology, audio assets, or project management software, and develop only those components that constitute their projects' competitive advantages. This reduces risk, shortens development time, and improves morale by letting people work on what they care about.

Prudence

Finally, game development is a risky business. Technology changes, platforms come and go, people get sick or quit, etc. As a result, predicting the flow of a project is hazardous at the best of times. Therefore, when in doubt, the prudent manager errs on the side of pessimism.

Again, if Project X can ship on time and under budget if and only if all staff members can sustain 72-hour work weeks for six months, then Project X should be cancelled. Other rules of defensive management inspired by [McConnell98] include:

- Make sure that at least two people know every piece of code inside out, in case one of them has to leave the project for whatever reason.
- Schedule risky jobs early in the project, and have backup solutions ready in case of failure.
- Make sure that the length of the critical path of linearly dependent tasks is shorter than the total duration of the project by a reasonable safety margin.

Other Perspectives

The articles in this last section of the book discuss the business of managing a game development team on a daily basis, and of turning a design document into a finished product:

- Game industry recruiter Barbara Walter answers the age-old question: How can we assemble a great development team, and keep it together until the end of a project?
- In a pair of articles, agent Jay Powell explains how to assemble a submission package that will attract the eye of a publisher—and then, how to negotiate a good contract for the development of your game.
- Bruce Onder approaches the contract negotiation problem from another angle: that of a freelance game designer looking to secure a service deal with a development studio or a publisher.
- Geoff Howland surveys effective management techniques that will keep the team motivated and working at peak efficiency during the long months of development.
- Tom Sloper discusses ways to manage remote developers, from a producer's perspective.
- Chris Campbell introduces the basic concepts of quality management, and how they can be applied to speed up game development while minimizing costs and risk.
- And finally, Charlie Cleveland applies the time-honored "focus groups" marketing technique to refine game design ideas throughout a project and maximize the final product's appeal.

Follow their advice, and the game development experience will have a better chance of being smooth and pleasant.

Bibliography

[Laramée00.1] Laramée, F.D., "How to Screw Up a Perfectly Good Game Company in 10 East Steps," *Gamedev.net*, February 2000.

[Laramée00.2] Laramée, F.D., "Ten More Easy Ways to Screw Up a Game Company," *GIGnews.com*, October 2000.

[McConnell98] McConnell, S., *Software Project Survival Guide*, Microsoft Press, 1998.

Building (and Keeping) a Great Game Development Team

Barbara Walter

walterco@earthlink.net

What is an article about staffing doing in a book about game design? Before the designer can bring his game concept to fruition, he first needs a team—programmers, artists, producers, and other professionals providing the intense effort required to ship a commercial game.

Assembling a game development team in today's job market can be a monumental task. Maintaining the team's interest and excitement during a project of many years' duration can be even harder. So before beginning to recruit, a savvy designer tries to answer this question: What makes a game developer happy? Some of the answers, found below, are expected. A few are surprising.

Designing a Great Development Team

Designers and their bosses putting together a game development team typically follow this pattern: First, they invite people they have enjoyed working with in the past on game titles to come on board to the new company. Then, they use their recruitment network by asking game developer friends for referrals to *their* friends and former coworkers. If positions still remain open, they turn to advertisements (free and paid) on sites that cater to game developers. Last, they may give the job order to a search firm (also called a recruitment agency or headhunter). Some game development firms shorten the process and go directly to recruiters. These may be larger shops with many openings to fill, smaller shops with no internal HR rep and no time or expertise to screen candidates, or shops of any size that have a solid business reason for keeping their search confidential.

Because team members can make or break a project, a company's personnel selection process is critically important. The first step in the process is one that many smaller game development firms skip—writing a clear, concise, and accurate job description. The job description does not have to be lengthy or written in bureaucratese; one page in plain language will do. Some basic information it should include: the position's title, the title of the immediate supervisor, the job duties and responsibilities, the job requirements—desired education, experience, and skills—and the salary range. There are a number of employment law books and Web sites that can provide templates, help ensure compliance with labor and equal opportunity laws, and suggest salary ranges. Once the job description is written, it should be distributed to everyone involved in the hiring process, well in advance of interviews.

Also important is that companies use a standardized set of questions, and/or test, for each position, so that all candidates for that position are treated equally. Extra questions are sure to be asked, because interviewing is an art, not a science, but having a list of questions each candidate has answered helps in the screening process.

Candidate Selection

Companies use a variety of methods to screen candidates, from a lengthy (but effective in lowering turnover) interview process allowing everyone in the company to talk to the candidate and vote on hiring, to the more usual method of having a candidate talk to his potential supervisor and members of his future team.

Companies that do not allow candidates to talk to prospective team members should raise a red flag for a potential employee.

Designating one person to be "HR rep" for the company is useful for smaller game development shops and helps to keep track of people and events. It also gives candidates a consistent contact point.

Whichever interview process is employed to build your team, please ensure that candidates are treated with confidentiality and respect. And if you interview them, please give them an answer, even if it is just "Sorry, we need more experience." No news is worse than bad news.

Keeping the Team Happy

The way to keep a game developer happy varies with the individual developer, but there are core elements that constitute a satisfying work environment in most people's minds.

To dig out these core elements, I conducted a very informal survey. Creating a short questionnaire, I asked some professional game developers to rate, in terms of importance, several aspects of their job and their work environment. I chose topics from issues frequently raised in conversations with both happy and disgruntled game developers. Respondents were given anonymity so they could speak freely. Full survey results can be found in Table 8.1.1, at the end of this article.

A disclaimer: This is not a statistically or mathematically precise survey. Rather, it is a snapshot of what was important to these particular game developers on a particular day. The respondent sample was small but represents a good cross-section of game developers. Unfortunately, no -senior managers responded.

The Surveyed Population

The individuals who responded to the survey occupy most job categories of game product development: programmer, artist, designer, composer, producer, project leader, manager/director of development, technical director, studio head. Some perform a dual role, such as designer/writer. The respondents' game industry experience ranges from 2 to 12 years, with an average of about 6 1/2 years. Some of the companies they work for have fewer than 20 employees, others, more than 200 employees.

Respondents rated job elements in terms of what is most important to them on the job, using the rating of 1=least important, 10=most important. They were also asked to describe the best job they have ever held in the game industry, and to tell what made it best. Some took the time to do so, and their remarks are revealing (see Table 8.1.1).

The Ratings

Anyone who knows game developers well would expect "Fun & Challenging Projects" to finish in first place. And it did. But, surprisingly, the rating for "Base Salary" was much farther down the list. In fact, "Base Salary" rated above average in importance, but well below the top three most desired work elements.

The popular press likes to portray today's workers as independent agents mostly interested in compensation. However, in this survey, the three least important work benefits were "Stock Options," "Royalties." and "Equity." One 10-year industry veteran gave royalties a high rating but added wistfully, "I've never had a royalty agreement in my life."

Next to "Fun & Challenging Projects," the two other most important components of a great game job were "Good Team Members to Work With & Learn From," and "Opportunity to Learn New Things, Technology, Techniques." This is good news for managers who have new projects and new technology to offer their team members, bad news for those who do not.

According to the survey, experienced, talented, and cooperative coworkers are a major factor in attracting and keeping new hires. This is not so surprising in an industry with frequent mergers, acquisitions, and layoffs. Loyalty to one's coworkers becomes more important than loyalty to one's company.

A positive note was that many respondents rated their current game industry job the best one they have ever had. These respondents said what makes them happy on the job is:

- "Interesting projects, great team."
- "Creative freedom, a growing company, great coworkers, convenient location to home."
- "Small team, talented people, freedom to make technical decisions, lots to learn, and everyone noticed and appreciated my contribution."
- "Good team environment, friendships, good coworkers, high salary."
- "Am able to work with the best and brightest in my division"

- "(Our lead designer is) a brilliant guy and working with him is great. We have rock solid financial support."

One respondent described what would be his dream game job, if he could combine the best elements of several:

- "Industry recognition, a monster hit title that your mother would have heard of. (If you've never had it, you'll never know how good it feels to be in the top ten.)"
- "Freedom to innovate *and* publish the results in *Game Developer* magazine or online. No trying to hide important staff for fear of headhunting. Make them happy to stay."
- "Good people to work with, focused, helpful, teamwork, realistic, funny, diverse."
- "Strong leadership. Working under a lead who knew what they wanted was a joy."
- "Recognition of your results—not the 'hacking through the night to fix my own stupid bug' crunch heroes, but the day-to-day, get-the-job-done-well-the-first-time people. (It'll never happen!)"
- "Support from the publisher. Know[ing] that your product will be given the respect due [it] and support needed all the way down the pipeline to the shops."

Some respondents cited a previous job as their best:

- "Best quality people I ever worked with, flex time, good planning, decent office environment, challenging project, excellent salary. Would work for those guys anytime"
- "I most enjoyed my tenure as studio head just after the acquisition of my development company. I was able to use my skills and experience in both business and creative sides of the industry"
- "Six years ago, working as game designer/lead programmer on a game with a very small and cohesive team, and with almost no outside intervention. The company wasn't that great; I quit later."

Along those lines, one respondent plaintively added: "I've had a lot of bad professional experiences so far, so I'm looking to have some much better experiences in the future."
A few job elements drew pithy comments in addition to their ratings:

- "Sensible Development Schedules: 5, never happen."
- "Sensible Development Schedules: 9, I *hate* crunch born out of stupidity."
- "Balanced Life, Professional & Personal: 10 (or higher)!"
- "Balanced Life, Professional & Personal: Team morale is the single most important determining factor of schedules being kept. A workplace that has mandates for weekend work/long hours/crunch time is a workplace that is destined to miss milestone after milestone."

Bosses who seek self-managed team members still may not agree with the respondent who rated "Participatory Management" as 6 on a scale of 1 to 10 and added, "only needed when things are going wrong."

Conclusion

Game developers are a relatively content group. They put up with last-minute changes in features and technology. They endure deadlines that require them to work crunch hours. They willingly develop the twelfth iteration of their company's leading game title, earning less pay than other commercial software developers—all for the sake of the personal satisfaction they gain working on games. One of the respondents said it best: "The main reason for staying in the games industry is that it provides new challenges and new problems all the time."

Companies that offer their teams these challenges and many of the other top-rated job elements have a much better than average chance of finding and keeping great game development team members.

Survey Results

Table 8.1.1 Survey Results

Criterion (1=least important, 10=most important)	Rating
Fun & Challenging Projects	8.65
Good Team Members to Work with & Learn From	8.41
Opportunity to Learn New Things, Technology, Techniques	8.29
Balanced Life, Professional & Personal	8.06
Sensible Development Schedules	7.00
Base Salary	6.82
Participatory Management	5.24
Recognition for Achievements (other than money or promotion)	5.06 (tie)
Flex Hours and/or Telecommuting	5.06 (tie)
Bonuses	4.71
Equity/Ownership	4.18
Promotional Opportunities	4.06
Royalties	3.88
Stock Options	3.65
Other: location (two respondents), support by competent marketing and PR professionals, intelligent leadership, trust between team members.	n/a

7.2

Showing Publishers What They Want to See

Jay Powell

jay@octagon1.com

With the growing need for titles to fill release schedules for three different consoles and the PC market, developers who can present publishers with the best package possible maximize their chances of securing a deal. This article reviews some of the basics of package submission, and presents a few of the new requirements that are being instituted by some of the world's top publishers.

Product Information

The most important part of a package will be the information on the product itself. A submission will be reviewed by a variety of departments and people within the larger companies, so it helps to provide information targeted towards each group. While the acquisitions group will need to know about the overall concept of the game and its expected budget, the marketing group will be interested in reasons why the game will sell, and the testers will need as much information as possible to properly evaluate the title.

Game Overview

Start building the package with a brief overview of the game. This should be kept to 10 to 15 pages, because it is meant to convey a high-level view of what the game is about.

The acquisitions manager and marketing departments are the primary audience for this overview, which should include a detailed concept of the game, a description of its look and feel, gameplay details, a timeline for completion, the target platforms, and a budget. These are the most important points in the evaluation of any game being submitted today.

Technical Design Document

Prepare a technical design document, which will serve as a companion to the overview. This document should describe the specifics of the engine being used for the game. If the engine is unique, the document should compare it to the other engines that are on the market: let the publisher know why yours is better or worse, and in what areas. If an existing engine is being licensed, then the document should state the changes that were made to the existing code to make this game stand out technically. Regardless of whether the engine is proprietary or licensed, the publisher will need to know how it compares to the engines powering the best-selling games on the market. Deals have been closed based on engines alone, so this is a key part of your package.

This document is also the place to outline the steps for porting a game from one platform to another. Publishers will want to know if this step has already been planned for, or if a separate version of the game will have to be developed from the ground up.

Finally, if you are presenting a PC game, do not forget to include the end-user system requirements in the technical design document. The publishers will want to know if the game will be playable on machines at launch time.

Project Outline

The next key components of a package are a time scale for the game's development, and the budget involved.

This document should describe the content of the milestones in detail, tell when they will be accomplished, and specify how much money is due after each of them. Extremely detailed budgets are not often required at this point, but if the publisher is going to be investing a large amount of money into the title, they will want to make sure it is justified.

One thing to remember about a budget is that once a title is evaluated for quality, the publisher will create a Profit and Loss spreadsheet (P&L). This P&L will determine how profitable the game will be, based on sales projections. The more that a developer knows about the publisher's business model, the easier it is to work out a deal that is profitable for both parties. To help the publisher, include sales figures of similar products if you have access to this information. Such figures lets the publisher know that there is serious consumer interest in the type of title being presented, and what to expect at retail when the title is released.

Remember to keep the budget and timetable reasonable. If there is any uncertainty in the "industry norms," consult with other developers to see where they have had success.

Localization

Include as much information as possible about the game's localization costs. How many words are there in the game and in the manual? How much dialog? How many actors are needed to contribute to the final product? Any international publisher will need to include this information in their P&L, as this is additional cost that they will need to invest in the game.

This document is also a good place to add any copyright information necessary for the game. If the intellectual property is licensed, make sure to include the appropriate documentation. For more information on the legal aspects of a submission package, see [Powell02].

Game Demo

The most important part of the product information section of the package is the game demo itself.

An effective demo will highlight the key selling points of the game and show them to the publisher. The demo should accurately depict the game's user interface and the engine that will be used. Many developers make the mistake of creating a demo on a freeware engine and promising a product based on an engine they have yet to license. This does not help the publisher, as they cannot see an accurate depiction of the graphics and environments of the final product. The demo should also include at least some of the artificial intelligence (AI) that will be present in the game. Strong, accurate AI is a key feature in video games today; a publisher wants to know that the product they are purchasing will be up to the industry standard. Most importantly, the demo should be polished and *stable*. A demo that crashes repeatedly or fails to deliver components that the publisher is expecting has a much higher chance of being rejected.

Every publisher is going to have their own idea of what should be included in the game demo, so there is no "sure bet" as far as content is concerned. In an ideal world, the developer would be able to show the entire game and have the publisher make their decision based on that. Obviously, this is rarely possible, but at the very least, the demo should contain:

- Unique selling points the developer has identified in their game.
- Accurate depiction of the user interface.
- Multiplayer play if included in the final game.
- Technically sound gameplay. The art may not be 100 percent complete, but the game should operate smoothly.

Ask yourself if your demo accurately represents the game you want to make. If you are not happy with the demo, chances are the publishers will not be either.

If it is impossible to create a demo, at least include a movie that shows the same key points that the playable demo would.

Competitive Analysis

The final aspect of the product portion of a package is the competitive analysis. In addition to the sales figures of similar products, developers must look to the future. Let the publishers know which similar games will be released at about the same time as yours.

This research will also help identify which publishers to approach with a game. Sending a game to a publisher with a competing product may give away some of the key selling points that the competing title is lacking. Explain why your own product is better than competing games. A list of features in the engine, design, and gameplay of all competing products should be compiled, to let the publisher know immediately which are included in your own game, which are on the "nice to have" list, and which will not be in the game at all.

Developer History

The second half of a complete submission package will discuss the team creating the game, their history, and their strengths.

This portion of the package must prove to the publisher that the team can complete the product and that it will be up to industry standard when finished. Many publishers require that the team members of a development project be named in the contract to guarantee the quality of the final product.

Establishing the development team and providing the publisher with this information will be a great asset, both for this project and for your company's long-term future. Often, publishers will approach teams whose projects they have rejected with the opportunity to work on an intellectual property that they have acquired.

Track Records

Packages should always include the track record of both the team and the individual team members. Include a description of all the titles that have been shipped by the company, the platforms on which they were released, and their sales numbers if possible. A history of being on time and under budget is a major asset in this industry; if your team has met this kind of success, bring it to the publisher's attention immediately! Even a title that sold poorly shows the publisher that the company can complete and ship a title. Publishers can research this information anyway, so it is a good idea to provide it up front in the package.

If the company is a startup, or has new team members, a complete breakdown of the titles each person has worked on in the past and of their role in that development should be included. Having the lead programmer or artist from a successful project working on your game carries much more weight with a publisher than hiring someone who provided very little input on the product.

Team Breakdown

The package should state how many people are involved in the project and the roles of the people involved. This information helps the publisher evaluate the budget of the game and the potential weak spots. Some genres or platforms need more artists or programmers than others and publishers need to know that a development team is sensitive to this and are prepared for what they are about to begin.

The number of people employed by a developer can also provide information on the company's financial stability. Publishers are more comfortable dealing with teams that have business experience and have proven themselves capable of balancing budgets. Along the same lines, developers that have stayed together for long periods of time and show significant amounts of company loyalty and unity catch the eyes of publishers more often.

Unique Technology

Finally, let the publisher know if you have any unique technology that you can bring to the table. Whether the technology is a complete engine or a modification to an existing engine, it is a powerful incentive and could be the key to signing the deal. Publishers always want to be a step ahead of the competition, and a technological edge is the best way to do it. If possible, show these unique features in your demo.

Package Presentation

How a developer presents a package can be just as important as the contents of the package itself.

All submissions should always be as professional as possible. Publishers see hundreds or thousands of submissions a year. A package that looks great, with professional printing and binding, will attract a publisher's attention before the game is even reviewed. In today's industry, where developers come and go every day, publishers want to find professional teams who they feel can properly manage a business as well as a game project. Having a professional-looking package on the publisher's desk will help build this credibility.

Package Checklist

Here, again, are the components that should be included in your package:

- Game overview
- Technical design document
- Project outline
- Localization information
- Game demo
- Competitive analysis
- Team and team member track record
- Size of team with breakdown for programming, art, etc.
- Information on unique technology

Optional Additions

In addition, you may add:

- Copies of any press the game has received
- PowerPoint presentation summarizing the entire package.
- Video tape version of gameplay and movies

Conclusion

The submission package you send to a publisher could be a first and last chance for a deal with that company. The old saying about never getting a second chance to make a first impression could not be truer in this industry.

Your package should strive to answer every question a publisher could possibly have and even some they do not. Once a publisher rejects a project from a developer, it is very difficult to get them to look at that project again, so make certain that all the features and benefits of the team and project are plainly stated in this package.

Bibliography

[Powell02] Powell, J., "Introduction to Contract Negotiations," *Game Design Perspectives*, Charles River Media, 2002.

7.3

Introduction to Contract Negotiation

Jay Powell

jay@octagon1.com

Contract negotiation is never fun, and as a general rule, the bigger the publisher, the longer the process will take. This article outlines the major components of any contract between a publisher and a developer, and discusses how to structure a deal that will be beneficial to all parties.

Preparing for Negotiation

There are two key questions that you must answer prior to any negotiation:

- What does my team need in a contract?
- What is our negotiation position?

Knowing what the team needs from the beginning will help you establish a negotiation position. Look at several factors before you start talking about a contract:

- What is the lowest budget on which we can finish this game?
- What intellectual property rights need to be retained? Characters, worlds, technology, etc.?
- What royalty rate is expected?
- How much development time do we still need to finish the project?

These are a few examples, but a developer who does not need very much money to complete the game is in a much better position than one who will have to rely on deep commitments and investments from a publisher. By knowing what portions of a contract you can give way on, you stand a much better chance of winning the points you are really interested in. Contracts for developers who only want to get their finished game in the market with a launch and great marketing will have little in common with contracts in which a developer is seeking a publisher to fund a multi-million dollar budget.

Obviously, teams with a stronger starting position can look forward to better contracts. It is easier to get the terms the developer is seeking if the developer has already demonstrated an ability to do what they promise. By knowing the needs of the team in advance, a contract can be tweaked and polished to benefit the developer and publisher and the lay the groundwork for a satisfying relationship. For example, some developers find that it is worth the lost advance to take a higher royalty rate and guarantee more marketing dollars for the game. This is the kind of decision that should be made early in the process.

Advances

One of the first questions a publisher will ask is: "What is the price?" The answer to this question will depend on the type of deal for which you are aiming.

With a development project, the response is quite simple: the price is the budget you have calculated. Be certain that your budget is realistic. When publishers are asked to invest a large amount of cash into a project, they will be very careful in evaluating budgets. Developers should be aware of the typical price for a game in the genre and platform they are targeting, and be prepared to provide interested publishers with a list of the people on the team, their experience, and their role in the project. This will help substantiate the budget being presented.

Also consider the relationship between advances and royalties. Typically, the higher the advance, the lower the royalty. Publishers want to make sure the game will be profitable for them. The actual budget for a publisher can actually be twice as high as the developer's advances when marketing, shelf space, manufacturing, technology support, and other factors are calculated in.

Net Receipts

If you are seeking a distribution deal for the game, or licensing a product that is near completion, more research could be needed. Know from the beginning how much revenue you need to recoup on the project, find out how similar titles have sold in the territory you are discussing the contract for, and base your initial proposals on these numbers.

A licensing deal for a full-price product should usually come to $4 to $6 per copy sold. If the publisher wishes to base royalties on a percentage of *net receipts*, aim for 25 percent or higher, and pay careful attention to the definition of net receipts in the contract or letter of intent. The more a publisher is allowed to subtract from gross sales numbers, the lower the royalty will be, regardless of percentage. *Net receipts* should usually be defined as the amount billed by the publisher for the sale, lease, or license of each product, minus a deduction for credits or returns that should not exceed 15 percent. Do not allow publishers to deduct expenses like manufacturing, insurance, shipping, withheld taxes, and marketing from the net receipts. There may be resistance to the marketing deductions; if so, at least put a cap on the recoupable part of this budget.

Helping Publishers Helps Developers

Publishers will use a Profit and Loss sheet (P&L) to decide if a project is feasible from a financial perspective. If you are seeing real interest in the project from the publisher but the budget seems to be out of reach, ask the publisher how you can make the deal work. It is always better to take a little less money up front and work with a publisher who is enthusiastic about the team and believes in the project than it is to take more money and risk being just another title in a catalog.

Many variations of the payment schedule can be implemented to help a publisher. Developers who are financially stable can spread the payments over a longer period of time, although all advances should be paid no later than 60 days after the game ships to retailers. It is also possible to lower the advance in exchange for a higher portion of the royalties. This shows the publisher that a team has complete confidence in their product and that they are willing to prove it in the contract.

Be honest and open with the publisher. They should understand the needs of their partner and work to make a contract that makes everyone happy. Large egos or unrealistic expectations can be a severe hindrance in negotiations.

For a straight distribution deal, the payment schedule is well defined. There are still milestones to be met, but they are consistent across all distribution or licensing deals. When a developer has nearly completed a game and does not need funding each month, they should expect to negotiate payment based on the following list of milestones:

- Signature of letter of intent
- Signature of contract
- Receipt of gold master by the publisher
- Receipt of localization kit by the publisher
- Receipt of localized gold master by the publisher
- Release of the product
- 30 days following the release of the product
- 60 days following the release of the product.

Royalty Rates

The royalty rate is the second half of the monetary equation. As mentioned earlier, advances and royalties are directly related and should be negotiated at the same time.

There are many factors involved in the calculation of the royalty rate, but as a general rule it should never fall below 15 percent for a PC title. The higher the better, of course, but most developers will find that they will ultimately see around 25 percent. Console titles can be a little more difficult as the console manufacturers take their share as well. With most consoles, developers will see a royalty of between 9 and 11 percent on sales. This may seem low, but the sales volume of console games versus PC games will certainly make up the difference.

Be very careful when negotiating console contracts. Find out whether the publisher is factoring the console manufacturer's royalty into the net receipts or not. If the manufacturer's cost is deducted prior to the division of royalties, a much higher rate should be sought.

Sublicensing

If the publisher does not have direct distribution in some territories, negotiate a separate royalty rate for these deals. Otherwise, you may have to make do with a small percentage of a small percentage.

If the publisher plans to sublicense the game, aim for a royalty of 50 percent of their net receipts from these territories. Be especially aware of companies that promise "developer friendly" royalties in the 35 to 50 percent range. If contract terms look too good to be true, they probably are.

Ask how the distribution is handled and contact other developers that have worked with the publisher. This question is important in any case, but especially important here. Most publishers will not give a hard number when it comes to the amount paid out to other developers, but most of the time a friendly call to the developer will yield that information and an accurate account of how the relationship with the publisher is working . If the situation is still unclear, negotiate a set dollar amount per copy for the royalty instead of a percentage. This negotiation can solve many of problems.

Protect yourself against the possibility that the publisher might not find a sublicensing partner in a particular territory. Insert a clause that states that, if the game is not released within a specific period of time after the first market release, all rights for the unreleased territories revert to you.

Other Options with Royalties

When a flat royalty rate is negotiated, be sensitive to the realities of the retail market. If the retailers demand a price drop, the publisher may not be able to afford to continue to pay the same royalty, and the title will be completely removed from the shelves. Always be prepared to renegotiate the rates in these situations.

You may want to look at the option of escalating royalties as well. In the initial discussions with publishers, find out how many copies the publisher must sell to break even on the title and reach an acceptable profit. (Making a profit at all will not usually sell a publisher on a game: as with any business, companies need to show a certain percentage profit to "green light" a project.) Then, discuss the option of having the royalty increase when the project breaks even, and again at certain sales milestones or when the publisher achieves the profit they anticipated. This rewards both companies for a job well done. Some of the greatest games made will not sell well if the publisher does not market and sell the title properly. Great success should be viewed as an achievement by both companies, not just one.

A frequently overlooked portion of the contract that will affect the royalty rate is the number of copies that a publisher gives to the media and retailers as samples. These promotional copies will generally hurt the publisher more than the developer, as they are manufacturing copies of the game on which they receive no revenue. While getting the word out about a game is useful, free copies should be limited to around 100. As with many other aspects of the process, you should discuss this with the publisher and see how many free copies they typically send out.

Localization

All developers should begin planning for the localization of their game very early in development. By the time a game is ready to be shown to publishers, it is usually too late to change the underlying code. Games should be prepared for double-byte characters from the very beginning of development. Care and attention should also be given to languages such as German, which require more characters per word than others. Failure to support languages such as these will certainly result in lost revenue: Germany is the second largest Western World market (behind the United States) for video games, and Asia is fast becoming a major market for PC games as well as console titles. Korea, in particular, has excellent support from their government for the gaming industry; the country is home to scores of publishers and literally thousands of developers.

Localizing Content

Aside from simple language issues, actual content must be carefully examined as well. Many countries are becoming more vigilant against violent video games. Korea, China, and Germany already have strict laws regarding video game content; these laws focus on violence and little else. Video games in Germany cannot show violence toward people at all: for example, enemies in shooters must be robots or aliens, and they cannot shed red blood when shot. Germany also has very strict laws regarding the portrayal of the Third Reich or Nazi propaganda in any way. On the other hand, the U.S. market is more concerned about sexual content than violence, and censorship happens at the retail level as opposed to government committees.

Localization Responsibilities

When developers approach publishers with games, the cost and job of localization need to be carefully examined. The contract should state that the publisher will pay for and provide localization for the game, and that the developer will be responsible for the integration of the localized content into the game. In practice, the developer will send all text and art which needs to be localized to the publisher. The publisher will then translate these files and return them to the developer, who will create a localized master of the game for each language. Occasionally, publishers will want to do all the work themselves; only agree to this if you have an excellent relationship with the publisher, because it usually involves giving them access to the game's source code.

Marketing

Marketing can make or break a game. Some of the best games in recent memory did not sell well, due to insufficient or bad marketing. Do not overlook this part of the contract.

Research the publisher's past marketing campaigns and request a marketing proposal prior to signing the contract for the game. This marketing proposal should outline what the publisher plans to do for online, print, and possible television marketing, along with the budget allocated to these plans. You need to know the publisher's strategy to secure prime shelf space and end caps (i.e., the spaces on the end of shelves that are shown in the aisles of a store), and how the game will be sold to the retailers.

A good general figure for the marketing of a North American launch is $150,000. Obviously, the more a publisher will commit to the marketing effort, the better, but this amount will buy a title a good campaign. Pay close attention to how the money in the budget is allotted; a good box design by itself can cost $10,000, so make sure the money is well spent. And finally, do not allow this money to be recoupable against your advances: this is the publisher's cost of doing business, not yours.

Name Recognition

Developers should always make sure that a clause in the contract states that the logo for their company must be displayed any time that the publisher's logo is shown, and that it should be the same size. Consumers are more likely to build brand loyalty to a developer than they are to a publisher. Even when a major publisher franchise is handed to a different developer, there can be uncertainty in the minds of the consumers. By guaranteeing that your logo is shown with the publisher's, you can invest in your future in two ways:

- **Player recognition:** Even if a different publisher handles your next game, the public will remember the quality of your previous titles and be interested in this one.
- **Publisher recognition:** Other publishers will take note of the great job you did on a particular game and pay close attention to you down the road.

Both of these points of recognition could result in opening doors that were closed earlier, or in contracts from publishers to work on licenses they have secured. Finally, once a developer is known to have shipped a best-selling game, their negotiating position is much better for the next contract.

Supporting the Publisher

Finally, developers need to remember that to ensure excellent marketing, they must support the publisher. The publisher is going to need artwork, demos, selling points, and time from the developer in order to create the appropriate buzz for a game.

Most publishers will want to start marketing a game no less than three months from launch. If a publisher wants to rush a title to market sooner than three months from signature, the developer should closely evaluate the situation and make sure they are making the right decision. In this pre-launch period, the publisher may bring the press to the studio; the team should make sure that the producer knows the game inside and out, because she will be handling the majority of the press inquiries and needs to know exactly how to sell the game. It is also a good idea to have the art assets ready for marketing and packaging, and to prepare a list of frequently asked questions and answers to help the publisher with typical queries.

This work will help the publisher properly support the game. Without serious support, the game will fail at retail, regardless of its quality. Know from the beginning of the negotiations how the publisher plans to support the game, and provide any help that is necessary to assist the publisher with this support.

Intellectual Property and Technology Rights

Negotiating who retains the rights to what assets can be one of the trickiest parts of the entire process. The publisher will want to retain all rights from the beginning, but you should be very careful with what you give away.

The *intellectual property* (IP) rights to the game will most likely end up in the hands of the publisher. Contracts that prevent this are possible, but not very common. In this context, intellectual property includes the names of the game and its characters, the story, trademarks and logos, artwork, and music.

You may want to push harder to retain IP rights if the game is a role-playing game (RPG) or involves a world that the designers have put a lot of effort into. However, if you cannot retain the rights, you should at least be compensated for them, and a clause should be placed in the contract stating that you have first rights to develop any sequels or spin-offs—and a last match option, meaning that if you are willing to perform the work under the conditions that the publisher is about to sign with another team, the assignment is yours. This may be the best possible situation: a publisher will have more incentive to promote a license they own, but you should simply make sure your team continues to develop the property.

As with the marketing and sales of the game, if the publisher is not using the rights, they should revert back to you.

Technology Rights

Technology rights are a different issue. The developer should always retain these rights, especially if the engine was created in-house, because licensing the engine underlying a successful game can provide a significant stream of income. With this in mind, document the engine from the beginning of development, and make sure all tools associated with the engine are easy to comprehend.

Developers will not want to devote a lot of resources to engine support unless a serious amount of revenue is being generated through technology licensing. Good game engines usually sell for $250,000 to $500,000, plus a 2 to 5 percent royalty on net income. With this added revenue, developers can easily begin additional projects and support a small staff to help other developers with questions. Tools will also be necessary if an editor is shipped with the game; an avid community of players developing new content ("mods") for a game can greatly increase its shelf life, but if the consumers do not comprehend the editing tools, it will be no benefit at all.

Note that the publisher may wish to impose an exclusivity clause on the games developed with your new engine. If the technology is groundbreaking, the publisher will not want a competing title to be released that may damage sales. This is a common request, but developers should make sure that the term of exclusivity is realistic; it should not exceed six months from the launch of the game.

Term

The final major component of a contract is the *term* and the rules governing its extension. Some games can have a very long shelf life, and publishers will plan for this entire life when they are working with their P&L statement. A game that releases at a $49 price may see sales at $39, $29 , $19, and $9 dollars before it is officially pulled from the shelves. Even at this point, the game could be bundled with similar titles for additional revenue.

In order to give the publisher the time they need to run a game through its complete life cycle, a term of five years is standard. If the game is still selling at this point, contract extensions should be added, at one year increments.

By cutting the term of the contract short, a developer runs the risk of losing sales that a good publisher can extract from games that are four or five years old. However, as with many other points in the contract, if sales are nonexistent for a period of time, usually three months, the rights should revert back to the developer. It may be possible to find a partner who can revive the sales using tactics or connections that the primary publisher did not have.

Points to Avoid

The following are points to be aware of and to avoid when negotiating a contract:

Cross-Collateralization

Developers should always be extremely cautious of this term. There are situations when cross-collateralization can be beneficial, but for the most part it should be avoided.

Cross-collateralization will only fall into a contract when more than one title (or more than one version of the same game for more than one platform) are being sold. If a contract includes the cross-collateralization of two different games, the publisher will not be responsible for paying royalties until the guaranteed number of units is sold through a combination of the sales for both titles. For example, if a publisher guarantees 500,000 units of two games, they would need to sell 400,000 of one and 100,000 of another in order to meet their commitment. This is a poor situation for the developer because they would already be seeing royalty checks for one game if the contract was negotiated in a different manner.

For contracts containing two different games, each game should have its own guarantee for units. This prevents a publisher from holding royalties on a strong-selling game to make up for a lack of sales on the other. If the example used here were negotiated to say that there was a 250,000-unit guarantee for each game, the developer would have already seen a significant amount of royalties for the title that sold 400,000 units.

Cross-collateralization can be useful when a title is released on several platforms. Developers should still be very cautious, but having one platform cover for the lack of sales on another is not nearly as bad as the two-game situation. For one thing, it may be the best way to obtain funding for development on a new platform, and the expertise gained can be worth the financial risk. Agree to cross-collateralization in this case as a last resort, but do not avoid it as earnestly as with two separate games.

Management Fees

On rare occasions, publishers try to insert the deduction of management fees, trade shows, travel expenses, and such items into the contract, usually under the definition of "net receipts." Under no circumstances should you agree to these terms. Publishers should always be responsible for these costs, and unless they are going far out of their way for a game, there is no reason for the developer to pay for them. The publisher has complete control over these expenses, after all.

Canceling without Warning

Make sure that a clause is inserted to protect you in the event the publisher decides to cancel a project with no warning. This happens quite frequently in the industry, most often when the publisher is purchased and the new owner has a competing project or no interest in the game.

A protection clause should state that in the event of cancellation, the publisher must pay the current and next milestones of the contract to the developer. This gives the development team sufficient time to find a new partner and does not leave them in a situation where they are instantly out of cash.

Protecting Your Team

There have been cases of publishers recognizing great talent in a team and hiring those members away for their own internal teams. All contracts should state that the publisher will not hire any member of the development team from the company during the process and for a set period after release. This clause is even easier to insert in a contract if the publisher wants to define the team members for a project in writing.

Besides, any publisher that would poach staff is one you would not want to work with in the future. This clause is also a good test of the potential partner's good faith.

No Defined Time Restraints

Finally, make certain that each milestone's acceptance and payment is tied to clearly defined time periods in the contract. For example:

- "Payment is due within five days of milestone acceptance."
- "Publisher has five business days to review the milestone or the milestone is considered accepted."

For all deliverables, define a due date, a time table for review and response, and a set amount of time for corrections. Including these definitions in the contract ensures that payments are made swiftly and that nothing is lost in the shuffle.

Conclusion

There are countless numbers of points a company can negotiate in a contract. The ones selected here are the key points that a developer would be certain to focus on.

The most important thing to remember is to know what the company or team needs. Then, remember that the company you are negotiating with will be your partner for some time to come. It does no one any good to start a long relationship on bad terms because of an acrimonious negotiation.

7.4

Negotiating a Freelance Game Design Contract

Bruce Onder

bonder@digitalarcana.com

Negotiating a game design services contract is not exactly pleasant. However, it is important to consider which clauses that you want, which clauses you will accept, and which clauses you must refuse in your contract with the software developer or publisher.

A Word about Lawyers

First, this article does not represent legal advice. We present the thoughts in this article to help shape your thinking as you enter negotiations for a game design contract. You are responsible for your own decisions.

A good lawyer versed in entertainment business practices and law can be a tremendous asset on your side of the table. Conversely, a bad lawyer can be worse than no lawyer at all. Having negotiated deals both with and without lawyers, we recommend hiring one for a few very simple and practical reasons, which we will now discuss.

Separating Negotiation from the Business Relationship

You will eventually be working closely with the people on the other side of the bargaining table (or at least, the people who work with or for those people), so you should maintain some emotional distance from the negotiation process once the work starts. Unfortunately, bad feelings have a habit of not remaining at the negotiation table; if one side or the other holds grudges, the negativity can permeate the working relationship. A lawyer can help you maintain distance by playing "bad cop" during the negotiations while you wait to be the "good cop" when it comes time to begin the actual work on the project.

Higher Authority

If you use a lawyer to represent you during negotiations, he cannot agree to any proposal himself—he must consult with you, which gives you time to consider the deal.

This time can be priceless, because as a game designer, you are probably over-eager to agree to any proposals so that you can start on the project. But when the game is on the shelves and you discover that your publisher does not have to pay you royalties for all your hard work, you will wish you had looked the contract over more carefully. The best way to avoid future disappointments is to stay out of the room or conversation during negotiations.

Legal Finesse

Some lawyers, including many corporate attorneys, do not always know the best legal methods. You want the ones who do, because these lawyers will better understand when it is in your best interest to reword clauses, and when it is in your best interest to let the publisher's wording stand.

Preliminary Work

Before you begin negotiations, you should put together a list of "deal points" that must be resolved acceptably. In this context, *acceptable* is not necessarily synonymous with *satisfactory*—chances are that at least some of your deal points will not be satisfactorily negotiated at all. Only you can decide what you can live with.

Deal points break down into two broad categories: deal killers and negotiable points. You and the publisher will have a list of both.

Deal Killers

Deal killers are any clauses that you absolutely cannot and will not accept. For your own economic happiness, you should keep this list to the bare minimum, but sometimes you must stand firm. Here are some potential deal killers you should think about:

"Favored Nation" Status on Credit

You will be working as hard as other creative people on the team (sometimes harder), so you want to make sure that you receive proper credit on the game. *Favored Nation* means that you get the best terms being offered. Specifically, strive to tie your company's credit to the director's (for individual credit) or the developer's logo placement. Ask for similar presentation style, size, and (for screen credits) duration. You can also try to negotiate specific placement of your credit, such as just after the director's, or on the last title card. A good entertainment lawyer will know how to word your wishes in this matter appropriately.

Payment on Delivery

Many contracts are worded such that a payment is not actually due you until the client accepts the *deliverable*, which means that you could be agreeing to provide unlimited free rewrites. Instead, outline the benefits of an interactive design cycle, such as the one presented in [Onder02], and insist that payments begin with the delivery of a first complete draft of the game design document to the client. In fact, enclose an invoice with the document and cover letter. The publisher will most likely want some type of qualifier to this to ensure that the material is well done and acceptable on some specific level.

Indemnifications

You should have the client indemnify you for any materials they provide to you as research or inspiration. This is critically important if you are being asked to take over a project midstream—you do not have the time or the resources to find out if the client legally owns the existing materials. Get the indemnifications. You will be expected to give the client the same, so make it a mutual indemnification.

Negotiable Points

Almost everything else on the contract is a *negotiable point*, which means that only the broad outline of the deal point is known, and you will have to fill in the details to the acceptance of both parties. Here are some sample negotiable points:

Price

Price is not a deal killer, except to the extent that you must get paid. (If you are ever presented with a contract for game design services that suggests no payment for services rendered, run, to the nearest exit.) That said, only you know what kind of price you will and will not accept. A general rule of thumb is that over time, you want to see your project rates go up for projects of equivalent size. However, another rule of thumb is that you should not walk away from a good project just because of price. It can be a tricky issue.

Flat Fee Versus Hourly

First, few publishers will work with hourly billing, unless you commit to a capped number of hours. If you are going to cap hours, then you are better off with flat fee pricing, for three reasons. First, billing by the hour actually hurts you because, over time, you learn to do a better job in fewer hours (unless you raise your rates constantly). Second, flat fees are easier to package—if you do not believe the client will pay three equal installments, take a bigger payment for the final draft (where most of the details have to be written). Finally, it is more satisfying to live in a world in which you are paid for producing an excellent, polished, and finished design document, not for putting in so many hours of effort. Not having to punch a clock can be a great morale booster.

Start of Services Fee

The purpose of the *start of services fee* is twofold: first, it helps get the relationship off to a good start by showing the client's good faith, and second, it provides you with some money right away. Sometimes you will negotiate for the start of services check to be available at signing of the contract, and other times you will invoice the client and get paid in a specified time period.

Payment Terms and Schedule

Obviously, you will want your payments as soon as you make delivery based on the schedule negotiated; in the real world, however, companies have accounting departments that process invoices in a set amount of time. In the contract, try to negotiate for "net 15" payment terms and fix real consequence for the publisher if they miss the payment. Do not expect to be successful in trying to charge interest on late payments—tracking interest is a hassle, and the client usually tries to avoid paying it anyway. It could also be a deal killer from the publisher's perspective. However, if you can, contractually tie payment to the work schedule on a day-for-day basis. If you were supposed to get paid on April 5, and you were not, halt the work at the end of the day, and wait until you receive the payment. That means that if payment is delayed one week and your next delivery deadline was originally May 15, it is automatically pushed back to May 23 (one week later).

Producers dislike having their schedules compromised by accounting glitches, so if you give them a gentle nudge a few days before the payment is due, they will probably strive to ensure that the check does indeed reach you on time.

Travel and Lodging Expenses

You may be asked to travel to take part in team meetings, brainstorming sessions, and other meetings. If you live in the same city as the client, this should not pose a problem. However, if you must travel to another city (or country), then you should consider how this travel will affect your other work and your life. If you do not want to travel, try to get the client to state explicitly that no travel will be required. If you can not negotiate that, try to put restrictions on the travel requirements. For example, on one of my projects, we agreed that the designers would fly on one week's notice, but only if first-class travel and accommodation were prepaid by the client (not expensed to the client). On another deal, we made weekly day trips from Los Angeles to San Francisco to review graphic designs and technology prototypes. No first-class treatment there, but all tickets were purchased by the client and all cab fares and meals were reimbursed. How travel expenses are covered definitely varies from project to project and can be a deal killer on either side, so keep that in mind during your negotiations.

Exclusive Service

It is never a good idea to grant *exclusive service* to a single client if you can help it. One way to avoid this point is to state that if you are unable to take on additional work as it becomes available, then you will need to charge higher rates on this project. Another solution is to offer "favored nation" status instead—they will not receive any less attention than other active clients (percentage-wise), and if you miss a deadline, you will accept a substantial penalty.

If you can not avoid exclusivity, you risk not being available for another job until after you completely wind up your current client's work, so consider this carefully in your planning.

Contributor's Copies

Ask for four times as many contributor's copies than the client initially offers. You will usually end up with twice as many as offered, or you can offer them back as a bargaining chip when you need something with a higher priority. At any rate, when you receive your contributor's copies, use them as promotional materials to promote you and your group by giving them to producers, publishers, and anyone else you would like to work with (or work with again).

Insurance

When a client asks for insurance, they want protection against anything out of the ordinary. Depending on the importance of the deal, you can either decline to provide any insurance, or agree to buy it for the term specified, but only if an advance is paid to cover the costs of such insurance.

Credit Arbitration

To ensure that you receive the proper credits, be sure to clarify possible issues. For instance, consider this scenario: you make an extraordinary effort for your client, working 18-hour days for three months to finish their big-budget adventure game design document on time so that they can start production. Then, the client pulls you off that project and puts you to work on their next troubled title. But, when the adventure game comes out, you find that some other designer received top design credit because of political issues in the company over your being moved off the game..

You will have little recourse if you let deal points such as credit arbitration slip. However, if credit is not that important to you, you can use it as a bargaining chip to get something that is more important to you than fair credit.

However, you can always try to negotiate some relatively objective credit determination scheme, such as a separate "Additional Design by" credit for any other designers who contributed less effort than you did.

Deliverables and Milestones

Make sure your contract specifies exactly what you will be delivering to the client. Almost everyone has their own ideas about what goes into a game design document, and these ideas are not standardized by any means. It is best to clarify what the client wants, and then capture those requirements in the agreement. Make sure you understand each of the elements agreed to. For example, if you do not know what a gameplay matrix looks like, have an example attached as an addendum. Likewise, if the client wants elements that you can not produce (character sketches, isometric level designs, et al), state that up front.

Delivery Schedule

As with pricing, only you know how quickly you can work to produce the level of quality expected by the client. Make sure, however, that you know (do not just assume) the client's expectations. A fix-up job on the current design document to be completed within three weeks requires a different level of effort than a complete rewrite.

Set a reasonable schedule given the amount of work, and try to divide the work into several phases:

- An **initial design phase** in which you flesh out the best ideas you or your team have generated for a game.
- One or more **revision phases** (specify how many in the agreement) in which you review the client's notes on your initial design.
- A **detailing phase** in which you write a first draft that includes all the detail behind your revised design notes.
- And finally one or more **polish phases** (again, specify how many) in which you incorporate the client's notes on the design.

Make sure that you get paid for every phase of the delivery schedule—it is just good business.

Client Notes

How many sets of notes should you need to collate to arrive at a checklist of issues to address? Only one. Your agreement should specify that the client is responsible for providing you with a single integrated set of notes, which you will then discuss with the client at length to arrive at the final checklist of revisions required..

Don not make the mistake of presuming that all the client notes should be incorporated into your revisions. First, some notes are, in fact, merely questions; second, some notes will suggest a course of rewrite that might lead to danger for the project. Try to negotiate a discussion period, during which you can work with the client to make sure everyone understands what the needed revisions will (and will not) be.

Additional Services

Sometimes you will be asked to perform tasks that are not covered by your agreement. For instance, my company is typically asked to review character and setting sketches or models. Usually, we do it, because we want the final product to be as close to our vision as possible; however, we like to have language in the agreement that makes it clear that we perform these services only if they will not impede our ability to provide the contracted ones, and that we reserve the right to refuse work we are not qualified or interested in doing (such as, asset management on one project) and the right to bill the client for this supplemental work. A high flat daily fee for optional additional services usually keeps the client focused on the contracted work. However, anything you can do easily to keep product quality high, do for free; the client will appreciate your extra work and it keeps things friendly. Be sure you describe these services in your invoice though, even if you write "no charge" in the amount column.

Conclusion

As stated above, we are not presenting legal advice, but advice from a business person who negotiates contracts in order to set a baseline description of the working relationship and expectations. However, your relationship with your client should evolve to be much deeper, more meaningful, and more rewarding than any contract could hope to indicate. If your client asks you to do something, and it is not in your agreement, strongly consider the potential upside of saying "sure" before you say "no."

This is a small industry, and people prefer to work with people they already know, like, and trust.

Bibliography

[Onder02] Onder, B., "Writing the Adventure Game," *Game Design Perspectives*, Charles River Media, 2002.

7.5

Keeping Your Team Motivated

Geoff Howland

ghowland@lupinegames.com

Many factors contribute to the success of a project: the experience of team members, the amount of time allocated to the project, and the technical boundaries and limitations of a platform are but of few of them. However, unless the constraints of your project are completely unreasonable or your team woefully inadequate, the largest problems you will face are organization and motivation.

While it is obvious to anyone running a non-trivial project that they need to be organized if they expect to have any hope to succeed, motivation is often dismissed as something project members should bring to work with them, and not something the project leads need to concern themselves with. The problem with this approach is that it equates motivation to professionalism, and takes no responsibility for situations and actions that can erode motivation—or expand on motivation already present.

Too often, motivation's potential impact on a project is overlooked. Who will contribute more to a project: an experienced developer who is not motivated to finish, because he has other problems on his mind while at work, or an experienced developer who is looking forward to completing the project and is not distracted by unrelated issues? We will ignore the argument that junior staff can produce more than experienced developers who are not interested in working, because in any large project you will have a spectrum of experience, and the point is that a properly motivating environment will drive contributors of all levels to produce more.

Let's look at some guidelines for inspiring motivation, and at the problems that can happen when motivation is lacking.

Visualization of Progress and Completion

The purpose of working on a project is to finish it. Anything that helps workers see that their project is moving toward completion will increase their motivation. With that in mind, let's look at some ways you can reinforce this visualization process.

Prototype Building

A working prototype is a good way in which to establish a common vision among your team: everyone can see that the project's basic premise works, and they will have a benchmark against which to compare their production builds.

Prototypes also help prevent wasted work, because the flaws in the gameplay are visible before production development time has been spent on them. Having one's work thrown away can seriously reduce motivation, and who can say that it will not happen again? Many long hours spent that did not move the project any closer to completion can make the final goal seem much farther away.

Several factors influence a prototype's desirability, including how much time you have for the whole project, and how much of the prototyping code and artwork could be salvaged for the final product. In any case, consider it.

Continuous Integration

The project's production code should be brought to a fully operational (if incomplete) state early and often.

An architecture that always functions can be seen as a succession of prototypes. If the initial prototype is designed properly, it can form the basis of the production code. (Depending on the project, it may be necessary and beneficial to separate the prototype from the production code.)

The continuous integration process allows everyone to see how the project is moving closer to the status of a finished product each time code and art resources are added to it. Add new content to the build regularly, and the team will have proof that the project has made another step towards the goal.

Scheduling for Visualization

Of course, some aspects of development (like engine architecture) are inherently non-visual, but they are the foundations of the work and must be completed first to ensure project completion. However, beyond these essentials are a number of components that can be crafted in any order. When scheduling, take into consideration the tasks that will bring the most visible results and plan accordingly.

A schedule that regularly makes large visible steps towards being a finished project will be more inspiring to work on than one where all of the components come together at the end. You may want to consider staggering visible improvements (even delaying some on purpose) to guarantee motivational rewards throughout the project and to save the developers from having to look at an apparently stagnant game for most of the duration of development life.

In addition to being beneficial to the team's motivation, visual-oriented scheduling will also be a boon to your publisher milestone demos. Being able to show visible progress can only help relations, and may even protect your team against cancellation if and when the publisher starts looking for titles that will slip deadlines or are not progressing as well as others.

Clear Vision of the Path

When you sit down in your car to go on a trip, how can you do it with confidence if your directions end with the first stop light? Hopefully, when you get to the stop light, you will be able to decide which way to turn, but it would still be nice to have a clear itinerary before you got started.

Developing a game works in much the same way. When developers are only told what they need to do in pieces, they are unsure of how each piece will fit into the whole. They may worry that the integration will be difficult and that part of their efforts will have been wasted.

A clear and visible plan must be provided, so that everyone can contribute and feel good about their work moving the game towards its completion.

Having a clear path of work and a solid destination can also reduce the number of changes that come from outside the team. Changes requested by a publisher or other outside force can make the team feel uncomfortable and worry about how their work will fit into a game with a shifting set of specifications. Having a prototype can also help here, as it communicates the intended functionality to the publisher clearly and reduces the likelihood of misunderstandings.

Well-Defined Jobs

Every member of the team should have access to the game's development roadmap and be provided with a clear list of responsibilities. If the roadmap (usually a document created with project management software) fails to specify who handles which pieces of code, or which subjects of art, or which levels, there will be confusion, and possibly frustration and lost time, as work is duplicated or ignored and people argue over ownership.

If everyone is aware of their roles and responsibilities in development, they can be aware of those of the other team members as well. If there is a problem, they know with whom they can discuss it. This leads to better communication and less time wasted trying to figure out *how* to solve the problem, instead of solving it.

Precise Scheduling

Responsibilities can be broad and fairly vague in nature. They will almost always need to be broken down into specific tasks to be organized and completed. Making a list of these tasks available to other team members not only helps in the understanding of how things work, but can also assist in visualizing the project's motion towards completion.

As tasks and sections of work are completed, the team moves closer and closer to their goal of finishing the game. The ability to see tasks being marked as completed can be motivating, as not all work is apparent from running the game. Architectural code that deals with internals, making systems more robust, or improving details of artwork may not jump out at people, but a list of what has been accomplished this week and what is left to be accomplished is hard evidence of progress.

Open Communication Lanes

People resent not being able to be heard. They also resent having problems and not being able to seek solutions to them. Not all problems can be resolved to everyone's satisfaction, but if there are no lines of communication open, they will not even have a chance to raise the issues.

There are several theories on how much communication should be allowed. Some people feel that anyone should be able to talk to anyone else at any time. Others believe that too much free communication can consume valuable work time while making it difficult to track the flow of information, and that strict chains of command should be enforced to prevent chaos.

However you define your balance on this problem, you should outline ways in which different groups can communicate with each other in timely ways. People who work inside a group may need basically unlimited access to each other. People in different groups may need certain times allotted during the week to air concerns, or be asked to send them via email. Impromptu discussions should also be possible in case of emergency.

Of course, if the project is progressing well and informal communication policies work without any significant complaints, rules can be relaxed and people allowed to communicate as they feel best. However, some teams are too large for ad hoc policies. In any case, if problems arise, the guidelines can be enforced more strictly to keep the project moving along while still giving the workers their say.

Shared Commitment

People who work in a team can accomplish far more than a collection of individuals. Teams build on the strengths of their members and support the weaknesses of their members. Not everyone on the team needs to be an expert on everything the team will do. But when not everyone acts in support of the team, more is lost than just the effort of a single person.

People Who Do Not Pull Their Weight Drag Others Down

For every developer who does not perform his job, there is a domino effect of consequences that can damage the team and the project.

In the best case, one other team member must stop doing his own work to do the offender's. This leads to a single negative impact in the project moving forward, as a week's worth of work must be put off to complete a week's worth of work—assuming the offending member can become effective elsewhere or is taken off the project entirely.

If the slacker is in charge of a task on the critical path to project completion (i.e., if the task is required to move the project past a milestone), the situation is far worse. If the delay is not discovered before the component is due, it could effect the entire team instead of just a single member who has to stand in to do the work. Everyone will be left waiting to move on before the project can resume as scheduled.

Beyond the frustration felt by all the workers whose time is being wasted, a distrust of other team members may emerge. This can lead to workers feeling less inclined to do their own job, or feeling as if they need to check up on others all the time. Both of these scenarios will reduce motivation and productivity.

Obviously, such project "choke points" should be avoided during planning if possible, but that cannot always be done, and some systems always need to be integrated last. Keeping these potential problems in mind when doing the initial planning, and highlighting what areas can become choke points, will help avoid the worst.

Bad Attitudes

Not doing their job is not the only way that members can pull a team apart. Frequently, when a developer becomes dissatisfied, they will begin making negative comments about the project, other team members, or the company, which can destroy the cohesiveness of a team and undermine the motivation to work on the project. Keeping these negative behaviors from becoming habits is not easy to do, as disgruntled employees usually talk to other rank-and-file staffers and not to team leads. However, it is easier to keep them from happening or escalating if everyone is on the lookout for sources of discontent, the most common of which include lack of open communication with the team leads and management, and worries about job stability. Anything you can do to ease these problems will help greatly.

Some people will also feel inclined to try to gain political favor with leads or management. You must be very careful not to reward this sort of activity implicitly, and to actively discourage it when you think it is taking place. Politicking undermines the concept that working on the project should be the goal of the team members.

Close-Working Teams Keep Motivation High

Just like football players after half-time speeches in movies, highly motivated developers may inspire excitement in others. At the very least, they do not suck excitement out of other people, as depressed coworkers can do.

Teams that have good communication, can see their project moving toward completion, and watch it becoming more like the game they saw in the prototyping stage, will reap the benefits of job satisfaction. Because we cannot all visit the beach or go snowboarding every day, having a job from which we can gain satisfaction is a wonderful thing.

Workplace Environments

The debate on the best ways to organize physical work space is just as controversial as the one on the most effective lines of communication. Whether you choose cubicles, closed offices or open spaces, make sure that the environment does not become an obstacle to productivity.

For example, programmers will often desire quiet one- or two-person offices, so that they can concentrate while they work, but this not always the case. Talk to your team, find out what they would like, then implement it and see if it actually works.

The only office elements that seem to be universally despised are half-cubicles, as they are seen as existing for the sole purpose of allowing management to spy on workers.

Remove or Reduce External Worries

How can you work if you cannot concentrate on working?

There are sources of stress that are outside of a company's control. You will never be able to solve family problems, sickness, etc. These, however, are constants, and people learn to deal with them as best they can. Problems that are directly related to the workplace are much harder to keep from becoming distractions.

Worries About Getting Paid or Losing Jobs Crushes Motivation

Why work if you are about to be fired, or are not getting paid? No matter how much you love your job, you almost assuredly would not show up to work every day if you had to do it for free.

If the company has money problems, let the employees know. If it will be tight, but hard work can pull you through, tell them. They may suffer from additional stress because of the extra work, and some of them may even leave for other jobs, but at least you will not completely erode the motivation of those who remain. Team cohesion might even increase as everyone pulls together and less interested people leave.

Cuts and money problems create rumors that can quickly get out of hand. Rumors that you may not be getting paid will bring productivity to a halt. And an actual bouncing paycheck is a long-term disaster: workers will distrust management, and even if the cash-flow issues are solved, the confidence will never return.

Do not play with people's livelihoods and expect them to give you anything but their minimums, if that.

Not Knowing Where the Company Is Going Can Reduce Motivation

If workers have no idea where the company is going in terms of projects and direction, it creates an uncomfortable tension about the future.

You may not actually know where you will be in the future, but you can outline where you think you are going and what you are trying to do to get there.

If you do not feel comfortable sharing all that information with the employees because they might leak it, just look at all the companies and government agencies with very strict rules on information flow—their most private memos leak constantly. The harder you try to protect information, the more people will want to get their hands on it. You will fare better with employees who feel like part of a team than with people you keep at arm's length, because they have less incentive to betray you.

Do not be afraid to be unable to predict the future. Tell them what you are trying to do, and if that idea fails, let them know and tell them about the new plan. They will learn to trust you, and trust is a powerful asset.

Getting Away from the Project

Working your employees over 40 hours a week on a regular basis is giving them reasons not to concentrate for the time they are there.

No one is able to concentrate and be truly productive 10 hours at a time. If a lot of your developers' time is chewed up by unproductive meetings, try to cut down on this nonworking time so that it can best provide communication without impairing active development of the project. Discourage staying after 5 PM. Instead put the emphasis on *working* while at work, instead of surfing the Web or playing *Quake* on the network, so there will be no reason to stay late.

Because games are projects with seasonal deadlines, there may be times when work loads have to be increased to finish the project on time. This should be considered a failure in the planning and time management process of the cycle, because it should be possible to complete the project without overtime. However, if it does happen, reduce overtime to a minimum, and immediately go back to normal hours when you can.

Under no circumstances should anyone ever lose normal sleep time because of work. This is not the way to ship a project, especially one without bugs. When someone is tired and hurried, they are more likely to make mistakes than when they are operating normally and are well rested. Discourage these kinds of "heroic" efforts.

To increase motivation, you want to make the project something that can be looked forward to. If the workers can never get away from the project, there is no feasible way of looking forward to working on it. At the very least, you do not want to make the project something the workers would rather avoid. If they are stuck at work for long stretches of time, and have their weekends and free time cut into, that is exactly how they will feel.

Motivation Is Not Just Cheerleading

Having excited and enthusiastic people working on a project is a great thing, but motivation is also about having incentive to work, and ways that the work can be meaningful, substantial, and rewarding. No one has to beam about it to feel as if they are doing a good job and work in a highly optimal way.

Keeping Motivation Going the Entire Project

It is more important to have *consistent* motivation than to have *high* motivation. Do not aim for workers to be jogging between desks because they are so vitalized by the work, aim for having a place of work where people are not frustrated, and where they can view what they have accomplished at the end of the day and see that it has meaning.

A project in which a group of people can get along without bitterness or power struggles, week after week, and where each member is completing his tasks on time and knows that others are doing the same, is a success. Anything beyond that is icing.

To Bonus or Not to Bonus

How do you reward employees for successfully completing a project? Specifically, should you give monetary bonuses? Other types of compensation? This decision mostly depends on what the company can afford, and to making sure that the reward does not skew the concentration on the project.

The first issue is the biggest one, because if you cannot afford a bonus, you should never offer one. Failing to deliver on a promise will frustrate workers, and it will affect your future projects. If you promise a bonus, pay it. It is a better idea to not even mention a bonus if you are unsure of your ability to deliver, unless it is based on a percentage of income from sales, which are out of your control.

The question of what to reward with is another problem. No one will turn down money, but perhaps what workers can use most after a project is time off. If everyone wants to go on a trip together, that could be a great release for the team, but do not make it a requirement. If some people want to go on their own, or spend time with their family and friends instead, fine. People are different, and some need time away from coworkers to wind down, instead of time with them after work.

Conclusion

Motivation and productivity go hand in hand. If you have a team that is unmotivated to work, it does not matter how experienced they are, they are not going to be giving you as much as they could.

Do not try to fix problems in a vacuum. Pay attention to what is happening within your team. Tailor your solutions to problems that are actually occurring, and do not try to build a "perfect environment" without regard for what your employees need, since everyone is different and one person's gold may be another's lead.

There is no single way to provide a workplace in which people can be motivated, and no one can transfuse motivation to anyone else. You can only try your best to remove sources of frustration and encourage positive behaviors, and let your workers' talents shine.

7.6

Managing External Development Teams: Hand Me the Remote

Tom Sloper

tomster@sloperama.com

Internal development costs have skyrocketed as games have become more complex. Increasingly, there are good budgetary reasons for developing games with external studios, but there is often resistance to the idea of developing externally. The usual objections to remote development are:

- Fear of the loss of direct control
- Time delays in transferring documents, data, and builds
- Distance (travel expenses, time zone differences)

This article deals with each of these points, with special emphasis on the first. The majority of the 78 unique released game titles that this author designed and/or produced at Sega, Atari, Activision, Datascan, and Western Technologies (and all of the 17 other completed projects) were developed externally. Many of the concepts in this discussion also apply to producers managing an internal project or outsourcing parts of the project.

Choosing a Developer

In the ideal case, the choice of developer is up to you. You have a project to produce, and you must find and hire a developer.

Never choose a developer based on cost alone (or on relationship or familiarity alone). Always follow normal developer selection procedures. In other words make sure you cover the following points.

Get and check references. Talk to other publishers for whom the developer has made games. Ask about their capabilities on your target hardware platform. Ask about their timeliness—did they deliver milestones on time? Was the game finished on time? If it fell behind, did the developer take steps to catch up? Ask about cost—did the developer finish the game on budget? If there were cost overruns, was it due to changes requested by the publisher or to factors within the developer's control? Ask about the management process—was the developer easy to manage or did they require a lot of handholding? What is the developer's management style? In the case of a console game, how did the approval process with the hardware manufacturer go? Were there many turnarounds or did the game sail through? Your company may have other issues you will wish to explore through the developer's references.

Review past products made by the developer. Obtain a copy of the games, and play them yourself. For each game, consider the following: Does it look and sound good? Is the interface intuitive and easy to pick up? Is the gameplay fun and engaging? Was the game well reviewed?

Visit the developer's office if it is feasible to do so. The typical development house has a lived-in, kind of hodge-podge look to it; computers and development equipment on desks and even stacked in corners. You want to see a busy place where everyone has a businesslike attitude (probably working on a project for someone else). If you are experienced in the business of making games, you know what looks familiar and normal. A developer with a different look may actually be in a different business entirely, requiring some additional background checking on your part.

Occasionally you may come across a developer who has not been in business very long. Obviously, it is always best to hire developers with a proven track record, but sometimes it makes sense to give at least a small project to a new, unproven developer. Find out about both the person at the top of the company and the individuals who would be doing the work on your project. How much experience have they had in the industry, and what kind? The more experience, the better. Big and/or crucial projects should go to a very experienced developer. The less experience the developer has, the smaller the project you want to try them out on.

If You Are Assigned a Developer

Sometimes, though, you have no choice; perhaps a superior has assigned a particular outside developer to work with you. When this happens, you simply must work with the developer the best you can. As soon as the project is given to you, it is your job to take command.

Taking Control

The first step in working with a developer is to establish a relationship with them (especially if they were assigned to you).

You are now the main contact between the developer and your company. *You are the client.* If all is right with the world, the developer should immediately attempt to accommodate you. In that case, it should be easy for you to assume command right away.

Sometimes, however, you may find yourself working with a developer who has his own agenda. Or there may be some other reason why taking control is not as easy as it should be.

For example, at one time a manager had contracted a project with an up-and-coming developer in order to foster a relationship with them. The developer had a track record of making hit games for personal computers, and now wanted to work on an original console game that our company would publish. We traveled to meet the project leader in person, and our first question for him was, of course, "What is the game?" They responded by providing a manifesto that discussed videogames versus computer games. We were to manage and schedule their project, but they came up with their own original game in their own time, and were not particularly inclined to give us any control. Likewise, the boss was inclined to give them free rein. Needless to say, the position was awkward.

As it happened, fate solved the problem: the company assigned the game to another producer. This story to illustrates that sometimes when you are assigned a developer , taking control is not a given. This loss of control can happen particularly if you are a junior producer dealing with a well established developer, and particularly if your company has a second agenda (such as the idea of "relationship building" behind this particular project).

Usually, the producer can take control of the publisher-developer relationship through careful planning, interdepartmental coordination, hard work, clear communications, confidence in his developer, and confidence in his own ability to manage the process.

Careful Planning and Coordination

Make a detailed plan, working with the developer to do so. As you unearth the details, the process becomes clearer not only for you but also for the developer. Plan everything through to the end. (And beyond—but that is beyond the scope of this article.)

- **Preproduction:** Plan who will create the design and how long it should take. Plan for the approvals and signoffs on the design and the technical plan. A licensor is involved, plan for licensor involvement as well.
- **Production:** Establish a formalized process for approving assets, builds, and milestones. Plan for subsequent visits at key milestones. Plan for changes in the plan. If your game will involve voice talent or video acting talent, decide when work on that component needs to take place, and plan to have your developer's technical people at the shoot.
- **Marketing:** Coordinate early with your company's marketing department. Make sure you plan for demos, images for magazine articles and covers, strategy guides, and trade shows.
- **Post-production:** Plan for the Entertainment Software Rating Board (ESRB) rating and the console manufacturer's approval cycle (if it is a console game). Even plan for the box production and documentation cycle.
- **Quality Assurance (QA):** Coordinate early with QA to make the test cycle a part of the plan from the beginning. Plan for international versions; anticipate possible Original Equipment Manufacturer (OEM) versions and ports. Make sure the

developer understands the importance of clearly documented code and asset packs.

Develop the plan with your developer to ensure that both parties (and various departments within your company) all agree on the plan. Consensus-building is an important part of planning and communication.

Clear Communications

Knowledge is ammunition, both for you and for your developer. Remember that you are on the same side: the best way to ensure that the two of you survive the battle is by sharing ammunition.

Clear communications does not mean enunciating clearly when you talk, or typing with proper use of the Shift key. It means sharing thoughts and ideas, and clarity between both parties.

If the developer tells you something and you are not certain what he means (or if he could mean one of several things), ask. Conversely, if you say something that could be interpreted in several different ways, do not wait to be asked for clarification. State your point again using different words, so that you are very clear. Asking questions about small points, or speaking or typing a thought twice, might seem like an unnecessary waste of time, but a small time investment early could save a large amount time later.

There are several methods of communication, each with its own purpose. In decreasing order of effectiveness, they are:

- **Face-to-face meetings:** For relationship building, multimember coordination, and (a bonus) for handing off of documents or builds or other materials.
- **Telephone calls:** For quick exchanges of short back-and-forth information, and the added benefit of relationship maintenance.
- **E-mails:** For conveying longer packets of information than can be transferred by telephone.
- **Faxes:** For official documents, or longer pieces of information that need illustrations.
- **Snail mail:** For official documents and for delivery of assets or materials.
- **Instant Messaging:** For quick exchanges of very short bi-directional pieces of information, when both parties are at their computers.

It is easy to lose the personal touch when writing emails, faxes, snail mail, or using instant messaging. Always be aware of your tone when sending written communications. However, when you have much information to convey, email or fax can be more useful than the telephone.

When using written communication, it is useful to number your points for reference for later replies, whether via phone or in writing. It is much easier to write: "3. Okay, we'll do that," than: "In regard to your request to color the heroine's hair red and the hero's shirt blue, okay, we'll do that."

Confidence

Confidence in a project usually comes from experience, but having done your homework is also a prerequisite. When you have examined your developer's track record, you have planned the project carefully, your boss trusts you, and you have universal agreement on the plan, you can reasonably feel confident that the project will go smoothly.

However, be ready to deal with any emergencies that may arise: expect the unexpected. As long as you have control over the standard process, you can probably handle any emergency that may come along. Your confidence in your project will carry over to the developer's confidence in you to manage it.

Keeping Control

Having taken control, you need to keep it throughout the project.

As before, clear communication is extremely important. Make sure you always understand what the developer is saying to you. Make sure they always understand what you are saying to them. Ambiguities must be avoided at all costs!

Keep your finger solidly on the pulse of the real world, and never ignore "red flags." In fact, be constantly prepared for them.. The most common red flag is a project's milestone either late or not fully meeting the agreed upon specifications. Discuss the problem with your developer; ask what he recommends to remedy the situation; discuss all the possibilities. Perhaps the next milestone could come in on time, or the missing feature could be included in the next milestone, or both.

A good developer will acknowledge their own mistakes and take the consequences, volunteering to fix the problem without adverse consequences for the project. But you should have money for emergency travel in your budget. If the developer does not come through and there is red flag on the project, you can simply tell them you will pay them a visit.

Typically, the last thing the developer wants is for you to visit their office because of a problem: a producer dropping by can be highly disruptive, and they must take time to come up with a solution to the problem to present to you face-to-face. Another way of keeping control is by being flexible. Stand ready to make adjustments to the plan as needed. Adjustments require the agreement of all affected parties—not just you, your boss, and the developer, but marketing, sales, the licensor, QA, and so forth. Therefore, at the first sign that there may be a change coming, get casual feedback from the affected parties, which is sometimes called "management by wandering around." Walk over to marketing, and mention the problem to your marketing counterpart. Wander to sales, tell the vice president the problem, and get his input. Move on to QA and chat with your lead tester. Call the licensor. You must use your best judgment and your interpersonal skills to determine how best to approach sensitive topics. But when a change is coming, face it head on, because it will almost never go away if you ignore it.

One favorite technique for keeping control is the "pincer" movement, which means to attack problems from multiple angles whenever possible, because there are usually multiple possible solutions to a single problem. Instead of grasping the first solution and hoping it works, set one plan in motion, then another. The goal is to make sure you get the problem solved.

A very powerful weapon in your relationship with your developer is your control over the milestone check. The developer knows that he will not be paid if you are unhappy with the product at each milestone. The ultimate weapon for keeping control, however, is the ever-present threat of cancellation. If the developer does not keep his promises of deadlines or quality , the publisher has the option of canceling the project with that developer and hiring another. Canceling is an extreme, last-resort solution, but the existence of the possibility helps to keep developers on schedule.

Data Transfers

This is the Internet age. The very best method for transferring game builds is via file-transfer protocol (ftp). Preferably, use your company's ftp server to maintain control over the storage transfer site. If your company cannot provide an ftp server, your developer should provide one. The developer will probably a Web site, and if they have enough space on their site server, they should be able to host the data transfers.

With ftp and fast connections you should be able transfer builds within a few hours. Without ftp, you must resort to courier services—FedEx, DHL, or local messengers if the developer is within a half hour's drive or so. Ftp is the best method, however, because the only time involved is that of transferring the data from their computer to yours.

Coming Down to the Wire—The Final Weeks

When the project deadline nears, plan for last-minute QA emergencies. When a tester finds a fatal bug, act immediately Can you call the developer right away, or do you have to wait to call during their business hours? How long will it take to make the fix, compile the code, and upload it? How long will it take you to download the new build, burn CDs, and redeliver to QA? Try to have your developer send you modules rather than a complete build each time. This way, the developer has to send you only selected files rather than the entire game for each fix.

Travel

It is possible to complete the game development process without ever traveling to the developer's location—if the developer is good and if the producer effectively manages the project. For instance, we developed three games with an Australian developer, and never traveled to Australia; likewise, we worked with a Russian art house once and never visited Russia. But expect to travel to domestic developers many times; and we have also been to Japan and England several times while working with developers in those countries. Travel is normal when working with a remote developer—if you do not go to them, they may well come to you.

Travel Costs

As the producer, you are responsible for all costs associated with your project. Only travel if you need to, and when you do travel, make every attempt to keep the costs down. Schedule airfares in advance when possible, and fly coach: it is irresponsible to fly business class (much less first class) in today's cost-conscious atmosphere.

You can sometimes save money staying at a bed and breakfast, though this may not be feasible if you need Internet access. In that case, find a hotel with the minimal services you need.

Most domestic hotels today provide easy access to the Internet; check with your ISP or your company's MIS department for the local phone numbers in your destination city before you go. A cell phone is also a must when traveling domestically. When traveling outside the country, however, Internet access may be unavailable and your cell phones may not work—do your research before you go.

Look for ways to enjoy the trip without impacting the budget. If your relationship with your developer is good, they will probably take you out for meals and show you some of the local sights. And of course, you should do the same when they visit you: the relationship is important.

The three phases of a project offer us a guide to determining when travel is necessary.

Preproduction

Preproduction is the most crucial phase of every project. In preproduction, you must make and coordinate your plan, laying out every step of the rest of the project. During this step is, therefore, the most likely and propitious time for travel. The usual reasons for travel in the preproduction phase are:

- Evaluating the developer
- Establishing a relationship
- Setting ground rules
- Agreeing on details of the project and of its coordination
- Discussing working styles and opening lines of communication
- Planning the timing of subsequent visits

Production

If all is going well in the project, you probably will not need to travel during the production phase. If you do, you might for these reasons:

- Review of first playable and pre-Alpha
- Coordinate a change in plan
- Evaluation/tweaking of features and/or gameplay
- Maintain/refresh relationship

Post-Production

Normally, you will not need to travel during post-production, unless the project has major problems. It is vitally important that you maximize the effectiveness of your visit when traveling during post-production; either stay until the project is completed, or do what you absolutely must and leave immediately.

Time Zones

When your developer is located in a different time zone than you, you must make a few adjustments. When your developer is located east of your company, you must come to work early and your workload is heaviest in the morning, until their day ends. When your developer is located to the west of you, your workload will become heavier toward the end of the day, and you may have to stay late. Give the developer your home phone number—and tell the developer the names of any other persons who live with you.

There are also some adjustments you can ask your developer to make. You can ask (but not demand) that your developer adjust work hours in tandem with a concomitant adjustment on your part, to allow extended hours during which both parties are at work. You can ask for the developer's home phone number, but be considerate of the time. Try to find out the names of any other persons who may answer the phone at that number.

Conclusion

The following is a checklist to help you take and keep control of the external development process:

- **Choose the developer wisely:** Check references, review past products, visit the developer's company to see it for yourself.
- **Begin by establishing a working relationship:** Visit the developer or invite them to come to you. Make a detailed plan for every phase of the project. Discuss your working style. Work out your lines of communication. Establish the method for transfers of builds. Set up a formal approval process for assets and milestones.

- **Coordinate the plan with other departments (and your licensor, if there is one):** Set up consensus-building review meetings. Plan for approvals and signoffs of your progress.
- Having established a detailed plan, **expect the unexpected and be flexible:** Plans are road maps to help us decide how to get where you are going, but be prepared to navigate roadblocks.
- **Keep control by means of regular communications with the developer:** Visits are best, but expensive and often a little disruptive. The telephone is second best, but not suitable for communicating large amounts of detailed information. Email and fax are very useful; use numbered points, but be cautious of losing the human touch. Instant messaging is good for short, back-and-forth factoids.
- **Make sure communications are crystal clear:** Request elucidation when something ambiguous is said; repeat your points, rephrasing them to remove any doubt as to your meaning.
- **Keep internal departments in touch** with ongoing events by the technique of "management by wandering around."
- **Never ignore red flags, or try to hide them:** Red flags never go away on their own. Use pincer movements whenever possible.
- **Your most potent weapons** in keeping control are:
  - The threat of a visit
  - Control of the milestone check
  - And the ultimate weapon: the power of cancellation.
- **Ftp is an excellent method of transferring data and builds:** Calculate the time it takes to transfer builds; for those crucial last couple of weeks in QA, try transferring modules rather than entire builds.
- **Preproduction is the phase during which travel is most useful:** Travel during the production phase should be mostly for coordination and maintenance of the relationship. If travel is necessary during post-production, you probably have a major problem to take care of.
- **Keep travel costs down:.** Plan ahead for the best airfares. Do not fly first class or stay in four-star hotels.
- **If you must travel, research what Internet access you will have and make sure your cell phone will work:** The last thing you need is to lose touch due to a technical glitch.
- **Time zones have some impact on the process,** but you can work around it if you are flexible.

Producing projects with external teams is ultimately easier than producing them with internal teams. When producing internal projects, you must closely manage every person on the team. When producing external projects, you manage only the manager at the other end of the phone. Following the above points should help keep this management process smooth.

7.7

Total Quality Control in Game Development

Chris Campbell

torgo@home.com

> *Before Myth II: Soulblighter hit the shelves, Bungie discovered a problem which warrants a recall of the title. Though the problem is likely to affect only a small number of Windows users, it nevertheless could be serious for them. Recalling a product is a difficult decision to make, but Bungie believes strongly it is the right thing to do.*

> —Press release from Bungie after they discovered that uninstalling the demo or game installed elsewhere than in the default directory could wipe out the root of a hard drive.

The above is a game developer's nightmare: You have spent several years developing a design, programming the code, and polishing finished product, only to have one "killer bug" thwart the game's success at the last moment. In the case mentioned above, Bungie felt it prudent to have the game pulled from the shelves and replacements made.

But what if this mistake had been found earlier in the development process? The cost of recalling and destroying game media would never have occurred. The reputation of a fine game developer would have remained unmarred. How many sales could have been saved?

Today's game development climate frequently seems to gloss over quality; quality assurance is usually relegated to the end of the product cycle. The formula for quality control adopted by many large publishers seems to be to hire a few college students for slightly more than minimum wage, have them play the game for a few hours, and ask them to fill out feedback forms.

Game testing using this method becomes only a fraction of the development equation. Quality is and should not be an afterthought. Your finished product represents your innovation, creativity, and above all, your quality of work. So why does quality in gaming seem to fail so often? The solution lies in how quality control is instituted in a company.

Quality from the Top Down

The quality process in game design and production should be no different than it is in other industries. Manufacturing has long since discovered that quality is not an action, but a process. This process is not localized in one specialized group; rather, it permeates the entire company, from the top down.

There are several steps to take to achieve total quality in game design. The goal of this process is twofold: first, to reduce development cost while maximizing the end quality of the product, and second, to strengthen the development team for future projects. It might be surprising exactly how little the process involves *design*, and how much it puts the emphasis on *people*. As we will soon discover, the investment in people quickly pays off in the quality of the resulting game.

Step 1: Make Perfection Your Goal

The following example is taken from a well-known quality case study about a steel mill in Colorado. Working in a steel mill is inherently dangerous: large machinery and hot liquid metal can both be deadly if precautions are not taken. The plant's safety record was abysmal; therefore, the manager set a new goal for the plant: to have only two deaths occur per month. Various procedures were implemented to accomplish this goal. One procedure required employees to carry an injured worker to the front gate so he could be picked up by an ambulance. Then, if the injured worker died on the way to the hospital, his death would not technically have occurred at the mill, thus maintaining the company's quality goal. Sound like a company at which you would like to work?

Yet, how often do we in game development follow the above way of thinking? In the aeronautical, medical, and military industries, perfection is not just a wishful thought, it is a *requirement*. One faulty O-ring caused the *Challenger* disaster. A mistake in a medical chart could send the wrong person to the operating room. Bad targeting information can lead to innocent people being killed.

Granted, people's lives are not on the line in game development, but the importance of striving for perfection remains the same. Having zero defects sounds like an impossible goal, and it is: in the real world, such a record is simply unattainable. However, anyone who works on the project must believe that a better quality product will increase the game's market share.

In game development, perfection is measured by comparing the final game build against the design documents. Do not make the mistake of simply changing the design document to work around a problem after the fact; this action is comparable to carrying an injured steel worker out to the curb so that he will not appear on your plant injury reports.

Step 2: Be Single-Minded in Your Purpose

A variety of people usually work together on a game project, and each person brings a unique perspective and personality to the game. While these unique perspectives are important , it is essential that everyone works toward the same goal: perfection. People working on the project for other reasons, such as using the opportunity to pad their resume or to make ends meet until a better job comes along, are a liability to the game.

Some project managers and designers, however can distort this idea into making virtual slaves out of employees. One of the worst mistakes that a company can make is to expect or require long work days of 10 to 12 hours on a regular basis. Other managers produce fear in the workplace by hunting out those who are not "with the program" or by committing character assassination when mistakes are made.

It is important to remember that what needs to be achieved is perfection in the end product. If mistakes are made, correct them and move forward. Do not let the punishments of long work hours, reprimands, and project changes get in the way of that goal.

Step 3: Build Quality into the Game Design Early

Far too many development houses leave the testing to the last possible moment. Worse yet, the Quality Assurance (QA) department is sometimes regarded as the lowest rung on the ladder in the company structure.

But quality does not begin and end with the QA department. Quality control begins before the first word is written on the design document. A quality process that touches every area of the game should already be in place before any work starts. Quality controls should be designed for programming, art, sound, and networking; likewise there should be quality processes for playtesting, equipment procurement, hiring, and even for stocking the soft drink machine. Establish a set of standards or metrics against which to measure your later development. These benchmarks need not be the size of a telephone book: the simpler, the better.

During the development of *Age of Empires II*, the art department created a set of perfect pictures. Before any game art was begun, a team set out to establish what they thought would be the look of a perfect game, using Photoshop and real-world photos. One resulting image represented our vision of a perfect shoreline: it had a white sandy beach clear blue-green water through which the ocean floor could be seen, waves further out to sea with turbulent white caps, and a blue whale sending a spray of water into the air—all in 32-bit color using several filters. The artists would then evaluate all art against the set of perfect pictures. If the art did not look good enough, they would go back and try again. By the end of the project, it was amazing how closely the game artwork resembled the perfect pictures, despite the artists working with only a 256-color palette.

In another example, in the first *Age of Empires* game, the Japanese building set was based on the restaurant next door to the office. The artists compared all of their buildings against the real-life building next door, and strove to perfectly represent it.

By building in quality from the beginning in both cases, we were able to measure progress immediately, thus reducing the time spent hurriedly putting together pieces that were either forgotten or incomplete at the end of the project. And we were able to make two games that were still top 10 sellers two years after their release.

Step 4: Eliminate Fear in the Workplace

The meaning of the word *fear* has changed much since it entered the English language. In the twelfth century, *fear* meant a certain sense of awe or respect. Today's manager in the game development workplace tends to instill the modern-day meaning of fear: anxiety, fright, and trepidation.

Managing through fear and uncertainty is not only unhealthy, it is also counterproductive to your goal of perfection. Workers would much rather spend time updating their résumés than work for someone who threatens employees when mistakes are made. Fear is not a motivator. Fear makes you run from a haunted house that also happens to be where you are employed.

Return to the original meaning of fear: *respect*. Building respect in your workplace should be a cornerstone of your company's foundation. Respect for your workers only brings out the best in people. It motivates. -

Psychologists have been aware of the motivation of respect for years. In Abraham Maslow's study on human beings' hierarchy of needs, the need to be loved and comforted appears in the third step of Maslow's schematic. The fourth step is self-esteem: according to Maslow, having the respect of one's peers is something that everyone desires. The fifth and highest step in Maslow's ladder is self-actualization, meaning a constant striving to be the best person one can be. This last step is the embodiment of quality.

Fear only occurs on the very first step of Maslow's hierarchy: the need for food, water, and shelter. Fear in the workplace drives the worker to find shelter, and nourishment, in other places of employment.

One example of how fear seems to be commonly used in the tech sector is in the number of working hours expected of an employee. What was once a cruel method of reducing the cost of labor has been twisted into a game of honor: pulling 36-hour shifts is the noble thing to do—and failing to put in 60 to 80 hours of work a week can lead to unemployment.

Numerous studies have shown that the more hours an employee works, the more mistakes that employee is liable to make. This is a serious problem in Japan, where the language actually contains a word, *karoshi*, for people who die from overworking. In an interview, lawyer Hiroshi Kawahito, secretary general of the National Defense Council for Victims of Karoshi, stated that at least 10,000 people die every year from overwork.

While the Western game development industry does not have people dying from *karoshi*, there is a problem when workers are sacrificing their health and productivity out of a needless fear that, unless they work 60 hours a week, they will lose their jobs.

The results of eliminating fear quickly become apparent. Employees working a regular 40-hour week are more rested, happier, healthier, they make fewer mistakes in their work, and, best of all, studies show that they use their time more effectively to get work done. Instead of wasting money ordering pizza in every night, send your workers home—and keep them busy during the day.

Step 5: Tear Down the Walls between Departments

Departments are meant to be a way of quickly organizing groups of people, but too often they become a barrier to development. When departments are compartmentalized and segregated from each other, communication becomes difficult and stagnation sets in. Once this segregation happens, one department does not know what the other is doing. Duplication of effort, work slipping through the cracks, or conflicts are too often the result.

Because an employee is a programmer, an artist, or a tester does not mean that they wholly own the process they belong to, or that their input should be limited to it. Once we have become single in mind and purpose, we leave a larger and more complete goal in mind. We are all working toward the same thing: perfection. Building communication and trust between departments is essential.

Implement a process analogous to the line stop used in manufacturing, where any employee is given the power to shut down the production line when there is a problem. Richard Schonberger gives this real-world example:

> *At Kawasaki's U.S. plant, assembly lines are strung with yellow and red lights; workers press the yellow when there is a problem and the red when the problem is serious enough for a line stop. Sometimes the line stops are necessitated by direct quality problems, such as parts not fitting quite right, and the problem needs to be noted and immediately forwarded to the work centers that made the poorly fitting parts. In nearly all cases the stop assures that the assemblers will take enough time to make sure that they are not the cause of bad quality.*

Line stop gives everyone in the company the power to stop development when a problem is found, regardless of what department they are in. This means that an artist who finds a problem in the programming code has the right—in fact, the responsibility—to raise the issue. Even the front desk clerk should have the power to question quality—everyone gets involved in the process.

Step 6: Use Everyone in the Company to Work on the Project

One of the things enjoyed while working at Ensemble Studios is that everyone playtested, not just myself as the Quality Assurance lead. We had a schedule telling everyone in the company when to play, what to do, and what to look for. The administrative assistant, the president of the company, and the systems administrator all took part in the playtesting processes, and each person brought their own perspective to the overall project. As a side benefit, all employees were kept up to date on the game's progress: at E3, everyone in the company could demonstrate *Age of Empires II* and answer questions from the press.

No matter how large your company or how many game development projects you have, everyone should be involved in the process at some point. Coworkers are thus able to share their knowledge with others, which builds a stronger, more informed workforce.

By now, we have eliminated fear and established respect for one another; once everyone is involved, and everyone's opinion is valued and treated with equal weight, team members will feel free to speak on any issue related to the project.

Step 7: Everyone Must Take Ownership and Accept Leadership Responsibilities

It is not enough to work on a project—you must *own* it. Usually, development of a AAA title can require two or three years, from design to shelf. With so much time invested, it makes no sense build anything less than the best product you can. It makes no difference whether you name is on the box, as is Sid Meier's or John Romero's, or at the bottom of the last page of the manual. If your name is in the credits somewhere, this is *your* game, and it is a reflection of yourself and your workmanship.

A part of ownership is the ability to accept self-responsibility. You are responsible for your part in the greater whole, but you also must rely on the help and expertise of others.

In successful game development, having *leadership* means doing that which you would like others to do. If perfection is the goal, then it will take everyone with leadership to carry it out. Part of that leadership is to continue fulfilling the vision of perfection, long after the initial excitement is over.

Step 8: Install Pride of Workmanship

The average gamer will choose a product released by Blizzard, id Software, or Ensemble Studios over most competitors, because these developers have consistently produced quality games that sell like mad. Consumers, with their dollars, recognize the effort made by each of these developers.

Team members at each of these companies know that they need to give their best work to their project. If their work is not satisfactory to themselves, they try again. It is not enough for them to simply program a workable 3D model or a software routine: they must work *perfectly*.

Pride of workmanship means that you are not ashamed of your work—you know that this work represents the best that you are capable of. You have reached your full measure and are ready to show the result to the world. If you are unsure about the quality of your work, then you know it is not ready. Pride comes not from being forced to do something, but from *wanting* to do it.

It takes very little to install pride of workmanship. In a Gallup poll conducted in September 1999, only 38 percent of employees were satisfied with the amount of recognition they received for their work. If you refer back to Maslow's hierarchy of needs, his fourth step was self-esteem. All workers crave recognition. Part of being a leader is to be able to recognize the contributions of those around you, and to help them achieve their goals. Help them understand their role in making the perfect game.

Step 9: Establish Training and Leadership Programs

We recently had a friend leave his position as a database administrator because he felt he was not getting the training that he needed to do his job better. His manager was angry at his departure because the manager felt he had spent so much money training him. There is an obvious conflict here, but who is right?

Because the worker quit, the manager obviously was unable to recognize the worker's need for further training. We later discovered that the manager had given the employee *one* training class on SQL server management and believed that was adequate for everyone involved.

Managers must realize that training is a constant process. If an employee is not challenged enough, he will seek satisfaction elsewhere. We strive to make our games exciting and fresh each time we play them; we need to take the same approach to our jobs. Training fills this need by providing new information and giving new perspectives. This training does not necessarily have to apply to the worker's current position: a C++ programmer who has an understanding of graphical user interface design is at least as valuable as one who can code binary programs in his sleep, but can do little else.

For example, do not be afraid to give programmers training in art design or management skills. When implementing your game design, versatile employees will save time and money by having the foresight to see how all the elements ultimately fit other. Cross-training bridges gaps between departments, reveals all sides of an issue, and reduces the occurrence of mistakes due to misunderstandings.

Step 10: Strive to Always Improve

Once you have a proper foundation for your work, you should always be looking for ways in which to improve quality.

Do not wait until the end of the project to perform a postmortem of the processes involved. The end is too late. Do it now. Identify areas that could be performing their functions better without losing quality.

Conduct personal interviews with the people who work with or for you. You do not need to make these interviews formal: take a few minutes every month to have a conversation with every person, during lunch, a social outing, or in the hallway. Use these meetings to identify problems and help the person think of solutions. People are frequently full of good ideas, but have no one with whom to share them. Ask the question: "If you had a magic wand of wishes (+2) and could change anything you wanted in the company to make it perfect and help improve your work, what would it be?" You will get good, honest answers about what needs to be improved: fewer hours, better equipment, more training, sympathetic management, etc.

There is no reason for any of these wishes not to come true when you use total quality management. Consider methods for implementing these changes. All the above wishes actually pay for themselves when implemented correctly—a healthy, equipped, trained employee under the right management will always make a quality product.

Conclusion

Many tools exist to help you make a better product, but the best tool you could have is your workers. All the databases, automated testing, and equipment in the world are not going to help you, unless you and the development team are committed to building a perfect game.

7.8

Using Focus Groups to Proof Design Ideas

Charlie Cleveland

flayra@overmind.org

In a closed environment like a game development studio, focus groups are vital to proofing design ideas and providing a reality check for new game concepts. Focus groups can speed development and increase end-product quality at little cost. In the fuzzy space that is game design, players are the only source for answers to such questions:

- Is this user interface understandable?
- Is my weapon customization system too complex?
- Will this nested circular level layout work?
- Is the artistic look we have chosen appealing to players?

Focus groups can be called upon at all stages of game creation in order to prevent misconceptions and allow the designer to innovate with confidence. This article describes how to use focus groups effectively to build better games methodically.

What Is a Focus Group, and How Are They Run?

Holding a focus group means bringing together a small group of people and obtaining their feedback. Usually, you will want them to play the game, but sometimes you will want them to test the user interface, examine the artwork, or comment on a specific aspect of the design. Only you as the designer can know where the group's assistance can be most useful to your project.

Who to Invite

The focus group can include any number of people, but the process tends to work best when groups are split into sessions small enough to allow everyone in the group to talk—typically, one to a few people at a time. Ideally, most of the testers will be fresh subjects who have never seen or heard of your game—not even in previous focus group sessions.

Members of a focus group can include friends, family, or strangers, but when inviting people who are close to you, select those who will not be afraid to be honest with you. Biased or tainted feedback is of little value.

Preparing the Session

Tell the subject or subjects that they can stop testing the game at any time, and also that you will not answer their questions or provide help of any kind. Make sure they understand that any bugs or problems they uncover are not their fault, and that all feedback is useful and will help improve the product.

While sessions can include a variety of activities and last as long as necessary, it is usually a good idea to keep them short in order to capture valuable first impressions and find the largest problems immediately.

Justification and Explanation

While feedback from your future audience is always good, focus groups are not for bug-hunting or beta testing. Focus groups provide feedback on innovation and design and help you ensure that your finished game will be understood and accepted by the market.

As a designer, you should realize that all projects will contain defects that a game designer or programmer might not notice, but that will be immediately obvious to people who have never seen or played the game. Developers who are "close" to the game and have seen it in many different stages can no longer view the game objectively, as a new player will. Strange but true: for the purpose of unearthing design flaws, developers are less useful than complete strangers who know nothing about the game.

Focus groups should be considered part of the prototyping process. Without focus groups or prototypes, the feedback loop for designers is a long and painful one: develop a game for a few years, receive feedback from beta testers and reviewers, and then work feverishly in a short period of time to fix the problems they uncover . This process makes growth and experimentation slow and difficult, and management is likely to reduce the risk of a schedule slip during finalization by forcing the design to follow tried (and tired) conventions. Using focus groups early helps designers quickly, easily, and inexpensively explore new gameplay ideas, and gives designers more freedom to take chances.

Finally, it is worth spending significant time obtaining feedback from focus groups because, otherwise, the final product's quality will be dependent on talent, guesswork, intuition, and other factors outside the team's control. Focus groups mean methodical improvement.

Focus Group Checklist

Here are some issues that should be explored by focus groups at different stages of the project. Be careful, though: do *not* ask overly specific questions during sessions.

Instead, watch and listen for feedback that can give insight into these topics, both during and after the meetings themselves.

Early in Development

Here are key questions to pinpoint early in development:

- Do the core game concepts sound like fun?
- Is the art style and brightness level appealing for long periods of time?
- Is the game world understandable and appealing? Does the player care?
- Does the game concept excite the player, provoking a such responses as: "Great idea, why hasn't this been done before?"
- Does the game immediately draw negative comparisons to another existing game or movie?

Middle of Development

The following questions are useful for focus groups in the game's mid-development stage:

- Are the core game concepts fun? If not, what tweaks would make them fun? Are there any fundamentally "broken" design concepts?
- Do the levels or missions seem repetitive?
- Does the player care about the story?
- Do many users have trouble with the interface? Where? How can the problems be fixed?
- Does the game grow in complexity too quickly? Too many creatures, too many options, too many races, or too many weapons? What can be done to begin the game as simply as possible then gradually add more complexity?
- What does the player think of the game's new features? If this is person has participated in earlier focus groups, does this feature seem to resonate with the person?
- What is the overall expression and mood of the player?

End of Development

Here are key questions to keep in mind near the game's completion:

- What game concepts or rules do players consistently have trouble understanding? How can they be more easily explained?
- What is the initial experience of the player after 15 to 30 minutes of playing for the first time? Is there extensive configuration, installation, or tweaking that must be done before the player can get into the game?
- Is a player's first multiplayer experience enjoyable. How can we improve it?
- Is the player excited by the experience and now awaiting the game's release?
- Is the game too easy or too difficult?

- Are there problem areas in which many people get stuck?
- If the player could choose one thing to change about the game, what would it be and why?
- As the focus group facilitator, did you find yourself ashamed, embarrassed, confident, or proud?

Caveats, Disadvantages, and Pitfalls

Focus groups do not work well in all development environments. Some designers are hostile to feedback, especially from average users, and believe that negative feedback means "they don't get" the grand vision. Focus groups also are not as useful for genre games that rely heavily on well-established formulas.

However, a designer's job is to make sure players "get it." Designers need to decide if it is more important to achieve every detail of the original concept or to make sure that the idea behind the grand vision is seen, understood, and enjoyed by many people. For a game to be true to its vision and for the average player to appreciate it, the design may have to change.

There are also times when focus groups provide thoroughly unpleasant feedback, for instance, that the entire concept on which an innovative game is founded does not work. If this is the case, decide why the concept does not work and keep trying different approaches until it does.

Finally, make sure to leave time for feedback and reworking features. Organizing focus groups so late in development that nothing can be changed when problems are discovered is a waste of time and effort. Focus groups work best when they are made an integral part of the design process and consulted regularly, and when their feedback carefully considered.

Focus Groups and Corporate Culture

The most difficult task facing you when using focus groups might be getting your employer to buy into them. Potential intellectual property right infringement, public relations "leaks," and perceived costs can make management wary.

You must convince your employer and publisher that focus groups' insights into how a game will be received by the marketplace will directly help sales. If necessary, have every focus group participant sign a nondisclosure agreement; if nondisclosure is a large issue for your company, it is better to "reuse" people for feedback on different parts of the game then it is to not get any feedback at all. If management considers the cost of a focus group unwarranted, explain that the cost of releasing an unfinished, unusable, or incomprehensible game is far worse. Most negative comments found in game reviews could have been prevented by focus groups long before release. Further, it takes very little time to meet with a few people every few weeks and conduct an informal session. User interface research indicates that feedback from as few as three users is all that is required. Do at least basic focus testing at all costs.

Conclusion

Focus group sessions do not have to be dry, corporate affairs with feedback forms and Styrofoam cups. Sessions can be as simple and informal as inviting a person from outside the office to come in and look at a specific design issue. Watch their reactions carefully and look for things that confuse them or stop them playing the game. Set up the session well in advance, and do not ask them to provide a written report; encourage the free flow of ideas by taking notes for them. Often you will not even need to take notes, because the feedback will be prompt, uniform, and (perhaps painfully) memorable.

Using focus groups is the best method for pursuing innovation without undue risk and to achieve mainstream acceptance. Reworking fundamental ideas as a result of focus group feedback does not reflect poorly on the designer: it is a sign of maturity and confidence, and means the designer is pushing boundaries. A bad designer will refuse to fix a problem out of hubris. A good designer will constantly try new ideas and expect that many ideas either will not work without extensive alterations or will not work at all.

Committing to the idea of focus groups means committing to redesign and committing to the premise that some ideas or features will simply not work. Programmers and artists have long since learned that improvement sometimes requires ridding yourself of conventional wisdom and restarting with a fresh approach. It is time for designers to do the same.